CLASS, RACE, AND
THE CIVIL RIGHTS
MOVEMENT

Blacks in the Diaspora

Darlene Clark Hine and John McCluskey, Jr.,
General Editors

CLASS, RACE, AND THE CIVIL RIGHTS MOVEMENT

JACK M. BLOOM

INDIANA UNIVERSITY PRESS
BLOOMINGTON AND INDIANAPOLIS

Manufactured in the United States of America

Library of Congress Cataloging-in-Publication Data

Bloom, Jack M.
Class, race, and the Civil Rights movement.

(Blacks in the diaspora)
Bibliography: p.
Includes index.
1. Afro-Americans—Civil rights. 2. United States—
Race relations.   3. Racism—United States—History—
20th century.   4. Southern States—Race relations.
5. Social Classes—Southern States.   I. Title.
II. Series.
E185.615.B557   1987   305.8′00973   85–45983
ISBN 0–253—31212—4
ISBN 0–253–20407–0 (pbk.)

5 6 7 8 9 00 99 98 97

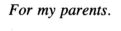

For my parents.

CONTENTS

FOREWORD

Class, Race, and the Civil Rights Movement: The Changing Political Economy of Racism makes an important contribution to the body of literature dealing with the struggle for black equality. Using a class analysis, Professor Jack Bloom has focused on the historical developments that in the 1950s led to the birth of the civil rights movement. Through careful documentation, he has shown that the civil rights movement was the culmination of a political struggle that began with the Reconstruction period of the 1860s. Preceded by great people's movements based on progressive Populist ideology, the civil rights era was also linked to a shift of black political allegiance from the Republican party to the Democrats in 1936 with the emergence of the New Deal policies of Franklin Delano Roosevelt.

In all of that, Bloom clearly reveals the roots of racial and class oppression. Analyzing the ongoing relationship between the monied classes of the South and the North, he examines the ties between the post-Reconstruction planter class and Northern banking interests that resulted in the impoverishment of small farmers, both black and white, through control of land ownership and the imposition of the sharecropping system. Additionally, Professor Bloom contends that it was these same classes that funded racist organizations such as the Ku Klux Klan and the White Citizens' Councils, whose actions were to terrorize and intimidate the black population while blunting unity between the black and white poor of the South.

A striking example of how racism was used to disfranchise both blacks and whites in Mississippi came through a change in the state constitution and imposed voting restrictions through property qualifications, literary requirements, and poll taxes. While touted as a way to eliminate the black vote, the result was that not only were blacks disfranchised, but whites were, as well. Subsequently, the right to vote became the sole property of the white upper classes. It would take the weight of the civil rights movement, a massive march in Selma, Alabama, and passage of the Voting Rights Act in 1965 to reverse this unfair and antidemocratic history.

Calling the civil rights movement the Second Reconstruction, Bloom cites several key factors that led to its development, including the landmark 1954 *Brown v. Board of Education* Supreme Court decision that reversed the racist separate but equal doctrine handed down in the 1896 *Plessy v. Ferguson* case. The fight to implement *Brown* through integration of the Southern school system became the rallying cry of an emerging black leadership under the banner of the National Association for the Advancement of Colored People (NAACP).

The second key factor was the organization in 1956 of the Montgomery bus boycott. Led by Dr. Martin Luther King, Jr., the boycott laid the basis for a deepening unity among blacks, whose expectations, heightened twenty years before by the more enlightened federal policies of the New Deal era, were now fired by a determination to end the fundamental indignity and repression of segregation. The initial demand for equal access to public facilities and conveyances grew into demands that challenged basic economic policies, and the fight for jobs, housing, and health care eventually became the issues of the mass movement.

The involvement of the masses of black people in the Montgomery bus boycott opened the door to new forms of resistance that sprang up all over the South. A bright star shining in the gloom of the McCarthy period, this broad-based, black-led movement became the mother of other significant forces, including the student movement of the 1960s and the anti-Vietnam War and women's movements, in addition to providing the springboard for the first independent black-based political party of its type, the Mississippi Freedom Democratic Party (MFDP).

Tying together the issues of economic exploitation, racism, and war, the civil rights movement raised basic class issues and eventually carried out a social revolution that changed the political fabric and economic policies forever. Professor Bloom contends that state-sanctioned segregation and second-class citizenship are relics of the past and not likely to return, owing to the proven social power of blacks and their historic and potential allies among the white working class. He has amply provided the research to support a general thesis that the denial of political rights to blacks and forced segregation were products of the class, economic, and political system of the South. For this reason, *Class, Race, and the Civil Rights Movement* invites thought and comment, as well as provides an excellent secondary source for scholars of the era.

RICHARD GORDON HATCHER
MAYOR, CITY OF GARY

ACKNOWLEDGMENTS

Many people were generous in providing help and support to this project. Their aid sometimes included sharp criticism and insightful suggestions. Some provided needed personal support. The contributions of five people were particularly significant: Herbert Blumer, Troy Duster, William Wilson, James Geschwender, and Jack Weinberg. I also wish gratefully to acknowledge the contributions of R. Stephan Warner, John Martin, Mary Glen Wiley, Bert Useem, Ronald Cohen, James Lane, Kathryn Johnson, Robert Catlin, Marty Zusman, Ed Escobar, Gayle Gullett, Eric Hirsch, Ann Williams, Morris Janowitz, Sydney Wilhelm, and John Leggett. Of course, I take full responsibility for the final product.

I wish to thank Olivia Gross, Helen Southwell, Michele Yanna, and Gayle O'Connor for their skills and effort in putting this manuscript into the word processor. Without their help it never would have seen daylight. Tim Sutherland, who ran the interlibrary loan desk at Indiana University Northwest, and Robert Moran, director of the library, provided aid that was invaluable.

CLASS, RACE, AND
THE CIVIL RIGHTS
MOVEMENT

INTRODUCTION

This study seeks to explain what the civil rights movement was about, why it happened and why it was successful. It is an analysis, not a history, of that movement, but it explores the history of the movement and that of the preceding era. It examines the interrelationship of class and race in America and analyzes the ways in which the politics of class and the politics of race shaped and affected each other. I contend that the racial practices and beliefs that the civil rights movement confronted—the denial of political rights to blacks, forced segregation, and the degradation of blacks to second-class citizenship—were embedded within the class, economic, and political systems of the South. Southern racial customs emerged from that class structure and were retained because they were necessary to its functioning. The interest group that, above all others, depended upon black subordination and suppression was the agrarian upper class of the Southern black belt.* This class had both the need to subordinate blacks and the power to do so, albeit in conjunction with other classes. The racist practices that the civil rights movement challenged were basically constructed by and for this agrarian elite. When this class system was undermined, the emergence of the civil rights movement became possible. Overturning the South's *racial* policies necessitated pushing aside what had been the dominant *class* in the region.

This study of the structural roots of Southern racism provides the basis for answering some of the central questions with which an analytical account of the civil rights movement must come to grips:

1. Since blacks had been unable to alter the terms of their subjection previously, what changed to make their successful intervention in history possible?

2. Why did the civil rights movement arise in, and remain centered in, the South? Further, as the movement changed its focus from civil rights to black power, why did its geographical location shift from the South to the North?

3. What interests underlay the vehement opposition to the black movement?

4. How did the movement affect the structure of power within the South?

---

*The term *black belt* refers to the plantation area of the South. That region was the black belt in two senses: it contained the fertile black soil that was the most productive farmland in the South—the heritage of the power of the slaveowning class. And it was where most black people resided; they often constituted the majority of the population of a district.

The answers to these questions make up the first part of this book, which deals with the changing structure of Southern racism.

The industrialization and urbanization of the South provided the context for the changes in racial patterns. A new elite and a middle class based on the new urban, commercial, and industrial economy developed as an economic, and ultimately as a political, competitor to the agrarian upper class. This situation provided new opportunities for blacks, but there was no simple relationship of cause and effect. Barrington Moore, Jr. and others have pointed to the possibility of the "Prussian route," whereby a society industrializes while maintaining its repressive political and social system under the continued domination of the agrarian upper class. Moore examined the United States in this light, and he argued that the Civil War was a revolutionary war in which industrial capitalism defeated and destroyed the slaveowners, eliminating them as a force in national politics and paving the way for the further development of democratic rule in the country.[1]

Moore was concerned with national developments, and his analysis of the transition from agrarianism to industrialism stops there. But in the postbellum South itself, the agrarian class, while subordinate to Northern capitalism, retained its dominance and set the political tone for the region. In its benign days that meant black subordination and white paternalism. In times of stress, agrarian dominance meant aggressive acts against blacks, including outright guerilla warfare. When the agrarian elite was finally faced with the political and social ramifications of the trend toward industrialism in the region, it dug in its collective heels to fight, and it was defeated.

The Supreme Court ruling of 1954 outlawing segregation in public schools was followed by tumult. The turmoil came about because in challenging Southern racial practices, blacks were effectively threatening the social system on which those practices were based, and the Southern elite whose position depended upon that system. In the end, the black movement was responsible for the transfer of political power from the rural and small-town cliques to the business and middle classes within the cities. That was the historic accomplishment necessary to gain equal legal rights for blacks. Had this process taken place in a nation rather than a region, it would be called a social revolution.

This political upheaval helped to complete the modernization of the South and to assimilate it into the rest of the country. Increasingly, the social and political structure of the South became like that of the rest of the nation. The civil rights movement was thus the producer of these sociological changes as well as their product. The social and economic changes created new centers of power, which did not have the same vested interest in the maintenance of the old racial patterns as the traditional Southern elite. In addition, the new international situation after World War II, in which the United States was competing with the Soviet Union in a world where the hue of more and more political actors was dark, weakened the ties of the federal government with Southern racism. The black vote in the North began to shift the orientation of the national Democratic party. These structural shifts provided new opportunities for blacks in the South to act.

The Class Basis of Racial Politics

The racial patterns that developed in the South were shaped in an economic system that depended upon cheap, plentiful, and easily controlled black labor. When the class system that relied upon racial supremacy was superseded by one that utilized other means to provide adequate supplies of labor, the patterns of racial domination could be abandoned. Racial patterns and racial consciousness have as their foundation particular class structures, and they develop and change as these structures themselves change. White supremacy, then, was the ideological foundation on which the Southern elite created a ruling coalition that it dominated; thus, class *and* racial struggles often took the form of political battles over white supremacy.

The concepts of class and class structure that I use here in explaining the dynamic of race are not narrowly construed. The concerns of classes, while shaped by their material existence, are political as well as economic, because the political system is so important in setting the framework within which economic struggles are carried out. Therefore, political conflicts frequently express class conflicts as well, even though they may not be phrased in those terms. Political interests, while necessarily conscious and organized, often present their goals in terms of the broader society rather than of a particular social sector. It is political suicide in the United States for a political party to announce itself as upholding the program of a special sector of the society. Parties seek to speak for the society as a whole and to become the legitimate representatives of classes and sectors other than their own. They attempt to obscure the differences between their own and broader social interests, and in the words of John W. Cell, they "make their special class concerns appear identical with the desires of the politically represented sections of society. Making such an identification is the very nature of the politician's profession."[2]

My emphasis on the economic sphere is not to deny that racial issues have had a life of their own. Class structure may set the parameters of racial action, but it cannot reduce race to class. All classes of whites participated in various ways in the oppression of blacks; this oppression may have been shaped by the class system, but it had its own independent character.

What, then, provided the dynamic of racism? Recently Edna Bonacich has contended that it was primarily the working class (broadly construed) that was responsible for that dynamic. Bonacich's analysis is based on her work on split labor market theory. A split labor market is one in which there are at least two groups of workers who are technically distinct, with one being more highly paid and generally better off than the other. According to this theory, racial antagonism emerges from the three-cornered conflict between the employers and the two labor groups. Capital seeks the cheapest labor and may attempt to use the lower-priced labor either in lieu of the more expensive labor or to force the cost of that labor down. At the same time, the better-off labor group emphasizes ethnic or racial antagonism in order to constrict the ability of the lower-priced workers to compete, either by driving them out of the labor market altogether or by restricting them to jobs that are lower-paid, are more arduous in their working conditions, and offer lower status. Through these efforts they thereby create a caste system.[3] Split labor market theory tends to ascribe the primary dynamic of racial discrimination to white labor's policies. Bonacich says: "The theory predicts that the class most overtly antagonistic to blacks is white labor, not white capital."[4] Thus white labor is presumably not only more antagonistic to blacks, but also able to impose its policies against the wishes of capital. An increase in black degradation should be the result.

William Wilson rejected Bonacich's contention that white labor imposed its policies during the antebellum period in the South, when the slaveowners were manifestly in control. But he accepted her analysis for the period after the Civil War, and historian C. Vann Woodward has presented a picture that in many ways supports Bonacich's. Woodward contended that lower-class whites provided the main impetus for the imposition of restrictions on blacks, stating that "the escalation of lynching, disfranchisement and proscription reflected concessions to the white lower class [on the part of the upper class]." He saw the lower-class whites as the active agents in this process. It was they who wished to suppress the blacks, but they were held off from doing so by the upper class, which, soon after the Civil War, ceased to view blacks as a threat: "By and large, the blacks still 'knew their place'; with a few exceptions, mainly political, roles were still defined by race and so was status; social distance prevailed over physical propinquity. The ancient racial etiquette persisted with few breaches, and so did personal relationships, and so did the dominance-submissive pattern." These circumstances helped to create what Wilson termed an "unholy alliance" between blacks and upper-class whites. The latter protected the blacks against the lower-class white demands for their subjugation. In return, said Woodward, the protectors received support they badly needed against the lower-class whites:

> Black votes could be used to overcome white working class majorities, and upper
> class white protection was needed by blacks under threat of lower class aggression.
> Many reciprocal accommodations between upper class whites and blacks were
> possible under the paternalistic order.[5]

It was the threat of joint action against the upper class, especially as manifested in the Populist movement of the 1890s, that broke up this arrangement: "The top people of the South *were* in this instance frightened to some degree, all right, but they were frightened by the white lower class, not by the blacks"[6] (emphasis in original). Faced with this menace, the upper class deserted the blacks and capitulated to the racist demagogues who emerged from, and who represented, the lower-class whites. It was these whites, held Woodward, who were responsible for the rise of the post-Civil War system of racism.

> The barriers of racial discrimination mounted in direct ratio with the tide of political
> democracy among whites. In fact, an increase of Jim Crow laws upon the statute
> books of a state is almost an accurate index of the decline of the reactionary
> regimes of the Redeemers and the triumph of white democratic movements.[7]

While the tendencies identified by split labor market theory are real, I contend that the theory ignores the central dynamic of racial oppression. It does not explain how this split labor market was created, nor does it adequately explain the vested interests of the upper class involved in maintaining the racial lines. For most of the second half of the nineteenth century, black and white labor were not primarily in competition with each other. They existed mainly in different geographical locations. The bulk of their labor was farm labor—rural labor, while segregation was basically an urban phenomenon. Black degradation was not primarily the product of upper-class capitulation to lower-class demagoguery. Rather, the upper class created the atmosphere that promoted attacks on blacks and often actually carried out lynching and other forms of terrorism. It did so as a political response to the challenge to its authority and power that emerged from the Populist revolt. The upper class bore the main responsibility for black disfranchisement and accomplished it, for the most part, when it wished to do so. While segregation is not unambiguously a product of upper-class effort, it came into being only after the framework of white and upper-class supremacy had already been established, mainly after the defeat of the Populist uprising in the early 1890s. Woodward himself points out some of this trend: "In their frantic efforts to stop the [Populist] revolt and save themselves the conservatives lost their heads . . . [and] themselves raised the cry of 'Negro domination' and white supremacy." It was this class, still in power and still defending its interests, that blacks had to confront and defeat by creating the political coalition that could effectuate the new balance of power.[8]

Creating a New Movement:
The Emergence and Development of the New Negro

The new class structure only provided new possibilities for blacks. Structural change alone does not fully account for the ability of the Southern black population to use its newly acquired social weight with such effect. Blacks could not have accomplished their ends alone; they were not sufficiently powerful to do so. But they were able to bring together a coalition of disparate social forces, which ultimately included Southern business and middle classes, the Northern middle class, the national Democratic party, and the federal government, in support of their efforts to change the racial practices of the South. *This new coalition*, made possible by the sociological and economic changes mentioned above, *was the key to the victory of the civil rights movement*. Through the coalition blacks were able to restructure racial politics in the South. The coalition cohered in response to the fight led by the agrarian upper class against desegregation, first of the schools, which that class saw as the beginning of the end of the existing Southern racial order, and hence of its continued political dominance.

That blacks could create such a coalition was remarkable in and of itself. The

Civil War and Reconstruction were the last occasions during which a powerful grouping of forces had toiled on their behalf. At that time, the Northern armies and politicians set their own agenda, and when in their view it was completed, the blacks' allies retired from the field. It was almost a century before these allies could again be enlisted. This time it was blacks who led the movement and shaped it for their own ends. In doing so, they challenged the power of the racists within the national Democratic party, and they transformed Southern politics.

Of themselves, neither the Southern urban businessmen and middle classes nor the federal government and Northern Democratic party would have pressed for the substantial and rapid changes in Southern racial practices that actually took place. Southern businessmen did not have the same need to suppress blacks as did the agrarian upper class, nor were they necessarily disposed to upset the status quo. The same reluctance to act was exhibited by the federal government and the national Democratic party, both of which drew back from racial confrontation whenever possible.

If the new structural conditions were to eventuate in a changed racial and political order, blacks had to actualize the potential coalition. Doing so meant creating sufficient chaos and disorder that blacks could not be ignored; it meant making it more costly to maintain the status quo than to accede to their demands. Using the growing political power of blacks in the North, the same strategy was successfully invoked to enlist the federal government, the national Democratic party, and Northern middle-class public opinion. The civil rights movement succeeded in pitting one section of the Southern elite against the other, effectively splitting the heretofore solid white Southern leadership. The movement also set the federal government against state and local policies and thus brought victory within its grasp.

How blacks were able to accomplish this task makes up the second set of questions that must be answered to understand the success of the civil rights movement. These are primarily questions of social psychology, dealing with the development of black consciousness. Blacks were the most important element of the coalition. The task that lay before them, of confronting Southern racism and white power, was not an easy one. The consolidation of Southern racist practices that took place at the turn of the century had meant for blacks the suppression of dignity, autonomy, and independence. The emergence of the black movement required a reversal of this pattern, and of the personalities and social relationships it had engendered. A psychological reconstruction of black individuals and of the black community in its relationship to white society as a whole was necessary.

1. How, then, were blacks able to carry through this change? Some people stepped forward before others; some opposed the move. There was a struggle within the black community, and the winners, those who led toward a new direction, redefined the black community in its relationship to white society. What was the inner turmoil occasioned by this change, both for individuals among the black population and for the black community as a whole?

2. Sociologically, who were the participants, who the leaders of this movement, and who among the black population opposed it?

3. How do we account for the outcome of the struggle—the emergence of the "New Negro" in the South, and of a leadership stratum that represented this new trend?

4. How did the class dynamic, invoked to shed light on the structural changes that underlay black motion, affect the composition and development of the movement, including its ultimate transformation from a movement for civil rights to one for black power?

These questions provide the framework for the second part of this study, which examines the black movement of the 1950s and 1960s and the development of black consciousness in that period.

The transformation of blacks was not a simple matter of grievances' being felt, since these are known to have been there for a long, long time. Neither was it merely a question of the development of an ideology to give shape to these grievances—though this perspective did emerge and did provide black and white supporters alike with an understanding of the legitimacy of their endeavors. Nor was it simply a matter of the development of what Marxists refer to as consciousness, either of class or of race, although racial solidarity did grow significantly in this period and was a part of the necessary changes. The development described by James Coleman in his summary of the "revolutionary transformation theorists" was not a complete description of what took place, but it is relevant: "The revolutionary action itself and the rewards of success it brings to hard work create men who are no longer bound by traditional customs, inhibited by ascribed authority patterns, and made apathetic by the lack of hope."[9] All of these elements played their part, as victories fed the black sense of power.

The most important development went deeper than any of these partial explanations. It involved the self-transformation of the black participants and of the black community as an entity. One of Karl Marx's great insights was that people could not change the world without changing themselves in the process. Marx saw that it was through men's and women's actual struggles that they would grow, develop talents and potentials of which they became aware only in retrospect, and eventually alter even their consciousness and self-concepts. He phrased it in the following way in *The German Ideology*:

> The alteration of men on a mass scale is necessary, an alteration which can only take place in a practical movement, a revolution; this revolution is necessary, therefore, because the class overthrowing it can only in a revolution succeed in ridding itself of all the muck of ages and become fitted to found society anew.[10]

Blacks had to overcome the patterns of action and the self-conceptions that decades, and even centuries, had imposed upon them. In the course of the civil rights movement they made this profound change, and they thus transformed themselves.

In the 1950s, the black movement for change and the white movement of reaction shaped each other. When the decade began, whites had the power in the South. The *Brown* ruling of 1954, outlawing segregation in public education, upset the balance of power by placing the federal government on the side of the blacks. But the immediate reaction of the whites showed them to be both intransigent and on the offense. Their response to the *Brown* ruling, in turn, shaped the choices for the blacks. Each participant's move was affected by the lessons learned in its previous efforts and by the other's response. Each sought to impose its version of reality on the society, and thereby each hoped to shape the reality within which the other had to function.

By the end of the decade of the fifties, the white resistance movement had lost in this struggle, and blacks had the momentum. The black movement began with tentative probes, with fits and starts. As it was tested against the white power structure and at crucial junctures emerged victorious, blacks' resulting self-confidence and courage allowed them to pursue their quest for equality irrespective of the repression and vilification they encountered. In this process, the black population came to define itself in a new way, as makers rather than victims of history. Crucial to this trend was the development of a new leadership that could reflect and articulate the new black attitudes, as well as lead and define them.

As the black movement further developed in the sixties, and as many of its participants continued the struggle for black equality, they perceived that the specifically Southern brand of racism was not the only source of black suffering. American society was a class society, and blacks were on the bottom there, also. As that became evident, and as lower-class blacks were increasingly able to make their social weight have an impact, the demands of the movement for change broadened. The black movement began to call for social and economic alternatives not just in the South but throughout American society—changes that would involve a redistribution of wealth and power. But for such a program there were no white allies of significance to be found. The civil rights coalition foundered on this political rock. Hence, blacks were left in isolation. The cry for black power was a response to these conditions.

Structure and Consciousness

My approach to the civil rights movement draws on, but differs from, two traditional ways of treating social movements in American society. One has tended to treat movements as part of the field of collective behavior and has emphasized what social movements have in common with panics, crazes, fads, and hysteria. From this perspective, movements are treated largely outside of the realm of social structure. A crowd is the prototype of such analysis, and in this crowd the structural origins of the participants are not important. Whether the individuals in a lynch mob are mill workers, farmers, storekeepers, or preachers does not matter; rather, their momentary and intense involvement creates the crowd's own emergent concerns, definitions of reality, and social relationships. They get "swept away." Harkening back to its origins in the reaction to the French Revolution, the collective-behavior tradition tends to perceive the actions of the crowd and its participants as irrational. Such a perception is surely reasonable on the assumptions of this tradition: if there is no structure, if on entering into the field of collective behavior the participants' background, social base, concerns, and needs become irrelevant, then there are no socially rooted *interests*, and choices of action therefore become capricious. It is difficult, under such circumstances, to imagine what rational action would be.

Another conventional approach is to focus on the structure itself. This approach sees the social structure as defining, shaping, and limiting the emergent social movement. It tends to see the structural components as moved by their interests: class, race, nationality, or status group. But such an approach tends to ignore the active construction of group cohesion and the conscious definition of group interests. These issues of definition are often hotly fought over and are an essential part of the development of group action in social movements. It is not, after all, fated that a black sharecroppers' organization will present itself as a farmers', workers', or blacks' movement; or that blacks will define themselves as having more in common with other blacks of different classes than with whites. Thus, another element that tends to be missing from the structural approach is the *interaction* of collective actors in motion. If the lines of action of any group must be constructed, then the explanation of the construction of those lines of action must include an examination of the interaction of and within the collectivities. The words and actions of one group can affect significantly those of the other.

It is this interactionist element that provides the necessary corrective to structuralism. One can find the theoretical basis for this approach in the teachings of Herbert Blumer and in the influential work by Peter Berger and Thomas Luckmann *The Social Construction of Reality*.[11] The action of groups is constructed within the framework of structures that define and limit the possibilities for social actors; yet, those structures themselves have been humanly constructed. This understanding provides the strategy that governs this analysis of the civil rights movement: it examines the interaction within and between classes and races, first to observe the process by which the class and racial structure of the South was attained after the disruption of slavery by the Civil War. That structure shaped the actors who were part of it. When it was weakened, the various collective actors had to create a new social reality, which would in turn shape those who lived in that society. In the case of blacks, I examined closely how this collective process was mediated through and sometimes within individuals. For that reason, there are frequent references in part two of this study to the experiences and thought processes of individual actors. A good deal of that section examines the interaction within the black community in order to grasp the process by which a new collective identity was created.

Previous Analyses of the Civil Rights Movement

Four analyses of the civil rights movement have made particularly important contributions. The first was Anthony Oberschall's *Social Conflict and Social Movements*. Oberschall held that the Southern rural black population lacked the capacity to change its situation by itself. "Unless massive resources are poured into them," he contended, "and protection from physical violence is extended to the first blacks who break the pattern of subordination, protest against the segregation structure is not likely to come about simply from within."[12] Therefore, to explain the rise of the black movement, he called attention primarily to new allies who came to support the black struggle, and to the movement of blacks to the cities, where they were able to build their own organizations, including the black church and, in the North, the NAACP and the Congress of Racial Equality (CORE).

Oberschall saw the civil rights movement as the product of a growing black middle class, in which students, who were particularly unencumbered by responsibilities and therefore uniquely free from threats of reprisal for their participation in protest activity, often took the lead. He contrasted this movement to the Northern ghetto riots of the late sixties, which, he argued, were a lower-class upheaval that tended to isolate the black movement.

Both of these insights are important. Allies were essential to the success of the black struggle, as was the movement of blacks to the cities, where they were less isolated than in rural areas. And examination of the class influences within the black movement helped to explain its direction and character.

Francis Piven and Richard Cloward also examined the civil rights movement in their 1977 study *Poor Peoples' Movements*. Their treatment was based on an examination of the political economy of racism. Piven and Cloward contended that the Southern patterns of racism were rooted in the class structure of the post-Reconstruction period. Blacks were reduced to a status of serfdom through economic controls supplemented by mob and police violence. Segregation and disfranchisement followed, with the acquiescence of the federal government. Piven and Cloward argued that it was changes in the Southern social and economic structure, resulting from both federal agricultural policies during the Depression and agricultural and industrial modernization beginning in World War II, that prepared the way for a new racial settlement. As they put it: "In the largest sense, political modernization in the South followed from economic modernization."[13]

This analysis provided Piven and Cloward with the basis for grappling with the key question: What had changed to make the successes of the civil rights movement possible? They argued that the new capitalist class that arose with Southern industry did not need the mechanisms formerly used to control the labor market. They further proposed that the acceptance by big business of unions in the North had undermined the utility of racial cleavages to American capitalism and thus loosened the ties of Northern capital to the Southern racial patterns.

They noted that the cold war put pressure on the federal government to withdraw its support of Southern racial practices.

Piven and Cloward viewed blacks as playing a much more active role than Oberschall did. They saw "mounting unrest among masses of blacks, eventually culminating in a black struggle against the Southern caste system" to which "national political leaders finally responded . . . and imposed modernizing political reforms on the South." Like Oberschall, they recognized that black urbanization both freed blacks from the constraints of the tight social control prevalent in rural areas and provided the base for the development of a much more independent leadership and population at large. They provided a valuable account of the development of black consciousness and black action: in response to frustration with the pace of change, students initiated the sit-in movement, which escalated the pace of struggle and inspired other audacious tactics such as freedom rides. This campaign culminated in the massive demonstrations in Birmingham and Selma, which forced the federal government to enact the civil rights legislation that, they said, "finally dismantled the feudal apparatus of the post-Reconstruction era."[14]

Doug McAdam's *Political Process and the Development of Black Insurgency, 1930-1970* explained that to comprehend the emergence of the civil rights movement, it was necessary to examine the broad historical processes "that rendered the political establishment more vulnerable to black protest activity while also affording black the institutional strength to launch such a challenge."[15] McAdam began with the joint interests of Southern planters and Northern industrialists to restore cheap black labor and the cotton economy, and he asked what changed to permit the black movement of the mid-twentieth century to emerge. He stressed two changes: the decline of King Cotton in the South, which lessened the planters' need for cheap labor; and the growing need for black labor in the North. These developments permitted blacks to depart from the farms to Northern and Southern cities, where they became an increasingly important political factor and less subject to terrorism. In the North, McAdam showed, blacks were able, through the use of the electoral system and mass action, to pressure the president and the Supreme Court to act more favorably on their behalf. McAdam argued that the structural roots of racism had been substantially weakened. Thus, he observed, the conditions in which blacks operated had changed, and an effort to alter their terms of existence became feasible.

McAdam next examined the change within blacks that enabled them to take advantage of their new situation through what he called "cognitive liberation," which he defined as "the transformation from hopeless submission to oppressive conditions to an aroused readiness to challenge those conditions." What social conditions will bring about such a change in attitudes? McAdam emphasized a combination of the changing circumstances themselves and the configuration of organizational strength within the black community. He noted that blacks were quite able to perceive the changes around them and that these perceptions rendered "the process of cognitive liberation more likely." Before, under the old conditions, blacks had "widespread feelings of pessimism and impotence." Later, they became more optimistic and developed a greater sense of political efficacy in dealing with these phenomena.[16]

McAdam built upon Oberschall's work in his analysis of the organizational strength of Southern blacks. He argued that Southern black institutions in the earlier period—churches, colleges, and the NAACP—had all been weak. But the same developments that altered the conditions in which blacks existed also augmented the strength of these institutions: churches expanded and developed a better-educated membership and pastoral leadership; so did black colleges and the NAACP. That was important because these institutions provided much of the base on which the civil rights movement drew for participants, leadership, and support.

McAdam saw much of the decline of the movement in the late 1960s as having occurred because the process that had formerly advanced blacks' efforts now ran in reverse. Whereas in the early sixties the main civil rights organizations had dominated black activities, now the movement became organizationally dispersed and became concerned with a much broader range of issues, each emphasized by one or another group. Factionalism, which became particularly intense with the emergence of the black power ideology, weakened the black movement as the disagreement over goals and other tactics became more heated. Coincidental with these trends was a move by whites away from suppport for black needs, largely in reaction to the growing militancy of blacks and to the tendency of the movement to make demands regarding racial issues that were no longer limited to the caste system in the South. McAdam held that this white reaction weakened the power of the black vote and increased pessimism among blacks concerning their prospects for political gains. Like Oberschall, McAdam perceived that the issues being raised by the black movement became increasingly infused with a class content. He argued that this change was, in part, what lay behind the diminution of white support and, with the outbreak of the ghetto riots, the turn of the federal government away from supporting black demands and toward suppressing their more militant organizations.

Alden Morris's *The Origins of the Civil Rights Movement*, published after this manuscript was written, has a different slant on the movement from that of the other works considered.[17] Morris does not concern himself with the structural basis of the civil rights movement. His focus is on the movement itself. Morris's book argues that blacks led and created the civil rights movement themselves. The book is a careful demonstration of this proposition, showing the sources and sustaining elements of the movement in and around the institutions and organizations of the black community. With that focus, Morris also provided an effective critique of Piven and Cloward's contention that organization impeded black gains.

Morris was concerned with the emergence of the black movement of the fifties and sixties. He showed in detail how that movement grew out of the already existing organizations of the black community, especially the church, but also the NAACP and black colleges. The church was the centerpiece of the movement as Morris saw it. It provided independent leadership for the black community; it sustained the developing movement; it provided organization and financial resources; and it provided a communications network that helped to spread knowledge of the movement and its strategy of nonviolent direct action. It educated and often organized the activists in the movement. The church became the instrument through which other organizations were mobilized. When the NAACP came under sustained attack in the South during the late fifties, the church provided the base for an alternative movement and an alternative organization, the Southern Christian Leadership Conference, which became the source of a more militant approach than that of the NAACP. The church often educated the students who initiated the sit-ins, and it played a substantial role in organizing those confrontations. Morris showed that at almost every stage, the black church was central to the movement. He also explored other sources of the movement, including the Congress of Racial Equality and what he called "movement halfway houses"—where people were trained and connected to a network of other activists.

These studies provide a good basis for understanding the civil rights movement, and this study builds upon them. It roots the Southern practice of racial domination in the economic system that evolved during the Reconstruction period, and it sees the black-belt elite, not Northern capital, lower-class whites, or all whites, as the primary agent in creating and maintaining black oppression. The concentration here is on changes in the class structure as the central element that made a black movement possible. I contend that new classes came into being whose relations to blacks were based on different considerations than in the old system, and that it was this development that made possible the black victories of the mid-twentieth century. Oberschall drew attention primarily to the new allies who came to aid blacks in the fifties, without examining the social changes that underlay the new political attitude of these allies and without recognizing that black leadership had cohered the movement. Piven and Cloward, who were aware of the broader process of social change, felt that all classes of Southern whites had lessened their opposition to the transformation of the "place" for blacks, and specifically to granting to blacks the right to vote. McAdam also emphasized the universal white participation in black subjection; where he employed a class analysis, it was Northern capital that was presented as the main shaper of economic and racial structures, with little mention of the Southern agrarian elite. But it was this elite that was the primary force that created the economic and racial structure of the South, even though it had to operate within the constraints of Northern capital and the federal government. (It also felt pressures from lower-class whites, and from blacks.) It was that same elite, decades later, that led the resistance to the civil rights movement. The old interests did not fade away—they had to be shoved away.

This study emphasizes the black community's leading role in overcoming Southern racial domination, beginning with an examination of the ways in which white power had been able to insinuate itself into and to shape the black community. These aspects of the black subjective experience are important because they indicate what blacks had to overcome if they were to confront white power in the South. The struggle that ensued was key to the emergence of the "New Negro" who challenged white power in this period. The white movement to resist desegregation was defeated in the fifties, and its defeat was crucial to the élan and self-confidence of the black movement. It was on the basis of their own victories that blacks were able to begin the decade of the sixties with such momentum and audacity. A sense of élan was part of the subjective experience of blacks that was necessary to sustain them in their movement.

This interactive development of the black movement meant also that black power grew out of the experience of the civil rights movement, though not in any simple way: the movement was both continuous and discontinuous. It was continuous in that the experiences of the civil rights movement radicalized the black activists and opened them to the new ideology of black power. This effect was more broadly felt as it infused the blacks in the Northern ghettos with a new sense of self, of potential power and militancy, as well as anger with the brutal treatment they saw delivered to the civil rights demonstrators. It was discontinuous in the social base from which it emerged and to whom it appealed. Stokeley Carmichael, the leader of SNCC, proclaimed black power in a rally in rural Mississippi. But he was responding to the self-assertions of lower-class blacks in the mostly Northern cities. These blacks had already exploded in several areas, and it was plain that they would do so still more. The rise of black power and the decline of the black movement, if they are to be properly understood, must be approached in the same way as the civil rights movement itself, using a combination of analysis of the political economy and the developing consciousness and élan of the black movement. Blacks moved beyond asking only for their rights as citizens in the South, and their new demands were unacceptable to the white allies who had stood with them against Southern opposition to desegregation; the black movement became isolated. This isolation was the soil out of which grew both the call for black power and the factionalism on which McAdam focused. Factionalism was less a cause than a symptom of the decline of the black movement.

The organization of this book reflects the approach presented here. Part one deals with the changing social, economic, and political structures within which blacks operated. Chapters one and two deal with the structure within which Southern racial discrimination was embedded. Chapter one provides an analysis of the emergence of a new class system after the destruction of slavery, and of how racial practices fit into this system. My contention is that these customs and the power structure of which they were a part were the substance that the civil rights movement had to confront in the mid-twentieth century. Chapter two details the undermining of this class structure and the laying of the foundation of a new structure. In chapter three I turn to another critical component that prepared the way for the emergence of the civil rights movement: the process of bringing the federal government into the civil rights coalition. The concern here is on the demographic and political changes that enabled blacks to affect the racial policy of the government. In chapter four I examine the rise and fall of the white reaction and how Southern businessmen and the Southern middle class came to support the new coalition.

Part two examines the growth and development of the black movement. Chapter five is concerned with the rise of the leadership of the coalition—the black movement—and with the transformation of Southern blacks. Chapters six and seven examine the experience of the 1960s and the transformation of black consciousness that took place in that turbulent period. Chapter six focuses on the Southern movement in the first half of the decade, with an emphasis on the broadening of the social base of the movement, its growing militance, and the radicalization of black youth. Chapter seven is concerned with the ghetto rebellions of the middle and late sixties, the emergence of black power, and the disintegration of the civil rights coalition.

Part One
The Changing Political
Economy of Racism

I

THE POLITICAL ECONOMY OF SOUTHERN RACISM

> Racism did not overwhelm class; racism became
> an organizing principle for social strata fearful of
> class-based political action.
>
> —Armsted Robinson[1]

To understand how the civil rights movement came into existence, how blacks successfully challenged racist practices, it is necessary first to grasp the root of this racism. Doing so will make it possible to understand what blacks had to confront in the mid-twentieth century. The civil rights movement encountered bitterness, resistance, even murder. Why? Why did the whites cling so tenaciously to segregation and the racial oppression associated with it? What was at stake in this struggle?

The civil rights movement was centered in the South. If black rights and dignity were to be won, it had to be in that region, because it was the base and source of the racial practices of the nation. "The South," wrote Martin Luther King, "was the stronghold of racism. . . . There could be no possibility of life-transforming change anywhere so long as the vast and solid influence of Southern segregation remained unchallenged and unhurt. The ten-year assault at the roots was fundamental to undermining the system."[2] Southern racism marked blacks with the badge of inferiority. It deprived them of political rights, economic opportunity, social justice, and human dignity. Why? How did these racist practices come to be embedded within the Southern social system? C. Vann Woodward pointed out that the position blacks came to occupy in the south was not inevitable and did not emerge immediately after the Civil War.

This chapter is an analysis of the creation of the racial system of the post-Civil War South. It argues that the racist beliefs and practices that the civil rights movement confronted were inextricably intertwined with, and shaped by, the class structure and class struggles of the latter part of the nineteenth century. More specifically, white supremacy became, more than anything else, the means used to maintain the dominance of the Southern upper class. Because of the importance of white supremacy in maintaining the class structure, this elite, based on the ownership of land, had a vested interest in perpetuating racism. Southern racism was thus intertwined with the class structure of the South and was, in fact, its lynchpin.

Post-Civil War racism did not develop under ordinary circumstances; rather, it took form in a period that can only be described as revolutionary. The South's defeat in the Civil War and the sudden emancipation of the slaves threw the social system into chaos; the destruction of slavery had ended one order, but it did not immediately create another. What the new economic arrangements would be, what social forces would predominate, and what was to be the basis of new racial relations were all unsettled issues. The Civil War and the era of Reconstruction destroyed the class system of the old South, and the result was a prolonged struggle over the social system that would replace it. "Emancipation," wrote James L. Roark in his study *Masters without Slaves*, "confronted planters with a problem their deepest convictions told them it was impossible to resolve— the management of staple-producing plantations employing free black labor."[3] The new racial practices were created in the course of carrying out this struggle, and racist oppression was made into the glue that held the whole system together.

In this situation, virtually all possible combinations came into being at one or another point. Upper-class whites developed a paternalistic relationship with blacks, which they used to hold back the class aspirations of lower-class whites. Upper- and lower-class whites allied to suppress blacks whenever blacks sought to challenge the economic and social arrangements that were the basis of the oppressive conditions of their lives. Lower-class whites and blacks united against the class prerogatives of the upper-class. But the main dynamic in this process was provided by the upper-class whites' successful effort to retain their economic and political domination of the region.

A new order eventually emerged from this period of social upheaval, an order that established a new class system. Upheavals of this magnitude often take decades to resolve, and so it was in the South. A stable system was not fully attained until after the turn of the century, by which time the Southern landowning class was once again securely in control.

It was not a foregone conclusion that whites would join in concert against blacks. White small farmers had long borne their own grudges against the wealthy slaveholders, and the economic squeeze they felt after the Civil War reinforced their anger against the upper class. The newly freed slaves had similar interests. Separately, each group constituted a problem for the planters; together, especially with the support of the federal government, they were a genuine threat to the existence of the landed aristocracy.

These problems were intensified by the South's poverty and by the efforts of the planters to retain as much of the old social system as they could. These circumstances forced the landowning class to change its character and to become bourgeois in order to make possible a settlement with the North. The new merchant-landlord class had its roots in the old planter class, and as it groped toward new class relations, it did so with the aim of recapitulating the old.

The form that white supremacy took was not a product of a coherent strategy but involved ad hoc responses to chaotic circumstances. White supremacy was directed primarily toward removing blacks from political power. Without political power, blacks could more easily be forced into economic subservience and become the controlled labor force that the merchant-landlord class felt it needed. White supremacy did not mean that all whites were to be supreme. It became the "code word" and the strategy for the domination of the region by the merchant-landlord class of the black belt, the traditional plantation area. In the name of white supremacy, lower-class whites were asked to sacrifice their well-being and eventually even their right to vote. That was ostensibly for the purpose of avoiding the danger of "Negro domination"; but in reality this *racial* danger was raised at any time that the merchant-landlord class felt its *class* position threatened. As a consequence, the merchant-landlords emerged from the turbulence occasioned by the South's defeat in the Civil War as powerful and secure in their region as the slaveholding class itself had been.

The Southern landed elite did not create the Southern racial system alone, though it was the primary mover. Lower-class white racism is not in doubt here, but it was not primarily responsible for the system of racial domination. Left to themselves, the merchant-landlords might have preferred a more genteel system, based on their own paternalistic relationship with blacks. Such a relationship enabled them to create the unholy alliance between themselves and the blacks in which wealthy whites "protected" blacks and enabled them to retain the right to vote and to use public property, so long as they stayed in their "place." In return, this white upper class was able to use the blacks as a buffer against the demands of lower-class whites and to play each off against the other. But the possibility of black and white labor's joining to challenge the political and economic structure was a constant threat. When the threat turned into a reality, the Southern elite acted to end the danger once and for all. It consolidated the hegemony of its class by removing all political rights from blacks, and, as it turned out, from many whites as well.

The first section of this chapter, "Survival of the Landowning Class," traces the economic and social evolution that the region underwent in the latter part of the nineteenth century. The conditions that existed in this period established the framework within which the battle for political power took place. This section delineates the major protagonists: the planter class, the merchants, and the evolution of both into the new merchant-landlord class; white farmers; the newly freed blacks. It demonstrates the problems each of these social groups faced and the evolutionary outcome of their efforts to respond to these problems. It does not, for the most part, show the process whereby a new social and economic system of exploitation was created, for that discussion requires an explication of the political struggles of the period. The subsequent two sections, "The Challenge of Reconstruction" and "The Threat from Below," trace this political process. The last section, "Shadow of the Plantation," discusses the class system of the South as it solidified out of this chaotic period and entered the twentieth century.

Survival of the Landowning Class

Poverty was the supreme reality of the post-Civil War South. It deeply affected everything about the South and cast a pall of desperation on everyone's endeavors. In this period the very survival of the plantation came into question. The former slaveowning class had suffered serious economic losses as a result of the war. Much of its capital had been invested in slaves. Most of the remainder had gone for land and war bonds. The victorious North repudiated the bonds, and the land that escaped damage had only a potential value without a stable labor force to work it. The physical destruction of cities, railroads, bridges, ports, navigable streams, even food and livestock added to the seriousness of the economic damage. Total destruction has been estimated in the billions of dollars. Moreover, the tariffs that the South had long opposed had been substantially raised during the war—up 47 percent, and steadily rising thereafter.[4]

All of that was compounded by the lack of liquid capital available in the region for planters to borrow. In 1880 the South had 35 percent of the nation's population but only 8.5 percent of the banking deposits. By 1895 there was only one bank for every 58,130 inhabitants of the South, while the comparable national figure was one per 16,000. In Georgia alone, 123 of the state's 137 counties had no banking facilities whatsoever. Neither did most of the parishes in Louisiana, where, historian William Hare wrote, "rural banks simply did not exist." The banks that did exist were short of funds. As late as 1937, savings deposits in the South were only 6 percent of the national total; of the sixty-six largest banks in the country at that time, only two were Southern, and they were on the bottom of the list. The weakness of the banking system was exaggerated by the cyclical demands upon it. Deposits tended to be largest in the fall and winter after the harvest, and smallest in the spring and summer, when the need for farm credit was the greatest.[5]

The Reconstruction regimes heavily taxed the planters. Throughout the South, property taxes were four times higher in 1870 than they had been in 1860. In Mississippi the property tax rate was fourteen times higher in 1874 than in 1869, the last year of Democratic party control. As taxes went up, so did the assessed value of property. Previously much of the planters' property had been assessed at less than its value for tax purposes; now that tendency was reversed. In some cases the aim of the taxation was frankly confiscatory. These taxes were directed primarily against the planter class, who, in its turn, provided most of the opposition, and certainly its leadership, to Reconstruction. In South Carolina a heavy tax was put on unused land to force the planters either to sell it or to cultivate it, thereby putting to work laborers or renters. The planters charged that their taxes were a result of government corruption, and indeed there was plenty of corruption; but more significant were the new social services provided by the state reconstruction programs.[6]

The planters' most serious problem was the rising cost of labor. Under slavery, "labor was like the air or the sunshine—it was on hand to be used at will." All at once, "when the slave was set free, this labor supply vanished, it had been confiscated and given back to the negro to use as he pleased.'' Labor became the planters' most pressing concern. From the very first, they tried to return to the kind of control over black labor that they had previously enjoyed. Blacks were urged to stay on their old plantations, but if they should do so, a Georgia planter advised his former slaves, ''they should work as they always had done.'' W. E. B. DuBois cited the case of a planter who told his slaves that they were free but that he would like them to remain and work for him. When one refused, ''his son James flew at him and cuffed and kicked him; . . . after that they were all 'perfectly willing to stay'; they were watched night and day; . . . Bob, one of the men, had been kept chained nights; . . . they were actually afraid to try to get away.''[7]

The planters tried to consolidate their control by a modified version of the wage labor system in which they would organize gangs of wage laborers to work under overseers, as under slavery. Planters attempted to act in concert to keep wages down, but blacks refused to cooperate with this system which so resembled slavery. Blacks hoped for better—for land of their own, or at least improved conditions. Historian Leon Litwack concluded that ''no matter how enticing the offer or how desperate their own situation had become, they might choose to cling stubbornly to whatever degree of separation from the old way of life they had managed to attain.'' ''I'm goin' to my own land just as soon as I git dis crop in, an' . . . I'm not goin' to work for any man for any such price [twenty-five cents a day],'' said one.[8]

The former slaves could and did move from the plantations where they had lived, often to leave agriculture altogether and to go to the towns, or even to depart from the state. The uncertainty and scarcity of the labor supply that resulted increased the bargaining power of blacks. They refused to work the daylight-to-dark, and sometimes even longer, hours that had been customary under slavery, and they also refused to allow themselves to be pressed as hard as they had been as slaves. They circulated among the planters in search of better terms, thus forcing employers to compete with one another to get the labor they needed. Even then they sometimes broke contracts. They went on strike occasionally to demand higher wages, better working conditions, the right to rent land, or in some cases the payment of cash wages instead of provisions. Their efforts were effective: economists Roger Ransom and Richard Sutch calculated that the black share of the agricultural product rose from 22 percent under slavery to 56 percent under the sharecropping and tenant farming system. Black income actually increased in dollar amount by about 30 percent, though the output was smaller, so the planters' share was reduced substantially.[9]

The cost and supply of labor remained a constant problem in the South for decades. When Ray Stannard Baker toured the South in the early 1900s, he found: ''If the South today could articulate its chief need, we should hear a single great shout: 'More labor!' ''[10] The South's leaders devised many solutions to the problem: they tried to encourage whites from the North to come South; they urged European immigrants to look to the opportunities in their region. They even tried importing Chinese laborers. All to no avail.

In truth, there was plenty of labor in the South: the region managed to export millions of its population to the rest of the country over decades and still have sufficient labor. What the planters really complained of was that labor had become so much more expensive with the end of slavery. Their various schemes were devised with the aim of forcing the former slaves "to choose between competition and starvation." "If white labor is generally introduced into the Upper District it will drive the Negro down and then the competition for labor will oblige them to work for very little," a South Carolina planter wrote hopefully. But the efforts to drive down the cost of labor, and so to increase profits, failed because the cost was already so low, the living and working conditions so poor, that other workers would not tolerate them. The experience of a South Carolina planter with a group of German laborers illustrates the problem. He fed them better than his other hands and "even gave them coffee and sauerkraut when, what would they do but demand butter for their bread and milk for their coffee, and the next thing the whole crowd left. . . ."[11]

As a result, what had been the prewar ruling class endured severe economic hardships that continued for years. "There were no rich left now," argued W. J. Cash. "At best there were only the land poor." That was an exaggeration, but there is no doubt that the planters were hard pressed. Life was much closer to the margins, and they were forced to struggle for what luxuries they could obtain, and in the process to abandon the luxury of *noblesse oblige*. Many were forced into bankruptcy or had to sell their land or mortgage their crops to pay their debts.[12]

But if much of the planter class did not survive, the plantation certainly did. In fact, the plantation economy was strengthened. By 1880, every Southern state showed an increase in its large plantations. In Marengo County, Alabama, 10 percent of the landowners held 63 percent of the real estate; in Dallas County, 10 percent held 57 percent of the land. In Louisiana there were three times as many plantations in 1880 as there had been in 1860. Cotton and tenantry had increased, and self-sufficiency among small farmers was disappearing. By 1900, 2.4 percent of the landowners held 45.3 percent of the land acreage, worth 27.4 percent of the total value. In North Carolina 4 percent of the landowners controlled the agricultural output of 20 percent of the tenants. One analyst argued that control both of the land and of labor was more concentrated in the South in 1900 than it had been in 1860. A 1910 Census Bureau study of 325 black-belt counties found that plantations covered over a third of the land area studied, Mississippi, Alabama, and Georgia each had plantations covering over five million acres of land.[13]

Some of these plantations changed owners. An estimate in 1881 held that less than a third of the cotton plantations in the Mississippi Valley were owned by their immediate post-Civil War owners. Sometimes they were run by corporations, and absentee ownership became far more common. Recent evidence, however, suggests that the decline of the planter class has been overestimated. A study of Alabama planters showed the top layer of the planter class to have increased its landholdings by 1870 both relatively and absolutely. But in order to do so, planters were forced to change the way they lived and operated; they had to join the ranks of the growing merchant class and thus to become transformed into a commercial, bourgeois class.[14]

The supply merchants arose out of the desperate need in the South for credit. Credit was essential both for living supplies and for the materials necessary for a new crop: seed, fertilizer, farm implements. Though the former planters, now turned landlords, provided some of this credit for the renters and tenants, they were unable to bear it all. Indeed, in the immediate postwar years, many of them desperately needed credit, and at first most of the merchants came from outside the planter class. It was somewhat later, in the 1870s, that the former slaveowners began to meet the merchants on their own ground, and to triumph. The country store emerged to fill the need for credit for the blacks and the white farmers. The merchant would lend or "advance" the goods to the farmer in exchange for a lien on his crop. That meant that the farmer had to settle his debt with the merchant by marketing his produce through the store where he had gotten the lien. In most cases, the merchant took the value of what he had lent the farmer before paying him. Through this system the merchant began to grow into an alternative economic power to the planter.[15]

Planters and merchants frequently found themselves at odds with one another. The planter-landlords felt that the merchant's credit offer was a threat to their profits and to their control over labor. Indeed, in the late 1860s the threat was greater than that. In the conditions of tight credit that existed, the merchants possessed leverage that gave them an advantage over the landlords and that thereby enabled them to challenge the landlords' control over the basis of their power—the land itself. They could refuse to finance the tenants unless the landlord countersigned the lien. Few landlords were prepared to finance their tenants themselves, so they had little choice but to acquiesce. The low value of land and high taxes virtually ruled out the alternatives of selling or merely leaving the land unused. This competition provided some advantages for the tenants, who tended to prefer the merchant system: it provided them an escape from the closer supervision of the landlord. And if the landlord countersigned a lien, the merchant might encourage the tenant to overspend, which would permit the merchant to attach the landlord's share—up to and including his land and money. "A man could start up as a rich planter with a large plantation and thousands of dollars but end up impoverished if he were forced to countersign his tenants' liens," wrote Michael Schwarz.[16]

These conditions had a real impact. In Alabama, the former planters' economic situation deteriorated relative to the merchants'. The value of the real estate of the planter class fell from fifteen million to five million dollars between 1860 and 1870. At the same time, the merchants' small land value increased. Merchants with large landholdings increased from 1 to 6 percent of all black-belt merchants, and that was at a time when the total number of merchants was growing rapidly. In the South as a whole, 43,000 merchants in 1860 expanded to 69,000 in 1870.[17]

But in the next decade, the planters were able to adapt and to triumph. They themselves became merchants, and they ended by owning most of the country stores in the former slaveowning areas. They pushed the independent merchants out of the plantation region. These merchants were then allowed to make their fortunes only in the hill country, where the white farmers lived. Lester Salomon found that in Mississippi the old planter class continued to be hegemonic. "The result," he said, "has been economic backwardness, the 'closed society,' and limited economic development." According to Gail O'Brien, in one county in North Carolina, landed slaveholders persisted in power despite emancipation and Reconstruction. Dwight Billings, Jr. found that in North Carolina as a whole, the old slave interests continued to dominate the economy, including its industrialization.[18]

Thus, the class that controlled the Southern economy and society after the Civil War was still a class of landowners, and in fact it appears to have been dominated by the antebellum slavocracy. No longer slaveowners, they had to exist under conditions that required careful attention to moneymaking. As merchants and landlords, they had to deal with customers and tenants; and it was from them that they had to accumulate their fortunes. However much they might wish to return to slavery, they could not do so, and the social and economic relations within which they were constrained to work were utterly different.[19]

The credit advanced by the merchant-landlords was extraordinarily expensive. One estimate held that the cost of credit ranged from 50 percent to 125 percent. Cash contended that it averaged 40 percent to 80 percent. Economists Ransom and Sutch estimated that between 1881 and 1889, interest rates ranged from 44.2 percent to 74.6 percent and averaged 59.4 percent per year. As late as the 1930s John Dollard reported tenants' commonly being charged a flat rate of 25 percent, "whatever the length of time they [the loans] are made for." A loan made in June and paid in October would still pay the 25 percent. Costs included the rate of interest, as well as the mark-up for goods sold on credit rather than for cash.[20]

These charges slowly provided the means for the merchants to prosper, though Southern poverty made it a difficult process:

> Thousands would attempt it and fail; hundreds of others would barely hang on. But let a man have a firm eye for the till; let him have it in him to remember always that the price of sentimental weakness was disaster, to return a quiet no to the client who was hopelessly involved, not to flinch from the ultimate necessity to which he must often come: the necessity of stripping a father of ten children of his last ear of corn—and his prospects of growing rich were bright.[21]

The merchants themselves were under a great deal of pressure. They had to pay harsh terms to their own creditors, and they went without payment for many months. Interest rates of from 12 to 36 percent per year were normal, and occasionally they had to pay even higher rates.[22]

The merchants served as brokers for Northern capital because ultimately that was where the money came from, either directly from Northern manufacturers or wholesalers or indirectly through the banks. The Southern credit line worked its way back to the New York banks. Thus, Northern capital played a significant part in shaping the post-Civil War economy, with the merchants in effect serving as its agents. The merchants transmitted the Northern banks' terms throughout the South, while grasping for their own well-being.[23]

Northern capital's dominance was evident in pathetic, if symbolically important, ways. People whose prestigious names derived from their leadership of the South before its defeat lent those names to the new moneymaking institutions, mostly owned by Northerners, for a good price. Much more significant was the sale, after Reconstruction, of millions of acres of publicly held land at very cheap rates to lumbermen and speculators—as cheap as from 12.5 to 75 cents per acre. Large amounts of this land were given away to the railroads: Texas granted over 32 million acres to twelve railroad companies. Most of this largesse was for the benefit of Northern capital.[24]

Most of the economic pressures were transmitted to the farmers by the merchants. The merchants bought the farmers' crops and sold them their goods. They bought low—when everyone was selling farm goods—and sold high. If cotton was held to get a better price, it was by the merchant.

Through the lien they obtained on the farmers' crops, the merchants became virtual overlords of their clients' lives. Once a merchant had a lien, no other merchant would sell the farmer anything, except in return for cash. The merchant would grant to the farmer what goods he thought he would be able to pay for, and he would often ride out to the fields to keep tabs on his clients. Frequently at settlement time the farmer would be told that he had not earned enough to pay his debt. His contract then required him to renew his lien with the same merchant the next year.[25]

In this way a form of peonage was created that approached, as closely as the South dared, the old slave system. DuBois reported that in one black-belt county in Georgia in 1898, only 75 tenant families out of 300 made a profit—which totaled only $1,600. The rest ended the year with a loss totaling $14,000. An 1896 study of Southern farms found that the overwhelming majority lost money in that year. With prices tending to drop regularly, and with the steep appreciation of the currency, farmers consistently tended to drop into insolvency. A federal government report from the Senate Committee on Agriculture and Forestry in 1895 gives some indication of the extent of misery in this period. In 72 percent of the counties the committee examined, the majority of the farmers were insolvent; in 28 percent over three-quarters were. Only 10 percent of the farmers were entirely out of debt. Merchants were often free to manipulate accounts so as to enable those whom they did not wish to have continue as tenants to be out of debt and free to go, and to compel the more desirable (i.e., more productive) to stay because they remained in debt.[26]

Those still in debt who sought to leave were treated like criminals. So were the labor-hungry landlords who tried to encourage them to leave (by "decoying" or "persuading" or "enticing" them, as the law read). And when outsiders tried to recruit blacks for industry, they frequently met with violence. A railroad emigration agent at the turn of the century testified:

> I know of several counties not a hundred miles from Atlanta where it's more than a man's life is worth to go in to get Negroes to move to some other state. There are farmers that would not hesitate to shoot their brother were he to come from Mississippi to get 'his niggers,' as he calls them, even though he has no contract with them. I know personally numbers of Negro men who have moved West, and after accumulating a little, return to get a brother, sister or an old father or mother and they were compelled to return without them, their lives being imperilled. . . .[27]

Bourgeois as the merchant-landlords may have become, they were certainly not out to introduce a free labor market into the South. The lien system, combined with legal and extralegal methods of coercion, was a key part of the solution to their problem of maintaining an adequate labor supply at low cost. One landlord articulated the ideology: "Unless you have power to compel them, they'll only work when they can't beg or steal enough to keep from starving." More than half a century later, researcher John Dollard found little to have changed: "The planters say they have to keep the Negroes poor to keep them here."[28]

The merchant-landlords controlled what the farmers planted, and they demanded cotton. Cotton was a cash crop that could easily be sold on the market; cotton was money. That meant that under the post-Civil War system, the South became more of a one-crop economy than it had been under slavery. Production of corn and hay declined even as that of cotton steadily advanced. Farmers were not permitted to borrow seed to grow their own food, and thus they became even more dependent on the merchants. This system tended to create overproduction of cotton, which helped drive the prices down, causing further misery for the Southern farmer.*[30]

Blacks were not alone in suffering from these conditions. For if the rich planters had been impoverished as a consequence of the Civil War, the white small farmers, who had little between themselves and mere subsistence, suffered far more. When the war was over, since many of them were already in debt they also needed credit to live, and to farm. And they had to turn to the merchant to get it. In order to get credit, they had to enter the cotton crop economy. They, or many of them, had previously been self-sufficient. Now they began to encounter the same conditions as the newly freed blacks:

> Here was an end for these people of the independence and self-sufficiency, the freedom from direct exploitation and servitude. . . . The relation of master and man, patron and client, was pouring over into the taboo confines of white men.[31]

From the census of 1870 on, white sharecroppers outnumbered black. While in 1860 blacks had produced 90 percent of the cotton crop, by 1876 they were

---

*According to economist Gordon Wright, "The main reason for the slow recovery of Southern incomes after the Civil War was the drastic slowdown in the rate of growth of demand for cotton." Apparently, the lien system made Southern farmers and merchants "blind to a market that signaled a cut rather than an increase in cotton production.[29]

responsible for only 60 percent, and by 1900 their share had dropped to only 40 percent. In 1900, 36 percent of all white farmers were tenants and share-croppers, and by 1930 this figure had risen to 45 percent. These figures tell the story not only of immiserization but also of a potential problem for the Southern upper class as it tried to attain and consolidate its political control over the region.[32]

The Challenge of Reconstruction

These economic trends set the parameters within which political struggle took place in the South. The poverty of the region and the net flow of capital outward left little room for generosity. What was beneficial to one man or one group was necessarily detrimental to another, and so each was arrayed at various times against the others: landlords versus merchants, yeoman farmers and blacks against the upper classes, and often against each other. The intense struggles that these antagonisms involved took place in the political as well as in the economic arena. For decades, the planters and their successors, the merchant-landlords, could not rest without fear of losing control. For much of this time they were under attack, and they responded with the program of white supremacy to make themselves preeminent. The actions that assured their continued pre-dominance were also those that took from the black population many of the fruits of Civil War victory.

There was a struggle for political hegemony in this period, in which no holds were barred. This struggle, which grew out of and was shaped by the economic circumstances, in turn helped to fashion the new economic structure. State power was fought over so intensely because it was used by all sides as an instrument favoring whichever group was able to hold it.

This relationship between political and economic power became clear im-mediately after the war, before Northern policy toward the newly defeated South had solidified. The Confederate states, under the mild terms of presidential Re-construction, set about to create as close a replica as possible of the slave system. That was done through a series of laws that came to be known as the "Black Codes." These laws usually included provisions that criminals—those who vio-lated the Black Codes—could be hired out to save the state the expense of keeping them, with first preference given to the former owner. Such penalties were even attached to vagrancy. Vagrants included those who had "no lawful employment or business" or who were "unlawfully assembling together"; who couldn't support themselves and their dependents and still refused to work for "usual and common wages"; or who couldn't pay their poll tax. In Mississippi, anyone who was without a written labor contract or who broke a contract "without good cause," who spoke obscenities, or who misspent his wages or neglected his work, was legally a vagrant. All of these measures created a large population of "criminals" who were made available for labor under deplorable conditions.

Children whose parents could not support them, or who were in danger of "moral contamination," could be bound out as apprentices without their parents' consent—again with preference to the former owner. It was made a criminal act to break a contract. If one did so, he could be arrested by anyone. The returned laborer then had deducted from his wages the legal compensation due to his captor. In Mississippi that amounted to five dollars, plus ten cents for each mile traveled.[33]

These moves were part of the planters' broader political offensive, which sought to reestablish their power, in part by seeking Democratic party hegemony nationally. With slavery abolished, so was the three-fifths constitutional rule that had limited the enumeration of blacks for apportionment of presidential electors and of representatives to Congress. Thus, the Democrats were able to increase their political power on the basis of black bodies who were not themselves eligible to vote. Their effort raised the specter of the Southern planters' gaining through political maneuvering what they had lost on the battlefield.

The Northern coalition of radical abolitionists and industrialists that had waged the war held together under the continuing menace of the unrepentant former slavocracy. But now its leadership passed to the radicals, who, in response to the Black Codes and the political maneuvering of the Southern landed elite, sought once and for all to destroy the power of the planters. To this end, they enfranchised blacks and disfranchised some 100,000 whites and made 200,000 ineligible to hold office. They thus displaced the planters from political power and began a protracted struggle over the right to vote which did not end until the twentieth century, when blacks were effectively disfranchised. Granting blacks the vote was a necessary act to challenge the planters on their home turf.[34]

The Emancipation Proclamation had made the Civil War into a revolutionary war. It began a process of expropriating billions of dollars of (human) property without any compensation, an act never again contemplated by the United States. More important, it utterly changed social relations in the South. People who had been slaves, who had been ordered and who had obeyed, who had had to demonstrate subservience, were now their own masters.

> The day the war ended, Prince John recalled, "wagonloads o' people rode all th'ough de place a tellin' us 'bout bein' free." When the news reached Ocona, Georgia, Ed McCree found himself so overcome that he refused to wait for his master to confirm the report of Lee's surrender: "I rushed 'round dat place a shoutin' to de top of my voice." Whites viewed the downfall of the Confederacy and slavery as fastening upon them the ignominy of bondage. Either they must submit to the insolence of their servants or appeal to their Northern "masters" for protection, one woman wrote "as if we were slaves ourselves—and that is just what they are trying to make of us. Oh, it is abominable!"[35]

Until passage of the Reconstruction Acts in 1867, virtually no Southern state had a Republican party organization. When the party organized itself, its primary base was among the blacks, but its appeal and support were by no means limited to blacks. The party often frankly and unabashedly advanced a class program directed against the planters. An appeal from the Georgia Republican party read:

> Poor white man of Georgia, be a man! Let the slaveholding aristocracy no longer rule you. Vote for a constitution which educates your children free of charge; relieves the poor debtor from his rich creditor; allows a liberal homestead for your families; and more than all, places you on a level with those who used to boast that for every slave they were entitled to three fifths of a vote in congressional representation.

In Arkansas: "Do you want good roads throughout your state? Do you want free bridges? Do you want free schools and the advantages of education for your children?" In North Carolina the party spoke of the laboring people who had been "imposed upon socially, politically and pecuniarily by Southern aristocrats and secession oligarchs." And in Mississippi at the constitutional convention, the president noted that "this hour brings to a final end that system that enriches the few at the expense of the many. . . ." In Georgia, Republicans advanced a program that included issues such as debtor relief, homestead exemptions, state social services, and the eight-hour workday.[36]

In Louisiana, Tennessee, Texas, Virginia, and South Carolina, similar class issues became the subject of serious divisions and the source of support for the Republican party among lower-class whites. In South Carolina, white farmers organized to protect themselves against their rapidly mounting debts. They tried by use of physical force to stop sheriffs from seizing their property for failure to pay their debts. Their efforts created enough of a stir that they forced the governor to petition (successfully) the military commander of the region to issue a military order staying all foreclosures and putting an end to debtors' prison. In Mississippi, whole new services were established by the Reconstruction regimes: a public biracial school system where no public schools had been before; aid to colleges; establishment of state hospitals; expansion of the facilities for the blind, deaf, dumb, and insane. Free public education appeared in many of the states for the first time, as did many other reforms, including a general democratization of the South.[37]

The new Reconstruction governments established conditions that were more favorable to the lower classes, black and white. They set aside some of the Black Codes, tried to enact a free labor market, established the conditions and to some degree regulated the contracts for labor, and tried to protect black civil rights. In some cases racial discrimination was specifically forbidden. The new governments repudiated the war debts and opened some land for homesteading, thereby making available an alternative to tenantry. They modified the lien laws to the benefit of the debtors. In South Carolina and Alabama, for example, the laborers' share came first before other liens could be executed. And, they significantly raised the level of taxation on the large property owners, while at the same time exempting most small farmers from property taxation.[38]

The Reconstruction governments, which were based on the black vote, began to shift the economic balance away from the planters. They were thus partly responsible for creating the conditions that enabled the merchants to challenge the planters' dominance. The political power and civil rights that their governments guaranteed for blacks provided these same blacks with greater bargaining power in the economic sphere and made it possible for them to seek better terms.[39]

One need not sympathize with the planters to recognize that their circumstances were desperate: they were under the boot of the federal government, besieged by their economic rivals, assaulted by black and white labor alike. If they were to survive, individually and collectively, they had to act ruthlessly. The planter elite responded to the challenge by seeking to undermine the Republican offensive and to destroy the Reconstruction regimes. They initiated a titanic struggle which did not end until the removal of federal troops in the late 1870s.

Some, seeing the danger the Republican party represented to planter interests when it was backed by the federal government, sought to blunt its thrust by entering the party to take it over and subvert it; as historian Carl Degler put it, they intended "to control its excesses." Joseph Bennett of Mississippi gave as his reason for joining the party his intention of watering down its program. The former chief justice of the North Carolina Supreme Court saw this course of action as the way to put an "end to that alliance between the Negro and the lower class white." The Hinds County, Mississippi *Gazette* "wanted white Southerners to work to contain the revolution from within rather than to resist it ineffectually from without." The Montgomery *Advertiser* voiced a similar sentiment, encouraging conservatives to enter the party so as not to let "so much power go into the hands of their enemies by default."[40]

These efforts apparently succeeded in blunting the class assault. The Republican party's appeal to lower-class whites became increasingly ambiguous, and the party itself became increasingly factionalized, which was in reality class struggle within the Republican party. The result was, as intended, that the white farmers became discouraged and turned away from the party.[41]

To render the Republican party ineffectual, an alternative had to be provided. Many planters relinquished their paternalistic approach to blacks to emphasize racial division as the political alternative to class divisions. They waged their fight around the slogans of "white supremacy" and "home rule," which, because of the importance of blacks in upholding the Reconstruction governments, amounted to the same thing. Home rule meant white supremacy, and the latter was the key to attaining home rule.

The Democratic party had to be made into the alternative to the Republican party; it did not automatically become the party of the white South. Prior to the Civil War, the slaveowners had tended to look to the Whig party; after the war, planters and businessmen often chose to avoid the Democratic party, many of them looking to the Republicans. To gain increased respectability among these, the Democratic party often called itself the Conservative party. But by whatever name, they made the Democratic party the party of the region, the party of all classes of Southern whites. To do so they had as much as possible to make the Republican party a party of the blacks, of "negro domination," and thus leave no other alternative*. In North Carolina the papers emphasized the prominence of blacks at the Republican party conventions. Historian Frenise Logan noted that that was "just what the Democrats wanted because they could then point to the large Negro element in the convention and present the Republicans as traitors to our race, aliens, an infamous, degraded set trying to put the state under Negro rule.' "[43]

Northern whites had to be driven out of the region, and those Southern whites who had become Republicans—some of whom were "influential" or "leading citizens"—had to be forced to leave the party or be repudiated as "scalawags." Thus, it became impossible for whites to be associated with any party but the Democratic party. White Republicans were ostracized or called "white niggers" to their faces. One Republican in Mississippi wrote that "even my own kins-people have turned the cold shoulder to me because I hold office under a Republican administration."[44]

The Ku Klux Klan was an instrument of the struggle. All classes in the white South appear to have been involved in it and to have used it for different purposes. In the predominantly white counties, which were usually located in the hills away from the fertile plantation areas, the Klan was used to drive blacks out so as to eliminate them as competitors with white laborers. In the black belt, the upper classes sometimes opposed the Klan because its violence was disruptive to labor and investment alike. Nonetheless, the upper class used the Klan to control black labor, even to the detriment of white labor. Blacks who tried to leave the area were threatened with murder, and some of them were killed. When they did leave, they were sometimes pursued and dragged back, even across state lines. An Alabama planter told a congressional committee that the Klan was necessary because blacks "are told by some . . . that planters do not pay sufficient wages for their labor." The Klan often went out of its way to cooperate with the planters: during planting season, blacks were left alone. Sometimes planters used the Klan against the poor whites. "These bands are having a great effect, in inspiring a nameless *terror* among Negroes, poor whites, and even others," a Republican editor wrote. In Mississippi, "prominent and respected Conservatives were immune from vigilante attack no matter what they did (as were the few Democratic Negroes), but poorer and more insignificant whites were visited without much regard to political learning."[45]

What was most important in winning upper-class support for the Klan was its political character. Allen Trelease wrote in his historical compendium of Klan activity, *White Terror*:

> The one really new ingredient of regulator activity after 1867 was political opposition to the Radicals. And so far as the Klan loomed larger than the earlier vigilante groups, this was undoubtedly the reason. Only now did upper class elements and Conservative political leaders take much interest in the idea. In many

*As in the Richmond *Daily Dispatch* of 1873: "The Conservative Party is the white man's party, and the Radical Party is the negro party. The former proposes to keep all the offices in the hands of the whites, and the latter is forced to divide the offices with the negroes."[42]

places some took over Klan leadership, at least temporarily. The Klan became in effect a terrorist arm of the Democratic Party, whether the party leaders as a whole liked it or not.

Threats were made and sometimes carried out against whites, as in a case in Tennessee in which a Confederate veteran who had voted Republican "'was seized by the crowd, put on a block, and offered for sale as a 'white nigger.' '' But overwhelmingly it was the blacks who bore the brunt of the attacks.[46]

These terrorist organizations and their actions frequently received the support of the whole white community. Their perpetrators were not prosecuted; when they were brought to trial, juries would not convict them no matter what the evidence. Such activity was another indication of the active support given the KKK and its sister organizations by "influential citizens" in the South who, even when they publicly deplored the actions, often indicated their support for them in private. The Klan was aided by the Democratic newspapers, which sometimes openly cheered it on: "Run, nigger, run, or the Ku Klux will catch you!"[47]

Whether the intent of the terror was political or economic, the effect was the same. Every political defeat the blacks suffered also meant economic setback for them. If the blacks had no rights, no protection, then they couldn't stand up to the landlord or the poor white. That was why "every sign of manhood was an invitation to Ku Klux attack."[48]

If these measures were not sufficient, the campaign for white domination brought massive fraud and violence to elections. In Louisiana, many parishes with a black majority went Democratic: In Nachitoches Parish, Louisiana, for instance, the vote was 2,800 Democratic, 0 Republican in 1878. In another majority black parish, "not a single Republican vote was counted in 1878, more than fifty Negroes were killed and others driven from their homes during the campaign, according to a report by the local United States District Attorney." In Alabama economic pressure was used, including the compiling of blacklists of those blacks who were active Republicans. Alongside the pressure was the use of "intimidation, ostracism, violence and murder," which included assassinations, bands of armed men, and mobs. Ballots were destroyed or thrown out along with whole ballot boxes. In one county, the polling place was stormed as the ballots were being counted; the judge who was counting was fired upon, his son was killed, and the ballot box was stolen.[49]

The political campaign that the planters led for "Redemption"—home rule— succeeded. Its success was due, in part, to acquiescence by the federal government. The government agreed to pull the troops out of the South and allow it to go its own way while there were still Republican administrations in Louisiana and South Carolina—administrations that soon toppled. The troop withdrawal was agreed upon by a complicated deal in the disputed Hayes-Tilden election of 1876. After extensive bargaining, Southern electors agreed to cast their votes for the Republican Hayes in return for the agreed-upon withdrawal, thereby creating the Compromise of 1877.

Although the precipitant of the bargain was the close election that permitted behind-the-scenes maneuvering, it would not have been struck had important changes not taken place in the South—namely, that the region's dominant class had become reconciled to industrial capitalism. There was no longer an alternative program or set of interests. This important change made possible two significant developments in national politics. The Republican party leadership perceived that the Reconstruction governments had failed to keep the South in alliance with Northern Republicans; it saw the conservative Redeemers as potential allies and sought to lure them into the Republican fold. Northern commercial interests, no longer faced with a serious threat to their hegemony and living through a serious depression that began in 1873 and persisted for most of the rest of the decade, longed for peace between the regions. Calm, they felt, would enable trade and commerce to grow, and the prerequisite for calm was that the North cease to champion blacks. And labor unrest in the North helped to create a climate of reaction that was favorable to an accord with the Southern elite. So they pressured Congress, the president, and their party to reintegrate the South into the nation. While the attitude of the Republican party toward blacks and the South remained a continuing source of controversy for more than a decade, the Compromise of 1877 was not overturned. By the late 1870s, the radical Republicans in every Southern state had been defeated and removed from power, and blacks were left to their own devices.[50]

The significance of this change in the South went beyond the removal of the federal government and black influence. The changes enacted by the Redeemers were, for the most part, for the benefit of the upper class. Home rule meant the reimposition of much of the Black Codes and convict leasing. This latter change became a serious bone of contention, with white workers bitterly opposed to it because it undercut their own labor. Redemption meant the dismantling of most of the social programs initiated by the Reconstruction governments. In Texas, for instance, the school system was replaced with one that was far less adequate, and the all-white Texas Rangers were established to replace the state police force, which had employed blacks. In Virginia the conservatives were prepared to sacrifice Reconstruction. Said the governor as he vetoed the debt adjustment bill: "Free schools are not a necessity. . . . They are a luxury, adding . . . to the beauty and power of the state, but to be paid for, like any other luxury, by the people who wish their benefits." The Redeemers, said Woodward, "frankly constituted themselves champions of the property owner against the propertyless and allegedly untaxed masses." That meant the subjugation of blacks and the continued use of terror when it was felt necessary. It meant, for example, that if blacks were to organize a strike, the leaders would be jailed and the strike crushed.[51]

The victory of white supremacy included serious efforts to circumvent popular votes. To consolidate their political control, the landlords sought to nullify the franchise of the blacks in the black-belt counties where they had a majority. In general, that was done by vast centralization—the appointment of many local officials by the governor. In Florida, the governor appointed the tax collector, assessor, treasurer, surveyor, school superintendent, county commissioners, sheriffs, court clerks, judges, and justices of the peace, "leaving to the uninhibited franchise of the Floridians," wrote Woodward, "the choice of constables."[52] Similar arrangements were found in the other Southern states.

White supremacy now meant that whoever controlled the state government controlled the whole state. And, since only one party was of any significance, whoever controlled it controlled the state, including most local government. In Mississippi, the governor, secretary of state, and attorney general acted as the board of election commissioners. They appointed a registrar in each county and the county election boards. These officials determined where the election sites were, who was qualified to vote, which votes were counted and which thrown out on technicalities. In North Carolina, the office of justice of the peace ceased to be elective. The now-appointed justices in their turn appointed county commissioners who set up the county courts. In Alabama, of the elected governments, some black-belt counties were abolished and replaced by gubernatorial appointment. The parties and the local and state governments came to be dominated by the "courthouse cliques"—bosses who effectively picked the party candidates and who could veto those who refused to accept party policy. It was, noted one observer, an "easy matter for a few aggressive, resourceful men to control a county."[53]

Control of the state party machinery was held by the landlords in the black belt. Since representation was based on the total population, the landlords were able to use the large number of blacks who did not vote, or who were subject to landlord control, to attain overrepresentation. Thus, in 1880, Lowndes County, Mississippi, with fewer voters than Jackson County, got three times as many legislators because of the large nonvoting black population. And, since party representation was based on the state legislative districts, the black-belt landlords were also overrepresented in the party. Black-belt representation in the Alabama Democratic party convention increased from 26 percent in 1876 to 34 percent in 1888, all based on a black electorate that had no representation in the convention. The population in these counties in the same period decreased from 38 percent of the Alabama population in 1879 to 32 percent in 1890, and the white population dropped from 21 percent to 14 percent of the total population in the black-belt counties. The Brandon, Mississippi *Republican* lamented that "the few white men in the negro counties will name our candidates, and the white counties will have to elect them."[54]

To assure their control, the conservatives set about to limit the suffrage. They used rigid residence requirements, payment of taxes as a prerequisite for voting, and ballots that required literacy. Extensive rights of citizens to challenge other citizens' rights to vote, together with procedures that made responses to these challenges difficult, were employed almost exclusively against blacks. Wide-ranging powers of election judges to count the votes; costs of bonding for political office so high that Republicans in particular and lower-class people in general could not meet them; and changing the location of polling places limited the exercise of the franchise. So did economic pressure, terror, deceit, and fraud.[55]

With political power wrested from the Republicans, a process that took place from the early to the late 1870s in different states, the plight of the planters began to ease. The federal army was withdrawn from the South, and the class threat from blacks and from white farmers diminished. As that happened, the planters turned their attention to the threat posed by the merchants. Jonathan Wiener, in a study of Alabama, found that hand in hand with the crippling of Reconstruction went attacks on the merchants' economic challenge to the landlords. Laws increasingly favored the latter. They gained the first right to the lien on the tenants' crop for rent and advances; later was added their right to attach not only a tenant's crop but his furniture, household goods, and personal effects. Finally, they repealed the right of non-land-owning merchants to hold crop liens at all in the black belt. The field of activity of the merchants became increasingly limited to the white counties, where they became lords over the white farmers. The number of independent merchants in the black belt declined in the 1870s, and they do not appear to have prospered, while the opposite was the case in the hill counties. So in the black belt those of planter origin remained dominant, while in the white areas the new merchants became the power.[56]

As the Democrats grew stronger, they began to turn away from their policy of race baiting and to extend their paternalistic hand of protection toward the blacks in return for black cooperation. "The best friends of the colored men are the old slaveholders," asserted Wade Hampton, leader of the Redeemers in South Carolina. This trend often began early, under Reconstruction, because the Democrats were forced to compete for the black vote. The Democratic party election platform in Louisiana in 1873 promised "to exercise our moral influence, both through personal advice and personal example, to bring about the rapid removal of all prejudices heretofore existing against the colored citizens of Louisiana. . . ."[57]

In state after state, the triumphant conservatives reached out to the blacks, promised to protect their rights, and urged them to look to the Democratic party for their protection. Conservative victory meant the return of paternalism. In Mississippi, they applied the dual policy of creating organizations of black Democrats and of terrorizing black Republicans. They developed the policy of "fusion," in which they would divide up offices with the black Republicans, each promising to support the other, thus leaving out the white farmers. Blacks were often conscious of what was happening, and many approved, feeling that with the defeat of Reconstruction their best hope lay not with the "poor white trash" but with the "well-raised gentlemen." Thus began the unholy alliance that strengthened the hand of the white upper class against the white lower class. This tendency of blacks to support Democrats was strongest in the Deep South states of Alabama, Georgia, Louisiana, and South Carolina, where the pressure was most intense.[58]

The Threat from Below

The position of the merchant-landlords was not yet secure. Though they sat atop the class structure, theirs was a political balancing act which left them with the ever-present possibility that they might yet be toppled. Once Reconstruction ended, the class divisions between the whites began to reassert themselves. Although the Democratic party was the party of all Southern whites, not all whites laid equal claim to it. Anger from the white farmers below often focused on the political monopoly established by the merchant-landlords over the Democratic party. "Discontent is the order of the day," warned one newspaper. "The great cry is that of 'rings' and star chambers and some argue that the Democratic Party is composed only of tricksters and demagogues." W. J. Cash noted that with the establishment of the one-party system, and with that party having become the political monopoly of one class, there was no way to give political expression to the conflict of classes: "the masses were stripped of every possibility of effective political action for the amelioration of their estate." In North Carolina, political domination by the upper class continued as a live issue throughout the 1880s. If the Democratic party could not be made into a political instrument for lower class whites, was it not reasonable that they would look elsewhere?[59]

Given the economic difficulties facing Southern farmers, it is not strange that opposition to the Democratic party persisted after Reconstruction. The Redeemers did not hold power without worry. There were numerous occasions when independent, Republican, or other parties threatened their control. "From 1880 through 1896 the Democrats in North Carolina never won more than 54 percent of the gubernatorial vote," wrote Dwight Billings. In that state Republicans came close to winning in 1880, taking 48.7 percent of the vote, and they got the same figure in Tennessee in 1884. Democrats in Alabama worried that they might lose to the Republicans. Seven states gave 40 percent or better to parties other than the Democratic party at some point in the eighties, and all but South Carolina, which had very restrictive voting laws, gave better than 30 percent at some point.[60]

These parties campaigned on class issues. In Mississippi, for example, the farmers sought to repeal the lien law. Independent movements and parties raised the issue of machine rule by the black-belt elite; they urged expansion of state services, especially free schools; they flourished on rage directed at the political power of the corporations, which the farmers felt were robbing them.[61]

The earliest significant challenge to the rule of the black-belt landed interests was in Virginia in 1879. Insurgent forces there captured control of the state legislature, and two years later they secured the governorship. The Readjuster party that took power in those years was a response to the fiscal conservatism of the Democratic party. The merchant-landlords, in their zeal to pay the state debt with interest, were using funds otherwise earmarked for the schools to pay the debt. The result was that many schools were forced to close. The Readjusters proposed to scale down the debt and apply the money saved to needed social purposes.[62]

The issues were of such importance that the Readjusters, in their efforts to defeat the conservatives, reached out beyond the forbidden boundaries of white supremacy to appeal to the blacks: "Without them, we can do nothing within ourselves, for we are weak as yet, and need all the assistance we can possibly get." The movement was a *class* movement directed against the landed and business interests. When once it came into office, it showed its roots. Readjuster government actions were far-reaching. They scaled down the debt, increased taxes on businesses, lowered property taxes on farmers, and collected delinquent taxes from the wealthy. They vastly expanded public services, almost doubling the number of schools, and paid salaries owed to teachers; they chartered labor unions and established a black college and an insane asylum for blacks. They expanded suffrage by removing the poll tax as a voting prerequisite. It has been estimated that, the blacks notwithstanding, the poll tax had eliminated as many as one-quarter of the eligible white voters.[63]

The Virginia Establishment took this new threat to its power and well-being very seriously. According to historian Raymond Pulley, "The forces of old Virginia believed [General William] Mahone's new party represented just as great a threat to the honor and respectability of the state as had the Radical policy of Reconstruction days." The effort they embarked upon to defeat the Readjusters was cast in the mold of the battle against Reconstruction: the Democratic party promised to accept the adjusted debt and therefore made race the sole issue in the campaign. They revived the rhetoric of Reconstruction, raising once again the specter of rule by carpetbaggers and scalawags ("a few unnatural Virginians, who are enemies to their State and renegades to their race"). "Every white man who votes for Mahone and his gang," read an election circular, "goes for making the negro his equal socially, and gives Mahone a legislature to carry out the African plan."[64]

Shortly before the election, an inflammatory circular appeared, speaking of black rule in the town of Danville, where blacks were a majority. It was alleged that blacks were insulting whites there and dominating the town. A few days before the election, a riot, which appears to have been provoked deliberately by the whites, broke out in Danville. The Democratic printing presses began working overtime, flooding the state with "news" concerning the riot too late to allow a response by the Readjusters. The result was that though the blacks held solid, the whites caved in to the propaganda assault: "The 'Nigger cry' was kept up so incessantly and howled so fiercely," wrote one participant, "that many of our people became really frightened, and some men who have been true Republicans since the war voted against us." Still, the Readjuster defeat came about not only because of whites' caving in to racist propaganda. Wholesale fraud, intimidation, and terror were practiced, as they had been during Reconstruction. The Democrats then set about to make sure that nothing similar would happen again by establishing tighter control over the election process—appointed election boards would make sure that only those who were reliable voted and only the right ballots were counted.[65]

The events in Virginia, isolated though they were, constituted a warning. The existence of the Independent and Republican parties in other states gave added importance to that warning. In general, however, while the black-belt elite did not enjoy the kind of political monopoly that was theirs for the first half of the twentieth century, during the 1880s these movements did not seriously challenge their power.

But in the 1890s a serious national depression struck and made conditions measurably worse. Cotton, which had sold for the greatly inflated price of a dollar per pound after the Civil War, dropped to 20 cents in the seventies and 9 cents in the eighties and then fell even further. In 1891 it went for 7¾ cents per pound, which was below the cost of production. An additional factor was the appreciation of the dollar, which amounted to 200 percent between 1865 and 1895, a devastating blow to debtors such as Southern farmers. Southerners were hit far harder than Western farmers by these events. In the same period in which the price of corn had fallen 32.8 percent, cotton dropped 47.7 percent. Under these conditions, farmers fell more deeply into debt and tenantry increased.[66]

The great trusts that formed in this period had a huge impact on the Southern farmer, and none more so than the railroads. The latter, in many cases owned by Northern capitalists, cooperated in setting artificially high prices for transportation. Where they had a monopoly on local lines, prices were jacked up even higher. Rates in the South were often substantially higher than they were in the North, the differential averaging 50 percent. The trusts in cotton, tobacco, fertilizer, and jutebagging all leached what they could from the Southern farmer. Southern business leaders were deeply implicated in these activities.[67]

This period was one of great unrest in the nation. It was the period that produced the Pullman Strike, the Homestead Strike, and a march on the capital by the unemployed. In the South there was a virtual war in Tennessee over the issue of using convict labor in the mines; in New Orleans there was a general strike; and in Alabama miners struck, once again over the use of convict labor. All of these outbreaks were occasioned by the economic crisis of the 1890s. Among farmers, this movement was channeled mainly through the Populist party. The Southern wing of this party was far and away the most radical section; the Populist movements in the Far West and in the Midwest were moderate compared to the Southern Populists.[68]

The Populist party in the South created a serious threat to Democratic rule for the first time since Redemption. The party made an assault on the financial and corporate interests that were ruining the farmer—Wall Street speculators, railroad owners, manufacturers, trusts, and the middlemen. Its program included regulation of the trusts, revision of the lien laws in favor of the farmers, lowered interest rates, and extension of the public schools. The party called for the removal of convict labor, an end to child labor, and state regulation of the measurement of the production of miners, who were paid by the ton. In Alabama,

Populists voted against proposals to punish black tenants for breaking their contracts. In North Carolina, they lowered bank interest rates to 6 percent per year, and they restored elective government to local areas. They greatly expanded public services and called for public ownership of the railroads. In Texas, they called for an eight-hour day and an end to prosecuting laborers for vagrancy when they could find no work. They excluded from membership landowners who were also merchants, and thus most of the plantation owners. But that was unnecessary, as the latter usually opposed the Populist movement with great vigor.[69]

The Populist movement was the most serious effort yet to recast the terms of economic activity, to shift wealth and its benefits away from the wealthy to the exploited. Inevitably, a contest of this sort, where such great interests were at stake, could not be contained within the bounds of white solidarity; it could not be expected to leave the enormous potential of the black vote untouched. The left Populists formulated and won support for a program unique in Southern history before or since. They proposed to organize a political coalition around the growing similarity of the economic conditions facing both black and white farmers. The expression of a Texas Populist: "They are in the ditch just like we are," succinctly gave voice to the sentiment. Indeed, many white farmers had already noticed that measures devised to restrict the black franchise were being applied against them. In Mississippi, enactment of the poll tax dropped the number of qualified white voters from 130,000 to 68,000.[70]

Tom Watson, the most articulate and best-known representative of those who sought racial unity in politics, boldly asserted:

> You are made to hate each other because upon that hatred is rested the keystone
> of the arch of financial despotism which enslaves you both. You are deceived and
> blinded that you may not see how this race antagonism perpetuates a monetary
> system which beggars you both.

Serious efforts were made by the Populists to promote racial unity: in Kansas they nominated a black for state auditor; in Arkansas, "It is the object of the People's Party to elevate the downtrodden irrespective of race or color." In Texas, two blacks were named to the party's executive committee, and many blacks to the county committees, while the state convention of the party proposed black school trustees and demanded proportional representation in the legislature for minorities. In Georgia, which at the time led all states in lynchings, the Populists announced their intention to "make lynch law odious to the people." These words could be backed up with dramatic action: when a black Populist was threatened with lynching in Georgia, two thousand white farmers assembled for his protection. In Alabama they rejected any warning of the danger of black domination: "The negroes are not asking for office. They want justice. They want the right to work for the betterment of their race. We don't fear negro domination." In Mississippi, Texas, and North Carolina, Populists promised free public schools for blacks and whites. In Louisiana: "We declare emphatically that the interests of the white and colored races of the South are identical. . . . Equal justice and fairness must be accorded to each." Blacks and whites mixed together at parties and conferences. In Texas, a white Populist sheriff appointed black deputies. In North Carolina, the Populists redistricted to allow a black Congressman to be elected.[71]

At the same time, many blacks were growing disillusioned with the Republican party as it attempted to find a base among Southern whites. Woodward reported that by 1890 over one million blacks were in the Colored Farmers' Alliance. Many of these responded to the new party. This movement became powerful enough to threaten the ruling regimes. It held mass meetings of thousands. The party in Texas was estimated to have 70,000 members. In Tennessee it elected a governor in 1890, five of ten congressmen from Virginia, eight of nine from North Carolina, two of seven from Mississippi, and four of eleven from Kentucky. Louisiana Populists won the election in 1892, and in Alabama the Populist candidate for governor won support of almost half of the voting population. In 1894, the People's party polled 44.5 percent of the vote in Georgia despite massive fraud and vote manipulation. They took two congressional and many legislative seats in Alabama, and in Mississippi they won a third of the vote. In 1896 they won control of the senate in North Carolina in a clean sweep and shared control of the House with the Republican party. In that year, the Populist candidate for governor of Louisiana won 44 percent of the vote.[72]

Faced with such a threat to their continued rule, the Democrats returned to the same methods they had employed against Reconstruction: fraud, terror, and the specter of black domination. They held the Populist menace to be the same as that of Reconstruction, and the threat they felt was not particularly a *racial* threat. It was their *class* position that was endangered. Thus, in Alabama the reformers lost support in the black belt while they were still operating within the Democratic party and making no appeal to the blacks. They were mobilizing whites around their economic problems and their political discontent with the black-belt monopoly over the Democratic party.[73]

The danger of "negro domination" was raised once again, and once again, note, it was by the upper-class whites. What was at stake, said the Southern leaders, was white supremacy itself. In North Carolina this leadership carried out a newspaper campaign of "prejudice, bitterness, vilification, misrepresentation and exaggeration." Lurid headlines appeared: "Negro Control in Wilmington," "Unbridled Lawlessness in the Streets," "Greenville Negroized." A story entitled "Nigger! Nigger! Nigger!" spoke of black office holding; "Is a Race Clash Unavoidable?" asked another headline ominously. In Georgia there was a similar campaign. Populism would end white supremacy, which, said the Atlanta *Constitution*, was more important "than all the financial reform in the world." A similar line was advanced in Mississippi, where the Democrats warned of the dangers of black domination and the ever-present threat to white women. Indeed, wherever they were faced with partisan opposition that even potentially threatened black-belt domination, they raised the charge of racial treason, as in

Louisiana, where the Populists were the "most dangerous and insidious foe of white supremacy."[74]

The hatred and intensity of the Reconstruction era were revived, and along with them the violence employed during the army occupation of the South. Terror became common once again. "In North Carolina the Red Shirts were riding," said Cash. There the Ku Klux Klan tradition of Reconstruction was followed. The Red Shirt clubs drew their membership from "respectable and well-to-do farmers, bankers, schoolteachers and merchants—in many cases the best men in the community." Whites were advised by an upper-class former congressman to "go to the polls tomorrow and if you find the Negro out voting tell him to leave the polls and if he refuses, kill him, shoot him down in his tracks." The terror was not limited to North Carolina. In Georgia, Mississippi, and Alabama, serious attacks and sometimes murders were perpetrated against Populists and their supporters. In Texas, blacks were murdered and at times besieged and ordered to leave the area by armed bands of marauders. In 1892, lynching reached its height—162 blacks. Where economic power could be used to deny a job or to fire a third-party adherent, it was.[75]

At the same time that the Democrats were preaching racial hatred, they also reached out to encourage blacks to join them. In Alabama many black leaders openly endorsed and supported the Democrats, apparently viewing this approach as the means to attain racial peace. These leaders even established an Afro-American Democratic League to woo voters to the Democratic party. The Democrats bought black votes, sometimes with pardons for convicts, more often with money. In North Carolina they used bribery, too, sometimes offering jobs in return for black support. In South Carolina, Democratic-Republican fusion continued through the Populist upheaval, and blacks, particularly those who were better off, continued to work in the Democratic party.[76]

Their efforts appear to have borne fruit. The Populists were beaten by the overwhelming Democratic majorities racked up in the black-belt counties. A historian wrote that in Mississippi, "had it not been for the presence of the Negro the Populists might have swept the state in the early 1890's." In Alabama the same was true.[77]

In this circumstance, the alliance of the upper-class whites and the blacks appears to have held against the class threat posed by white and black farmers. And yet the evidence is ambiguous when examined more carefully. For the most part the black-belt victories were won by terror and fraud. "In 1892, we gave (Governor) Jim Hogg 4500 votes, over 3000 more than he was entitled to," admitted one activist in Texas. In that state, as in Virginia, the blacks did not acquiesce in the Democratic tide; they stuck to their guns. In Alabama, ballot boxes were stolen and tallies altered; returns were announced and later altered; illegalities were "open and obvious." Democrats were heard boasting that black votes that had been cast one way were counted another. In North Carolina, the black vote was overcome by the combination of fraud and a vicious race riot in Wilmington, which was fermented in a manner reminiscent of the riot in Danville,

Virginia in the eighties. In Wilmington, as in Danville, the riot took place on the eve of the election. In Mississippi a leader of the convention noted: "It is no secret that there has not been a full vote and a fair count in Mississippi since 1875." In Virginia an observer stated that after the polls closed, the election judges, who were Democrats, locked themselves in with the ballots. "In the black counties this enabled them to change the ballots to suit themselves." In Texas they simply altered the ballots to obtain the count they wished. The importance of these cases increases when placed beside the fact that relatively few examples of fraud are reported in the Populist victories.[78]

The campaign created a racist atmosphere and a momentum that continued on its own. Atlanta and New Orleans joined Wilmington, each with its own vicious race riot around the turn of the century. The disfranchisement of blacks followed the defeat of Populism. A series of devices were established to keep the black vote out. Black voters numbering 130,334 (50.5 percent of the state's registered voters) in Louisiana in 1896 fell to 1,342 (0.6 percent of the registered voters) by 1904. In Alabama a black electorate of over 100,000 before 1900 declined rapidly to only 3,700.[79]

Jim Crow now swept quickly across the South.* Prior to 1900 only passenger trains were segregated, and they not universally. But in the next several years, segregation appeared everywhere: in travel, restrooms, state institutions, amusements, sports, housing, telephone booths, elevators, even (in Atlanta) separate Bibles for court witnesses and (in New Orleans) separate districts for prostitutes.[81]

This movement found a good deal of acceptance from an American society that was tiring of sectionalism. The last major Republican effort in favor of blacks was the attempt in 1890 and 1891 to pass a voting rights bill, sponsored by Henry Cabot Lodge. The Lodge Bill was strongly opposed by Northern business interests, and it was defeated. According to Stanley Hirshon,

> More than any other Northern groups, merchants engaged in Southern trade and Eastern industrialists frustrated Republican attempts to stress the war issues. . . . The former argued that agitation of the race question would ruin their profits. The latter persuaded influential Republicans . . . that if the Negro theme

---

*There has been a sharp historical controversy over this question. Woodward put forward the thesis that segregation became widespread in this period, emphasizing the advent of legal segregation. Others have challenged this emphasis and have maintained that the *customs* of segregation were already well established. One of these went so far as to state that "the Jim Crow laws . . . did scarcely more than to legalize an existing and widespread custom." I have taken Woodward's side here. Even if his critics are entirely correct that segregation was widely practiced long before the Jim Crow laws were passed, the solidification of these customs through legislation marked a significant change. That was so in a number of ways. It indicated an end to the wavering, to the possibility for change, and to the struggle for power that had been ongoing in the South for a prolonged period. Moreover, there is evidence that these laws marked a real change in the actual ways of life of blacks and whites. The late historian Dale Somers found a whole number of ways in which blacks and whites worked and played together in New Orleans in the 1870s and 1880s. But as Jim Crow triumphed, these disappeared. The same has also been found in Georgia and most of the rest of the South.[80]

was dropped from politics Southern high tariff advocates would join the Republican Party for business reasons.

The Populist movement, to which the Southern elite had responded by driving blacks out of politics, may have caused a similar reaction in the North. The movement was, after all, directed against Northern business interests, and it sought to unite the South and West against them. Leaders in the North may well have felt that it was necessary to side with Southern reaction to preserve their own interests. [82]

Giving added strength to this trend was the growth of racist ideas outside the South. Out West in California, working men who were confronted with the competition of Chinese laborers pressed for legislation to exclude them, and justified it with racist arguments. In the East, workers felt threatened by the competition of new waves of immigrants from Southern and Eastern Europe, while their employers felt similarly threatened by their fear that the immigrants were radicals. America's belated entry into the business of colonialism with the Spanish-American War called for the doctrine of racial superiority to justify it: "The Declaration of Independence applies only to peoples capable of self-government. Otherwise, how dared we administer the affairs of the Indians? How dare we continue them today?" argued Albert Beveridge. Rudyard Kipling's 1899 poem "The White Man's Burden" was seized upon by the American press at this time. Many newspapers printed it on their front pages. This trend was supported by the spread of scientific racism that became prominent at that time and by the rise of the doctrine of Social Darwinism, which saw the "fittest" as those on top of the social order and those on the bottom as there inevitably. [83]

Racial antagonism in the North was heightened by the deliberate efforts of the employers who, with growth of large industry and industrial warfare, employed black labor as one means of undercutting unions. Blacks were brought in as strikebreakers in almost all major strikes, and the result was a bitter residue of racial hatred.

These tendencies help to explain why the Supreme Court quickly ratified the segregation movement in the South. In 1896, the Court ruled on the segregation statutes that required separate and supposedly equal conditions in the famous *Plessy* v. *Ferguson* suit: "A statute which implies merely a legal distinction between the white and colored races . . . has no tendency to destroy the legal equality of the two races or reestablish a state of involuntary servitude." Speaking of the Fourteenth Amendment, the Court said:

> The object of the amendment . . . could not have been intended to abolish distinctions based upon color, or to enforce social, as distinguished from political equality, or a commingling of the two races. . . . Laws permitting and even requiring their separation in places where they are liable to be brought into contact do not necessarily imply the inferiority of either race to the other. . . . We cannot say that a law which authorizes or even requires the separation of the two races in public conveyance is unreasonable. . . .

With these statements the Court robbed the amendment of its original Reconstruction intent, which was precisely to abolish distinctions between the races. The Court went further:

> We consider the underlying fallacy of the plaintiff's argument to consist in the assumption that the enforced separation of the two races stamps the colored race with a badge of inferiority. If this be so, it is not by reason of anything found in the act, but solely because the colored race chooses to put that construction upon it. Legislation is powerless to eradicate racial institutions or to abolish distinctions based upon physical differences, and the attempt to do so can only result in accentuating difficulties of the present situation. If the civil and political rights of both races be equal, one cannot be inferior to the other civilly or politically. If one race be inferior to the other socially, the Constitution of the United States cannot put them upon the same plane.[84]

The Supreme Court thus gave the go-ahead to the South that it was free to proceed with its program of suppressing blacks under the guise of separate but equal, in which equal conditions were never approached. It was after the *Plessy* ruling that most of the segregationist legislation was passed. This legal ruling held for nearly sixty years, until 1954, when it was reversed. By granting the approval of the federal government, the Supreme Court helped to stabilize the emerging racial order in the South.

A national consensus had gelled. Its character was indicated in the prestigious *Encyclopedia Brittanica* of 1903, under the heading "Negro":

> Weight of brain, as indicating cranial capacity, 35 ounces (highest gorilla 20, average European 45); . . . thick epidermis . . . emitting a peculiar rancid odour, compared . . . to that of a buck goat; . . . cranial sutures which close much earlier in the Negro than in other races. To this premature ossification of the skull, preventing all further development of the brain, many pathologists have attributed the inherent mental inferiority of the blacks, an inferiority which is even more marked than their physical differences. Nearly all observers admit that the Negro child is on the whole quite as intelligent as those of other human varieties, but that on arriving at puberty all further progress seems to be arrested. . . . The Negro children [on plantations] were sharp, intelligent and full of vivacity, but on approaching the adult period a gradual change set in. The intellect seemed to become clouded. . . . We must necessarily suppose that the development of the Negro and white proceeds on different lines. It is more correct to say of the Negro that he is nonmoral than immoral. All the social institutions are at the same low level, and . . . seem to have made no perceptible advance except under the stimulus of foreign influences. . . . Slavery continues everywhere to prevail, both as a local institution and a branch of the export trade, where not checked by European Governments. . . . The arts . . . are exclusively of an industrial character, and restricted mainly to coarse weaving, pottery, the smelting and working of metals, agriculture, and growing. . . . No full-blood Negro has ever been distinguished as a man of science, a poet or an artist, and the fundamental equality claimed for him by ignorant philanthropists is belied by the whole history of the race throughout the historic period.[85]

As W. E. B. DuBois charged, histories and textbooks were written extolling the white South and its sufferings at the hands of the Reconstruction regimes and adopting that same white South's attitude toward blacks until that view came to be the conventional wisdom. It was not seriously challenged until after World War II. This point of view also came to be expressed in plays, movies, and novels.[86]

Thus, it was no mere coincidence that in 1895 Booker T. Washington gave the speech at the Atlanta Exposition that won him national fame. He asserted that blacks "shall prosper in proportion as we learn to dignify and glorify common labor and put brains and skill into the common occupations of life." He promised "at all times the patient, sympathetic help of my race." And, he assured whites, "in all things that are purely social we can be as separate as the fingers, yet one as the hand in all things essential to mutual progress." Washington's statement came just after the Populist movement had crested and was already in decline, and racist propaganda was ubiquitous. It was a statement of political defeat, a recognition of the meaning of that defeat, and a strategy for moving ahead based on accepting that defeat.[87]

Shadow of the Plantation

The persistence of the planters as the South's dominant class was the key obstacle to the establishment of liberal democracy in the region during the century which followed the Civil War.   —Jonathan Wiener[88]

Just who was defeated in the 1890s? The Populist movement was white-led, and its greatest support came from the white counties. It would certainly appear, therefore, that blacks were not the only losers, that their loss was shared by lower-class whites. And yet, Woodward affirmed that "political democracy for the white man and racial discrimination for the black were often products of the same dynamics," implying that lower-class whites won political gains at this time. Historians Thomas Clark and Albert Kirwan argued that the group of demagogic race baiters who began to take power early in the twentieth century "carried forward the Populist program after the Populist Party had disappeared," also implying lower-class white gains. Did the lower-class whites manage to escape the defeat of Populism and emerge more powerful, while only the blacks were submerged? If so, there should be some demonstration of their power, some indication of benefits gained. Woodward argued that these were to be found in the segregation laws, especially those governing employment, and this view fits Bonacich's theory. The argument is that such segregation was to the advantage of white labor because it eliminated black competitors, and that it was to the disadvantage of employers because it raised their labor costs by decreasing their labor pool.[89]

Let us, then, begin with an examination of the distribution of power in the

South. Control over the franchise is always a key to power. American history in the nineteenth century is characterized by a general broadening of the franchise and presumably, therefore, a democratization of power. But in the South after Reconstruction, and much more seriously after Populism, the franchise was substantially reduced, and black voting was virtually eliminated.

Who was responsible for this drastic change in the distribution of power, and what was its impact? Did the upper classes merely acquiesce in it, as Woodward asserts and as Bonacich would predict? Because of the control the black-belt elite held over the voting process, it was often able to cast black votes for the Democratic candidates, no matter how blacks had actually voted. The Populists were thus doomed to defeat, even though they frequently carried the white counties by large percentages. That makes the poor white farmers, the base of the support of the Populists, the prime candidates for the role of disfranchisers, because if the black vote was eliminated if could not be used against them. And there certainly were times when the scenario suggested here was indeed what took place. Historian Carl Degler cited one:

> Before the Alabama Populists sought out the Negro vote they tried to interest the Democrats in the idea of a white primary, thus eliminating the need for Negro votes. But the Democrats twice rejected the overtures because they wanted to use the Negro voters in the Black Belt counties to outweigh their Populist opponents in the northern white counties of the state.[90]

Here it is evident that it was not the lower-class whites who set the agenda or the timing. In the case of Alabama, when disfranchisement did not accord with the interests of the merchant-landlords, it did not occur. Later, when they wished it, they were able to put it through even over the objections of the lower-class whites. Woodward himself stated flatly that in the struggle over the franchise, "the real question was *which whites* should be supreme" (emphasis in original). He also indicated the role played by the upper-class whites in the disfranchisement process:

> In order to overcome the opposition and divert the suspicions of the poor and illiterate whites that they as well as the Negro were in danger of losing the franchise . . . the leaders of the movement resorted to an intensive propaganda campaign of white supremacy, Negrophobia and race chauvinism. Such a campaign preceded and accompanied disfranchisement in each state.[91]

The evidence is unmistakable that it was the merchant-landlord class from the black belt who led the movement to eliminate blacks as voters. These voting restrictions came in two waves: one coinciding with the emergence of a renewed strength of Republicanism, the other after the defeat of Populism. In 1880 the Republican party captured a majority of both houses of Congress and the presidency for the first time in six years. This victory coincided with renewed efforts to field Republican slates in some Southern states. In Congress, the Republican party proposed a bill to extend federal control of elections. If enacted, it might have upset the political order that the Southern ruling class had so painfully created. In response, Florida, Mississippi, Tennessee, and Arkansas instituted measures for disfranchising blacks. After the clear defeat of Populism, starting in 1898, Louisiana, North Carolina, Alabama, Virginia, Texas, and Georgia did the same.[92]

Five states carried out these measures by conventions. In none of them was the convention held unless the threat of lower-class insurgency either did not exist or had passed. Where the white elite faced the menace of a black and white lower class united against its rule, it did not act until it was secure. The upper classes did not seek to disfranchise blacks until they were once again thoroughly in control of events, and when they did so they accomplished their end in such a way as to eliminate from the voting polls a large percentage of the lower-class whites, as well. In that way they were able to keep the disfranchisement of blacks from diminishing their power relative to the white farmers. Thus, the removal of blacks from the voting rolls, far from diluting the power and control of the Southern ruling class, became the means by which it confirmed and consolidated that power at last. The result was that the Populist movement marked the last real threat to upper-class hegemony. The chaos and political instability that had marked the region intermittently since the Civil War were over.[93]

In every state but Texas, the leadership in the fight for disfranchisement came from the black belt. Historian J. Morgan Kousser, who carried out a careful study of the disfranchisement movement, characterized this leadership:

> Not only did the vast majority of the leaders reside in the black belt, almost all of them were affluent and well-educated, and they often bore striking resemblances to antebellum 'patricians.' Indeed, almost everyone was the son or grandson of a large planter, and several of the older chiefs had been slaveholders before the war. To trace a composite picture of these men is to discover the classic Southern politico—a leading landowner and member of the county clique. . . .[94]

Opposition to black disfranchisement came, for the most part, from the dissident whites. The Populists did not usually support limiting the vote. Among whites, those who stood with the blacks tended to be from the lower classes. Said Kousser: "The principal white opponents of limitations on the electorate were so obscure that we know little of their lives." It is clear that opposition to voter restrictions was centered in the white counties. In Alabama, for instance, a new constitution was carried by the black belt; counties that had gone Populist voted against the constitution. In Virginia, despite a promise to submit the new constitution to a referendum, the convention followed the lead of Mississippi and merely proclaimed it law out of fear that it would fail. In Texas, a poll tax proposal was defeated by the votes of poor whites. When the proposal was finally passed, said a historian of the period, "predominantly Mexican counties along the Rio Grande and strong Populist and labor union counties, mainly in West Central and Northeast Texas, cast the only majorities against the amendment."[95]

These whites had good reason to oppose the disfranchising measures directed against blacks. The Fifteenth Amendment to the Constitution barred the states from enacting legislation that would deprive blacks of the vote because of their race. If such measures were to be permitted, they would have to be of more general application. The Constitution never barred class legislation, and it was to such measures that the patricians turned: Mississippi led the way by introducing property qualifications, literacy requirements, complicated registration procedures, and poll taxes that served as barriers to the right to vote. These acts would, by their very nature, eliminate many white voters, as well as black. Political leaders were aware of this effect and intended it. Mississippi congressman Eaton Bowers stated that the new constitution had "disfranchised not only the ignorant and vicious black, but the ignorant and vicious white as well, and the electorate in Mississippi is now confined to those and those alone, who are qualified by intelligence and character for the proper and patriotic exercise of this great franchise." In Alabama, they wished to discourage the "ignorant and vicious" whites from voting. In North Carolina: "The struggle of the white people of North Carolina to rid themselves of the danger of the rule of Negroes and the lower classes of whites is being watched with interest outside the state."[96]

The Southern upper class knew what it was about. The disfranchising measures it introduced had the desired effect of virtually ending black voting, and they drastically curtailed white voting, as well. Thus, in Louisiana, even as the black vote dropped by 90 percent, the white vote fell off by nearly 60 percent. In Florida, a white participation rate of 75 percent became less than 40 percent after voter restrictions were introduced. In Arkansas, 75 percent of white voters went to the polls before suffrage restrictions were introduced, less than 60 percent afterwards. In Virginia, "the restriction of the electorate and partisan domination of the electoral bureaucracy paved the way for the Byrd machine. The active electorate was so small that from 1905 to 1948 state employees and office-holders cast approximately one third of the votes in state elections." In Texas, 80 percent of whites voted in 1900, and 62 percent in 1902. These figures fell to 46 percent, 27 percent, 39 percent, and 29 percent in succeeding elections. A poll tax enacted by the city of Houston reduced the potential electorate of 12,000 by some 7,500. The ultimate result of the disfranchisement movement in that state was to produce a voter participation rate of under 50 percent for the first half of the twentieth century. In North Carolina, voter participation dropped from 75 percent to less than 50 percent, and politics moved to the right. In Mississippi, the Vicksburg *Commercial Herald* editorialized that "the poll tax gets rid of most of the Negro votes there, but it gets rid of a great many whites at the same time—in fact a majority of them. . . . the law 'discouraged' probably 6,000 negroes who would have been qualified . . . but it discouraged 60,000 or more white men from voting." The Southern leadership certainly appeared to be consolidating its power.[97]

Nonetheless, it was shortly after the disfranchisement that a significant reform was introduced into Southern politics: the primary. A primary limited to whites had the potential of easing some of the undemocratic practices that had prevailed in the region until then. It certainly seemed an improvement over the closed convention system that was controlled by the black-belt upper class. And, in fact, it did increase somewhat the political power of the lower-class whites. In particular, it meant that they had a much greater say over the selection of the party's gubernatorial candidate, who, since there was only one party, was effectively elected in the primary. Moreover, as a result of this primary system, a series of reformers emerged in most of the Southern states. These new men, who did not come from the old elite but rather had to fight their way into political office, often against the wishes of the Southern ruling class, had a dual program: vicious race baiting, and social and economic reform. In office they made some reforms in the convict-leasing system, in working conditions, and in child labor; and they adopted the rhetoric of Populism, railing against Wall Street, the Cotton Exchange, and the rich. All of that would seem to indicate growing political power of the lower-class whites.[98]

But why would the white upper class, after having just gained the goal for which it had striven for decades—stable control of the Southern political and economic system—countenance such a concession to the lower-class whites? In part, having won the main issue, they saw fit to compromise and thus to win the allegiance of those who might otherwise be alienated. That was not merely a gesture of magnanimity. It was shrewdly designed to undermine any further moves to a two-party system: whites would fight it out within the Democratic party and then present a united front in the general election. The key to the development of the primary was that with the disfranchisement of large numbers of whites, the merchant-landlords had little to fear from any insurgence within the Democratic party; they controlled it now. Even the new rebels did not threaten their power. They were not of the Populist stamp: they were challenging not the socioeconomic structure, as the Populists had, but rather the closed nature of the system of political succession, which was genteelly administered by the hierarchy. Their electoral support did not come from the same sources as that for the Populists. The new breed fought their way into power, but once there did little to upset the existing order. Said historian T. Harry Williams, biographer of Huey Long:

> The demagogues forced their way into the seats hitherto reserved for members of the hierarchy and grasped the power of office. But then—after the tumult and the shouting died—nothing much happened. The average demagogic leader did not enact the program he had promised, did not create that better life he had held out to his followers. At the most he pushed through a few mild reforms and subsided into inaction.

Historian Jack Temple Kirby was more blunt:

> [Cole] Blease [governor of South Carolina], purporting to be the champion of poor whites, was an utter fraud. . . . In Texas during the 1890's, rural Democrat, James S. Hogg, co-opted Populist issues and as governor presented a familiar reform program: improved education, farmer relief, a tough state regulatory commission for corporations. However . . . Hogg soon mellowed and drifted into a com-

fortable relationship with his erstwhile corporate antagonists; frustrated farmers and reformers had to look elsewhere for leadership.[99]

The reformers fought their way into office, but once there they did not seek to destroy the old political machinery; rather, they came to terms with it. The changes they introduced never challenged the prerogatives of the upper class. And, in their turn, these upstarts were accepted, though grudgingly, and sometimes even endorsed. Moreover, the lower-class whites were never able to use their supposed growing power to aid them in winning the many strikes in which they were engaged. So the black-belt merchant-landlord class continued to dominate the region, continued to set the political character of the South, and continued to benefit from its economic system. However much lower-class white political power may have increased in this period, and the evidence for it is slight, it did not challenge the political domination of the merchant-landlord class.[100]

There remains, then, segregation as an indicator of white lower-class power.* Segregation emerged as a full-blown system only after and because of the political defeats and disfranchisement blacks had already suffered along with many whites. Historian Dale Somers wrote: "Blacks in postwar New Orleans moved toward equality in stages, seeking first to win basic political rights, especially the vote. Once that victory appeared secure, they began emphasizing the right of equal access to all public facilities." The reversal of this process appears to have proceeded in the same way: blacks lost first political rights and later (or at the same time) some of the more substantive gains, as well. Legal segregation was one of the results of this process. It was basically a post-Populist phenomenon, and it occurred after the massive rise in racist propaganda designed to turn back the Populist threat. Thus, for example, as late as 1886 the North Carolina Supreme Court declared unconstitutional legislation that sought to divide school funds between blacks and whites on other than a per capita basis. "Only in the new century . . . did the South—from Maryland to the Southwest—consolidate a final racial settlement and a new orthodoxy. . . . The great inconsistencies of the 1870's, 1880's, and 1890's had virtually disappeared," wrote Jack Kirby. John Dittmer contended that "during the first two decades of the twentieth century segregation in Georgia reached a new plateau: the color line gave way to a color wall, thick, high, almost impenetrable." As table 1 illustrates, the large bulk of these laws were passed in the twentieth century. Before 1900 only two states (Georgia and Mississippi) had passed a law segregating prisoners; three states segregated buses (Arkansas, Georgia, and Mississippi); and ten states had laws segregating railroad cars and/or waiting rooms (Florida, Louisiana, Georgia, Tennessee, Texas, Kentucky, Mississippi, South Carolina, North Carolina, and Georgia), with two of them passed in 1898 and 1899. Most of the rest of the legislation and city ordinances came later.[102]

The most significant gain for white labor would come from employment seg-

---

*Woodward himself took a different approach in a review of John Cell's *The Highest State of White Supremacy*: "Far from being the crude work of 'rednecks' segregation is the subtle, flexible, complex fabrication of sophisticated elites."[101]

TABLE 1[103]
Segregation Laws by Year of Passage

Time Period	Handi-capped	Delin-quent	Prisons	Hospital	Trans-portation	Railroad	Employ-ment
Before 1881			Miss	S.C.			
1881–1885						La; Ga	
1886–1890		Ga					
1891–1895					Ark; Ga; Miss	Tenn; Tx; Ark; Ky; Miss	
1896–1900	Va					S.C.; N.C.	
1901–1905	Md	Ark; Fla		La	S.C.	Md	
1906–1910		S.C.	N.C.	Miss	Miss; Tenn; N.C.; Fla		
1911–1915	Tenn		Ala				N.C.; S.C.; Tx
1916–1920		Miss	N.C.				Ark
1921–1925	Md; Ark	Md		Ala	Ala	Ala	Tenn

regation, which would eliminate blacks as competitors for jobs. In some places these laws segregated tiny minutiae. Woodward cited the South Carolina code of 1915, which required workers to be in separate rooms, and use separate entrances, pay windows, exits, doorways, stairways, windows, lavatories, toilets, water buckets, pails, cups, dippers, and glasses. It served the purpose of making it too cumbersome and expensive to hire blacks. But how much did even these laws indicate the growth of white lower-class power?[104]

Only six states had state laws calling for employment segregation (Arkansas, Oklahoma, Tennessee, Texas, North Carolina, and South Carolina). If such laws are a measure of the rise of lower-class white power, then in most of the Southern states, especially in the Deep South, they show that this power was lacking. Much of the employment segregation was done through city ordinances. But there the power of the black-belt upper class was not being contested. Moreover, if these ordinances were to have hurt the employers (rather than just hurting blacks), they should have raised wages. There is little evidence that they did so. Wages in Southern industry were so low that often every member of the family, including small children, had to work to survive. Rupert Vance, writing in 1927, said of the Southern textile industry:

> One is forced to the conclusion that the basic resource of the Southern cotton textiles is not management, nor nearness to raw materials, not necessarily improved

technology but labor that works long hours for low wages. The differential between New England and the Southeast is then the differential between a highly industrial area and an area of decadent agriculture.[105]

The mill owners guaranteed jobs to whites only, and in doing so they won the loyalty of those who were thereby protected. But this gesture was premised on self-interest. "As long as the white labor supply remained adequate and made no demands," wrote Melton McLaurin in his study of the cotton mills, "management relied upon it almost exclusively." John Coffin, vice-president of the Southern Industrial Convention, stated the policy to the Industrial Commission in 1900: "If labor is reasonable, if labor will work for anything within reason, white labor will dominate the South forever; but they [management] will not submit to such outrages as have been frequently committed by organized labor." In other words, the job reservation scheme was voluntary; it was controlled by the employers and used to their own benefit. They retained the threat to abandon it if they needed black labor as an instrument to counter pressure from whites. The employers also made certain with this approach that they would cause no trouble to the black-belt agrarian elite because they were not competing for labor. That jobs were reserved to whites does not appear to be an indication of the power of the white lower classes. Yet, if there is any area in which Bonacich's prediction that white labor would impose its will on the upper class is borne out, it ought to be here.[106]

Another important measure of power was the distribution of school funds, which were paid for by state taxes and distributed to the counties on a per capita basis. Prior to disfranchisement, blacks got a relatively equal share. Table 2 illustrates the drop-off of benefits to blacks as a result of disfranchisement. In each state examined, the ratio between per capita expenditures and number of school days of whites and blacks rose dramatically between 1890 and 1910. The data in table 3, which looks carefully at North Carolina, are even more striking. Between 1880 and 1900, the black/white ratio of per capita expenditures hovered close to unity. Within the first five years following disfranchisement, it fell to 0.59, and in the next five years to 0.40, a total drop of 53 percent.

Once again, blacks were not the only losers from the disfranchisement. The data illustrate a clear class bias, as well. In table 4 it is evident that the greater the percentage of the black population in a county, the higher the ratio of white to black expenditures. These figures demonstrate that the black-belt whites secured by far the lion's share of these benefits, and they did so as a direct result of disfranchisement. The information in table 5 is especially interesting. That table shows that in North Carolina the disparity between whites in rich and poor counties jumped from $1.01 per capita to $3.57 within ten years of disfranchisement. It further shows that while blacks' per capita expenditures fell slightly relative to whites in the poor white counties (from 95 percent to 86 percent), their percentage dropped dramatically in the rich black-belt counties (from 92 percent to 19 percent of what the whites received). Moreover, until disfranchisement per capita expenditures on blacks in both the white and black belt

TABLE 2[107]
Race Differences in Expenditures per Pupil and
Length of School Year: 1890 and 1910

State	Ratio of White to Black Expenditures	Ratio of White to Black Length of School Year
Alabama		
1890	1.01	0.94
1910	3.74	1.35
Florida		
1890[a]	2.03	0.99
1910	3.72	1.24
Louisiana		
1890	2.00	0.97
1910	5.57	2.04
N. Carolina		
1890	0.99	0.97
1910	2.06	1.11
Virginia		
1890	1.44	0.93
1910	2.83	1.12

NOTE: Figures are weighted averages of county data. Weight = Average daily attendance in county/Total average daily attendance in state. Consumer Price Index (Historical Statistics, 1976: 212).

[a]1893/1894 school year.

TABLE 3[108]
Statewide per Capita Expenditures on Education by Race
North Carolina, 1880–1910

Year	White	Black	Expenditure Population Black/White Ratio
1880–1885	$0.93	$0.98	1.05
1886–1890	1.70	0.94	0.88
1891–1895	1.17	1.02	0.87
1896–1900	1.22	1.14	0.93
1901–1905	1.98	1.17	0.59
1906–1910	3.70	1.49	0.40

counties were greater than those for whites in the poor counties. After disfranchisement this situation changed. But while blacks in the poor counties fell only slightly behind the whites, the per capita expenditures on blacks in the wealthy counties plummeted relative to the whites in both the rich and poor counties as well. Nor was it merely a question of *racial* advantage, for while the monies

TABLE 4[109]

Ratio of Per Pupil Expenditures within States: 1910

Percent Black	0–25%	25–50%	50–75%	75–100%
State				
Alabama	2.23	3.00	5.61	10.04
Florida	2.78	2.89	5.10	13.88
Louisiana	2.21	4.72	7.36	17.45
N. Carolina	1.42	2.36	43.16	———
S. Carolina	3.78	3.52	5.91	7.78
Virginia	1.66	2.99	5.47	———

NOTE: Figures are ratios of white to black expenditures on teacher salaries per pupil in average daily attendance. The expenditure figures are weighted averages of the county data within county groups (i.e., 0–25%). Weight = Average daily attendance within county/Average daily attendance within county group.

TABLE 5[110]

Predicted Expenditures per Child by Race and Ratios of Expenditures in Rich and Poor Counties—North Carolina, 1880–1910

Period	Poor	Rich	Difference (Rich-Poor)
A. White			
1880–1884	$0.77	$1.15	$0.38
1896–1900	0.86	1.87	1.01
1906–1910	1.79	5.36	3.57
B. Black			
1880–1884	$0.94	$1.03	$0.09
1896–1900	0.89	1.23	0.34
1906–1910	1.71	1.40	-0.31
C. Ratio (Black/White)			
1880–1884	121%	92%	26%
1896–1900	95%	70%	25%
1906–1910	86%	19%	67%

NOTE: Poor counties are defined as those where the average white property value per white male adult was $400 in the first two periods and $600 in the last, and where the percentage of blacks in the population was 10 percent. Rich counties are those where white wealth was $1,400 in the first two periods and $1,600 in the last, and where the percentage of blacks was 50 percent.

available to the whites of the poor counties doubled, in what was plainly a period of expanding school revenues, those available to wealthy whites, who started from a higher base, nearly tripled. The inequities produced by this system were immense. The extremes are illustrated by two counties in Mississippi in 1907, one majority black, one majority white. The white county, Itawamba, had a per capita expenditure of $5.65 for whites and $3.50 for blacks. Washington County, whose majority was black, spent $80.00 per capita on whites and $2.50 on blacks.[111]

It is difficult to see where the great gains for lower-class whites are to be found in this situation. It seems, instead, apparent that the defeat of Populism and the subsequent disfranchisement of blacks brought about a severe setback for these whites, as well. Many of them lost the right to vote. They were subject to the harsh terms of their employers, and they remained without labor unions to counter the power the wealthy retained. When they did try to form unions, they found the region's tradition of violence turned against them. And while some of the segregation may have been instituted by the lower-class whites, or their representatives, it appears that where there was real economic benefit to be gained from it, it went to the upper class.

The segregationist wave completed the post-Civil War degradation of blacks. It permanently removed them from the political arena; it made them second-class citizens, with no hope of change: it turned them into pariahs. The upshot of it all was little change in the structure of power or the distribution of wealth: there were some reforms, and a few gains for lower-class whites in removing blacks as competitors in the job and status markets, but the old system, with the plantation at its center, remained.

Southern poverty persisted along with the plantation system, which appeared to prevent the South from progressing. Tenancy continued to increase among both blacks and whites—an indication that the farm system wasn't working for most. Between 1900 and 1910, the percentage of farmers who were tenants rose from 59.9 percent to 65.4 percent. In 1930, a Works Progress Administration study found, 87 percent of all black agricultural workers in the Southeast were wage laborers or tenants; so were some 750,000 white families. In 1935, over 3,000,000 blacks and 5,500,000 whites—one-quarter of all Southerners—were tenant farmers. In 1913 the South had 28 percent of the population but only 11 percent of the nation's taxable income, while by 1919 per capita income averaged 40 percent less than that of the rest of the nation, and by 1920, 60 percent of Southern families lived in mortgaged or rented houses. No surprise, then, that in the decade of the twenties some 6,000,000 moved from the rural areas to the cities.[112]

Despite this movement, the South remained a rural region. In 1900 four-fifths of its population lived in the country, and by 1930 two-thirds still did. Of 145 American cities over 50,000 population, only 21 were in the South. Only five Southern states had population densities greater than 50 persons per square mile: Massachusetts had 479.4; Pennsylvania, 278.4.[113]

More important, however, than the demographic pattern was the political control that continued to be exercised by the rural areas, and in particular by the black belt. Despite the movement of population to the cities, the legislators refused to reapportion legislative districts. Thus, in North Carolina, one district had a population of 5,400, while another had 51,305; Atlanta had about one-fifth of Georgia's population but elected only 1 of 35 senators and 7 of 106 representatives. Southern Alabama had far less than half of the state's population, but a majority in both houses.[114]

Even the development of Southern industry did not change this pattern. Industry found the Southern system of politics, race relations, and especially cheap labor to be quite compatible with its needs. Like Southern agriculture, the success of the region's industries was based on almost unbelievably cheap labor that required every member of the family to work in order to survive.[115]

The mills were organized like the plantations. The factories provided the workers with poorly built housing like "the 'quarters' of the antebellum plantation," with a commissary that provided advances of food and clothing on future earnings, and with schools and churches whose teachers and preachers were under the pay and control of the company.[116]

The ethos remained the same, even as industry advanced. The huge profits of the lumber industry, for example, were based on abundant supplies of cheap labor. Correspondingly, the lumberman actively discouraged the importation of new industry, lest it create competition for his labor supply and drive wages up. Small local industries in the towns had the same attitude.[117]

Industry and plantation found no important differences concerning the key questions that had been fought out in politics in the last decades of the nineteenth century. And they had an important common interest in the cost and supply of labor. But there was an important underlying potential difference. The patterns of racial oppression that had been developed by the plantation owners were essential to their continued political rule and economic well-being. For commerce and industry these patterns were convenient, because they regulated labor very effectively. But business had another means of regulating labor on which it could rely if these broke down, namely, the traditional free labor market. This difference was to become very important when, under the impact of a changing economic and social system, blacks began once again to challenge their oppression.

In summary: the post-Civil War South was impoverished, and that poverty imposed narrow constraints on the ways to acquire wealth. For the newly freed slaves, success could be gained only by damaging the planters' interests. The planters fought against this trend politically and adapted economically. Those who were successful became transformed into the merchant-landlord class, which the former planters came to dominate. For blacks and lower-class whites alike, this new arrangement meant economic misery and subjection to outside control through the lien system. The black-belt agrarian upper class fought to regain political power from the radical Reconstruction regimes. It used the framework of white supremacy, fashioned the Democratic party into its own party, and sanctioned and sometimes organized the use of the Ku Klux terror to gain its victory. Once having regained power, the Redeemers moved to establish a paternalistic link with the blacks and used them to tighten their hold on power against any challenge from lower-class whites.

The depression of the 1890s intensified discontent with the black-belt-run state governments, and the Populist party emerged in response. The party reached out to blacks and began to forge a coalition that enabled it to become the first real contender for power against the Democrats since Reconstruction. The black-belt elite responded to this menace by scrapping paternalism and resurrecting the specter of black domination to defeat this challenge to its power. It then proceeded to remove the threat that Populism had presented by disfranchising blacks and large numbers of whites, thereby assuring its continued power. Its campaign of racism set in motion a trend that produced riots and lynchings, the trend toward segregation, and the denial of any rights to blacks.

The outcome was to solidify the black-belt agrarian upper class in a position of power that remained unchallenged for a half-century. The case made here is that, regardless of the virulence of racism among the lower-class whites, the foundations for and dynamic of Southern racism as it was confronted by the civil rights movement rested upon the class system of the South. The economic and political domination of the black-belt elite required the suppression of the black population, and it was this class that provided the main dynamic in creating the racial system.

II

THE OLD ORDER CHANGES

Once, on a visit to Warm Springs, I'd heard Franklin D. Roosevelt say that Georgia was an unfinished state and the South was an unfinished region.
He explained, saying the development of the
Southern states had been halted by the Civil War
and that postwar recovery had been tortuous and
slow because of the corrosive poverty and the pressures of politics, prejudice, and economic exploitation which had developed after the
reconstruction years. There must be a beginning
again, and perhaps, he said, it will come out of
this depression. He was right about it. There was
a beginning again. It did grow out of the heart-
break of the depression years.

—Ralph McGill[1]

The plantation system lingered on. Worse, from about 1910 conditions began
to deteriorate dramatically. The boll weevil decimated cotton areas in the Southeast, causing great hardship. Responding to the decreased supply in the East,
cotton growing rapidly expanded in Oklahoma and Texas. By 1930 one-half of
the total cotton acreage was in these two states. That was not because of a decline
in acreage in the more traditional cotton-growing states to the East but rather
because of the immense expansion in the West. By 1930 the insect had passed
through the region, and the cotton areas had recovered. There was a net reduction
of 5 percent in the easternmost states, but that was more than made up for by
the 40 percent increase in Mississippi, Arkansas, and Louisiana. So, when cotton
recovered in the afflicted area, the whole region suffered from vast overproduction. Returns per acre dropped regularly during the teens and twenties. The
only exception was the temporary boom occasioned by World War I.[2]

Although capital both had been accumulated and had filtered into the South,
in reality little had changed. Indeed, Northern capital frequently promoted the
"development of underdevelopment"—its policies retarded the growth of Southern industry in order to enhance its own interests. For example, United States
Steel purchased the largest steel-making facilities in Birmingham and then pur-

posely priced their product out of much of its natural market. In this way the company prevented otherwise damaging competition to its Pittsburgh facilities, which were already in place.[3] And when the Depression struck, it deeply intensified conditions that were already unbearable.

But change did come—rapid change. By the 1970s the "Sun Belt," which included the South, became the most dynamic, fastest-growing section of the nation's economy. Even by the 1960s manufacturing had become the major source of income in every Southern state. In most of the states, construction, wholesale and retail trade, and government employment were all more important in the economy than agriculture, and cotton had lost its prominent role in the latter.[4]

The cities, too, had grown rapidly. By 1960 over half the Southern population—58 percent—were urban dwellers, and the farm population had declined to 11 percent. That was a big change from the 1940 figures of 35 percent and 23 percent respectively. In 1963 the South's per capita income was 74 percent of the nation's—up sharply from 58 percent in 1940. Economist Vivian Henderson wrote: "The South can no longer be characterized by an economic structure distinctively different from that of the rest of the country."[5]

That meant, of course, a sharp decline in the economic centrality of the plantation. It was reflected, as well, in the increasing social and economic strength of the black population. During the 1940s, blacks employed in agriculture dropped by 450,000—almost one-third of the whole black agricultural population. At the same time, jobs for blacks opened up in manufacturing—over 500,000; and in commerce—over 350,000. A similar drastic decline in the number of black domestic servants indicated that black fortunes were picking up. These changes were accompanied by the growth in black wealth: the median family income jumped from $489 in 1939 to $3,088 in 1963. In the early 1960s, black purchases were estimated to account for 15 percent of retail sales in Houston, 17 percent in Atlanta, 24 percent in Memphis. These changing circumstances and the growth of a specifically "Negro market" put pressure on businesses in the South to open up still more jobs for blacks in the 1950s. This growing economic power was but one—albeit very important—indication of the strength and importance that blacks were developing.[6]

But the recitation of numbers such as these cannot begin to give an understanding of the wrenching changes in social life that they involved. The changes naturally promoted a new hope and aggressiveness on the part of blacks to do away with the structure of power that had oppressed them for so long. But what must be emphasized here is that the changes occurred neither gradually nor naturally. They were abrupt,* and they were imposed from the outside—by the federal government, for the most part.

---

*Thus, in 1957 historians Thomas Clark and Albert Kirwan could write: "Tenancy and subdivision of farms seemed in 1930 incurable blights on the land, but they are no longer matters of primary concern."[7]

Depression Misery: The Need for Structural Change

The Great Depression of the 1930s was the turning point. In 1932, at the depth of the Depression, production in America was only slightly greater than one-half of what it had been in 1929. Unemployment was up to 25 percent—over thirteen million were out of work, with little or no unemployment compensation. Real nonfarm earnings dropped below the level they had been forty years previously, in 1890. People were losing their homes through foreclosures at a rate of more than one thousand per day.[8]

Agriculture was hardest hit, and the South, where agricultural income was two and one-half times as important as it was in the rest of the nation, suffered most. Moreover, the rate of decline in agriculture in the South was twice the national rate. That was almost entirely because of cotton, which suffered from a massive glut of overproduction on the world market. The overstock in 1932 reached some sixteen million bales in a world that consumed a total of only twenty-three million bales. When in 1932 prices for all agricultural products were down to 43 percent of the 1929 figure, the price of cotton had fallen to only 31 percent. Prices for cotton dropped from a high of over 20 cents a bale in 1927 and almost 17 cents in 1929 to 4.6 cents in 1932. As a result, farmers in Mississippi were losing their land at about double the national rate.[9]

The rest of the Southern economy followed. Banking suffered severely, and failures became common. That was partly a result of the now almost worthless mortgages the banks held. It was also a product of the colonial features of the Southern economy. Insurance companies and industries drained their capital out of the South. Two economists estimated that insurance companies alone withdrew at least $50 million between 1929 and 1934. In those years Southern banks lost a total of almost $2 billion, and this loss caused the South's percentage of the country's bank resources to fall from 9.7 percent to 8.7 percent. The result was a tightening of credit just at the time when people needed it the most.[10]

These circumstances had dire consequences for the already impoverished region. Gross farm income from cotton between the 1929–1930 and the 1932–1933 seasons fell from $1,470,000,000 to only $431,000,000—a total of over $1,000,000,000, or about 70 percent. The drop per family was from a high of $737 to a low of $216. In Louisiana, cash income went down from a 1929 high of $170,000,000 to the 1932 low of only $59,000,000; on a per capita basis the figures went from $415 in 1929 to $222 in 1933. In Georgia the per capita fell from $206 to $83. These figures consistently understate the impact on the most impoverished, the tenants and sharecroppers. By October of 1933, 500,000 families in Alabama, Arkansas, Georgia, Louisiana, Mississippi, North Carolina, and South Carolina were on relief. That was more than one-eighth of the families reported in the 1930 census. Almost 300,000 of these were in the cotton counties. By January of 1934, the percentage had increased to over one-sixth of the families included in the 1930 census. Blacks were more dependent on the cotton economy than whites, and thus they were hurt more by these trends.[11]

Rise of the Welfare State

These terrible conditions brought ruin and even starvation to many. They also brought change. The status quo was becoming intolerable to live with and impossible to bear. As the Depression dragged on, partisans on all sides began to develop programs to end it. And in 1933 this new mood came to fruition in the New Deal. Since the Civil War and the expansion in industrial growth to which it had contributed, the national program had been laissez faire. Business was to be regulated by the market—by the "invisible hand." But the unbelievable misery of the Depression that appeared to have no end did put an end to the old program—the free market had proved its uselessness.

Within a relatively short space of time, the New Deal brought forth a wave of legislation that began to change the way the country operated. The legislation made regulation by the federal government a way of life. The New Deal measures introduced and institutionalized centralization. The growth and development of the economy and of technology had made a truly integrated national economy possible; the Depression had made it necessary. These measures included federal regulation or control over banking, welfare, unemployment compensation, social security, agriculture, the stock exchange, the communications industry, and labor relations. They provided jobs for the unemployed, new sources of credit for farmers and homeowners, and the Tennessee Valley Authority, which provided a combination of reservoirs, electric power, and fertilizer.[12]

The advent of World War II inevitably meant that the processes begun during the Depression were greatly extended. As the federal government rapidly sought to mobilize the country for war, its earlier experiments at planning were dwarfed. The "dollar-a-year men" swarmed over Washington, and the War Planning Boards poked into all aspects of the American economy. The government reorganized the economy. It ordered industries to reequip themselves for war production, established whole new industries, such as the synthetic rubber industry, and told companies where to build plants, or built them itself. It regulated labor-management relations and told farmers what to grow. By the war's end, the welfare state was established; the American economy was profoundly and permanently transformed.

As the federal government increased its scope and authority, it inevitably focused much of its attention on the South—the region that had long been economically disadvantaged, the region that President Roosevelt was moved in 1938 to call "the Nation's No. 1 economic problem—the Nation's problem, not merely the South's." That proclamation arose out of the evident fact that Southern poverty was so intense that it was dragging the whole nation deeper into Depression: "We have an economic unbalance in the nation as a whole due to this very condition of the South," the president continued. "It is an unbalance that can and must be righted for the sake of the South and of the nation." And, he announced a commitment to a wide-ranging program to correct that imbalance:

That task embraces the wanted or neglected resources of land and water, the abuses suffered by the soil, the need for cheap fertilizer and cheap power; the problems presented by the population itself—a population still holding the great heritages of King's Mountain and Shiloh—the problems presented by the South's capital resources and the absentee ownership of the new industries. There is the problem of labor and employment in the South and the related problems of protecting women and children in this field, there is the problem of farm ownership, of which farm tenantry is a part, and of farm income. There are questions of taxation, of education, of housing, and of health.[13]

The commitment did not flow only from the sentiment of one who knew and was sympathetic to the South—though that described President Roosevelt. It could be made because there was a broader recognition that the South could no longer be treated as before. Before, it was a place to be exploited; now it was dragging the whole structure down. Therefore, the South was moving to center stage in terms of the economic ills that had to be treated. The New Deal, and later the war, saw a variety of programs and projects designed primarily to aid the region and to change it—to bring it into line with the national economy.

The Depression made it nearly impossible for Southern landowners to turn a profit, and the resultant precarious hold many had on comfortable living made for desperation. The resistance to change of the Southern governing class was weakened under these circumstances, even as everyone else's desires for change were heightened.

The region's economic and social practices came under unprecedented scrutiny; vast amounts of governmental aid and regulation were channeled into the area. These could not fail to have a lasting impact on the economic and social relations of the South. In the space of little more than a decade—from the start of the New Deal in 1933 to the end of World War II in 1945—these changes were set into motion. When they were finished, the South's course had been changed. What followed in terms of the *economy* was simply quantitative—a continuation of the new trends; in *politics* it was something else altogether.

The New Deal: The Changes Begin

The process began with the New Deal's efforts to remedy the country's ills. The new programs both helped to remove cotton from its central place in the Southern economy and prepared the basis for industry.

The Agricultural Adjustment Act provided for acreage limitation to curtail crop production and raise prices. Cotton land cultivation declined, as a result, by twenty million acres between 1929 and 1939, leaving a total of only twenty-three million acres in production. Cotton prices rose, and Southern cotton came to be priced out of the world market and geared to domestic production. As a result, the region began to diversify its agriculture. By 1939, cotton provided only 29.2 percent of cash receipts for Southern agriculture—down from its 46 percent contribution ten years earlier—and by 1946 cotton's share was only 21 percent.[14]

While these measures raised prices and thus helped Southern agriculture to recover,* they were of little benefit, and often proved harmful, to the tenants and sharecroppers. Many of the latter were now unemployed as a result of the cutbacks in production. Despite the legal requirements to allocate farm price support benefits to tenants in proportion to their share of production, they received few of the benefits of the legislation. John Dollard reported that "Negroes get a very bad deal on relief; it was said that in a neighboring town there is only one Negro man on relief out of three or four hundred families." Many tenants had their status downgraded to wage laborers and were thus ineligible to receive acreage cutback allotments. Sometimes they would be thrown off the land altogether. While these conditions often increased the tenants' misery, in the long run many were thus freed from the bondage they had had to endure. Under the conditions of surplus labor that prevailed during the Depression, landlords and merchants became less stringent about making their tenants remain in place to work off their debts—a posture they would come to regret when faced with labor shortages during the war boom.[16]

The federal provision of relief created real problems for the landlords. WPA jobs had relatively short hours and light work compared with cotton picking. On either WPA or relief, farm laborers' standard of living tended to rise, and that meant they were less dependent on the landlords and frequently less willing to work. "Ever since federal relief . . . came in you can't hire a nigger to do anything for you," complained one landlord. "High wages is ruinin' 'em." The New Deal programs did indeed force wages up, which, of course, made the existing labor system less useful because it was less profitable. More and more, the plantations were coming to be owned by banks and holding companies, who either took the land out of production and collected Agricultural Adjustment Act payments on it or introduced mechanization.[17]

Newly created government sources of credit began to undercut the local power of the merchants and bankers. The Reconstruction Finance Corporation was established to provide massive amounts of government money in the form of low-cost loans in order to put the economy into motion once again. According to Jesse Jones, administrator of the RFC, by 1936 the agency's offspring, the Commodity Credit Corporation, was owed some $286 million on cotton loans alone (but owed only $11 million for corn). A study done in the late thirties for the WPA found a decline in the number of loans from merchants and from banks in this period, even as reliance on government money grew.[18]

These measures began to undermine the political and economic order that the region had so painfully attained and endured. Other official acts began to prepare

---

*By 1935 cotton had climbed back up to almost 15 cents a pound. Southern income in that year was 90 percent of what it was in 1929.[15]

the way for a modern industrial alternative to emerge and to enable the South to develop in step with the rest of the American economy.

The then-controversial Tennessee Valley Authority was very important to industrial development. The electrification it brought increased demand for consumer goods both directly and indirectly, and by 1940 it was already selling one-third of its power to industry. One company indicated that savings in power costs from the TVA compared to Northern operations would save them the entire cost of the plant within ten years. War production rapidly increased this reliance on TVA electricity thereafter. According to two Southern historians, "the modern industrial South could not exist without this power resource."[19]

The New Deal program of rationalization and centralization—of making the South a genuine part of the national economy—also pushed aside some of the "colonial" fetters to industrial development that existed. Under government pressure, United States Steel reduced its rates on Birmingham steel to parity with Pittsburgh in 1938; other steel producers followed suit.[20]

Railroad freight rates had been established to make it inexpensive to move raw and semifinished materials from the South to the North and similarly inexpensive to transport manufactured goods North to South. But it was costly to move finished goods from South to North. That meant that it was difficult to build an industrial base in the South, because so much of the largest market was unavailable to Southern producers. In fact, these rates often enabled Northern producers to outcompete Southerners *in their own area*, and the increased business that Northern interests were able to generate under these conditions allowed them to take advantage of the benefits of large-scale production and to reduce unit costs. In that way they obtained another competitive advantage over Southern producers. Industries were thus kept from growing or locating in the South. "The real sufferers in such a system," wrote one analyst, "are the unborn industries." A campaign begun in the thirties against this rate discrimination, mostly by Southern politicians, resulted in the adoption of uniform rates in 1945.[21]

The New Deal thus began to change the character of the Southern economy: it began to prepare the way for industry. It helped to shift the emphasis in Southern agriculture away from cotton toward a more diverse mix. Moreover, it began to change relations among the rural and small-town classes. The government's aid in the forms of loans and relief made a real difference, even though these were locally administered, usually by white farmers and bankers who tended to favor the status quo. They could not prevent some portions of this money from reaching the black community, although fewer blacks got it than whites, and when blacks were able to get loans, they were usually smaller than the whites' loans. The government also insisted that tenants and sharecroppers, including blacks, vote in the AAA elections to decide on acreage limitations.* With these acts, the

---

*Here pressure for change did not come exclusively from the federal government; the times themselves were an important pressure on the landlords. One study, done in the thirties, found that landlords were encouraging their tenants to vote in the AAA elections in order to influence the outcome.[22]

federal government thus began to strengthen the hand of agricultural labor and to threaten the old established relations.

World War II: Creation of a New Infrastructure

It was during the war that the vast shifts were made that brought the South to the point of no return, to the "take-off" stage of industrial growth. The war ended the Depression and opened up jobs. The huge amounts of money the government spent, as well as the mobilization of the whole society for war, made possible rapid changes that otherwise would have taken decades. To get some idea of the magnitudes involved: between 1930 and 1940, total federal governmental expenditures nearly tripled—from $3.3 billion to $9.5 billion. Between 1940 and 1945 they went up almost ten fold again—to $92.7 billion.[23]

The pull of jobs exerted an enormous influence on the Southern population. Around 2.5 million people migrated out of twelve Southern states between 1940 and 1950. That was about one-third of the total emigration of 7.3 million between 1870 and 1950. During the war years, 4 million left Southern farms, so that despite the decline of civilian population in the South from 1940 to 1943, the cities grew: by 1950 the urban population had increased by nearly 36 percent. It was in the wake of this departure that the mechanization of Southern farming began to take off.[24]

Although at first jobs went to the North, where the industrial infrastructure was already established, it was not long before new establishments were brought to the South to get new sources of labor and to decentralize for security purposes. Altogether some $4.4 billion was spent on war plants in the south, with $1 billion coming from private industry, and another $600 million of investment that was not necessarily related to the war effort. Manufacturing employment increased from 1.65 million to 2.84 million and stabilized in 1947 at 2.4 million; effective industrial capacity was increased by 40 percent. The government ran an intensive program training workers for industry. By May of 1941 it was training 75,000 workers for fifty industries in the region. That was an important contribution: one of the features that had kept companies out of the South was the lack of skilled labor. The war experience provided a pool of trained workers, many of whom became available when the war ended and war industries were curtailed, and it showed that Southern labor could readily be trained.[25]

Governmental expenditures on the construction and maintenance of military camps, and on the military and civilian personnel who staffed and trained in them, were probably more significant, at least immediately, in accounting for higher incomes than the new industries. Over $4,000,000,000, or 46 percent of the allocations of military construction, was channeled to the South. Government payments to military and civilian personnel between 1940 and 1944 increased by almost 500 percent from $1,591,000 to $7,726,000. They accounted for 34 percent of the total increase and were, according to one scholar, "the most important factor affecting Southern incomes in this period.'' Because government incomes were so high relative to other sources of income in the region, the military camps created boom-town conditions and served as a magnet drawing people from the rural areas.[26]

The new military bases also had an impact on agriculture. The federal government wanted the South to feed the camps, and it set goals for agricultural production to make that possible. In the Southeast the government wanted increased production of milk (11 percent), eggs (11 percent), oats (32 percent), peanuts (78 percent), cattle (12 percent), and soybeans (74 percent). These guidelines could be very useful in helping the South to break out of its one-crop agricultural pattern. A 1942 study of the region stated: "In the opinion of farm adjustment specialists, the goals for the South stand out uniquely in contrast to those for some regions in that they are in line with desired long-range changes.'' In 1948, a survey of the region's farms found that the following changes had taken place since 1939: corn production was up 5.4 percent, cotton down 8.5 percent, hay up 40.9 percent, wheat up 79.3 percent, peanuts up 143.2 percent, soybeans up 554.4 percent, tobacco up 30.7 percent, rice up 93.8 percent, peaches up 19.9 percent, cattle up 76.6 percent, milk cows up 33.7 percent, sheep up 32.2 percent, hogs up 49.4 percent, mules down 39.7 percent. These figures indicated that Southern agriculture was finally breaking out of its established mold.[27]

The economic and social patterns of the South were changing rapidly. Prosperity was coming to the region. Incomes rose in this period by 187 percent, as opposed to only 150 percent in the nation as a whole. Out of this vast turmoil came a new South that was able to continue the growth begun during the war. That was so for a variety of reasons. The war produced trained, skilled labor that was high in productivity as well as a skilled and experienced managerial group. The prosperity that developed fed on itself. Rising incomes and concentration in cities generated markets for consumer goods industries. A study of eighty-eight major new manufacturing plants in thirteen Southern states in 1949 found that the growing market itself was the "major force attracting plants to the South in recent years.'' This growing market involved at least three features: the growing number and wealth of consumers; the increasing needs of the industries that were already established for suppliers; and the changing agricultural patterns that created a new market for specialized farm machinery. Plants were also found to be locating in the Upper South in order to supply the Northern market.[28]

The new industrialization relied heavily upon the most enduring feature of the Southern economy: its cheap labor force, and most particularly its antiunion climate. A 1949 study of the growth of Southern industry, commissioned by the National Planning Association, contended that the labor cost had little to do with the decision to locate a plant in the South. This assessment was based on what the authors were told by executives and may not be entirely accurate.[29] While the wage differential alone may not have been a compelling reason for choosing a Southern location, unions, which affected not only wages but, even more important, productivity, were. One large manufacturer, who said he paid union scale wages and even expected that his plant would become unionized in the future, stated his reason for locating in the South:

> It is supremely important to me that in the years during which I am organizing this new industry and training labor in the plant that I should not have to operate within the strait-jacket of union rules and regulations with respect to seniority, featherbedding and the like. . . . Some time I will have to accept these rules and regulations. But I will have got my plant going well by then. The rules and regulations will of necessity conform in some degree to the actual routine of operations which I will have established by that time. Then let the union come and organize my men, as come it will.[30]

By the end of the war, the new economic infrastructure had been laid and the South was ready to "take off." And it did. Between 1939 and 1954, Southern industrial output increased from $11 billion to $60 billion, which was several times the national growth rate. Between 1956 and 1959, almost 5,000 new plants were built in the South. Manufacturing employment in the fifties rose by 31 percent—over four times as fast as the rest of the nation.[31]

Thus, in a short period of time the economic base and character of the South were transformed. A foundation for a new economy was laid in the thirties and forties. As a result of the extraordinary prosperity created by the postwar boom, that foundation was rapidly built up during the fifties. By 1960 economic power had shifted decisively to the urban centers.

The Sociological Impact: The Black-Belt Elite under Attack

These changes had a profound impact on the social arrangements in the South, as well as the rest of the nation. Blacks moved to the North, following the jobs, and strengthened the political hand of the black community already established there. They moved to the Southern cities, too, and there they also found that things were different. Terror was missing from the city—as were the abject poverty and the isolation and its accompanying powerlessness of the rural areas. Individuals were not such easy targets for terror or intimidation as they were in the country, and when they encountered it they were more prone to fight back. In the cities, blacks were concentrated. They created organizations for self-help and for change; they began to get educated, and they developed purchasing power. A black middle class could develop in the cities, based on the black working class.

Changes were felt on the farm, as well. Indeed, by the mid 1930s, as the economy began to recover, the landlords were feeling the impact of the rising labor costs that resulted from WPA and relief. They began to turn against President Roosevelt and the New Deal. At harvest time they had bumper crops in their fields, and they could not find sufficient labor to harvest them at the wages they felt they could pay. They angrily pressured the WPA to close down its projects in order to eliminate competition during the harvest. But even with that source of income removed, Southern laborers responded so reluctantly that the landlords resorted to the old methods of vagrancy laws and armed patrols to get their workers.[32]

During the war, labor shortages raised wages. From 1940 to 1945, the average wage for cotton picking rose from $.62 per one hundred pounds to $1.93. And the problem was also felt in small ways by the better-off whites in the small towns and rural areas. Domestics—cooks and maids—began to disappear as jobs in war plants opened up for them or their husbands. "I can't wait for this war to end and to have [the cooks] come crawling back," wrote a woman to her local newspaper. Ralph McGill, former editor of the Atlanta *Constitution*, tells the story of a woman who "was outraged because her cook, who had worked for twenty years at wages from three to five dollars a week, quit and 'just sat on her porch and rocked' when her two sons went into the army and began sending home allotment checks."[33]

Indeed, the Southern rural elite—whom McGill called "a certain type, small-town rich man" and whom Southern political scientist Jasper Shannon called the "banker-merchant-farmer-lawyer-doctor-governing class"—was feeling itself under attack as it had not been in the twentieth century. These ruling elites in the rural areas who held political influence and dominance in the South, who knew the governor and the senators and representatives, who "owned the sheriff," who controlled credit and business, "hated Roosevelt, the New Deal, the triple A [Agricultural Adjustment Act], and the federal Land Bank, which took mortgages and farm loans out of his hands."[34]

They had, of course, weathered attacks before. But this situation was different—more difficult to deal with, more threatening, more subversive. In the past, threats to their power had come from the Republicans and from the Populists. They had been able to draw themselves securely into their party, the party of the South, the party of white supremacy, the Democratic party—and to fight off the attacks. Now, however, the threat came from within that very party, from a figure who enjoyed overwhelming popularity among the white small farmers and laborers. That made their task particularly arduous.

Meanwhile, the attack pressed on. In 1936, Northern blacks, who could vote, moved over into the Democratic party en masse for the first time. That year was also the first time black delegates were seated at the Democratic party convention. And at that convention the rules were changed, weakening the South's influence in the Democratic party. Until then, a two-thirds vote was required to nominate a president, giving the South an effective veto over the candidate. After 1936 only a simple majority was required.[35]

In 1937 the South struck back and played a pivotal role in defeating Roosevelt's plan to reverse the Supreme Court, which had been consistently ruling that his initiatives were unconstitutional. His idea was to expand the number of justices on the Court and to pack it with members of his own persuasion. But he lost his attempt. The battle lines were then immediately drawn over the proposed Wages and Hours Bill, which would establish a national minimum wage and maximum work week of forty hours. The coalition that had just defeated the Supreme Court bill was looking for another victory over the president's social and economic policies in order to turn the tide of events. And this bill—which would weaken the most important competitive advantage the South felt it had to attract industry, its cheap labor—was an appropriate target. Southern industrialist John Edgerton, a past president of the National Association of Manufacturers, claimed that "the NRA was devised, to a very large extent, to reform the South. . . . General Johnson practically told me that when he said 'we don't propose to allow the Negro labor of the South to debase the living standards of the rest of the country.' "[36]

Despite Southern resistance, the law was enacted in June of 1938. Roosevelt then proceeded, literally within days, to carry the fight into the South itself. By the end of 1937, Democratic party liberals had met to "explore the possibility of purging the party of its conservatives." After winning the Wages and Hours Act, Roosevelt openly joined them. In South Carolina, Maryland, and Georgia, he tried to defeat anti-New Deal senators in the primaries. As part of that strategy, he included an attack on the poll tax as well, reasoning that the increased political participation that would result from its repeal would only benefit him. He failed, but the sally did not endear him to those who felt threatened by his program. A confrontation was developing within the South's party for the first time.[37]

Counterattack: The Black-Belt Elite Begins to Organize a Response

The changes that were taking place in the economy were not reflected in politics. The previous chapter argued that the political relations—including racial practices—in the South were intimately a part of, and made necessary by, the plantation economy that emerged after the Civil War. That economy's basic structure was undermined and transformed during the Depression and World War II (although the fruits of the transformation were not fully visible until the 1960s and 1970s). But the political power of the black-belt landed elite did not automatically disappear. Rather, they clung to it tenaciously, even as the cities grew and industry and commerce became the heart of the region. Samuel Lubbell, writing in 1955, pointed out that the state legislatures were becoming increasingly unrepresentative, because although there were vast movements of population, there was no significant reapportionment. In Alabama, 28 percent of the people elected the majority of the legislature; in Florida it took 20 percent in 1950 and 14 percent in 1960; in Georgia, one-third of the population could nominate a governor. As the economic and political changes proceeded, the Southern ruling class became increasingly restive and belligerent.[38]

In the early days, their criticism of FDR and the New Deal was fairly isolated, and it tended to focus on the economic issues that were at the root of the malaise.

Senator Bailey of North Carolina: "It is un-American to prescribe by law what a farmer may sell, a manufacturer shall make or a consumer shall pay." Oklahoma senator Thomas Gore complained that "a paternalistic government is bound to destroy the self-reliance and self-respect of the people." New Deal measures were held to be unconstitutional (by a few), and their charges were vindicated by Supreme Court rulings that struck down many of the new laws.[39]

By Roosevelt's second term, things were heating up. The Democratic party had been an agrarian-dominated party. William Jennings Bryan, the several-times presidential candidate and powerhouse in the party for years, had represented the rural interests. However, in 1928 the cities had taken over the party apparatus and put in their candidate, Al Smith. In 1932 these same elements won with Roosevelt. The 1936 election deepened the party's roots in the cities. It was a resounding victory for the president, who carried every state but Maine and Vermont. The New Deal definitively made the Democratic party the party of the cities and had swept into it the laboring population. Even the Communist party was moved to call it "the American expression of the People's Front." Class struggle was accelerating in industry: general strikes had occurred in Toledo, Minneapolis, and San Francisco and in the Southern cotton mills in 1934, and the CIO explosion was taking shape. All of these events alienated and offended the Southern elite.[40]

At the same time, a measure of prosperity was returning to the South, which recovered more rapidly than the rest of the nation. The Southern ruling class was less desperate and more angered by the economic policies that were pressing it. Its hostility was fueled by its opposition to the sit-down strikes, the unbalanced budgets, and relief payments.[41]

The fight over the Supreme Court in 1937 began to unite the Southern bloc. Roosevelt's plan for expanding the Court was viewed as an effort to undermine Southern race relations at a time when they were coming under increasing legal attack. The Court had been invalidating the New Deal legislation; it still reflected the political and economic thinking of an era that was already gone. The collision between the Court and the chief executive occurred because the change had taken place so rapidly. Roosevelt was fighting for the New Deal program with his attack on the Supreme Court. But that program, with all of its social content and its emphasis on centralization, was in effect renouncing the compromise that had brought an end to Reconstruction. The Compromise of 1877, whereby the federal government agreed to the removal of troops from the South, had left the region to handle its own affairs undisturbed. That was the real content of the principle of states' rights. The New Deal was in reality saying that the old deal had come to an end. Senator Carter Glass from Virginia noted as much when he venomously charged that Interior Secretary Harold Ickes, who had been president of the Chicago chapter of the NAACP, was campaigning for the courtpacking bill: "This infuriated propagandist for degrading the Supreme Court practically proposes another tragic era of reconstruction for the South.[42]

By the end of 1937, at the same time the liberals were planning to purge the

Democratic party, the conservatives were planning much the same, with both sides looking to consolidate control in 1940. In fact, it was Roosevelt's vice-president, Texan John Nance Garner, who led the opposition. They circulated a manifesto calling for a balanced budget and states' rights. When Roosevelt tried to intervene in the primaries in 1938, he was met with a counteroffensive emphasizing states' rights: newspaper editorials with titles such as "Marching through Georgia" and the references to carpetbaggers invading the South.[43]

It should come as no surprise that the race issue became a focal point for opposition to government policies, given the history and the fact that to some extent the racial relations *were* being undermined. Thus, the complaint of the Jackson, Mississippi *Daily News*: "The average Mississippian can't imagine himself chipping in to pay pensions for able-bodied Negroes to sit around in idleness on front galleries, supporting all their kinfolks on pensions, while cotton crops are crying for workers to get them out of the grass." The Farm Security Administration, which tried to help tenants purchase land, was charged with resurrecting the old Reconstruction promise of forty acres and a mule, "the same promise the other Yankees made to the negroes during the other Civil War." But such charges did not become the general theme—not yet.[44]

Roosevelt's great popularity among Southern whites made it difficult to attack him directly. And for a time the war created a sense of national unity. The president swept the 1940 convention and demonstrated that he was still in thorough control of the party.

Still, as the war progressed and the Southern ruling class was pressed harder, opposition grew more forceful and indicated a sense of threat. The Mississippi Farm Bureau president spoke vituperatively in 1942: "We must realize that the present administration is not a Democratic Party. It is a New Deal party, a labor government." Journalist John Temple Graves noted that in 1942, "with a preponderant balance of political power in the South, the farmer was apparently swinging it against his New Deal patrons. . . ." After the 1942 elections, Governor Dixon of Alabama angrily charged: "It is [the Southern Democrats'] own party that is dynamiting their social structure." And, he warned, "ways and means are being discussed daily to break our chains."[45]

But Roosevelt, who won the support of 80 percent of Southern voters for renomination in a 1943 Gallup poll, remained secure. So, in 1944 they went after Henry Wallace and had him replaced as vice-president by Senator Harry Truman, a man who they had reason to believe would see things more their way. Even that success was not enough to placate the more extreme. Slates of unpledged electors were put on the ballot in Texas, South Carolina, and Mississippi for the 1944 election.[46]

In 1948 these swirling trends came to a head. Roosevelt was finally gone from the scene. A counterattack was now possible. The Southern ruling class shaped that counterattack into the form it had always found most useful and effective. The elite did not make it an election over the economic and political trends that had been so damaging to their interests. The issues invoked were the more familiar ones—what they called the unwarranted invasion of states' rights, and white supremacy itself. It was indicative of the source of the reaction that those who were pro-New Deal as well as prosegregation tended not to join them. They thus reverted to their old strategy of emphasizing race as the means of advancing their class interests. They tried to undo the damage they suffered by the Democratic party's being used as the instrument for reform against them by calling themselves "true Democrats" and "true Jeffersonian Democrats" (or "true white Jeffersonian Democrats"). And where they could, they put the States' Rights party on the ballot on the Democratic party line.[47]

This election both reflected and defined the developing trends and thus shaped the politics of the 1950s. In 1948 the rulers of the old order in the South focused their discontent around the issue of race. In doing so they found a means of enlisting much broader support for their cause. As it crystallized its position, the old Southern governing class undertook to lead virtually the whole region. It was that class's last hurrah. It mobilized the South in a massive struggle over what had been the key political rallying points for so long: white supremacy and states' rights. As in the past, the struggle was also over the political and economic hegemony of the agrarian ruling class. But it was already being displaced as the economically most central class, and in the course of the battle it was to lose its political leadership, as well. The Dewey-Truman-Wallace-Thurmond election of 1948 drew a sharp line between the old South and the rest of the national Democratic party. That was the beginning of a new era. In the 1950s the division would grow increasingly sharp.

III

NINETEEN FORTY-EIGHT
THE OPENING OF THE BREACH

On Tuesday, July 13, 1948, George Vaughan rose to speak to the nominating convention of the Democratic party. Vaughan, a black attorney from St. Louis, was a member of the convention credentials committee. He was delivering a minority report, urging that Mississippi be excluded from the convention because of her commitment not to support Truman if he was nominated and his proposed civil rights platform plank adopted. After making the case, he raised his fist and spoke angrily into the microphone: "Three million Negroes have left the South since the outbreak of World War II to escape this thing. I ask the convention to give consideration. . . ." Vaughan's voice was drowned out in the shouts and screams coming from the Southern delegations. The chair called for a voice vote, and although several Northern delegations were demanding a roll call, they were ignored. The motion was declared defeated, and the session was quickly adjourned for the night.[1]

This incident was remarkable in that it showed the Democratic party, the party of slavery and white supremacy, at war with itself over racial issues. The Northern and Southern Democratic parties were clearly bound in different directions. Tuesday was just a prelude to the tumultuous Wednesday session, when the platform was debated. After the party adopted a more militant plank than even President Truman wanted, the Mississippi delegation walked out, along with half of the Alabama delegation. They left calling for an all-Southern meeting of the "true Democratic Party." Within a few days they and others joined in a meeting in Birmingham to launch a new party, the States' Rights party, to run against Truman.[2]

This party was the second split-off from the Democratic party that year. Earlier, Henry Wallace, Roosevelt's vice-president from 1940 to 1944, had announced that he would run against Truman on the new Progressive party ticket. Wallace's was a left-wing split. So, in 1948 the Democratic party split into three parties. Nothing like that had happened since the election of 1860—the prelude to Civil War.

The treatment of blacks emerged as a central issue for the first time ever in a presidential election in 1948. It did so for a variety of reasons, but most particularly because blacks perceived that they had an opportunity to exert political pressure and to reap some important political gains. Seeing that opportunity, they acted.

The experience of the Great Depression—the worst depression in history, and of World War II—the most destructive and expensive war in history, also had profound and lasting effects. These began to make themselves felt seriously in 1948.

This election was the first since 1928 in which Franklin Roosevelt had not headed the Democratic ticket. The 1928 election had split the Democratic party in the South, with many Southerners voting for Hoover and against the Catholic candidate, Al Smith. The Depression had ended that episode, and the South had flocked home to the Democrats, but Roosevelt's economic policies had met with bitter opposition from the Southern leadership. In 1944 the South had led the effort at the Democratic convention to ditch Henry Wallace as the vice-presidential candidate. Wallace had become identified with the New Deal liberal economic and racial policies and the left wing of the administration. Many felt Roosevelt's victories to be his *personal* victories and that once he was gone his policies would be repudiated by the voters. The New Deal and the changes it had made in politics and economics were being fought over in 1948. That was one of the reasons the nation was seriously divided.[3]

The United States had emerged from the war deeply involved in international affairs. As the most powerful nation in the world, it was busily involved in the reconstruction of that world. That effort ranged from transferring control of much of the oil in the Middle East from Britain to America to refashioning the international monetary system to make the dollar the preeminent currency in the world, and to reforming the world trade system to greatly diminish trade barriers and therefore to give U.S. products access to all world markets. What became most significant was the competition with Russia—the cold war. This issue was central in the election.[4]

Splits and dislocations as the nation and the world came to grips with reconstructing political, economic, and social life were only natural. Structural changes in the world and within the United States brought about these splits, which in their turn provided new opportunities for blacks to influence the federal government, and through it to affect the South.

Black Political Power

But these were opportunities that blacks could take advantage of only from a position of strength. In 1948 they had potential power such as they had never before had—voting power, power to determine the outcome of the presidential election and of many local offices. Moreover, blacks were conscious of their power, militant, and better organized than they ever had been.

The simple movement of population is part of what created this new black political power. If Vaughan exaggerated in his claim that 3 million blacks had fled the South during the war, the number was still huge. Between 1940 and 1950, 1.5 million blacks left the South in search of jobs. These numbers increased the Northern black population of 2.8 million by over half. Moreover, this population movement was focused: in 1940, 90 percent of the black population outside the South was concentrated in urban areas; 47 percent of these lived in New York, Chicago, Philadelphia, Detroit, Cleveland, and Pittsburgh. The new migration continued and even accentuated that trend. In the Portland-Vancouver area, the increase of blacks was 437 percent; in San Francisco it was 227 percent; in Detroit it was 60 percent.[5]

The political division in 1948 gave blacks a potential importance in the election that their numbers alone could still not account for. In the 1944 election, with Roosevelt at the head of the ticket, four Northern industrial states were decided by less than a 1 percent vote: Wisconsin, Ohio, New Jersey, and Michigan. Another three were carried by less than 2 percent: Pennsylvania, Missouri, and Illinois; and four more had less than a 3 percent margin: Indiana, Massachusetts, and New York. In virtually all of these states, blacks were a greater percentage of the electorate than was needed to shift the results. By 1940 blacks were 4 to 5 percent of the electorate in New York, New Jersey, Pennsylvania, Ohio, Michigan, and Illinois. However, in that year Roosevelt was a sure winner and had no opposition organized in the Democratic party. In 1948 blacks were in a better position to demand that the piper be paid. Estimates of voting strength in 1948 saw blacks holding the balance of power in sixteen states with a total of 278 electoral votes, compared to 127 electoral votes controlled by the South. This fact alone was sufficient to suggest an important shift in the American political structure.[6]

It didn't take long for this political potential to begin to be translated into actuality. In 1942, Democrat William Dawson was elected to Congress from Chicago. He was joined by Adam Clayton Powell from Harlem in 1944. In 1946, black candidates ran credible campaigns in Los Angeles, Philadelphia, and the Bronx. In that same year, thirty blacks won seats in ten state legislatures. By 1947 there were black judges in Cleveland, Chicago, Los Angeles, Washington, D.C., and seven in New York City, some elected and some appointed. "An alert, well-organized Negro electorate can be an effective factor in at least seventy-five congressional districts in eighteen Northern and border states," argued an observer in 1948. Clearly, black political power was becoming something to contend with.[7]

Blacks and the Cold War

But politics is more than just numbers and votes. Conscious action and organization helped to make blacks into a cohesive and important political force. This strengthening occurred at the same time that changes were taking place in world politics that gave increasing prominence to black concerns and added to the pressures on the American government to do something about black treatment. America's increasing importance in world politics provided new leverage, which blacks were quick to take advantage of.

In 1942, a brutal racial lynching was picked up immediately by Japanese propaganda. The Japanese broadcast the news to the Dutch East Indies and India. It was presented as evidence of how those nations could expect to be treated under United States dominion. As the cold war took shape, Russia naturally picked up where the Japanese left off. The State Department estimated that almost half of all Russian propaganda against the United States at that time concerned racism. Secretary of State James Byrnes told of how the Soviet foreign minister had countered his attacks on Russia's activities in Eastern Europe with stories about racism and racist treatment in the United States.[8]

What gave this matter particular urgency was the emerging revolution against colonialism. The war had hastened the process of the disintegration of the vast colonial empires. Shortly after the war's conclusion, India and Pakistan attained independence, as did several colonies in Africa. By the late forties, the Communist forces in China were clearly approaching victory. The United States was about to be deprived of vast markets, natural resources, and opportunities for investment, not to mention an important element in the world struggle for power. This movement toward self-determination meant that a great deal of the American competition with the Soviet Union focused on gaining the allegiance of the former colonies. In these circumstances, American treatment of blacks in their own country could not help but be weighed by these emerging countries and create serious difficulties for the United States.

Truman openly admitted the problem. Clark Clifford, Truman's special campaign strategist and advisor, recalled the president's feeling that failure to assure equal rights to blacks was one of the nation's weakest points in the struggle with Communism. As Truman delicately phrased it when speaking to the Black Press in 1947:

> More and more we are learning how closely our democracy is under observation. We are learning what loud echoes both our successes and our failures have in every corner of the world. That is one of the pressing reasons why we cannot afford failures. When we fail to live together in peace the failure touches not us, as Americans alone, but the cause of democracy itself in the whole world. That we must never forget.[9]

Blacks could not help but be aware of the changing circumstances and their growing political importance. The NAACP not only saw the changes going on around the organization but directly experienced rapid growth. The association went from a membership of 50,000 before the war to 350,000 after.[10] This change, naturally, provided the organization with many more resources, both finances and personnel. By the middle of the decade, a new mood was clearly sweeping the black communities across the nation. It was fueled by an increasing sense of power that blacks now had and an increased indignation concerning treatment they felt they no longer had to endure. The growth and conscious use of the black vote in the forties was part of a larger process of motion in the black community.

In the early forties, blacks received few of the jobs that were created in the first part of the war boom. They were hardly inclined to submerge their struggle for equality during the war. Instead, they called for "Victory at Home as well as Abroad." In 1941 A. Philip Randolph had upped the ante by organizing the March on Washington movement to pressure Roosevelt to establish a Fair Employment Practices Committee in order to provide jobs for blacks. Randolph's statement was militant:

> The Negro's stake in national defense is big. It consists of jobs, thousands of jobs. It may represent millions, yes hundreds of millions of dollars in wages. It consists of new industrial opportunities and hope. This is worth fighting for. Most important and vital of all, Negroes by the mobilization and coordination of their mass power, can cause PRESIDENT ROOSEVELT TO ISSUE AN EXECUTIVE ORDER ABOLISHING DISCRIMINATION IN ALL GOVERNMENT DEPARTMENTS, ARMY, NAVY, AIR CORPS AND NATIONAL DEFENSE JOBS. (emphasis in original)

Randolph threatened to bring thousands of blacks to march on the capital demanding action. In the midst of the war, the movement organized mass rallies of tens of thousands of blacks in New York, Chicago, and St. Louis. They won their committee.[11]

Militancy continued after the war. Walter White, leader of the NAACP, testified before the Senate in 1945: "Throughout the Pacific I was told with grim pessimism by Negro troops that 'we know that our fight for democracy will really begin when we reach San Francisco on our way home.' " Black veterans in the South began to organize protests against their conditions. In January of 1946, over a hundred black veterans marched to the Birmingham courthouse to demand their right to register to vote. They were turned away, but their demonstration helped to unite black pressure on Truman. He responded by establishing the President's Committee on Civil Rights. The committee was told to prepare recommendations for government action to protect civil rights.[12]

The NAACP submitted a petition of grievances to the United Nations Committee on Human Rights. "This protest," it read, "is to induce the nations of the world to persuade this nation to be just to its own people." Though the petition was rejected, it caused great embarrassment to the United States government, especially when the Soviet Union used it as an opportunity to score propaganda points against the United States. The Soviets proposed making a crime of the "advocacy of national, racial and religious hostility or of national exclusiveness or hatred and contempt as well as of any action establishing privilege or discrimination based on distinction of race, nationality or religion."[13]

These acts were minor compared with the organization of the Committee against Jim Crow in Military Service and Training in late 1947, when, because of the developing cold war, the government was preparing to reintroduce the draft. A. Philip Randolph, once again in the lead, threatened to organize refusal among blacks to be drafted into a segregated army:

> I personally will advise Negroes to refuse to fight as slaves for a democracy they cannot possess and cannot enjoy. . . . I personally pledge myself to openly counsel and abet youth, both white and Negro, to quarantine a Jim Crow conscription system. . . .

When reminded during his testimony at a Senate hearing that such an act would be treason in time of war, Randolph responded that

> the Government now has time to change its policy on segregation and discrimination and if the government does not change its policy . . . in the interests of the very democracy it is fighting for, I would advocate that Negroes take no part in the army.

"I am prepared," he said, "to oppose a Jim Crow army til I rot in jail." Randolph led a picket line outside the Democratic Convention in 1948 demanding an end to segregation in the military. A poll of black youth in Harlem found 71 percent favoring refusal to be drafted into a segregated army. *Newsweek* reported that among Negro college students "there were indications of strong sympathy and support for Randolph."[14]

These were serious actions that indicated that blacks were ready and able to organize to pressure the government for equal rights. They were obviously aware of and willing to use the increased leverage provided by the pressures of the developing cold war. As Truman had indicated, with the United States trying to present itself as the leader of the free world as against the totalitarian Communists, the condition of blacks was the country's weak point. Henry Moon, voting analyst for the NAACP, wryly observed:

> Culturally and economically he [the Southern Negro] today surpasses the masses of the Rumanians, Bulgars and Poles for whom, ironically, former Secretary of State James F. Byrnes of South Carolina demanded "free and unfettered elections" at a time when this right was being denied to millions of Americans.[15]

The Wallace Threat

Truman, heading the Democratic ticket for the first time, was in trouble with liberals who had been discontent with him for some time. In 1944 he had been a conservative replacement for the enormously popular Henry Wallace, and he was then strongly supported by the South, whose leaders felt that Truman would be more sympathetic to their problems. Wallace's support had been from labor, blacks, liberals, and the left. It was not long after Truman succeeded Roosevelt that liberals began to be unhappy with his policies. The most crucial of these was the issue of relations with Russia. The two countries had enjoyed a close working relationship during the war. But six weeks after Roosevelt's death, when two leading liberals went to visit the new president, they were shocked to hear him say: "We have got to get tough with the Russians. They don't know how to behave. They're like bulls in a china shop. . . . We've got to teach them to behave." He replaced a number of liberal Roosevelt appointees, which upset many. He appeared sufficiently antilabor that the president of the Brotherhood of Railway Trainmen promised to spend the whole union treasury, if necessary, to defeat him for reelection after Truman urged the drafting of strikers during a railroad strike. Other labor leaders were unhappy enough with Truman that they tried to replace him as the Democratic party candidate. Blacks were so discontented with his policies that many voted Republican or simply did not vote in 1946. Many liberals saw Wallace as the rightful heir to Roosevelt. The 1946 election debacle, which brought about a Republican-dominated legislature for the first time since 1930, shook up the left and sent it casting in new directions. A third party was widely discussed.[16]

At the time Wallace was considering running against Truman, he had reason to believe that he would get some substantial labor support. Many unions had indicated their interest. But by the time he declared, at the end of December 1947, that support had disappeared. In part, labor's desertion of Wallace was due to a left turn that Truman had made after the 1946 mid-term elections. That election had brought serious losses to the Democrats in Congress, and it illustrated how far the president was from prevailing attitudes. In particular, his veto of the Taft-Hartley antilabor law was important in helping Truman to regain labor's support. But more fundamental were the cold war and the domestic red-baiting that went with it, both of which had a big impact on American politics.[17]

Truman was very conscious about his use of red-baiting to increase his popularity. His strategy was to use the antagonism with Russia that was growing as American and Soviet interests collided in order to create anti-Communist hysteria at home, and to use that hysteria against his opposition. This strategy was part of the overall election "game plan" developed for the president by Clark Clifford.[18]

In 1947, Truman had already instituted a loyalty program for federal employees. While it was ostensibly for the purposes of national security, in the program's implementation the division between espionage and political radicalism was obliterated. The president called opposition to his foreign policy an effort to "sabotage the foreign policy of the United States [which] is just as bad in this Cold War as it would be to shoot our soldiers in the back in a hot war." Although this particular barb was aimed at congressional opposition, it helped to create a general atmosphere that labeled dissent as being disloyal. He even suggested that the Republican party was soft on Communism because Republicans had expressed differences on foreign policy.[19]

Truman's rhetoric raised the level of hysteria. He rejected the support of "Wallace and his Communists." The Democratic National Committee labeled the Progressive party as "Communist-influenced." Jack Redding, Truman's publicity director, wrote concerning the 1948 campaign: "Wallace was smarting as we pinned red labels on him and his followers. Through every avenue we were pointing out that Wallace and his third party were following the Kremlin line slavishly.'' The formation of another liberal anti-Communist organization, the Americans for Democratic Action, was very helpful in the effort; these liberals served as frontmen for the president in the attack on Wallace. Indeed, as other support dropped away, virtually the only organized backing Wallace had was from the Communist party and the organizations it controlled.[20]

But if Wallace's campaign was weakened by this activity, it was certainly not destroyed. Although Wallace had few hopes of winning now, his political base could still affect the issues. In November of 1947, a Wallacite had garnered 40 percent of the vote in a Chicago judicial election. On February 17, a special congressional election in New York City produced a victory for the American Labor party candidate, who was backed by Wallace. The candidate, Leo Isaacson, took 56 percent of the vote and defeated the Democratic candidate by about two to one. A *New York Times* survey found that after the election, Wallace had increased support in the crucial states of Michigan, Pennsylvania, Illinois, and California. The *Times* argued that Wallace was a sufficient threat that it would be hard for Truman to win any of these states now. Polls taken before the convention showed the same trend. In Pennsylvania, Truman got 41 percent, Dewey 49 percent, Wallace 7 percent; in Illinois, it was Truman 44 percent, Dewey 43 percent, Wallace 13 percent; in New York, results were similar.[21]

Wallace's main issue was opposition to the Truman Doctrine, which defined Communism and Russia as America's main enemies—Wallace was for recognizing Russia's sphere of influence in Eastern Europe and maintaining a cooperative relationship with her. Nonetheless, he waged a hard-hitting campaign on other issues. He made serious efforts to woo labor and black support. Paul Robeson was made vice-chairman of the Progressive party; Joe Louis was a public contributor to the Wallace campaign fund; and W. E. B. DuBois and other blacks played a prominent role at the party convention in July.[22]

Indeed, because of his previous record and his campaign, Wallace's most important single source of strength was in the black community. The Associated Negro Press reported that in Los Angeles, ''thousands of Negro voters here began lining up behind Henry A. Wallace the day after he announced that he would run for the Presidency.'' Wallace deliberately went after the black vote. He and his vice-presidential candidate, Senator Glen Taylor, held election rallies in several cities in the South, including Little Rock, Memphis, Asheville, Greenville, Knoxville, and Chattanooga. At these rallies they verbally assaulted the segregation system and physically challenged it by refusing to hold segregated meetings. In doing so, they courted arrest and violence. Taylor was arrested in Birmingham by Eugene ''Bull'' Connor, who became nationally infamous in 1963 because of his treatment of civil rights demonstrators. Wallace and Taylor had to endure eggs, tomatoes, peach stones, and other sundries being hurled at them as they attempted to speak. Wallace was several times forced to cancel meetings.[23]

These efforts paid off. Though Wallace failed to win the support of the national black leadership, he gained the endorsement of the president of the Indiana NAACP and of officials in many of the large cities, including San Francisco and Philadelphia. Ward leaders in Brooklyn and Harlem thought that Wallace might get as much as 75 percent of the vote in their wards. Even as late as October 2, a poll taken in Baltimore indicated that Wallace was drawing a substantial percentage of the black vote—perhaps enough to hand the election to Dewey. The Chicago *Defender* was the only important black newspaper to endorse Truman, a fact that made the situation more worrisome for the president.[24]

The Liberals Respond

It was the very strength of the Wallace campaign that made the liberal opposition within the Democratic party important. Many liberals who refused to follow Wallace were still quite unhappy with Truman. They organized the Americans for Democratic Action early in 1947 with a double aim: to exclude Communists from the liberal movement ("a reconstruction of the liberal movement free of totalitarian influence from either the Left or the Right") and to strengthen their own position within the Democratic party ("All our efforts, all our own ingenuity must be thrown into the struggle to establish liberal control of the Democratic Party"). The content of liberalism came very largely to be shaped in the course of the campaign itself.[25]

The ADA was solidly behind the anti-Communist direction of Truman's policies at home and abroad. It was locked in battle against the Communists and their supporters for liberal supremacy in America. Nonetheless, the ADA was very much in opposition to Truman, because they felt he was not really a liberal, because of his antilabor policy, and because they felt he was a sure loser and would take the Democratic party and labor and the liberals down to defeat with him. Until shortly before the convention, the organization was engaged in a serious effort to deny the nomination to Truman. It was forced to abandon the effort when its candidate, General Eisenhower, announced that he would not accept the nomination.[26]

Responding to the pressure of the Wallace campaign, the ADA now sought to shore up the Democratic party's weakest flank by turning to civil rights, which blacks had made an issue before Wallace began his campaign. The Civil Rights Committee that blacks had pressured the president to appoint in 1946 had produced a report of its findings in 1947. Truman had delivered a civil rights message to Congress in early 1948 that was largely based on this report. This act caused the white South to respond in anger, and Truman soon backed off. He refrained from sending legislation to Congress and from issuing any executive orders concerning the matter.[27]

But it was impossible simply to placate the white South and ignore blacks. Truman himself had created expectations with his civil rights address to Congress; he had even had it broadcast over the Voice of America to make sure it would be used as a weapon in the cold war. Blacks were not letting the matter rest—Randolph was in the midst of campaigning against the segregated armed forces. And the Wallace threat continued.[28]

Truman tried to respond to both pressures by resurrecting for the platform a rewritten version of the civil rights plank from 1944, which was an innocuous statement that read:

> We believe that racial and religious minorities have the right to live, develop and vote equally with all citizens and share the rights that are guaranteed by our Constitution. Congress should exert its full constitutional powers to protect those rights.

Even the Republican party platform was stronger than this statement. It included a call for abolition of the poll tax and for ending segregation in the armed forces.[29]

Truman's proposal pleased no one. It certainly did not please the South, which wanted its own plank assuring states' rights. Nor did it please blacks, who felt it insufficient. Walter White, head of the NAACP, appeared before the convention platform representing not only the association but twenty other black organizations as well, with a combined membership of over six million. White said the plank was totally unsatisfactory and reminded the committee of the voting power of blacks, who, he said, would vote on issues, not party labels. The Truman forces continued to press on with their planned position, hoping to keep support of the South with it.[30]

But the ADA was unwilling to let things stand and determined to challenge the president on the civil rights plank, if necessary, in order to strengthen it. They took their proposal, which included the following points, to the floor of the convention after they failed to get it through the platform committee:

> The right to full and equal political participation, the right to equal opportunity of employment, the right of security of persons [referring to lynchings in particular], and the right of equal treatment in the services and defense of our nation.

They were backed in their efforts by several big-city-machine bosses, including those from Chicago, Pittsburgh, the Bronx, San Francisco, and Minneapolis, who were concerned about losing not only the presidential election but the local elections in which Wallace was giving them a hard time in competition for black votes.[31] Hubert Humphrey, who was facing a strong Republican opponent in his bid to be elected senator of Minnesota, and who was threatened by the Wallacites, was the public leader of the fight. He presented the case eloquently:

> There are those who say this issue of civil rights is an infringement on states' rights. The time has come for the Democratic Party to get out of the shadow of states' rights and walk forthrightly into the bright sunshine of human rights.

What was most instructive was his clear explanation of the issue in terms of world politics:

> Yes, this is far more than a party matter. Every citizen has a stake in the emergence of the United States as the leader of the free world. That world is being challenged

by the world of slavery. For us to play our part effectively we must be in a morally sound position. We cannot use a double standard for measuring our own and other people's policies. Our demands for democratic practices in other lands will be no more effective than the guarantee of those practiced in our own country.

Humphrey made the point clearly. He and his coworkers had set the liberal and the Democratic party agenda. In order to be able to wage the cold war effectively, they had to espouse civil rights at home. The pressures of international politics together with changes in domestic politics gave civil rights their day—at least in rhetoric.[32]

The amendment carried, and the states' rights advocates walked out. The ADA and their allies had carried off a remarkable feat. They had challenged a sitting president and defeated him within the party. They, rather than he, had determined one of the principal issues on which the campaign would be run. But it was black organization, activity, and power that had made it imperative to do and possible to accomplish. "Never since 1932," said the *New York Times*, "had there been such a material change in a party platform after it had reached the convention floor."[33]

Campaign and Election

Truman had little choice but to run on the platform, especially after the loss of the right-wing Southerners. Less than two weeks after the convention, he issued two executive orders that he had been sitting on for six months or more. He barred discrimination in federal employment and established a review board in each government department. Employees who felt discriminated against could appeal to this board.

Truman further announced a policy of "equality of treatment and opportunity for all persons in the armed services without regard to race, color, religion or national origin." It was unclear, however, if that meant a policy of desegregation in the armed forces, especially when he further announced that he would appoint a committee to study the problem. Two days later, General Bradley, army chief of staff, announced that the army would not be a laboratory for social reforms and that it would change "when the Nation as a whole changes." The president responded at a press conference that the policy indeed was to integrate the armed forces. In mid-August, when the civil disobedience campaign against the new draft was to have begun, Randolph terminated it, satisfied that the point had been won.[34]

In the end, Truman felt compelled to pursue the black vote openly. At the end of October, he toured the black ghetto in Philadelphia; and on October 29 he became the first president to speak in Harlem. On the anniversary of his receipt of the report of his Civil Rights Committee, he addressed some 65,000 people and affirmed his commitment to civil rights: "Our determination to attain the goal of equal rights and equal opportunity must be resolute and unwavering."[35]

Truman, of course, won. "Labor did it," said Truman. And it was true that labor had played a crucial role in his victory. But it was a very close election. The president beat Dewey by 2,000,000 votes, but he won three crucial states— Ohio, California, and Illinois—by a total of only 58,584 votes. If he had lost those states, he would have lost the election; if he had lost two of them, it would have been thrown into the House of Representatives. Blacks, who voted 69 percent for Truman overall, carried those states for him. The black vote in Los Angeles, Chicago, and Cleveland and Akron provided the margin of victory in those key states.[36]

Truman's strategy with regard to blacks was successful. He won their vote and appears to have gotten a better percentage of it than had Roosevelt. So was the black strategy a success. For the first time blacks forced the issue of race into the very center of national politics.[37]

The election was very much focused around the developing cold war, and Truman's strategy called for intensifying the emphasis on the competition with Russia. The emerging colonial revolution put extraordinary new pressures on the United States to develop an acceptable racial policy, while at the same time blacks were beginning to gain some power. Their activity and muscle forced the issue to public attention, thus making it a matter of international concern. These pressures persisted after 1948. As more colonies became independent, their presence encouraged American blacks to oppose their own conditions. The 1948 election demonstrated the new power and position that blacks had attained after depression and war. In that sense, it was a reflection of change, as well as a turning point that quickened the pace of events.

The election struggle had opened a breach in the Democratic party and in the nation. The country was becoming divided again. The strength of blacks in the North was pitted against the racists in the South, and the latter lost. Truman's appeal to blacks was a success, despite the States' Rights party, which carried four Southern states. That was an important lesson. It showed that it was possible for a Democrat to win by ignoring Southern racism and courting blacks. It was a lesson that would figure significantly in Senator John F. Kennedy's bid for the presidency in 1960. It illustrated, furthermore, how isolated the South's racist culture and political structure had become from the prevailing sentiments and political trends in the nation. Both of these perceptions would have an impact on the black community and, as they were reinforced in the fifties, would encourage black activism.

The breach was not to close before it was wrenched open much further. The events of 1948 were the beginning of the struggle that was to burst into open battle in the 1960s. Blacks were encouraged by what happened and became more self-confident and more demanding in the South as well as the North.

Black demands for equality were given legitimacy in the campaign. Three of the four candidates for president, including the nominees of the two major parties, announced themselves as being for civil rights and black equality. This new attitude among political leaders, in addition to the rising tide of black militancy, created an atmosphere that helped to propel the Supreme Court into rendering decisions that struck at the whole structure of racial politics. The Court had begun changing its decisions from endorsing segregation to finding it unacceptable in the late thirties, and had quickened the pace in the forties. But the most important judicial decisions were issued from 1948 to 1954, culminating in the famous *Brown* v. *Board of Education* case that caused such an uproar in the South. These decisions, in their turn, played an important role in creating the conditions that led to the civil rights explosion of the 1960s. Thus, this exercise of black political power, and the resulting realignment of the federal government, would have a major impact on the civil rights struggles of the coming decade.[38]

This process assured the continued alienation of those sections of the South that had led and supported the Dixiecrat revolt. The States' Rights movement of 1948 was the first step down the road to what became known as "massive resistance" in the 1950s, and to violent, brutal attacks on black and white integrationists in the 1960s. "The Dixiecrat movement . . . fixed the broad aims and many of the programs that were to carry over into massive resistance," said Numan Bartley in his study of the massive resistance movement.[39]

The election of 1948 illustrated the new strength blacks had attained, but it came before the massive and powerful struggles of the sixties, in which blacks sought to reap the gains their new power entitled them to. Because of the peculiar juncture of circumstances in the political arena during the first postwar election, new opportunities became suddenly available to blacks. It was as though a curtain had temporarily been drawn aside to provide a preview of the struggle that was yet to come, and to reveal the great historical changes that had already taken place.

IV

THE SPLITTING OF THE SOLID SOUTH

The civil rights movement began in the 1950s. That decade was a period of preparation for the turbulent and militant sixties, when broader and broader layers of people challenged more and more of the ideology, customs, and practices of white supremacy. But this movement did not appear out of a vacuum; it required preparation. Social movements demand leadership and involve "élan" and "momentum," qualities that, in the fifties, whites possessed far more than blacks. Southern blacks, who were to lead this movement in its early stages, had to develop a new, more militant leadership and become politically more tightly knit. They had to overcome the immense power of the white population in general, and of the white leadership in particular. As a political entity, the Southern black population emerged from the decade of the fifties prepared to lead and support a militant social movement. This political development was shaped by the response of the white South to black requests and ultimately demands for dignity, equality, and a share of power. That response was total, or, as it came to be known, massive, resistance: terror, economic coercion, and a call to the whole white population to maintain white supremacy. The effort was a conscious attempt to recapitulate the successful struggle against Reconstruction.

But the immense structural change brought about by the strains of the Depression and the war had reshaped the Southern economy. Its primary focus was now centered in the cities; its main activity was business. The latter no longer was merely an appendage to agriculture but came more and more to shape social life. That meant that the businessman was becoming an increasingly important and influential feature of Southern society.

The profound social and economic transformation that this change entailed did not, however, translate into any significant alteration in the racial practices or social relations, or in the allocation of political power, in the region. The elite that had emerged dominant in the South in the latter part of the nineteenth century continued to exercise political power, though even it had been affected by the changes and had become more "bourgeois" in its social outlook. The racial practices of segregation and the denial of political rights to blacks, upon which the political power and economic well-being of this class had rested, remained.

Had it been simply a matter of the dynamic between the agricultural and business classes, the latter might never have challenged the power of the former, and they almost certainly would not have chosen to upset the racial status quo. The businessmen were not reformers; they were not out to change the world. Their purpose was to make money, and the existing system of social relations, which kept the cost of labor down, was certainly no hindrance to their aim. Moreover, any effort to alter the racial and political structure of the South was bound to encounter tremendous resistance, as it did, and to create substantial instability, the notorious bête noire of business.

Nonetheless, the outstanding political development of the decade was the split that occurred between these two components of the leadership of the South. This split developed as a result of the tenacity of the blacks in their demands for equal treatment. They had been pressuring the federal government to act in their behalf and were persistently pressing the federal courts to diminish the stranglehold of segregation on their lives. But in the end what was to prove most important was that they were finding the strength and ability to stand up to the whites, even when they had to face terror.

It was in response to these pressures, and the impact they were having on a Southern social system that was becoming ever more strained, that the South's traditional leadership was forced to act. With the 1954 *Brown* v. *Board of Education* decision that outlawed segregation in education, it became clear that if the leaders did not take serious action, the racial order that had solidified by the beginning of the twentieth century would soon be obliterated. With it would go white elite political power. The implied threat was symbolized by the demand articulated by Martin Luther King, Jr. in the 1957 "Pilgrimage to Washington": "Give us the ballot!"[1] They therefore undertook to recreate the "solid South," with the intention of making the federal government back off from attempting to force black rights upon a region that was determined to resist such measures.

The business community did not have the same stake in the maintenance of the status quo. The free labor market, coupled with a political climate hostile to unionism, could provide them with the labor they needed at prices they could afford to pay. And precisely because of their concern for stability, they were not eager to defy the federal government. Acceptance of the law, and of the Supreme Court as its ultimate arbiter, was the banner under which they gathered.

Such was the opposition that the small-town "county seat governing class" had to contend with, in addition to the blacks themselves and the federal government. The business class constituted, at least potentially, an alternative leadership. But it was a reluctant and timorous alternative. When the agrarian elite turned its guns on the businessmen (usually figuratively), the commercial leadership was quick to back down, leaving the agrarian leaders free to press their offensive against the federal government and the black population. For blacks that meant a reign of terror such as they had not experienced for decades. Economic coercion, political murders, and even lynchings returned as blacks faced an all-out assault to drive them back to their "place" of subservience.

The offensive gained some results, as both the government and the courts began to back away. This response encouraged the Southern leadership to attempt open defiance. Little Rock was the arena within which this drama was enacted; the defeat of the segregationist forces there spelled the end to the strategy of open confrontation. Moreover, it weakened, though not yet decisively, the Southern political leadership.

That leadership then turned to its second recourse, the closing of schools facing desegregation. But this action meant a drastic upheaval, severe threats to the future of the region's youth, and the most significant menace to political, social, and economic stability that had yet appeared on the horizon. The South's Old Guard, in its zeal to uphold the established order, was undermining all order. It was that fact, which could be measured in strictly economic terms, that forced the business community and the middle classes into action. Despite their reluctance, they were forced to oppose directly the old leadership's policies and to seek to accommodate black demands. To accomplish that task, they had to fight for leadership itself, which meant an end to the "solid South" and to the old Southern elite's unified control over politics in the region.

The great economic changes that took place in the South in the decades of the thirties and forties had split the Southern upper class into two separate sections, whose interests lay along potentially different courses. The black community, by its determination and by its ability to use its leverage to gain support from the federal government, drove a wedge between these two sections and turned a potential split into an actuality. The process became a pattern that was repeated as the drive for black rights reached deeper into the core of Southern racism. The first victories were gained in the cities of the Upper South, and they set the stage for carrying the offensive deeper until not even the most Deep South black-belt rural areas could escape the determination of the black movement. This chapter traces the process by which that split took place; the following chapter will examine the effects of the struggle on the black population of the South.

The Second Reconstruction

Writing two years after the historic Supreme Court decision of 1954 that outlawed segregation in education, C. Vann Woodward compared the 1950s with Reconstruction. The White Citizens' Council, the main organization of white reaction in the South in that period, applauded this comparison. It warned that the "stark terror" of "Black Reconstruction" was stalking the region once again, and called for a determined resistance to it. The parallel has been noted by others, and it has become quite commonplace to refer to the period as the "Second Reconstruction." The *Brown* decision calling segregation unconstitutional evoked these images with particular clarity, but even before *Brown* there was considerable evidence of an assault on the South's racial order. Truman's decision to desegregate the military and the skirmishes over a new Fair Employment Practices Committee after World War II were examples.[2]

One indication of Northern concern with the South was the new interest in studies of the "Negro question" and of the South itself. In the late thirties and early forties, the Carnegie Corporation underwrote a study of American race relations carried out under the direction of Gunnar Myrdal and published under the title *An American Dilemma*. Its purpose, according to Frederick Keppel, then president of the trustees of the corporation, was specifically not limited to the "advancement and diffusion of knowledge and understanding." Rather, as Keppel said, "more knowledge and better organized and related knowledge were essential before the Corporation could intelligently distribute its own funds." The Myrdal study set the framework for the analysis of race relations in the United States and ended what little academic respectability remained in the racist camp. Whether so intended or not, it and the studies associated with it became important in helping to decide the *Brown* case. In 1946, the Rockefeller Foundation financed a landmark study under the direction of political scientist V.0. Key. *Southern Politics* examined carefully the political functioning and alignments in each of the Southern states with a particular interest in race and its impact on the politics of the region. These studies were ground-breaking, in that they represented the first attempts to examine the region carefully from the outside. They were followed by a plethora of others.[3]

Far more important in terms of their immediate impact were the court decisions that, even before *Brown*, were seriously eroding the institution of segregation. A series of decisions had opened up Southern graduate schools to blacks and disallowed any state-imposed restrictions. Other decisions had outlawed segregation in interstate travel on buses and railroads. Southern liberal Hodding Carter III wrote that before *Brown*, "it was an increasingly common event for the white Southerner to discover that a Negro was attending his state university or graduate school, or that Negroes were ordering meals in the white sections of railroad dining cars even South of Atlanta."[4]

In 1944 the Supreme Court had outlawed the white primary. Under the impact of that decision, black voter registration had increased 400 percent by 1952— up to 1 million voters—and by 1956 it was up another 25 percent, to almost 1.25 million. In Southern cities blacks were winning some local offices. The growing boldness of Southern blacks was reflected in the fact that the NAACP held its annual meeting in the South in 1951.[5]

The Southern leadership could see the handwriting on the wall. In 1950, one of Georgia Governor Talmadge's assistants predicted "that [the Supreme Court] will go all the way and say there can be no such things as separate and equal facilities." The governors of South Carolina, Georgia, and Mississippi had vowed not to countenance integration in the public schools.[6]

Still, when the decision was issued, it hit hard. "In the field of public education," it read, "the doctrine of separate but equal has no place. Separate educational facilities are inherently unequal. . . . Therefore . . . the plaintiffs and others similarly situated . . . are, by reason of the segregation complained of, deprived of the equal protection of the laws guaranteed by the Fourteenth Amendment." With these words the Court reversed the position it had taken in the *Plessy* case almost sixty years earlier, in 1896. In doing so, it returned the Fourteenth Amendment to its original Reconstruction intent, and it withdrew federal approbation of, and acquiescence to, the South's racial order. Supreme Court Chief Justice Earl Warren wrote that "the Court was thoroughly conscious of the importance of the decision to be arrived at and of the impact it would have on the nation." There were few on any side of the question who did not see that the ruling would apply not only to education but to every other area of life, as well. The decision certainly gave credence to the notion that a new Reconstruction was at hand.[7]

The Rise and (Rapid) Fall of the Moderates

Bob Smith, author of a study of the school-closing controversy in Virginia, asserted that there was "little evidence . . . that the man on the street and the man behind the plow reacted sharply to the Supreme Court decision." People were not ready to fight the decision, but it is impossible to say that there was acceptance of it or that there was not a deep hostility to it. Smith himself saw "a spirit of rebellion." In South Carolina, the white citizenry was "momentarily stunned." Nonetheless, the decision created a new situation, and the response of the white South was not a foregone conclusion. Sociologist Elaine Burgess found in her study of Durham, North Carolina that the white leadership was split: 25 percent favored desegregation without resistance, 20 percent preferred to fight it "regardless of consequences," and the rest "were in-between."[8]

Southern moderates attempted to shape the Southern response, stressing the importance of law and order and the inevitability of the mandated change. The Richmond *News Leader*, soon to be a leader of the resistance movement, editorialized that "if the Court were to fix, say a ten year period, and permit the states to integrate ten per cent of their schools a year . . . a solution might be found." The Nashville *Tennessean* said: "The South is and has been for years a land of change. Its people—of both races—have learned to live with change. They can both learn to live with this one. Given a reasonable amount of time and understanding, they will."[9]

Southern churches, including Southern Baptists, Methodists, Presbyterians, and Episcopalians, urged compliance with the ruling. The Presbyterian church stated editorially in its publication that many would "rejoice that Churchmen are courageously challenging an evil social order." The Virginia superintendent of public instruction stated on the day of the *Brown* decision: "There will be no defiance of the Supreme Court as far as I am concerned. We are trying to teach children to abide by the law of the land, and we will abide by it.'' The North Carolina school superintendent commented that ''integration is as inevitable as the sunrise,'' and the governor acknowledged that ''the Supreme Court . . . has spoken.'' Five days after the decision was issued, the Little Rock school board promised to comply. Within a short period, similar intentions were announced in Fayetteville, Arkansas, the District of Columbia, Baltimore, Louisville, and several counties in West Virginia.[10]

Three months after the ruling, a study in Florida found only a minority of whites objecting vigorously to the decision and a majority of both black and white leaders doubting that it would produce serious violence. Such indications led the Southern Regional Council, a liberal organization, to report optimistically a few months after the ruling that ''the South is moving—not always smoothly, but with seeming inevitability—toward an increasingly integrated society.'' The NAACP set the fall of 1955 as the tanget date for desegregation. The organization stated that ''the steady progress being made demonstrates the fact that integration will work even in the Deep South.''[11]

Nor did this trend simply disappear as the political tides turned. When, in Virginia, the possibility of abandoning the public school system was raised as a means of countering the Court ruling, many opposed it. A Richmond paper suggested that it was by no means clear that such a proposal would pass a referendum. ''The [Senator Harry] Byrd organization,'' said one observer, referring to the organization's support for closing the schools, ''suddenly found itself . . . with its back to the wall.'' Even in Mississippi similar measures at times encountered serious opposition. And the border states of Delaware, Maryland, Kentucky, and West Virginia began to implement the ruling.[12]

Businessmen provided much of the impulse for this approach. In Savannah, Georgia a rotary club meeting burst into applause when apprised of the decision. In 1955 the executive director of the Virginia Chamber of Commerce had suggested that integration might provide benefits to the South: the increased purchasing power it would ultimately create among blacks would bring a general prosperity. Martin Luther King, Jr. noted in his account of the Montgomery bus boycott that on more than one occasion businessmen expressed an interest in reaching an agreement only to be held back by more intransigent forces. Some businesses based in the North made some symbolic moves to win favor with the growing national black market. The Falstaff brewing company, for example, purchased a lifetime membership in the NAACP.[13]

Despite all this activity, it was not long before the forces of resistance were in command in the heart of the South. The moderates were silenced, and the South had solidified behind a leadership committed to ''massive resistance.'' Two observers who toured the South in the mid-1950s claimed that ''North and South, the W[hite] C[itizens'] C[ouncils'] defiant pronouncements have been heeded as 'the' voice of 'the' South.'' A prointegrationist remarked a few years after Brown: ''We felt that maybe Mississippi and Georgia would hold out awhile. But I don't think anybody foresaw a resolidification of an eight-state South. I don't think even the Segregationist leadership foresaw it. They were amazed at their own success.'' The chief justice of the Supreme Court, Earl Warren, voiced the same sentiment: ''The Court expected some resistance from the South. But I doubt if any of us expected as much as we got.'' The line had been drawn, and a fight was brewing—a replay, perhaps, of the battle against the first Reconstruction?[14]

The battle, however, was one-sided. Though moderates made a bid to shape a cooperative response to the inevitability of desegregation, they were not committed to fight for desegregation. Rather, as it became clear that they faced the traditional Southern leadership, united in its intention to repulse this assault on the South's customs, they quickly backed away. They began to stress that the problem was the ''extremists'' on both sides, while in actuality they turned their ire on the blacks, who were pushing to upset the established social order. The moderates chided blacks for going too far, too fast. They pointed to the progress being made before *Brown* and noted the abrupt turnabout and hardening of positions: ''Two short years ago . . . race relations were better than at any time since the turn of the century. Then the 1954 and 1955 Supreme Court decisions were handed down. In their wake have come ugly race tension stirred by hatred, bitterness and fear. . . .''[15]

They ignored the fact that progress had been tolerated only because it had not fundamentally challenged the system. Hodding Carter III himself admitted: ''This toleration existed only so long as the goals remained within the framework of segregation. . . . But,'' he added, ''it was tolerance nonetheless.'' Most significant, the voice of the moderates came hardly to be heard. Or, rather, what they were heard to say could hardly be comforting to blacks. Numan Bartley, historian of the movement of white reaction, wrote that ''even more progressively oriented 'moderates' usually felt compelled to avow their devotion to segregation before timidly suggesting token alternatives.''[16]

The Bogey of Communism

In its effort to attain Southern unity on its own terms, the Southern establishment was swimming with the stream. For, apart from the black victories in the courts and some executive actions such as desegregation of the armed forces, events of the time seemed to be moving in a direction favorable to Southern reaction—more so than for a very long time. There emerged in the late forties and early fifties a national movement whose aim was to reverse the changes that had taken place in the American economic, political, and social structure since the Depression. Known often as McCarthyism, the movement was not limited to the activities of the senator from Wisconsin and his associates. It had its origins in the cold war and in the reaction to the New Deal measures. It was already under way, though nothing like what it would become, before the 1948 election. In 1947 Truman had instituted a loyalty program; the attorney general had begun drawing up lists of subversive organizations.[17]

The movement had a profound impact on American society that lasted beyond

McCarthy himself. Fred Cook summed it up in his history of McCarthyism: "The entire nation ran cowed. A whimper out of the night could ruin a life, a career. Just to have a name similar to someone else's could be fatal. . . . In this atmosphere . . . any accusation was tantamount to conviction." Everyone became suspect, and everyone feared to speak out; not only Communists and left-wingers but even liberals were under assault. Things went so far that McCarthy, in his heyday, could charge that any Democrat, by virtue of being a Democrat, might be guilty of treachery.[18]

A pall settled upon the nation. The House Committee on Un-American Activities traveled from city to city holding hearings. People named as "suspects," or just subpoenaed to testify before the committee, often faced the threat of being fired. Refusal to answer questions by invoking the protection of the Fifth Amendment brought automatic dismissal from one's job in many cases. Workers who were Communists or "Communist sympathizers" were "walked out" of their plants—"escorted" out by other workers and told in no uncertain terms not to return. It is no wonder, then, that in this period the black movement for equality retired from the streets, from almost everywhere, and directed its energies almost solely toward the courts.[19]

The Southern political leadership was part of this movement of reaction. Cook described the Texas oil money that was directly tied to McCarthy. Alexander Heard, an associate of V. O. Key's, indicated that the Texas Regular movement, which fielded independent electors in 1944 because of opposition to the New Deal, dominated the 1948 Dixiecrat movement in the state. He suggested that their racist program was for the purpose of building a broader right-wing movement by "using such votes as they could find" at that time and which they "would not get in support of their economic position alone." One of the leaders of the White Citizens' Councils frankly stated that the movement was about more than just white supremacy: "It is fundamentally the first real stirrings of a conservative revolt in this country. . . ." A whole number of state legislatures made it clear that they were concerned with more than just race. A report to the Fund for the Republic on "The American Right Wing" suggested that "perhaps the segregation question may be the issue on which the Right will finally present a united front."[20]

Regardless of what actual direct links there were between Southern leaders and the anti-Communist hysteria of those years, the latter created a national mood that the South's leaders were not slow to take advantage of. Even in 1948, Strom Thurmond, governor of South Carolina and States' Rights party presidential candidate, contended that the Democratic party's "so-called civil rights platform" was "made to order for Communist use in their designs upon national security." Judge Thomas Brady, who had been a leader of the States' Rights party, warned in the foreword to his pamphlet *Black Monday* of the danger of forced integration by "Communist front organizations, the CIO and the NAACP." The attorney general of Georgia charged officials of the NAACP, including the president, the chairman of the board, the honorary chairman, eleven of twenty-eight vice-presidents, the treasurer, twenty-eight of forty-seven directors, the chairman of the National Legal Committee, the executive secretary, the special counsel, the assistant special counsel, the Southeast regional secretary, the West Coast secretary, the director of the Washington bureau, the director of public relations, and two field secretaries with ''affiliation with, participation in Communist or Communist-front, fellow-traveling or subversive organizations or activities.'' The White Citizens' Councils charged that integration was ''nothing more and nothing less'' than ''a strategic campaign of the world communist movement.'' In their organizing efforts, the councils stressed the job they were doing to stop the Communist plot for integration.[21]

Senator James Eastland of Mississippi, chairman of the Senate Internal Security Committee and of the Judiciary Committee, demanded an investigation into the ''subversive influence behind the desegregation decision,'' which he said was ''attempting to graft into the organic law of the land the teachings, preachments and social doctrines which can be traced to Karl Marx.'' Eastland distributed over 300,000 copies of the speech, and it and several other such pamphlets were widely read throughout the South. Eastland even had McCarthy—already censured by the Senate—testify before his committee. The two issued a joint statement claiming that Chief Justice Earl Warren was ''following the Communist line.'' Their efforts were aided by FBI director J. Edgar Hoover. When a civil rights bill was being debated in 1956, the FBI head contradicted his superior, Attorney General Brownell, and blamed the racial tensions in the South since *Brown* on Communist agitators. Hoover expressed such opinions repeatedly.[22]

The Southern Establishment succeeded in creating an atmosphere in which integration was thought of by many as subversive. Many others, who might have spoken up in favor of integration or in opposition to the resistance efforts, were intimidated lest their loyalty be questioned. Daniel Thompson cited the case of an interracial committee in New Orleans. The committee disbanded following the investigation of one of its members by the House Committee on Un-American Activities. Similarly, when the New Orleans Urban League was accused of being under Communist influence, Thompson reported that ''several influential white persons'' resigned from its board, and the organization was dropped as a recipient of United Fund monies. Even blacks were affected. The NAACP grew more conservative; in the 1960s Bayard Rustin was forced to leave Martin Luther King, Jr.'s staff because of his previous socialist affiliations.[23]

The anti-Communist thrust became a live issue in the South even as the hysteria was beginning to relax in the rest of the country. With a Republican administration in office for the first time in twenty years, and with the emergence of more conservative unionism, the business community withdrew its support from McCarthy. The postwar boom was also easing the pressure on all but the Southern ruling class. As it grew more isolated, this class became more fixed in its determination to fight back. The menace of Communism became simply one more in its bag of weapons with which to attempt to defeat the Second Reconstruction.[24]

Forging a Solid South

> Hegel remarks somewhere that all facts and personages of great importance in
> world history occur, as it were, twice. He forgot to add: the first time as tragedy,
> the second as farce. . . . The tradition of all the dead generations weighs like a
> nightmare on the brain of the living. . . . They anxiously conjure up the spirits
> of the past to their service and borrow from them names, battle cries and costumes.
> —Karl Marx[25]

After the *Brown* decision, the Southern ruling elite was preoccupied by the
fight to attain Southern unity around its program for a solid, defiant South. That
effort took over a year and a half to accomplish. While the Court ruling was
issued in May of 1954, it was not until early 1956 that a solid South was militantly
up in arms confronting "this illegal encroachment upon our sovereign powers."[26]
At that point the first phase of the resistance movement was over.

In order to create a solid white front against both the blacks and the federal
government, the Southern leadership drew on the historical precedent of the
Redeemers' successful battle against the first Reconstruction. In that earlier effort, there had been whites who had broken the united front against the former
slaves and against the federal occupation of the region. It had taken persuasion,
the coercion of the Ku Klux terror, and the opprobrium of public opinion to
coax them into a united front or cast them outside of respectability. Similar
measures were required for the threat that appeared in the fifties. A spokesman
from South Carolina said as much, recalling that

> Reconstruction days were harsh, but, notwithstanding the scalawags, the carpet-
> baggers and the federal bayonet, the basic principles for which the South fought
> were not destroyed. Today, we face a similar challenge. Perhaps, if we have the
> strength of character exhibited by the generation proceeding, the dawn of a new
> 1876 will arrive.[27]

It was only weeks after *Brown* that Judge Brady declared war on the ruling
in his *Black Monday* speech. Referring by the title to the day of the decision,
he made it clear to those inside and out of the region that peaceful acquiescence
was out of the question: "Oh, High Priests of Washington . . . pour a little coal
oil of political expediency and hope of racial amalgamation upon the flickering
blaze which you have created and you will start a conflagration in the South
which all of Neptune's mighty ocean can not quench."[28]

The Jackson *Daily News* stated the policy toward internal dissent: "Common
sense calls for a solid front. . . . An impregnable front is absolutely necessary."
William Simmons, head of the White Citizens' Council, underlined the point:
"Fence straddlers, condemning Council members as 'extremists' are nothing
more than spiritual comrades of Revolutionary War 'moderates' who doubtless
regarded Paul Revere as an extremist and hate monger." This program was
sometimes chillingly illustrated. In the center of Montgomery, two effigies were
hung, one white, one black. The black wore the label "NAACP." The white's

label read: "I talked for integration." This material was supplemented with sensationalist sexual propaganda.[29]

A few months after *Brown*, in the summer of 1954, Southern governors meeting in Richmond, Virginia promised "not to comply voluntarily with the Supreme Court's decision against racial segregation in the public schools." With this act they helped to set the framework within which the response of Southern whites would be developed. Late that year, Mississippi raised the stakes by passing a constitutional amendment that ended the state requirement for public education. The measure permitted the abolition of the whole public school system, or of any local part of it. Other Deep South states followed suit.[30]

The Southern leadership worked hard to dispel any idea that the South must accept change because it had been mandated by the Supreme Court. The Redeemers had refused to recognize the legitimacy of Reconstruction, so that it could be imposed only by force, by a standing army. Now the black-belt elite sought to develop support for a similar effort with a concerted campaign to undermine the court's legitimacy, and to suggest that any attempt to enforce such laws would be met with force. "If this constitutes disrespect or treason," Judge Brady had written, "then let the most be made of it. . . . We say to the Supreme Court and to the entire world, 'You shall not make us drink from this cup! . . . We have, through our forefathers, died before for our sacred principles. We can, if necessary, die again. . . .'"[31]

In April 1955, the editor of the Jackson, Mississippi *Daily News* told the American Society of Newspaper editors: "Mississippi will not obey the decision. If an effort is made to send Negroes to school with white children there will be bloodshed. The stain of that bloodshed will be on the Supreme Court's steps." That summer the paper warned in a front-page editorial that "the NAACP is dedicated to widening this wedge which was handed it by a subversive Supreme Court. . . . A mandate has been hurled at the white people of Mississippi." The Jackson *Daily News* entitled its editorial "Yes, We Defy the Law." Senator Eastland counseled a White Citizens' Council rally in Mississippi: "You are not required to obey a court which passes out such a ruling. In fact, you are obligated to defy it." Journalist John Temple Graves echoed this sentiment. Writing in the Birmingham *Post Herald*, he told his readers: "The Court . . . has taught us to disregard the law." The Richmond *News Leader* proclaimed the same sentiments in an editorial:

> These nine men repudiated the Constitution, spit upon the tenth Amendment, and rewrote the fundamental law of this land to suit their own gauzy concepts of sociology. If it be said now that the South is flouting the law, let it be said to the high court, you taught us how.

It was to the atmosphere created by such propaganda that a federal court referred when it noted ominously that "the attitude of the public authorities openly encourages opposition to the law of the land, which may easily find expression in the disturbances of the public peace."[32]

Brady not only had expressed his opposition to *Brown* in his *Black Monday* speech; he also had called for organization: he proposed the formation in each of the Southern states of "law-abiding resistance organizations which would in no way resemble the nefarious KKK." Brady was not alone in calling for organized opposition. That summer Senator Eastland of Mississippi proposed the formation of a "people's organization . . . not controlled by fawning politicians who cater to organized groups who are attempting our destruction . . . mobilize and organize public opinion . . . and attempt to pledge candidates in advance as they [the prointegrationists] attempt to pledge."[33]

On July 11, 1954, the White Citizens' Council was formed, in direct response to Brady's appeal. It originated in Indianola, Mississippi, which was the heart of the plantation county, and in the home country of Senator Eastland. With this move the ferment began to take shape. The White Citizens' Councils grew rapidly in Mississippi. By fall there were already some thirty chapters. And they began to spread to other states. Robert Patterson, the leader of the council movement, promised that Mississippi would keep segregation one way or another. The councils would do it peaceably, but if they failed, "We'll have violence and you know it."[34]

The growing movement was certainly not above using coercive pressures on the moderates to silence them or to force them to join the movement for white supremacy. Newspapers that editorially and in their reportage, did not support the resistance movement were attacked.* In some cases that meant slashed tires or nighttime automobile chases. Council members would withdraw their advertising and threaten other merchants that they would lose business if they did not follow suit. In at least one case, the White Citizens' Council collected money to start a rival paper in order to undermine one whose policy they could not control. Roy Harris, head of the Citizens' Councils of America, proposed driving Ralph McGill, publisher of the Atlanta *Constitution*, "clean out of the state of Georgia." Similar pressures were put on churches, individual ministers, businessmen, teachers, and educational institutions and any others who might stand in the way of a solid South. Journalist James Cook told of a physician who was driven out of a town in Mississippi for having protected a black youth against the sheriff. He was denounced before a crowd of 700 people; they then voted 698 to 2 to ask him to leave "in the best interest of the county." Though he vowed to stay, ten months later he had to leave because of a boycott against him.[36]

National businesses that did not act "properly" and that had a Southern market came in for their share of attack, as well. The Falstaff brewing company, for example, became subject to a council-initiated boycott which the council alleged cost the company four million dollars. Whether that was so or not, the company flew a vice-president to Jackson, Mississippi to confer with the Citizens' Council. Judge Brady claimed that the company offered fifty thousand dollars to call off

---

*The Montgomery *Advertiser*, for instance, labeled the council plan for using economic pressure against blacks as "rank, indecent and vicious."[35]

the boycott. This offer was apparently rejected, but the company was advised to issue a statement disavowing support for the NAACP, which it did. According to the Falstaff executive vice-president and general manager, the council had been "very cooperative since we explained our position." Similar economic blackmail was practiced against the Philip Morris cigarette company, Philco, and its parent firm, the Ford Motor Company. By late 1955 there were few voices heard among Southern whites to indicate that the South was not solidly in favor of resistance.[37]

Suppressing Black Aspirations

The propaganda campaign helped to create the climate of defiance that its authors were searching for. That was necessary because success in forcing the Second Reconstruction to retreat would require ruthlessness toward blacks. During Reconstruction, the instrument for terrorizing the black community had been the Ku Klux Klan. In the 1950s it was the White Citizens' Councils. Their main device was economic coercion to eliminate black challenges to segregation and to help prevent the rise of a black electorate. Through this method they could exercise their considerable economic power against those who broke the racial etiquette and reverse the trend of increasing black voter participation with its concomitant danger to their own political power. They consistently refused openly to endorse violence.

By using their control over poverty and credit, especially in the black belt, they literally were able to control people's lives. Judge Brady had originally called for the use of this power: "declaring a cold war and an economic boycott. . . . The Negro of the South should be forewarned, and when the next [desegregation] suit is brought in any of the remaining states, the economic boycott should begin." At their outset the White Citizens' Councils proposed "the careful application of economic pressure upon men who cannot be controlled otherwise." Blacks who tried to register to vote, who signed a petition for school desegregation, who belonged to the NAACP, who spoke out for equality received the treatment. Bankers would deny loans; black merchants couldn't get credit from wholesale houses or sometimes could not get supplies even with cash; insurance policies were canceled; employees were dismissed; renters were evicted from their homes; mortgages were recalled. Blacks dependent on whites for employment or credit were often forced to boycott black ministers or doctors or craftsmen who were violating the racial etiquette. A black minister who was active in one of the original school desegregation cases in Prince Edward County, Virginia described what they did to him:

> Suddenly I was notified that I had fifteen days to pay my fuel bill. When I went to buy clothes for the children or food for the family I was told I had to have cash. All of a sudden . . . this place and that place and places I can't even remember were serving warrants on me.

The heat was in his home only when he could afford to pay for the oil that he once had been able to get easily on credit. He walked about cold rooms, rubbing his hands and worrying about the running noses of his children. . . .[38]

In the summer of 1955, the NAACP initiated a rash of school desegregation petitions in the South. Yazoo City, Mississippi provided an example of the council's functioning. At the time, 1,500 of the town's 11,000 population belonged to the White Citizens' Council. The council ran an ad in the town paper listing the names of all the petitioners. The list of names appeared in the stores, in the bank, even in cotton fields around the city. White community leaders would visit individuals and suggest that their action was not proper for a "colored" who "wanted to live in peace." If that didn't work, it would be followed by visits to employers, creditors, and landlords. It was not long before the original list of fifty-three signators to the petition had been reduced to six, as people rushed to take their names off or claimed they had not known what they were signing. Similar treatment was given to blacks who sought to register to vote.[39]

In addition to individual intimidation, the council members gerrymandered the boundaries of cities and counties to reduce the black vote. In Alabama they even proposed eliminating some of the counties by parceling them out among their neighbors, and in Louisiana they embarked upon a purge of the voter registration rolls during a three-year-long operation. Spelling errors provided one of the most common excuses for removal from the rolls. In Mississippi, a new voter registration law made it much easier to eliminate blacks.[40]

Repression was not limited to the open efforts of the White Citizens' Councils. Pronouncements of respected political leaders encouraged opposition to the law. The councils created an atmosphere that gave the green light to others to carry out violence. Martin Luther King, Jr. pointed out in the case of Montgomery: "When people, especially in public office, talk about bloodshed as a concomitant of integration, they stir and arouse the hoodlums to acts of destruction, and often work under cover to bring them about."[41] The worst violence in that period occurred in Mississippi, but its effect—to terrorize—was felt beyond the state's borders. There were several murders in that state in 1955. These killings helped to build the white movement and to intimidate blacks.

In early spring 1955, Gus Courts, the head of the NAACP in Belzoni, Mississippi, was critically wounded by a shotgun blast. This shooting occurred after he had repeatedly refused to surrender his right to vote, despite serious efforts to ruin him economically. The sheriff listed the assailant as a "light-skinned Negro," even though courts and an eyewitness contended he was white.[42]

In May, a black minister in Belzoni who had refused to abandon advocating black voting was murdered while driving his car. The sheriff claimed at first that the pieces of lead found in his mouth and face were dental fillings. When he acknowledged that a murder had indeed occurred, he contended that another black was responsible. The supposed cause: an argument over a woman.[43]

In August a man was shot to death in Judge Brady's hometown. This incident occurred in the middle of the day, in front of the courthouse and several witnesses.

Lamar Smith, the victim, had been actively working to defeat a county supervisor, had himself voted in the primary, and was instructing blacks how to vote by absentee ballot to enable them to avoid violence at the polls. Despite the blatant openness of the murder, no one was ever brought to trial. Judge Brady contended that the reason was that no white man was willing to testify against another in the murder of a black man.[44]

Two weeks later, the most spectacular and infamous of these killings was perpetrated. This murder had no apparent connection with politics; it was an out-and-out lynching whose only purpose could be to terrorize. Emmett Till, a fourteen-year-old boy from Chicago, was accused of having "wolf-whistled" at a white woman. He was kidnapped from his grandfather's home "in the middle of the night, pistol-whipped, stripped naked, shot through the head with a .45 caliber Colt automatic, barb-wired to a 74 pound cotton gin fan, and dumped into twenty feet of water in the Tallahatchie River." The Till case became a cause célèbre, and the NAACP charged that Mississippi "has decided to maintain white supremacy by murdering children."[45]

Anne Moody, an activist in the Student Nonviolent Coordinating Committee, a militant civil rights organization of the 1960s, told of a murder by arson of a whole family. It was apparently a mistake, meant for a neighbor who had surreptitiously engaged in an interracial affair. Moody described its impact on the community: "I shall never forget the expressions on the faces of the Negroes. There was almost unanimous hopelessness in them." The FBI investigated, but "as usual in this sort of case, the investigation was dropped as soon as public interest died down."[46]

These killings, by no means the only ones, were acts of terror designed to force blacks back into their place. They were part of a larger process of violence and intimidation in that period. A study done for the Southern Regional Council, a liberal organization, found 530 such cases between 1955 and 1958. "The threats and illegal activities aimed at individual Negroes and whites who questioned the South's tradition of segregation undoubtedly deterred other Negroes from asserting their rights, including the right to vote," concluded the study's author. The study found a decline in black registered voters between 1956 and 1958 of 45,845, not counting Mississippi and Alabama. Before *Brown* there had been 265 registered black voters in three black-belt counties in Mississippi. By later summer in 1955 there were only 90. In the whole state, the number of black voters declined from 22,000 to only 8,000 between 1952 and 1956. Virtually all of the latter votes were cast in the cities.[47]

Black-Belt Rule

The impetus, the organization, the leadership, and the control of this movement rested in the hands of the traditional black-belt ruling class that had emerged after Reconstruction. That class was still centered in the black belt, though in most cases now in the small towns. Its members were businessmen and bankers in these areas, as well as merchants and landlords. They still dominated the South in every state but North Carolina, where power had already passed to the modern commercial and industrial leaders. The Supreme Court's one-man, one-vote ruling that forced states to redistrict was not issued until 1962 and not effectuated in most cases until 1964 or later. It was the old Southern ruling class that set state policy. It was, moreover, the Deep South states of Georgia, Mississippi, Alabama, Louisiana, and South Carolina that, in addition to Virginia, made up the core of the resistance. In these states the old Southern ruling class remained the strongest. In almost every single case where the White Citizens' Councils emerged, they were led and organized from the black belt. That was true in Mississippi, Alabama, Louisiana and South Carolina, Florida, and Virginia.[48]

The White Citizens' Council in Alabama was led by a wealthy planter with an aristocratic heritage that dated to before the Civil War. Journalist Hodding Carter III contended that in Mississippi, where the councils originated, their leadership was "drawn primarily from the ranks of the white community's business, political and social leadership." According to Carter, the top officials in that state were the president of a bank in Greenwood—in the heart of the black belt—a businessman from Jackson, the owner of a printing company from Greenwood, and a planter. These are the same people who made up the "courthouse cliques" that ran the South, the "banker-merchant-farmer-lawyer-doctor-governing class." In the local councils, the composition of the leadership was similar. That is especially important in view of the fact that the council movement as a whole was led, organized, and to a significant degree controlled by the Mississippi White Citizens' Council.[49]

The organization received its political impetus from the efforts of Mississippi Circuit Court Judge Thomas Brady, who was listed in *Who's Who*. His *Black Monday* speech became widely distributed in printed form and was the "inspiration and first handbook of the council movement." Neil McMillen contended that the council's members included governors, congressmen, judges, physicians, lawyers, industrialists, and bankers. It was black-belt leaders in South Carolina, Georgia, and Florida who organized the councils. In Virginia there was no significant White Citizens' Council, but its counterpart, the Defenders, was organized by "eighty-five prominent representatives from eighteen black belt counties." Virginia was historically a political leader of the South and played an important leadership role in the movement of the fifties. It is therefore important to note that in that state, geographically distant from the Deep South, the black belt (which represented "less than 15 percent of the inhabitants") dominated the state, especially with respect to race questions. In Arkansas the black belt surrounded Little Rock, which was the trading center of the area and economically dependent upon it. This area controlled the state legislature and the state Democratic party.[50]

The whole dynamic of massive resistance and the mobilization by the traditional ruling class to confront the government can be explained only in terms of the class dynamic analyzed in this chapter and chapters one and two. In its bitter opposition to desegregation, the traditional ruling elite was fighting not only to retain the racial settlement of the past but also for the maintenance of the traditional social order, which was the condition for its rule. It was the importance of the stakes involved that accounts for the calls to violence on the part of respected leaders, as well as for the failure to prosecute or otherwise discourage them. Their attitude and actions, or inaction, encouraged and supported the use of violence.

The Cities—The Southern Establishment's Achilles' Heel

White reaction was not as successful as it had been in the 1870s. Times had changed, and with them customs. The cities were at once the site the greatest strength of the blacks and the greatest weakness of the white leadership. In the cities, blacks were bolder and had the power of numbers, and the pressures of bourgeois mores were felt strongly. Especially in the cities, there were often efforts to minimize and prevent violence. Such measures could only inhibit the effectiveness of efforts to suppress the growing black movement. And, in fact, it was from the cities—particularly Norfolk and Arlington in Virginia, for example—that opposition to the white-supremacy hardliners came. In the manufacturing center of Greensboro, North Carolina, the school board voted 6–1 to begin desegregation, and this action was endorsed by the town's Jaycee chapter and by the Greensboro *Daily News*: "Segregation has been ruled out and the responsibility now is to readjust to that reality with a minimum of friction, disruption, and setback to the public school system."[51]

These new conditions made it difficult for the Southern leaders to press forward without inhibitions toward their program. The Redeemers had often openly led the terror and had created its organization, the Ku Klux Klan, and had campaigned to legitimize it. But the White Citizens' Councils felt it necessary to put a great deal of distance between themselves and the Klan. John Martin described them as having "a terrible yearning for respectability." Council leaders believed that "unless we keep and pitch our battle on a high plane, and unless we keep our ranks free from the demagogue, the renegade, the lawless and the violent, we will be branded, as we should be branded, a fearful, underground, lawless organization." In Alabama they fought to purge the council of adherents who favored a Klan-type program. Partly as a result, the efforts to suppress blacks who attempted to undermine the race system were not wholly successful.[52]

The Southern ruling class could no longer impose a wholly monolithic order. In some cases, blacks not only stood up to the whites but were successful in their resistance. In Orangeburg, South Carolina when blacks petitioned the school board for desegregation in the summer of 1955, the economic screws were turned on the signers. But blacks, who made up 63 percent of the population of the county, responded with their own counterboycott of the white merchants who were leading the movement. This economic warfare proceeded for the better part of the year, by which time the white business community was ready to call for a truce. Blacks lost on the desegregation issue, but they had shown the whites that the economic weapon was a two-edged sword. This and other less dramatic stands, which illustrated a new power in the black community, caused the councils to back off their stand on economic boycotts. Judge Brady said of them in 1957: "It's a terrible thing; a horrible thing to use and it can cut and hurt deep."[53]

Much more significant was the Montgomery bus boycott, which lasted for a year. In this action, which began in December 1955, blacks stood up to and ultimately defeated the entire white power structure. Using both their economic strength and their unity and élan, they stood against all efforts to crush the boycott; and ultimately they achieved their goal of desegregated seating on the municipal bus lines, even if it was with the help of the Supreme Court, which ultimately ruled in their favor. They had won a victory in one of the South's metropolises—one of its important political, cultural, and economic centers. The implications of that victory were profound, as many other Southern cities rapidly dropped their segregation barriers on buses for fear of facing a similar movement. In Montgomery itself, Martin Luther King, Jr. noted that the black victory had caused demoralization among the White Citizens' Councils: "That such organizations could not prevent this from happening was evidence to many of the dues-paying members that they could best use their own dollars otherwise."[54]

For the most part, however, the importance of Montgomery was in how it affected blacks rather than whites. The momentum was still with the latter. Massive resistance had not yet peaked. But these early cases of successful efforts of blacks to stand up to white pressure and white terror indicated the political weakness of the position of the Southern ruling class. When the blacks were able to win, it was in the cities. And now the cities had become the dominant feature of the Southern economy; their political significance was vastly greater than ever before. Ultimately, it would be in the cities that massive resistance would be put to the test—and in one city in particular, Little Rock, that it would reach its denouement.

The Federal Government Responds

The efforts of the Southern leadership were not directed solely to attaining a monolithic order in the region. Their intent was to back down the federal government in order to counter the pressures that were pushing it to refashion the South in the image of the rest of the country. Some of this effort had begun substantially before *Brown*, in the Dixiecrat campaign of 1948. That was a conscious attempt to repeat the successful Southern electoral strategy of 1870, when Southern intransigence had made winning a majority of the electoral college almost impossible. Then the election was to be thrown into the House of Representatives, where each state had only one vote, and the South used its bargaining power to end Reconstruction. Southern representatives cast their votes for the Republican, Hayes, in return for a promise to withdraw the federal troops from the South. The memory of that strategy remained, and in 1948 it was resurrected. The defeat in 1948 closed that door, though not permanently. In 1956, South Carolina and Mississippi attempted to go that route,* and in 1968 George Wallace made the last serious effort. Wallace spoke openly of plans to deadlock the election in the electoral college.[56]

Their efforts in the fifties had more success, and in both the executive and judicial branches of government, they were clearly having an impact. Despite the favorable court rulings, the Supreme Court seemed to vacillate on just how far it was prepared to go, and the president seemed ready to accommodate the South.

When the Supreme Court had issued the *Brown* decision, it had made no ruling concerning its implementation. Instead, it had set another hearing for a second decision on that matter. A year's time lay between the two decisions. That delay, during which virtually no desegregation took place, allowed the Southern leadership a lengthy period to mobilize and organize its supporters.

In the hearing that preceded the second ruling, the NAACP requested that the Court order desegregation to begin immediately. The South countered with the proposal that the cases be sent back "without instructions" to the lower courts for adjudication based on local conditions. Speaking for the defendants, the attorney stated to the justices: "I would have to tell you right now we would not conform." The government entered a friend-of-the-court brief that supported gradual rather than immediate desegregation and that followed the Southern position in urging that the cases be returned to the lower courts. On May 31, 1955, the Court sided with the South and with the government and sent the cases back to the district courts, stipulating that desegregation should commence with "a prompt and reasonable start" but should be allowed to proceed "with all deliberate speed."[57]

Southerners took heart at this move. Said the Richmond *News Leader*, expressing a renewed sense of power: "When the court proposes that its social revolution be imposed upon the South 'as soon as practicable' there are those of us who respond that 'as soon as practicable' means never at all." One of the leaders of the White Citizens' Council said that looking back, "there was a turning point in public opinion in the South, a turning from a feeling that 'integration is inevitable' to a determination that 'we ain't going to do it.' "[58]

President Eisenhower did nothing in this period to abolish the impression many had that he was supporting the South. He never made a public statement of support for the *Brown* decision. (Earl Warren later wrote: "I still believe that much of our racial strife could have been avoided if President Eisenhower had

---

*The leader of the Mississippi States' Rights party that year boldly proclaimed that "the master minds of socialism who control both major parties do not care which one wins. But the very thought of throwing the election into the House strikes terror in their hearts."[55]

at least observed that our country is dedicated to the principle that 'We hold these truths to be self-evident, that all Men are created equal. . . .' "[59]) He avoided commenting favorably about proposed legislation that would prohibit segregation in interstate transportation: "I am not sure. I would have to consult the Attorney-General. . . ." He stressed his hope that the matter would be solved within the states, without federal government interference; and he expressed doubts about the usefulness of laws to "change men's hearts." The president stressed the need to rely on education to achieve change rather than on the force of law, but he refused to use the prestige of his office for that purpose. Instead, he issued what could easily be understood as an apology for Southern intransigence by reminding the country that "the people who have this deep emotional reaction . . . were not acting over these past three generations in defiance of the law. They were acting in compliance with the law as interpreted by the Supreme Court of the United States under the decision of 1896."[60]

As the resistance movement grew, Eisenhower tried to ignore it. Indicating that he chose to stay out of the controversy, the president proclaimed that he "would not make any assumption that the judicial branch of the Government is incapable of implementing the Supreme Court's decision"—meaning specifically that he did not wish to send in government troops. And if the FBI was sent in to investigate some of the more spectacular occurrences, as Anne Moody had said, "the investigation was dropped as soon as public interest had died down." This state of affairs led one analyst to declare that "there can be little doubt that some of the South's political leaders took the President's continued neutrality to mean he was secretly on their side."[61] (Earl Warren later confided that before the *Brown* decision he had been invited to a White House dinner at which the president went out of his way to praise the South's counsel to the chief justice. "The President . . . took me by the arm and as we walked along, speaking of the Southern states in the segregation cases, he said, 'These are not bad people. All they are concerned about is to see that their sweet little girls are not required to sit in school alongside some big overgrown Negroes. . . .' Shortly thereafter, the *Brown* case was decided, and with it went our cordial relations."[62])

Virginia and the Southern United Front

Far from the Deep South, the members of the Virginia Establishment had a more formidable opposition and a less violent tradition. To win support for defying the Supreme Court, they had to frame their position defensively. They were not aiming to resist or to break the law but merely to guarantee "freedom of choice." A program was presented to voters as one that would allow local option: those school districts that wished to adopt it could do so; any that preferred to desegregate would have that right. The plan called for individual choice: "that no child be required to attend an integrated school," and for state-provided tuition grants to private schools in order to implement this provision. In arguing for the referendum, the resistance forces stressed freedom of choice and asked urban residents to respect the feelings of the population of the black belt. The governor campaigned for the referendum, suggesting that its defeat would be a prointegration vote, and Virginia's U.S. Senator Robertson argued for the bill as a moderate step short of all-out resistance.[63]

But once the measure had passed by a two-to-one vote in early 1956, the political climate began to change. When the Arlington school district came forward with a program for desegregation under the local-option feature of the program, State Senator Grey, whose commission had recommended the local-option provision, expressed his opposition to its use. A special constitutional convention held in early March rejected the local-option feature. It was not long before Arlington lost its right to have an elected school board. Now the results of the referendum were interpreted as a vote for total resistance to integration.[64]

The proresistance forces began to work out a program that they felt was politically defensible. While calling for resistance and rejecting the authority of the Supreme Court, the Richmond *News Leader* also rejected outright physical resistance as unworkable: "We tried that once before." Instead they proposed "to enter upon a long course of lawful resistance. . . . Litigate? Let us pledge ourselves to litigate this thing for fifty years. If one remedial law is ruled invalid then let us try another; and if the second is ruled invalid, then let us enact a third."[65]

The political leadership was searching for some such program—a justification for defying the Court that could be couched in legal terms. Such a program would be used as a means to rally the entire region in a joint response. The *News Leader* developed part of that program with what it called interposition. The doctrine of interposition reached back into pre-Civil War history. Essentially, it involved the state legislatures' placing themselves between the federal courts and the school districts and exercising their "states' rights" to declare the ruling illegal. Beginning in the fall of 1955, the newspaper ran an intensive propaganda campaign that was widely read throughout the South. By February 1956, five states had passed, or were considering, resolutions of interposition. Whether these had any legal standing was doubtful, but they clearly reflected the fact that the states were girding themselves for a confrontation and that Southern unity, both within and between the states, was fast developing.[66]

That same month, the South took a big step forward in its efforts at defiance by moving beyond talk and resolutions. Mobs turned away Autherine Lucy, a black woman, from attending the University of Alabama, and they had the tacit support of school officials and public authorities for their actions. Under the leadership of the White Citizens' Council, a mammoth rally of ten to fifteen thousand was held in Montgomery to build up support for the movement to keep out Lucy. People from all over the state attended. When Lucy later suggested that university officials were in complicity with these efforts, she was expelled. Now there was a concrete case of successful defiance of the Court order, and it encountered no adverse response. Rather, according to advisor Sherman Adams,

President Eisenhower "made it clear that he had no intention of interfering in the affairs of a sovereign state unless it was absolutely necessary for him to do so." Apparently Lucy's case did not make such interference necessary. That certainly seemed to be an indication that the government would not interfere with the segregationists' actions, even if those actions involved defying the courts.[67]

Momentum was now with those who were for resistance. The White Citizens' Council itself had by now become the dominant resistance organization. John Martin reported that the organization had 75,000 members in Mississippi, 60,000 in Georgia, 40,000 in South Carolina, and 20,000 in Louisiana. They met in downtown hotels, politicians paid attention to them, and they even had succeeded in silencing leading liberals. By early 1956, Samuel Lubbell reported that "throughout the South my interviews showed a rising belief that the Court could be defied completely, and the decision nullified." Governor Orval Faubus of Arkansas, considered a moderate on racial matters, stated publicly: "I cannot be a party to any attempt to force acceptance of a change to which the people are so overwhelmingly opposed." Less than two weeks after the Lucy incident, Senator Byrd of Virginia expressed his hope that "if we can organize the Southern states for massive resistance to this order I think that in time the rest of the country will realize integration is not going to be accepted in the South."[68]

On March 12, under the leadership of Senator Byrd, Southern unity was achieved. On that date almost the whole of the Southern congressional delegation—nineteen senators and eighty-two representatives—placed their prestige behind the movement with the issuance of what became known as the "Southern Manifesto." The doctrine called the *Brown* ruling "unwarranted" and a "substitution of naked power for established law." It was, they said, "a clear abuse of judicial power" and a case of the justices' injecting "their personal, political and social ideas for the law of the land." Its impact was to open the floodgates to "outside agitators" and "revolutionary changes." The signers commended "the motives of those states which have declared the intention to resist forced integration by any lawful means." And they pledged themselves "to use all lawful means to bring about a reversal of this decision which is contrary to the Constitution and to prevent the use of force in its implementation."[69]

Legal scholar Alexander Bickel called the document "a calculated declaration of political war against the Court's decision." *New York Times* journalist Anthony Lewis contended that its impact was "to make defiance of the Supreme Court and the Constitution socially acceptable in the South—to give resistance to the law the approval of the Southern establishment." The Southern Manifesto did have these effects, but it meant more. War had already been declared on the Supreme Court many times over this issue. The manifesto was the statement that the South was now unified, that with little resistance at home the Southern ruling class was joining in a united front to challenge the Second Reconstruction. It marked the end of the first phase of the resistance movement; the struggle for political leadership in the South was over for the moment, and the time for action had begun.[70]

Active Defiance

The South's leaders could not help but be encouraged by the reaction that their challenge to federal authority encountered on the part of the national political leadership. In the election year of 1956, the president noted the promise of the Southern Manifesto to stay within the bounds of the law and indicated its acceptability to him. His Democratic challenger, Adlai Stevenson, simply ignored the manifesto. This response was a victory for the white South. Just as the election of 1948 had indicated the growing power of blacks, this election showed the Southern white leadership to be on the offensive. In the next period, Southern reaction grew increasingly bold as it probed the limits of action it was permitted and found plenty of room for expanding those limits.

Having consolidated its power internally and having created the core of a united front, the black-belt upper class became more aggressive. "We must take the offense," said Senator Eastland. "We must carry the message to every section of the United States." Mississippi established a propaganda agency that distributed pamphlets to national media and sponsored a tour of the state for New England newspaper executives. Its purpose: to give Mississippi a chance to present its side of the story. The Montgomery *Advertiser* ran a five-month series on racial discrimination in the North and double-standard reporting in Northern newspapers. The paper argued that the rest of the country lived in a racial glass house and had no business throwing bricks at the South.[71]

In the spring of 1956, the Southern states began a series of legal assaults on the NAACP. This act was significant, for heretofore such actions had been carried out only by private citizens. Now the state governments themselves could intervene. Under the leadership of Virginia, several states passed laws requiring association membership lists to be given to the states. Legal charges were brought against the association, fines were imposed, and in some states the organization was temporarily driven underground. Known members of the NAACP were fired from their government jobs. And state investigating committees pursued the organization and its members with the same tactics and zeal with which the McCarthyites had hunted for Communists.[72]

Once again, with Virginia in the lead, the states began to harden their legal stance, in effect preparing the way for defiance. In the summer of 1956, two federal judges ordered desegregation in Charlottesville and Arlington, Virginia. In response, the governor—following the lead of the Virginia equivalent of the White Citizens' Councils, the Defenders of State Sovereignty and Individual Liberties—proposed new legislation that would permit him to withhold state funds from school districts "whenever it is determined the public interest, or safety, or welfare so requires." Speaking in favor of the proposal, a former governor told his supporters: "If [the other Virginia areas] won't stand with us then I say make 'em. We cannot compromise. . . . If you ever let them integrate anywhere the whole state will be integrated in a short time." Clearly, the Southern power structure was moving to tighten its control. Deep South states quickly followed Virginia's lead. Perhaps even more significant, the border began to fall into line. In 1956 and 1957, North Carolina, Texas, Florida, Arkansas, and Tennessee passed various forms of legislation designed to prevent or hamper desegregation and to harass the NAACP.[73]

In the fall of 1956, defiance reached new heights. In Texas, a junior college in Texarkana was ordered to admit two black students. Urged by the president of the college to defy the ruling, mobs refused to let the blacks in, and the Texas Rangers sent there to keep order refused to interfere with the mobs. The Court's ruling was defied, with official backing.[74]

At the same time, Mansfield, Texas was under Court order to admit blacks to the public high school—one of the first such cases in the South. Governor Shivers announced that he had urged the school board to "transfer any scholastics . . . whose attendance . . . would be reasonably calculated to incite violence." Once again the mobs appeared, and, again with the support of the Texas Rangers, the blacks were turned away. The governor defiantly taunted the Supreme Court: "I respectfully suggest . . . that the Supreme Court, which is responsible for the order, be given the task of enforcing it." Integrationists who were looking for a decisive rebuke to this stance from the federal government were to be disappointed. When asked about the matter, the president stated at a press conference that the case did not require intervention: "Before anyone could move the Texas authorities had moved in and order was restored, so the question became unimportant." He further elaborated that "until states show their inability or their refusal to grapple with this question properly, which they haven't yet . . . we'd better be careful about moving in and exercising police power."[75]

If the white South was searching for a signal, it certainly seemed to have it. Events were edging closer to outright confrontation with the federal government. And the resistance leaders in the South were growing more confident about its eventual outcome. Eugene Talmadge, recently elected senator and former governor of Georgia, expressed this mood in an interview: "They couldn't send enough bayonets down to compel the people to send their children to school with Nigras. You'd have another Hungarian situation."[76]

The newly formed civil rights organization, the Southern Leadership Conference on Transportation and Nonviolent Integration, sought to intervene by calling upon the president to exercise his moral authority on the matter. The organization wired President Eisenhower, asking him to come South and "make a major speech in a major Southern city urging all Southerners to accept and abide by the Supreme Court's decision as the law of the land." The request was denied, and when the president was asked about it at a press conference, he dismissed the idea: "I have expressed myself so often wherever I have been about this thing that I don't know what good another speech will do right now."[77]

That was the situation at the beginning of the school year in 1957. President Eisenhower seemed to be providing plenty of reassurance to the segregationists. On July 17 he appeared to give them the green light when he assured them that in his view the use of federal troops was not a live possibility: "I can't imagine any set of circumstances that would ever induce me to send federal troops into a federal court and into any area to enforce the orders of a federal court.''[78]

Little Rock

Five major Southern cities faced desegregation in 1957, all of them in the Upper South: the courts were probing at the weaker sections of the region. Three of the cities—Charlotte, Winston-Salem, and Greensboro—were in North Carolina, the only Southern state not under the control of the traditional Southern leadership. North Carolina's leadership was businessmen, and desegregation occurred there with relative calm, with the support of the state government. Much of the same was true of the fourth city, Nashville.[79]

In Little Rock, located in the heart of the plantation country in Arkansas, it was otherwise. Here, for the first time in a major city, the movement of defiance made its stand. One participant stated melodramatically: ''Little Rock is the last battle. If we win in Little Rock, integration is dead. If we lose in Little Rock, the Republic of the United States is gone forever.''[80] There was some truth to this claim. The resistance movement was bound to do what it had been preparing for: confront the government with the open refusal to heed the court order. Ultimately, either the government would have to respond with force—and the previous feelers put out by Southern resistance gave little indication of such a response*—or it would have to back down and ignominiously call a halt to the Second Reconstruction, as it had to the first.

From the point of view of the segregationists, Little Rock was not necessarily an ideal place for a confrontation. The city had already made some concessions to blacks, including seating arrangements on buses in the wake of the Montgomery boycott movement. But some small towns in the state had begun to accede to the *Brown* decision. And in the gubernatorial primary in late 1956, Faubus, facing a representative of the White Citizens' Council as his main opponent, had edged closer to resistance by promising: ''There will be NO forced integration of public schools as long as I am governor'' (emphasis in original). Little Rock, in the center of the black belt, the state capital, and by far the state's largest city, was a logical place to make a stand.[82]

With school desegregation slated for the fall, segregationists had begun organizing seriously for defiance in the spring of 1957. They tried to force Faubus to join them by publicly calling upon him to aid them. They organized an intensive propaganda campaign with leaflets and public advertisements: ''If you integrate Little Rock Central High School in September . . . would the negro boys be permitted to solicit the white girls for dances?'' They held rallies and letter-

---

*Governor Faubus certainly claimed that that was his sense when he telegraphed President Eisenhower after barring the blacks from desegregating the Little Rock high school: ''The Supreme Court recognized that conditions in each community must be considered and I have interpreted your public statements to indicate that you are in agreement with this premise.''[81]

writing campaigns, and they disrupted public meetings. They engaged in independent political action, winning 35 percent of the city vote in March and almost 50 percent in November.[83]

On August 22, two weeks before school was to open, the Capital Citizens' Council held a fund-raising dinner featuring Georgia Governor Marvin Griffin and White Citizens' Council leader Roy Harris. The governor termed those assembled "patriots," and he called for a national propaganda campaign to support their stand. He told the meeting that there would be no integration in his state, that if necessary he would "enlist every white man in Georgia" to stop it.[84]

Somehow, word from that meeting made its way to the home of Daisy Bates. Bates was copublisher, with her husband, of the city's black newspaper, a leader of the NAACP, and chief force behind the efforts to integrate the Little Rock schools. That night a rock came smashing through her living room window. It bore a note: "STONE THIS TIME. DYNAMITE NEXT." Governor Faubus felt the effects of that night, as well: "People are coming to me and saying 'if Georgia doesn't have integration, why does Arkansas have it?' " Bates wrote.

> Meanwhile, the hate campaigns sponsored by the Capital Citizens' Council, the White Citizens' Council and the Ku Klux Klan were gathering momentum. Speakers from Mississippi and Louisiana appeared before the Capital Citizens' Council and advocated "bloodshed if necessary" to keep the Negro children out of the so-called "white schools." Everywhere in Little Rock there were rumors that segregationist forces from hard-core states, the so-called "solid South" were organizing for a fight to the finish against integration in public education. Little Rock was to be the battleground.[85]

As the confrontation drew near, it was clear that the Southern leadership's offense was having success. In August and September of 1957, Gallup polls showed a decline in support for the *Brown* decision for the first time. The same polls showed a decline in support for the Supreme Court and in the percentage of Southern whites who thought desegregation was inevitable. Though the numbers were different, the former two trends were not limited to the South but were national in scope.[86]

Faubus called out the National Guard. The black students had to make their way through a gauntlet of white hatred to get to the school, only to find their way barred by the Guardsmen, who turned them away, repeating the action of the Texas Rangers. In the face of this action, President Eisenhower still extemporized. At his press conference the day the Guard was posted, he again stated his position that "you cannot change people's hearts merely by laws." He went still further, exonerating the whites by pointing out that their resistance was a result of their seeing "a picture of mongrelization of the race. . . ." After considering federalizing the Guard, the president rejected that option. It was three weeks before he took decisive action and sought and won an injunction against use of the Guard. Faubus complied and predicted that violence would ensue.[87]

On September 23, the black children entered the school, only to be driven out by mobs. Two black reporters were beaten and might have been killed had their attackers not been distracted by the cry "The niggers are in the school!" That night the Bates family sat at home in darkness, with friends and guns by their side. Bates now acted to force the president's hand. At every point where the segregationists had pushed, he had backed away. She now pushed back. The students, she said, "will not be out there again until they have the assurance of the President of the United States that they will be protected from the mob."[88]

The situation was now significantly different from what had occurred in Alabama and Texas. There the president had had merely to respond to a fait accompli. Here the students remained ready to go to school; the courts were behind them; mobs were keeping them out and the president was being challenged to assure their safety where no one else would. All of these events were taking place in a major metropolitan area, in front of the full public glare of the national and world press. There was no doubt that the outcome of this situation would shape race relations and even the federal system for years to come.

With the ball now firmly in his court, the president responded to the challenge by federalizing the National Guard and sending United States troops to the South for the first time since Reconstruction. Desegregation now proceeded, although opposition to it remained so strong that the troops were kept in the school for the remainder of the school year. The president's stance had a profound impact. Journalist Cabell Phillips wrote in the *New York Times Magazine*:

> There should be no doubt in anyone's mind that, wherever segregation is sanctioned, the mighty majesty of the United States Government is now committed to its eradication—not today or this year necessarily, but ultimately, and with bayonets if need be. Little Rock is more than an incident; it is a precedent. There is no likely turning back from this course, and intelligent leaders of the South admit it, however privately and ruefully.[89]

The Southern leadership had persistently tested the federal government and had consistently found it to be lacking in will. Each test had emboldened the upholders of white supremacy and gained them greater legitimacy in the South and in the nation. Ultimately they had come to the point where open defiance was both possible and necessary: possible because of the support they had and the apparent weakness of the federal government; necessary because without it desegregation would have proceeded. Legal defiance had worked its way out to illegal defiance.

In an open confrontation, powerful forces were pushing the president toward the action he took: the pressures of the cold war and the increased political importance of blacks had their impact. Perhaps most important was the need to bring the South into alignment with the rest of the nation. An area whose economy was becoming increasingly integrated into the nation's could not be left alone with its bizarre—for the modern world—social relations. So that version of massive resistance proved to be a blind alley.

The Solid South Cracks

This important tactical defeat did not spell the end of the resistance to desegregation. In fact, the resistance grew even more determined in outrage at the use of federal troops. Shortly after the federal intervention in Little Rock, the city council passed an ordinance requiring organizations to file membership lists and other information with the city upon request. The NAACP was the target, and when its officers refused to comply, they were arrested. Active antagonism to the troops continued during the whole of the school year. Governor Faubus easily swept into the nomination for a third term as governor of Arkansas in July 1958, following a campaign in which he reaffirmed his commitment to segregated schools. The Arkansas *Gazette* wrote in an editorial: "The moderate position . . . is now clearly untenable for any man in public life anywhere in the region."[90]

There was no evidence of a change in attitude as a result of the defeat, or of any significant section's breaking from the prevailing attitude. There was still no open challenge to the segregationist hardliners. Rather, gubernatorial elections in the fall of 1958 in Alabama, Tennessee, South Carolina, Georgia, and Texas tended to confirm an intensified mood of resistance. So did new legislation that called for the closing of schools when they faced integration or when federal troops were present. By the end of 1958, all Southern states had such laws except Tennessee.[91]

Those laws provided the second line of defense against segregation. If the South's leaders failed to prevent blacks from attending white schools, their next recourse was to close the schools themselves. On September 18, 1958, Governor Faubus closed Little Rock Central High, the focus of national attention the year before. That same day, Governor Almond of Virginia ordered the closing of rural (but not black-belt) Warren County High School to prevent its school board from complying with court-ordered desegregation. One week later the Virginia governor extended the closure to the city of Charlottesville; Norfolk followed shortly. Once again the arena was the Upper South.[92]

With these acts, the black-belt elite had played out its hand. Now, in order to maintain the old social order, it had to damage the future of white children, to upset social stability to a degree far surpassing what desegregation, especially the token desegregation that was proposed, ever threatened to do, and had to do it in the cities, far away from its own strongholds. The act of closing the schools seriously deepened the split between the countryside and the cities, between the black-belt upper class and the new business and middle classes.

When Samuel Lubbell interviewed in the South in early 1960, he found evidence of a change in mood. In the cities where the schools had been closed, opposition to token integration was the weakest. "In Norfolk an average of only one person in twelve preferred the schools shut rather than mixed." Lubbell sought out people whom he had interviewed earlier, and he found drastic changes in sentiment. In 1958 a factory worker in Little Rock had stated, "I'd rather see Central High School burned to ashes than have it infested with niggers." In 1960 he said, "It makes no difference whether the schools are mixed or integrated, as long as they're quiet." But in the rural areas, Lubbell found little change. The school closing forced the hand of those who had been willing to sit quietly back. It also provided a formula for opposing massive resistance that did not require being in favor of integration, but rather supported the public school system itself: "The alternative to public schools is unthinkable!" said a group of Virginia clergy.[93]

In Virginia, "Committees for Public Schools" began forming in the affected areas, and they grew quickly. On the day of the school closing in Norfolk, the clergy met and signed an open appeal calling for reopening the schools. The American Association of University Women and the League of Women Voters urged the same. Parent-Teachers' Associations began to get into the act, and in late October the Virginia PTA held its annual convention. Though badly split, it rejected support for massive resistance and called for local option. One week later the Virginia Education Association came out strongly for opening the schools. In early December, a statewide Committee for Public Schools was formed. In Arkansas a similar pattern developed. Women's organizations, PTAs, and the Arkansas Education Association came out firmly for the support of public education.[94]

What so far was missing was the alternative power to the traditional Southern elite, the businessmen, who had heretofore refused to challenge the former. The earlier efforts of moderates helped prepare the way for their entrance onto the scene. As the businessmen came to an understanding of what closing the schools meant to their economic well-being, they were moved to act. And they were able to swing the balance. In fact, the whole school controversy was proving to be an economic catastrophe. Little Rock had been the recipient of a great deal of investment in the postwar period. In the first eight months of 1957 alone, eight new plants, with a total value of over three million dollars, had opened. But the manager of the Arkansas Chamber of Commerce pointed out that since September of that year, not a single new industry had come to the city.[95]

A University of Virginia economist found the same results: no new industries in the state in 1958 and closure of some large plants. With the schools closed, there was the danger of qualified teachers' leaving the state and providing a long-term setback to the educational system. Furthermore, there was the increasing difficulty Virginia industries were having of

> bringing into their plants the highly trained personnel needed to guide production and distribution programs. Some skilled workers in these plants and industries have already left because they regarded the education of their children to be of paramount importance. They have returned to places where the situation is more dependable and stable than in Virginia. As more schools become subject to Federal Court orders to desegregate, more and more communities in Virginia will be

affected by this kind of situation. . . . Any environment which is unstable and in which public education is threatened is not conducive to business development or expansion.[96]

It was not long after the school closings were implemented that these powerful elements began to shift their weight against massive resistance, even as the moderates, who had already begun to organize, stepped up their pace. In Norfolk, Virginia, whites entered a suit against the school-closing laws.[97] In late October and November, the Virginia press began to turn from massive resistance. Even the Richmond *News Leader*, which had led the campaign for interposition, called for a return to the policy of local option. The editor explicitly recognized that that would mean that "some public schools in Virginia may be coerced into some degree of integration." In late December, in a private meeting with the governor, Virginia's "leading industrial and financial titans" warned of the dangerous effects of continuing the policy of massive resistance.[98]

Events moved quickly. In mid-January 1959, the Virginia Supreme Court struck down the state's massive-resistance laws. Not long after, the businessmen in Charlottesville and Norfolk publicly issued a "veritable power structure manifesto." It said in part: "the prolonged continuance of closed schools is intolerable and . . . it is in the interest of all our citizens to support a policy designed to reopen schools." Only days later, in the face of new federal court orders for integration, the Virginia governor, in a specially summoned session of the state legislature, called for retreat from massive resistance. Telephone polls in five major cities in the state found two-thirds supporting the governor's new approach and only 17 percent opposing.[99]

In Little Rock, though events moved somewhat more slowly than in Virginia, the course was substantially the same. In late fall, the Little Rock school board, which had attempted to comply with federal court orders, resigned, thus provoking a referendum over the issue. Hard-core segregationists opposed a businessman-sponsored slate of moderates. The election in December resulted in a 3–3 split, which resolved nothing. In January the Little Rock Chamber of Commerce called for reopening the schools, and in March the chamber openly stated: "The decision of the Supreme Court of the United States, however much we dislike it, is the declared law and is binding upon us." By spring each side forced a recall election on the others, with the business leadership actively involved on the moderate side. "They acted not . . . as defenders of human equality or social justice," stressed Numan Bartley, "but merely as proponents of order, stability and new factories in Little Rock." Though Governor Faubus urged the "good, hard-working, honest people" to watch out for the "charge of the Cadillac Brigade," the moderates carried the election. It was the turning point.[100]

In both Virginia and Arkansas, elections played an important role in registering public opinion. In Virginia, in the summer primary of 1959, the Defenders sought to defeat legislators who had supported the governor's retreat from massive resistance. They failed utterly. In Arkansas, in addition to the school board elections the state held a referendum in the fall on a constitutional amendment that would reintroduce massive resistance. The measure failed, providing the first such defeat in a statewide vote in the South.[101]

It is difficult to overestimate the significance of these acts. Myrdal had written that "the South votes for men . . . but rarely ever for issues, unless the issue is defined in black and white." Yet they had voted for issues: the issues were defined in black and white, it is true—but the whites had voted in favor of the black point of view. V. O. Key had said in his important study *Southern Politics* that "of all the American states, Virginia can lay claim to the most thorough control by an oligarchy. . . . By contrast Mississippi is a hotbed of democracy." Of Arkansas, he had said that "Arkansas's active electorate possesses a high degree of homogeneity. That homogeneity may contribute to a politics in which genuinely important issues are not raised." His work was published only a decade before the final events described here. Yet, clearly an immense change had taken place. In Virginia, the Byrd machine, which ran the oligarchy, was challenged and beaten, and in Arkansas the homogeneity had come to an end. Blacks had already begun to realign Southern politics even without participating much in the voting process itself. They had forced the new economic elite to challenge the political rule of the traditional Southern power structure. As a result, Southern politics would never again be the same.[102]

These events had a ripple effect. Miami and Houston desegregated in the fall of 1959 and 1960 respectively. So did Atlanta in the fall of 1961. In that city— the financial and cultural center of the emerging Southeast region—business leaders joined "virtually the united voice of respectability in the metropolitan area," to insist that the city abide by the law and keep the schools open. Lubbell had found in Atlanta that in 1960 "two out of every three parents favored token integration over closed schools." In New Orleans, when a big battle over school desegregation began to brew, an important businessman recognized the lesson of Little Rock: "We simply cannot afford to let our city become another Little Rock. Look what happened to business after the riots and everything. They may never get over the mess they made of the school business."[103]

Part Two
The Black Movement

V

THE DEFEAT OF WHITE POWER AND THE EMERGENCE OF THE "NEW NEGRO" IN THE SOUTH

White rule was consolidated around the turn of the century. It meant terror and poverty to blacks; it meant that whites were able to shape the society and economy, to decide what would be the rules, and to change those rules at any time. It meant that even if blacks took Booker T. Washington's advice and set about to earn the respect of the whites by prospering, they would find their hopes frustrated: respect was not forthcoming in a white-controlled world. Or if it was, it would be only within the framework of black subordination and segregation.

White power meant more than whites' controlling the world within which blacks had to live. White power was able to reach into the black community itself and to shape it, to help determine the goals the black community sought, the means devised to seek those goals, the leadership the black community had, the kinds of personal options blacks often felt they had, and even the view that blacks had of themselves. As a result of the victory of white supremacy, blacks had few options. They were not in a position to confront the white-created social, political, and economic world in order to change its terms; rather, they had to find a way to survive in it, to adjust to it. Accommodation meant looking to powerful whites as benefactors, requesting "favors," accepting paternalism and subordination. It meant that whites determined the black community's leaders by deciding with whom they would communicate and to whom they would grant their "largesse." It meant that blacks failed to challenge the view of themselves as inferior.

While these patterns of action were never fully realized, they certainly became the norm. As the economic changes proceeded in the decades of the thirties and forties, these racial patterns remained largely unchanged. Blacks were growing more aggressive and impatient, but they entered the decade of the fifties with the old system basically intact. It was in the course of that decade that the old patterns were challenged and began to be broken and that the "New Negro" emerged in the South. The New Negro was first spoken of in the 1920s in the North, especially in Harlem, the most highly developed of the urban black communities. The New Negro in the North was independent of whites, aggressive, and insistent upon equality and had cast off the sense of black inferiority. These new behavioral characteristics blossomed almost immediately upon blacks' attaining independence from direct white domination.[1]

It was another three decades until the New Negro began to appear in the South to present a significant challenge to the old style of black accommodation to white power. Southern blacks had to confront white supremacy far more directly and centrally than blacks in the North. They had to free themselves from fear and from the pervasive feelings of self-worthlessness. Instead of making requests, they had to steel themselves to make demands. They came to learn that requests to make real changes simply would not be granted without their demonstrating that the cost of not granting a demand would be greater than if it were granted. Even then, they were sometimes met with intransigence.

The new balance of power in the South made it possible to continue in the face of these circumstances. Structural changes meant that those who were determined to prevent change could no longer carry the day. Their power to affect regional and national decisions had been greatly weakened. Correspondingly, the power of the blacks had been strengthened, and part of the story of the emergence of the New Negro in the South is that blacks sensed these changes and began to act on their perceptions.

The transformation of blacks in the fifties was painful and difficult. It was spurred on by white brutality and viciousness as much as by black hope. It often took form as a struggle for leadership in the black community. In some places gradually, in others rapidly, the old style accommodationist leaders were shunted aside, and what happened in one place often had a big impact on the consciousness and organization in others. Certainly by the end of the decade there was little support for the old-style leadership in the Southern black population. Here was the death of white power *inside the black community*.

The *Brown* decision was very important in this process: it set the law clearly on the side of the blacks and thereby encouraged them to seek their rights more aggressively. By putting whites on the defense, it impelled them to organize in response, which widened the gulf between black and white and made it more necessary for the blacks to push forward.

The Montgomery bus boycott was a crucial turning point in the black struggle of the fifties—*the* crucial turning point where blacks scored an unequivocal victory over whites. A strategy, a new leadership, and a new consciousness among blacks were the product of this episode. The success in Montgomery, Little Rock, and elsewhere helped to create a new élan and leadership.

But blacks experienced more than white terror, or the victory over it, in the decade of the fifties. As they pursued their ends more aggressively, as they grew more impatient with their status, they tested the support that was forthcoming from sources many had thought to be their allies. The federal government and white liberals came to be seen as sorely lacking, and the result was more anger and frustration and the recognition that blacks had independently to set their own course. Thus, as a new decade approached, the impulse toward direct action was taking hold.

Accommodation to White Power

> Every Negro in the South knows that he is under a kind of sentence of death; he does not know when his turn will come, it may never come, but it may also be at any time. This fear tends to intimidate the Negro man. If he loves his family, this love itself is a barrier against any open attempt to change his status. . . . What matters is the fear of extralegal violence, not knowing when or how the danger may appear . . . and the mist of anxiety raised under such conditions. This threat is all the more pervasive and insidious the higher the class position of the Negro, since the higher positions tend to draw more hostile effect.
>
> —John Dollard[2]

The consolidation of power by the Southern ruling class at the beginning of the twentieth century set the terms of the Southern racial and political system for another half-century. The violence and terror that had been used to defeat Reconstruction and Populism became a normal part of the region's culture. Its use by almost any white under almost any conditions against almost any black without fear of legal reprisal was standard. Gunnar Myrdal wrote: "In the South the Negro's person and property are practically subject to the whim of any white person who wishes to take advantage of him or to punish him for any real or fancied wrongdoing or 'insult.' " Police protection was close to nonexistent and was, if anything, on the side of the blacks' tormentors. It was similar with the courts, whose judges were beholden to whites, not blacks, for their tenure in office and whose juries refused to convict when cases were brought before them. These circumstances created a generalized terror of whites that always affected blacks. John Dollard described his visit to blacks' homes accompanied by three Southern white men. "The Negroes were frightened and reluctant," he said. When he commented to his companions on how politely they were received, he was laughingly answered: "They have to be [polite]." Whites could, at any time, freely test and taunt the blacks.[3]

Acting properly—as defined by whites—was therefore essential, though by no means a guarantee of security. One black informant told sociologist Charles Johnson in the late thirties:

> I like some white people all right I just don't want to have no trouble with them. If I did get in trouble with 'em I wouldn't do nothin'. I couldn't do nothin'. They'd kill me. White folks don't play with no colored folks. You have to do what they want you to do or else your life ain't worth nothin'.[4]

If these grim conditions were not always sufficient to guarantee proper black acquiescence, whites had an array of other sanctions: control over jobs, credit, and mortgages. Charles Johnson pointed out in referring to school teachers and principals that "since most if not all of them hold their jobs at the will of white school officials and politicians, they are extremely careful to observe the racial etiquette as far as possible. . . ." Martin Luther King, Sr. described the situation as one where "the black man had no rights . . . that the white man was bound to respect. He wasn't nothin' but a nigger, a workhorse. He wasn't supposed to have any formal training, wasn't supposed to be bright."[5]

This condition of virtually unchecked white power was the reality to which blacks had to adjust. There was little room for independence; they had to take great care in the presence of whites. In general, black action and consciousness were shaped by these conditions. If such was not universally the case, if there was some room for individuals to maneuver or even, in some circumstances, to ignore the expected rules of conduct, most felt resistance to be hopeless. One man succinctly summed up the situation:

> The white man is the boss in the South and you got to talk to him like he is the boss. It don't make any difference how much money you have or how much education you have, he won't look at you as his equal, and there is no use in you acting like you're his equal if you want to stay here.[6]

Adjustment meant not challenging segregation in any of its manifestations: it meant not seeking to use the vote, or if voting was acceptable in individual cases, it was certainly out of the question to organize it. A black real estate operator in Atlanta told Charles Johnson: "At the Court House they have a colored elevator, but that don't bother me. It runs like the rest of them."[7] Hylan Lewis was told by an election official in the early fifties: "We've had a few niggers voting in Kent for years. They are good niggers—know their place. And there has never been any trouble about their voting. On election day, they always come to the polls as soon as they open, vote and leave."[8] It meant blacks' staying in their assigned "place" in the social order: "Negroes are practiced in saying 'yes, sir,' 'no, sir' to white people," reported Dollard. That place, he contended, was perhaps best portrayed by black movie actor Stepan Fetchit, who "always plays the part of a well-accommodated, lower-class Negro, whining, vacillating, shambling, stupid and moved by very simple cravings." Accepting one's place meant accepting continually demeaning behavior: not dressing well; not buying a new car or other expensive consumer items lest one appear "uppity" by challenging the status of lower-class whites; waiting in stores to be served until after the whites had been taken care of; avoiding looking whites in the eye for fear that this behavior would be interpreted as arrogance; being addressed as "boy," "girl," "aunty," "professor," but never "Mr.," "Mrs.," or "Miss"; even getting off the sidewalk and walking around to provide a respectful distance to whites. One informant told Charles Johnson: "When I see them, I let them have they side of the street, and I goes on."[9] John Lewis described what conditions were like in Alabama prior to the *Brown* ruling:

> When you went to go to the water fountain, you *knew* not to drink out of that fountain that said White Only, that you were directed to drink out of the one

saying Colored. You couldn't go to the soda fountain and get a Coke. Somehow
we grew up *knowing* that you couldn't cross that line. . . .[10]

Adjustment meant more, however, than just learning to avoid or to tolerate
unpleasant or dangerous circumstances. It meant learning how to get along, to
gain benefits in a world run by and for whites. Since whites controlled everything,
in order to get anything one needed to please them. "Tact" in dealing with
whites became a necessary mode of behavior. A component part of tact was
lying. Blacks would often tell whites what they felt the latter would wish to hear
and act as whites would wish them to act. These patterns of action were ingrained
into the children's consciousness by their families, who, as Hylan Lewis put it,
tended "to have the child seek satisfactions and goals within the framework of
the local situation." One woman explained it in the following way:

> It's like with cars and knives, you have to teach your children to know what's
> dangerous and how to stay away from it, or else they sure won't live long. White
> people are a real danger to us until we learn how to live with them. So if you
> want your kids to live long, they have to grow up scared of whites; and the way
> they get scared is through us; and that's why I don't let my kids get fresh about
> the white man even in their own house. If I do there's liable to be trouble to pay.
> They'll forget and they'll say something outside, and that'll be it for them, and
> us too. So I make them store it in the bones, way inside, and then no one sees
> it. . . .[11]

Because whites had the power, getting along often required getting their aid
and support. Attaching oneself to a white benefactor was the way one got breaks
and extras that might be impossible to attain without such support:

> The white folks look out for you. When I was sick I went to the hospital, but they
> said I couldn't get in. But Mr. _____ hisself went back wid me and tole 'em yes
> I was gonna get in; they have to find a place for me; and they did, too.

The condition for such aid was that the black ingratiate himself to the white:
"The 'angel' will protect only a properly deferential Negro," noted Dollard.[12]

The whites who could provide most of the benefits to blacks were those who
had the most power in society. Therefore, it is not surprising, though it is
somewhat ironic, that the whites who were looked to as benefactors were of the
very class that had led the battle for white supremacy in the past, and was to
do so again in the 1950s. It was the "quality folks," the "best people among
the whites," the "better class of whites" to whom blacks looked for protection.
These were the planters, merchants, and businessmen, who, secure in their
privileges, often deplored the racist "excesses" of lower-class whites. (One
prosecuting attorney told of instances in which planters had made agreements
with him by which the tenants would receive light sentences in return for a plea
of guilty.[13]) The latter, in economic competition with the blacks, frequently
insisted on enforcing some of the most demeaning conditions in order to enhance

their own poor status. Blacks often looked to upper-class whites for protection against these "peckerwoods."[14]

Reliance on powerful whites was not only a way of getting certain otherwise unattainable benefits; it was also an alternative to relying on other blacks. Many felt that their own people were simply not to be trusted: "I can't stand white people . . . but you can't depend on Negroes to stand by you." That meant that rather than developing black solidarity and organization, blacks tended to look to whites:

> I tell you one thing: You'll find that the Negroes here have been accustomed to lookin' up to the white man an' doin' what he tells them, an' it's a fact that these negroes here will follow a white man an' do what he tells them sooner than they'd follow any colored man. . . .

This attitude made some real sense. In a white-controlled world, there was much to be attained from having good relations with the whites. In the paternalistic relationship, where the black tenant kept his "place," the white planter took care of him: provided him with medical treatment, kept him out of trouble with the law, gave aid in times of illness, hard economic times, and death in the family, and generally treated him and his family like children who were his wards.[15]

Good relations with whites would provide prestige among other blacks, and even a certain amount of power. Thus, for example, those in a position to have the ear of important whites could be persons of some influence in the black community, and certainly people to be reckoned with: "You can get along all right just so you don't cross one of these white folks' cooks." Relying on whites often entailed reciprocal obligations. That involved not only acknowledging the deference due to whites but also sometimes displaying loyalty even to the point of betraying other blacks by informing on them.[16]

The gradual emergence of class distinctions among blacks only tended to accentuate these divisions and to make racial unity almost impossible. Blacks who were attaining what should be loosely called middle-class status tended to be individualistic, rather than race-conscious. Their achievements, then, were attributable to their own qualities and not a testimony to the abilities of the race. They often tended to adopt white standards in an exaggerated fashion. That led them to go out of their way to dissociate themselves from the white stereotype of blacks—namely, from lower-class blacks:

> Those niggahs don't know how to act or talk at a decent dance. It was terrible the crowd they had last night. It makes you feel sick.

> They appear to regard lower class colored persons as 'unclean' as revolting physically. . . .

Allison Davis and John Dollard saw this tendency as so pronounced that they held that "upper class and middle class Negroes often criticize lower class

Negroes for being loud, ignorant, black or dirty persons. If this charge does not appear in a case record, it is safe to assume that the individuals concerned are of lower class origin.'' Such sentiments did not go unnoticed by the lower-class blacks, who tended to view the middle class as snobbish, selfish, and disloyal to the race. Davis and Dollard reported of one of their subjects that ''with many other lower-lower class Negroes, he shares a distrust of the Negro middle class, and prefers white doctors and hospitals.''[17]

The attempt on the part of some middle-class blacks to exaggerate the differences between themselves and the bulk of the black population was part of a more general phenomenon: the pervasive feeling of black inferiority and the adoption of white standards of value. White power meant not only control but also the internalization of the view that whites were better than blacks, producing what Martin Luther King, Jr. called a ''corroding sense of inferiority, which often expressed itself in a lack of self-respect.''[18]

Numerous studies have found evidence of blacks' wishing to be white, or to be like whites, to have white or whiter skin, or ''white'' hair (''good hair''). Some of this material helped form the basis of the *Brown* decision that segregation was inherently discriminatory. Sales of hair straighteners and skin lighteners provided other testimony to this terrible effect of the Southern system of racial domination. It also helped to maintain that system by undermining the self-respect of blacks. This problem persisted into the fifties and sixties and was part of what had to be overcome for blacks to stand up to white domination. King noted in Montgomery, Alabama: ''Many unconsciously wondered whether they actually deserved any better conditions. Their minds and souls were so conditioned to the system of segregation that they submissively adjusted themselves to things as they were.''[19]

Blacks tended to turn their aggressions, which could find no outlet toward whites, inward, against other blacks. Dollard and Johnson both noted that tendency. It was encouraged by whites, who created a double standard of justice. Black aggression against whites was harshly dealt with; but when blacks acted against other blacks, they were frequently treated indulgently. Those blacks who could claim white benefactors might escape punishment entirely.[20]

Nor was that the end of the matter. The tentacles of white domination reached into and shaped the response of the black population in yet another crucial manner: whites chose the leadership of the black community in a variety of ways. Since whites had the prestige, those blacks with whom they dealt partook of that prestige. Myrdal noted that ''the Negro press eagerly records and plays up the slightest recognition shown a Negro by whites.'' More important than recognition by whites in making black leadership was white control of the purse strings. It was normally through the black leader that white generosity was channeled, making him a very important person in the community indeed.[21]

Having the power to pick their agents gave whites the ability to determine how those agents would act. Blacks who did not visibly accept the racial mores of the South, or who encouraged others to break them, were not acceptable.

What was required was "good Negroes" who encouraged and personified black passivity and acceptance, who discouraged protest. Such a "leader" would be given sufficient authority and material benefits to legitimate his approach among blacks and to discourage alternative styles.[22]

The means by which black leaders attained benefits for the community replicated the methods individual blacks employed to gain certain privileges—humbly supplicating the powerful white benefactor:

> Don't emphasize the Negro's right . . . don't *press* for anything . . . make him feel he's a big man, get to other white men to make him want to avoid seeming small, and you can make him jump through the barrel. You can make him a friend or a rattlesnake, depending on your approach.

> We *ask* for things, but never *demand*. They find me calm and reasonable.

When a black physician received the highest vote of all city council candidates in Greensboro, a vote that normally should have meant his selection as mayor, he declined the position: "I wouldn't do anything to lessen the progress that has come in these years and I am fully cognizant of the support that white people have given me."[23]

This tendency was powerfully reinforced by the many blacks, particularly middle-class professionals, who were dependent on whites for their jobs. Bayard Rustin told of his experience in the first freedom ride, sponsored by the Congress of Racial Equality (CORE), called then the "Journey of Reconciliation," in 1947. At Chapel Hill, North Carolina, a school teacher "actually got down on his knees and beseeched me to stop making trouble and move to the back of the bus." William Chafe described the plight of the president of a black college:

> What do you do? You can fight to get freedom and you can protest. . . . But how do you get the things that you need?" For the Blufords [the president] of Greensboro, the ultimate question was not what felt best, but what could be done to help the community. "If he had to go down to Raleigh [the capital] and suffer indignities, he would" one faculty member remarked.*[25]

This process did not exclusively involve submitting to whites. Blacks could use the process to manipulate whites by beguiling, flattering, bluffing, and outwitting them. But while such action might be satisfying to an individual, it really accomplished little, because it always took place within the framework of, and thus helped to reinforce, white supremacy.

That was virtually the only model of black leadership at the time. Through it whites were able to shape and direct black action. Without independent black leaders, whites were able not only to force blacks to acquiesce but also to make organizing any kind of alternative virtually impossible. At the same time, white power made it very hard for the black population to support an alternative:

---

*Elaine Burgess found the same problem confronting the president of a black college in Durham, North Carolina: "We are caught between the wishes of our own people and those of the white state legislatures which hold the purse strings."[24]

They need Negro leaders who can get things from the whites. They know that a Negro leader who starts to act aggressively is not only losing his own power and often his livelihood but might endanger the welfare of the whole Negro community. In Southern Negro communities there is apparently much suspicion against "radical," "hot-headed" and "outspoken" Negroes. Negroes do not want to be observed associating with such persons, because they might "get in trouble." A barricade will often be thrown up around them by a common consent that they are "queer." The Negro community itself will thus often, before there is any white interference, advise individual Negroes who show signs of aggression that they had better trim their sails.[26]

A complete picture of Southern race relations in this period is not presented here. Most of the researchers who produced these findings were white. In order to survive, blacks had to lie to whites and to hide from them what they (the whites) might find unpleasant. Anger, hatred, and militancy often seethed below the surface within many. Some blacks fought back or refused to accept the humiliations demanded of them. But these sentiments rarely pierced the surface; whites were seldom aware of them. Blacks often repressed them, or they existed side-by-side with self-hatred: "The colored man, I think he has to hide what he really feels even from himself. Otherwise there would be too much pain—too much," psychiatrist Robert Coles was told. Blacks were not really able to challenge the structure of white domination. If change was to come, it would entail a basic change in attitude as well as a change in leadership of the black population. Leaders would no longer be chosen by whites, or by white criteria. That change was to take place in the decade of the fifties.[27]

A New Beginning

The economic and sociological transformations brought to the South by the Depression and World War II prepared the basis for the emergence of the New Negro. But the war itself was the single most important catalytic event: it opened up jobs for blacks, took them off the farms, and set them in the cities; it put guns in their hands and trained them to use them; the war exposed blacks to education and to the world and made them more cosmopolitan. As a result, by the war's end blacks were becoming more self-assertive. Morton Rubin, who did a study of "Plantation County" in the late forties, noted the trend toward "a growing feeling of race consciousness and race pride. . . ."[28]

Black veterans were to play an important part in this change. In 1946 there was a riot in Columbia, Tennessee. It was precipitated when a black veteran knocked a white radio repairman through a plate-glass window after the white had slapped his mother. The veteran was arrested, and a lynch mob began to form. Efforts to post bond in a town that had had two lynchings "by invitation" in the past two decades were blocked by raising the amount of bail. "Let me tell you one thing, sheriff," said a black businessman in response, "there won't be any more 'social' lynchings in Columbia.'' They got the young man released on bond, and that night a white mob came into the black part of town. It was met by a determined population that included over 150 veterans and a number of chemical workers who held membership in the CIO Mine, Mill, and Smelter Workers' union. When the shooting was over, four police officers had been wounded, one seriously. A few years later one of the participants told Carl Rowan, "Before the riot Columbia was a hellhole, but . . . we've got a good city now." said another: "No, there ain't gonna be no more trouble. That's the one thing I learned from 1946. They know now that negroes have guts. . . . Blood was shed, but it paid off. A colored man used not to have the chance ofa sheep-killing dog. But 1946 changed that."[29]

In 1946 a black veteran arrived in Prince Edward County in Virginia to be a minister at a black church there. He had belonged to the NAACP in college, had been touched by the Wallace campaign the previous year, and "I thought religion ought to be lived up to, squared with economics, politics, all that. . . ." Leslie Griffin was to play a key role in creating the conditions that led to a student strike for better schools and ultimately to a court suit that became one of the cases consolidated into the 1954 *Brown* ruling.[30]

The ferment suggested by these events was fueled not only by black indignation at injustice but also by blacks' sense that things were going their way. Part of this feeling involved the legal victories that the NAACP was winning against conditions that were supposed to be separate and equal but that had no pretense of equality. Under the threat of integration, cities were building better facilities for blacks. Statistics on black incomes and jobs were up, as were those on home ownership and college attendance. These characteristics, indicating the rise of a middle class, were the very phenomena later associated with increased civil rights activity.[31]

Floyd Hunter noted a number of such gains in Atlanta: blacks on the police force; parks and other recreational facilities for blacks; new schools; black teachers paid on an equal basis with whites. In Greensboro, the Jim Crow signs were removed from public offices and facilities and large department stores. The signs came down in Houston, too, and the city golf course was desegregated; blacks were appointed to city boards and commissions, and black streets began to be paved for the first time. Hylan Lewis recorded in the town of "Kent" (a false name, provided to protect Lewis's informants) "indications of more equitable shares of public services and expenditures as seen in teachers' salaries, expenditures for school improvement and services, and improved streets and trash removal service." There were also a large increase in black voting and a decline in violence against blacks. Blacks were winning some elections, and the NAACP was aggressively organizing. Lewis found the NAACP to be the largest black organization in Kent by far, even if its membership was largely passive.[32]

Edgar French, secretary of the Montgomery Improvement Association, the organization that led a bus boycott in that city, recalled that on the eve of the *Brown* decision, "there was a peculiar kind of social unrest. . . . It was not at all uncommon to hear a colored citizen say 'We have been in this all of our lives! We are tired of this! We want somebody to lead us out of this! We are willing to do whatever is necessary. We want somebody to tell us what to do and to show us how to do it. . . .' " It is evident that this feeling came from a broader sentiment that was growing in the black community. Daniel Thompson found that as early as 1950, even black moderates, who tended to accept segregation, "increasingly voiced impatience with the slow progress being made in achieving civil rights for Negroes within the biracial social system. Some of them began to insist upon a frontal attack upon segregation *per se*." In 1950 the NAACP decided to stop bringing suits against segregated facilities simply because they were physically unequal, and to bring suit against segregation itself because it was inherently unequal. When they imparted this information to the people of Prince Edward County in a public meeting, one parent arose and responded: "We have known that in this county for a long time and we have simply been waiting for you and the NAACP to find out the same thing."[33]

Perhaps nothing was more indicative of the changing mood among Southern blacks than the 1951 student strike in Prince Edward County. Planned, organized, and executed by the students, it foreshadowed much of what was later to come. The leaders, having assembled the student body and gotten rid of the principal by subterfuge, told the students in order to firm up their support that "the jail was not big enough to hold them all and that, as long as they stayed together none would be punished." That was an idea that reverberated through the sixties. That they received almost unanimous support from their parents indicates how deeply these waters were running.[34]

The strife in Prince Edward County foreshadowed the future in yet another important way: it created a deep split among black leaders. Even before the strike, the Reverend Leslie Francis Griffin had recognized that if there was to be change, it would be necessary to "discredit the old, segregation-oriented leadership." He had already had some success in this matter before the strike, having replaced the most important of the accommodationist leaders on the PTA. When the strike broke out, the old leadership opposed it. Barbara Johns, the student leader of the strike, openly attacked them: "Don't let Mr. Charlie [the term for whites], Mr. Tommie [an allusion to Uncle Tom], or Mr. Pervall [one of the strike's opponents] stop you from backing us. We are depending on you." Her words drew tears from the listening adults, and she was met with loud applause. The new leadership triumphed in Prince Edward County.[35]

In general there was a sense that things were getting better, that perhaps the end was in sight. Hylan Lewis found in Kent "a promise and an expectation of improvement that is generally shared, even by the most skeptical." Black sociologist Charles Johnson surveyed the period with great optimism: "We are changing from a racial society in many respects to a human relations society," he said. Looking forward to the *Brown* decision, the head of the South Carolina NAACP thought that both blacks and whites in the state would accept the Supreme Court's decision.[36]

Brown: New Hope, New Militancy

When the *Brown* ruling was issued, its impact on the black population was electric. Louis Lomax called the day of decision a "black Monday," playing on Mississippi judge Thomas Brady's famous speech and pamphlet: "That was the day we won," he said, "and we were proud." A sixteen-year-old black student in Virginia broke into tears when told the decision by her teacher: "We went on studying history, but things weren't the same, and will never be the same again." The (black) Atlanta *Daily World* heralded that day as "one of the important days in the history of this country and the fight for freedom for all the citizens of the nation!" John Lewis recalled the impact upon him: "I was 14 and . . . as I recall we rejoiced. It was like a day of jubilee . . . that segregation would be ended. . . . We thought that we would go to a better school . . . get better transportation, better buses, and that type of thing." "This decision," said Martin Luther King, Jr., "brought hope to millions of disinherited Negroes who had formerly dared only to dream of freedom."[37]

New hope and courage appeared everywhere. Blacks were vindicated in their struggle. "Suddenly there was a voice, more impressive and resounding than that of any Negro leader, the voice of the highest court in the land, and it was saying in unmistakable language that segregation was wrong, was illegal, was intolerable, and that it must be ended," wrote Mrs. Medgar Evers. Roy Wilkins summmed up the meaning of the decision for many:

> We have been subject to the whims and fancies of white persons, individually and collectively. We went to back doors. . . . We stepped off sidewalks and removed our hats and said "Sir" to all and sundry, if they were white. . . . We could not vote. Our health and our recreation were of little or no concern to the responsible officials of government. In time of war we were called to serve, but were insulted, degraded and mistreated. . . . This school decision heralds the death of all inequality in citizenship based on race. . . .[38]

From the black point of view, the decision changed everything, and blacks became more aggressive. In Greensboro this new mood was noted at school board meetings. Visits from the NAACP and black parents were "more frequent . . . and more assertive, but less patient. They wanted it done boom, boom, boom." Jim Crow in the department stores provoked new protests, as did segregation in other areas. In Florida, black leaders reported getting pressure from the community to communicate to whites their wish for rapid implementation of the *Brown* ruling. In South Carolina, blacks began organizing to elect to office candidates who would support their needs. And in New Orleans, the movement against segregation picked up steam after *Brown*. The NAACP planned to make sure *Brown* was implemented; the organization looked forward to gaining "complete emancipation" by January 1, 1963, the one-hundredth anniversary of the Emancipation Proclamation.[39]

The new spirit was perhaps best illustrated in Mississippi. There, but two months after "Black Monday," the governor summoned a group of trusted (by whites) black leaders who were asked to endorse a proposal for voluntary segregation. Most denounced it; the few who did not were themselves ridiculed and denounced. Similar efforts were made elsewhere; whites simply could not believe that "their" blacks wanted it.[40]

Blacks had played the game according to white rules. They had gone through the white courts, and they had won. Now they expected—assumed—adherence to the rules. Thurgood Marshall, who had plotted the legal strategy, said: "Once and for all, it's decided, and completely decided." It was now assumed that school boards would comply, and the NAACP optimistically prepared to be magnanimous:

> It is important . . . that . . . the spirit of give and take characterize the discussions. Let it not be said of us that we took advantage of a sweeping victory to drive hard bargains or impose unnecessary hardships upon those responsible for working out the details of adjustment.[41]

"But we were naive," said Louis Lomax.[42] And indeed, looking back, these expressions of optimism certainly appear naive. Looking down the road, those standing on the crest of the Supreme Court ruling could see the end. They could not perceive the obstacles that yet lay before them. The next years would be a time of education, and the naivete would give way to bitterness, anger, determination, and organization. If the Southern ruling class would not give up the ground that it had legally lost, that ground would have to be wrested from it. The remainder of the decade prepared the black population to do just that.

Brown: "The Great Silence"

When the Supreme Court ruled, it was Southern whites who made the next move; blacks awaited the improvements they expected to be forthcoming. As detailed in the previous chapter, the white response was to resist the law. Instead, they attempted to undermine its legitimacy, to establish a higher authority—the south's (white) people and their customs—and to create the solid white South to confront blacks and the federal government.

They drew a hard line between white and black. Crossing that line was made very difficult, lest the line itself disappear; white solidarity had to mean increased hostility to blacks. Black-white associations suddenly became taboo. Race relations, with which moderates had been pleased, suddenly deteriorated. This change was felt in small ways: black college chorus performances before white audiences were dropped; black groups were excluded from holiday parades and festivities; proposals for intramural sports activities between blacks and whites, which had sometimes occurred in the past without anyone's taking notice, were now viewed with suspicion as efforts to begin compliance with the *Brown* ruling. In Orangeburg, South Carolina, the white ministerial alliance refused to organize joint prayer services with blacks.[43]

White paternalism, which was premised on unquestioned white superiority, began to disappear. Carl Rowan was told by a southern moderate in Mississippi that at Christmas time wealthy whites would no longer make contributions to buy presents for poor black children. The Urban League was excluded from Community Chest fundraising efforts in several Southern cities where it had previously participated, including Little Rock, Richmond, New Orleans, Jacksonville, and Fort Worth.[44]

Requests for meetings or for biracial committees to discuss problems were met with a cold shoulder. In Durham, North Carolina, despite a proliferation of formal organizational structures, both black and white leaders felt that communication was not as good as it had been prior to 1954. Virtually any request for better conditions was now viewed with hostility. Whites who might have acceded to such requests now rejected them. Although whites insisted that Southern blacks were perfectly content, they viewed every request, no matter how hat-in-hand, as a demand that threatened the existing system of racial domination.[45]

These actions hardened attitudes among the blacks. Those who might still be pulled by lingering ties of affection for or dependence on whites had their channels of communication shut off. White paternalism was severely curtailed, and with it went some of the whites' ability to shape black action. Perhaps most important was that the black accommodationist leadership was undermined by the new turn. The base of these "leaders" in the black community was their ability to produce, to bring home the bacon, to make gains. In an era when most blacks' backs were bent from stooping, their own bent backs were not out of place. But when the whites drew back and in effect labeled all blacks alike, as dissenters, and would grant no concessions, the whites removed the basis of the old leadership's predominance in the black community. They did so even as black sentiment was shifting away from the approach that many characterized as begging for crumbs, and as an alternative leadership began to appear. The hardening line of whites served only to stiffen the backs of blacks and to hasten the process of changing leadership.

Brown: White Terror and a New Leadership

The white response included economic coercion, violence, and terror, even murder. In four years a survey found forty-four people beaten, twenty-nine shot, and wounded, six killed. A compilation over the same period found 225 acts against "private liberties and public peace." Over time, as the campaign continued, a self-selective process took place in which those blacks who had the courage, the conviction, the inner strength, the independence, (especially economic), and the ability to stand up to the terror no matter what the cost—even possibly death—came to the fore and reshaped the attitudes of the black population. The process by which new leaders were tested and proven for leadership, so different from the accommodationist leaders of the past, trained them for a wholly different approach to whites and white supremacy. "Medgar [Evers] . . . came to have . . . respect for the Negroes who dared to accept positions of leadership throughout the state," wrote Evers's wife. Far from looking for white paternalism, this new leadership was selected and trained by defying the most vicious and sometimes brutal actions of the whites.[46]

Ruby Hurley, who opened the first NAACP office in the Deep South, described what conditions were like, what it meant to stand up to white supremacy in that period. she was investigating the Emmett Till murder in Mississippi:

> Those persons heard by way of the grapevine that I was investigating the case, and they passed the word back to me that they wouldn't talk to anybody but me. So I had to put on some cotton-pickin' clothes . . . and make my way on to the plantation. . . . I really got a feeling of what the Underground Railroad during the days of slavery was all about—how word would be passed by just the look in an eye, never the exact phraseology being used, never the clear language, always in some form that you have to sorta try to figure out what the people meant. And it was only after going . . . to four different places, did I finally get to the people who had sent word that they wanted to talk to me. You never went directly to a place. . . . You were cleared all the way. Protection was there for me all the way and I didn't know it until many years later. There were men all around with shotguns standing in various spots to be sure that I got where I was going and got back.[47]

The diversity of their weapons was great. A forty-seven-year-old dentist who was a leader of the NAACP in Mississippi was ordered by his local draft board to explain why he should not be classified 1-A. In 1958, it was discovered that the Internal Revenue Service was systematically harassing Southern opponents of segregation, black and white. For those who could not be intimidated, there was the threat of death: a list of names circulated by the White Citizens' Councils came unofficially to be known as a "death list," and at least one of the persons on it was murdered.[48]

The repression could be visited on anyone who refused to stay in his or her presumed place. That treatment was felt by those who dared to petition for desegregated schools. Anne Moody recalled a teacher who, following Emmett Till's brutal murder, told her about the NAACP and of the truth about relations between blacks and whites. The teacher had warned her: "Don't you dare breathe a word of what I said. It could cost me my job if word got out I was teaching my students such." She was fired.[49]

Such an atmosphere could not fail to have an impact on black attitudes, and ultimately on leadership and organization. Either the repression would curb the new tendencies and defeat them or it would spur them on. Because of the new strength that blacks were developing, and because of the trials they endured in the decade, they could not be turned around. Moody provided a revealing portrait of how sentiments were developing. After the slaying of Emmett Till, she began to change:

I was 15 years old when I began to hate people. I hated the white men who murdered Emmett Till and I hated all the other whites who were responsible for the countless murders Mrs. Rice had told me about and those I vaguely remembered from childhood. But I also hated Negroes. I hated them for not standing up and doing something about the murders. In fact, I think I had a stronger resentment toward Negroes for letting the whites kill them than toward the whites. Anyway, it was at this stage in my life that I began to look upon Negro men as cowards. I could not respect them for smiling in a white man's face, addressing him as Mr. So-and-So, saying yessuh and nossuh when after they were home behind closed doors that same white man was a son of a bitch, a bastard, or any other name more suitable than mister.[50]

With sentiments like these percolating, it became harder for white power to control black action. Still, the terror was effective. Moody said, "Every Negro man in Centreville became afraid to walk the streets. . . . Emmett Till's murder had proved it was a crime, punishable by death, for a Negro man to even whistle at a white woman in Mississippi." The terror still had its effects, but it was being shaken off. "I was choking to death in Centreville," said Moody. "I was sick of selling my feelings for a dollar a day."[51]

It was an agonizing process. The *Brown* decision, which put right and law on the side of blacks, pushed it forward. They were no longer asking for favors or seeking the benevolence of a "friend." They now demanded their due; it was the whites who were the lawbreakers. And with the change, those blacks who persisted in the old patterns came increasingly to be viewed as traitors. Repeated efforts by whites in Montgomery to divide the blacks finally persuaded one of their number to collaborate with the whites. But he was frozen out by the black community. In Durham, the first black city councilman, elected only a year before with the support of all black community organizations, responded cautiously to the court ruling. Implementation would take time, he said, and most black pupils would not go to white schools. Other black leaders disapproved of this statement; the councilman lost influence, and by the 1957 election he was replaced.[52]

But as a group, the old-style black leaders did not just disappear. They sometimes fought openly for their stance. The publisher of a black newspaper in Mississippi wrote almost a year after *Brown*:

It can be safely stated as a fact that 85 per cent of the Negro school patrons in Mississippi, and the South generally, are hoping and praying that no attempt will be made to enforce the Supreme Court decision. . . . Insofar as Negroes in the South are concerned, the NAACP is an enemy of the Negro race.

A black college president told a meeting of blacks: "I don't believe you are going to throw away your churches, schools, hospitals, businesses, insurances, newspapers . . . just to sit, eat, and ride with a white person." A school principal in South Carolina warned that the *Brown* decision would create "many perplexing problems and grave consequences" for black students and teachers and that educational opportunities for black children would "suffer for the next fifty years.'' There were blacks with livings dependent upon separate institutions who defended segregation.[53]

Nonetheless, more and more frequently blacks were refusing to be intimidated, were standing up to the white terror and facing it down. A seven-year-old boy asked to be sent to an all-white school. His mother: "If you got the guts to go I've got the guts to send you." An Alabama preacher had been threatened by a white gang with being beaten and thrown in the river: "I wouldn't advise you to do that," he warned. They didn't. In Greensboro, parents who were economically vulnerable applied for permits for their children to attend white schools. In Montgomery, over one hundred blacks were indicted during the boycott. One of the participants wrote:

> For the first time police . . . were confronted by Negroes who acted like men. . . . Many . . . reported to the jail voluntarily. Others . . . sat chatting leisurely in the cells long after bonds had been arranged. . . . All the threats which had been used to suppress the Negro had lost their potency. Iron bars and the prison cell would be a pleasant sight if such meant freedom and first-class citizenship for all unborn generations. . . . The thirst for freedom had pushed all fears into the background.[54]

In New Orleans, when the NAACP was driven underground the New Orleans Improvement League carried on its activities. If coercion and intimidation could force some blacks to back off from their urge for desegregation, as they did in Yazoo City, Mississippi, others refused to budge. The "Great Silence," the breaking off of interracial cooperation, helped to create a sense of unity that had previously been lacking and that many had vainly called for in the past. King noted that in Montgomery "the PhD's and the no 'D's were bound together in a common venture."[55]

Whenever possible, the black community in Durham tried to present a united front to the whites. In Tuskeegee, Alabama, site of Booker T. Washington's famous institute, middle-class blacks had set themselves apart from the black farmers and took middle-class whites as their point of reference. When blacks, who were 83 percent of the population, began to have an impact on local elections, however, the whites rewrote the rules and gerrymandered almost all blacks out of the city. Thus, blacks were reminded that, no matter what their achievements were, what was most important about them was their race. They struck back by organizing a boycott against local merchants. In the course of this effort, new unity was attained. Said a Tuskeegee professor:

> It was the gerrymander that brought us together. Before that, we professional people had the feeling that it was possible for us to go downtown to get special privileges. . . . We were shocked into the realization that we were still Negroes, with all the disabilities attached thereto. . . .[56]

In time these pressures, which caught the accommodationists between white intransigence and black impatience, squeezed them out. The time for Uncle Tom was drawing to a close. Polls indicated that opposition to segregation was becoming the mainstream respectable attitude among blacks. Daniel Thompson found that in New Orleans by the end of the decade, "more and more the Negro community rejects the Uncle Tom." The same was true in Durham. Referring to a segregated school, a moderate black leader there stated, "Not one of us would go back to our people and recommend the use of that old building. We would be repudiated and scorned if we did." A study in Little Rock after the school closing found much the same. In reference to an outspoken segregationist black:

> He used to do a lot of . . . speaking in the streets supporting segregation; but it is now too dangerous to do this for there have been threats of physical injury. Even the kids will stone his house or automobile when they pass going to school. A Negro leader who advocates segregation immediately draws the ire and dislike from negroes generally.[57]

Montgomery: Martin Luther King, Jr. and the Strategy of Nonviolent Direct Action

The actual changes emerged in counterpoint to the activities of the white supremacists, who themselves responded to challenges to their system. That was evident in the emergence of the White Citizens' Council as an immediate response to the *Brown* ruling. The organization languished in the early months of 1955. But, subsequent to the second *Brown* ruling when it was clear that all the voluntary compliance there was to be had already taken place, the NAACP began to act. The organization prepared a petition campaign calling for integrated schools. Once again the White Citizens' Councils grew.[58]

The summer of 1955 was the most violent of the decade. The murder of Emmett Till became a cause celebre and inflamed black consciousness. Blacks in Mississippi were being told to "agree and knuckle under, or flee, or die," said Roy Wilkins. Faced with such choices, blacks had little alternative but to push forward. Angered at being unlawfully denied their rights, confident that they had some backing in Washington, D.C., blacks grew in determination. "Toward the end of 1955," wrote one observer, "the spirit of rebellion and resistance was spreading among black people in every corner of the South." Confrontation was becoming inevitable. The questions were where it would be, what form it would take, and what its outcome would be.[59]

In Montgomery, Alabama blacks had made gains as they had elsewhere in the South: merchants had been pressured to eliminate separate drinking fountains and to begin addressing black customers as Mr., Miss, or Mrs.; the city had been induced to hire four black policemen; and efforts had already begun to gain equal recreational facilities for blacks. Martin Luther King's church had been conducting a voter registration drive to increase the political power of blacks in the city.[60]

But the structure of segregation remained solid, and the indignities continued.

As elsewhere, blacks were becoming increasingly unwilling to tolerate such conditions. In the year before the bus boycott began, five black women and two black children had been arrested for disobeying the segregation laws on the buses. One black man was shot; others were threatened with pistols by bus drivers; a blind man had his leg caught in the door and was dragged down the street. King had served on a committee formed in 1955 after a fifteen-year-old high-school girl had been arrested for failing to give up her seat to a white. The committee met with the the bus company and with the police but won no concessions.[61]

A boycott had been considered for a year, but a defendant whose character could not be impugned had not been found. Six days before Rosa Parks refused to give up her seat to a white, the Interstate Commerce Commission outlawed segregation in interstate travel. Though unplanned, Parks's act was no accident. A longtime outspoken activist and secretary of the state office of the NAACP, "I had almost a life history of being rebellious about being mistreated because of my color." Mrs. Parks's arrest in December 1955 sparked the Montgomery bus boycott. Speaking of her action, Parks said, "This is what I wanted to know: when and how would we ever determine our rights as human beings?"[62]

Parks described the ad hoc character of the action that brought about her arrest:

> At the time when I refused to move from this seat and stand up I didn't feel that I was breaking any law because the ordinances as far as I could recall didn't say a driver would have a person to leave a seat and stand. . . . When I was ordered by the driver to leave the seat, there was nothing I could do but either stand up and get off the bus, or stand up over this same seat that I had vacated because there was no where even to move back. The back of the bus was already crowded with passengers: people were standing in the aisles up to where I was sitting, and I didn't feel I was even violating the segregation law. Only thing I did was just refuse to obey the driver when he said, "stand up." so there were four people involved: a man in the seat with me . . . and two women across the aisle. so that meant four of us would stand for one person to occupy a seat and leave three vacancies unless another white person got on.[63]

The Montgomery effort was as important as the *Brown* decision itself in pushing the black movement forward. It was a long and difficult struggle in which the black population of the city took on the entire white power structure in a year-long battle, and won. That battle encouraged a rising tide of black militancy. It was the most important confrontation of the decade, in which blacks demonstrated to the world and to themselves the unity and the sacrifices of which they were capable. It inspired blacks to challenge white supremacy elsewhere and was a crucial turning point in the emergence of the New Negro and the eclipse of the old. It became a unifying point not only for blacks in Montgomery, Alabama but for blacks across the nation. Thousands of dollars were sent in to aid the boycott from many sources. In New York in the summer of 1956, a giant rally was held to build support and raise money. Those attending included Eleanor Roosevelt, Sammy Davis, Jr., Congressman Adam Clayton Powell, and A. Philip Randolph. Montgomery had come to occupy center stage in the struggle for black liberation.[64]

Out of the crucible of struggle in that city, Martin Luther King, Jr. emerged. As Montgomery rose to national attention, so did the leader of the struggle. Invitations for him to speak proliferated. In 1956, King appeared before the Democratic party platform committee. *Time* and *Jet* magazines ran cover stories on him, as did many other newspapers and periodicals. By the late fifties, King was emerging as the most important black leader in America. He became a symbol of the new black spirit and came to be generally acknowledged as *the* black leader—no one approached the prestige King enjoyed.[65]

King was a product of the new mood. The changing attitudes on the part of blacks and their newly developing sense of power encouraged his own proclivity to seek change. He, in his turn, helped to inspire blacks to reach for greater heights, to demand racial justice, and to do so with dignity and self-respect. The hastening pace of events that resulted from Montgomery, and King's self-conscious efforts helped to create a new stratum of leaders to push the struggle further. The formation of the Southern Christian Leadership Conference served both to build on this emerging new leadership and to extend it. Its establishment was very important, because it meant that now the new trend became organized.

When King came to Montgomery, he was not fully formed as the leader he would become. He was concerned about the matters that would soon come to dominate his life; that was why he had chosen "in spite of the disadvantages and inevitable sacrifices" to return to the South, "at least for a few years." He was shaped by the struggle in Montgomery as much as he shaped it. Andrew Young asserted as much: "I'm convinced that Martin never wanted to be a leader. I mean, everything he did, he was pushed into." Coretta King recalled King himself saying much the same:

> If anybody had told me a couple of years ago, when I accepted the presidency of the MIA [Montgomery Improvement Association, the organization that led the boycott], that I would be in this position, I would have avoided it with all my strength. This is not the life I expected to lead. but gradually you take some responsibility, then a little more, until finally you are not in control anymore. You have to give yourself entirely.[66]

It was not simply a matter of commitment. King was confronted in Montgomery with a continual series of realities and choices that he did not anticipate. His growth in response to these had a deep and lasting impact on him, and on the emerging black movement as a whole. Before Montgomery, nonviolence was not a worked-out program, nor was King fully committed to it. His application for a permit to carry a gun is one illustration. So were his doubts about the boycott as a legitimate tactic. On the day before the boycott was to begin, King confronted the argument that blacks' organizing a boycott was the same as the economic pressure employed by the White Citizens' Councils. "Now certain doubts began to bother me," he said. As he thought the question through, he recalled Thoreau's essay on civil disobedience and saw a relationship: "We were simply saying to the white community, 'we can no longer lend our cooperation to an evil system.' " A week after the boycott began, a white woman wrote a letter to the paper suggesting, for the first time, a comparison of the boycott with Gandhi's campaign in India. David Lewis, a King biographer, points out that it was under the influence of Bayard Rustin, who arrived two and one-half months after the boycott began, that King developed the ideas of nonviolence more systematically.[67]

King came to see the efficacy of mass action in Montgomery. He had doubts about what support the boycott would gain: the day it was to begin, "I was still saying that if we could get 60 percent cooperation the venture would be a success." The virtual 100 percent participation was a revelation: "As I watched them I knew that there is nothing more majestic than the determined courage of individuals willing to suffer and sacrifice for their freedom and dignity." When King was arrested on a trumped-up speaking charge, he got a demonstration of the power of mass action. The jailers sought to delay his being bailed out until a mass of blacks gathered outside the jail, whereupon King was hustled out "before I could half get my coat on." That action was a repeat of the massive turnout of blacks to Rosa Parks's trial, which had shocked the authorities[68]

King entered the Montgomery struggle with some illusions about its outcome. He had anticipated that negotiations with the authorities would entail honest discussion and a resolution based on the legitimacy and justice of the sides. The demands blacks raised at first were quite moderate and did not challenge the system of segregation. They asked only for courteous treatment for black passengers; seating on a first-come, first-served basis, with blacks seated in the rear; and employment of black drivers on predominantly black routes. Instead, it became clear that what was involved was a battle for power:

> Feeling that our demands were moderate, I had assumed that they would be granted with little question; I had believed that the privileged would give up their privileges on request. This experience, however, taught me a lesson. I came to see that no one gives up his privileges without strong resistance. I saw further that the underlying purpose of segregation was to oppress and exploit the segregated, not simply to keep them apart.

It was only then that blacks decided that they must demand an end to segregation itself, "because the basic purpose of segregation was to perpetuate injustice and inequality."[69]

King made many contributions to the Montgomery battle and to the black liberation struggle, but central to it all was his approach to the matter as a strategist. King kept his eye on the future, on the outcome, and sought to use all means consistent with his goals. He looked continually to the federal government, recognizing its power and potential to aid his cause; he tried to use whatever pressure he could to get the government to act. Noting the growing anticolonial movement, King linked it to his struggle: "The one thing they are saying around the world is that colonialism and racism must go." He cast the black struggle in terms that made it central to the national interest: "History has thrust upon our generation an indescribably important destiny—to complete a

process of democratization which our nation has developed too long, too slowly."
He reminded the "reactionary senators" and the president that

> the civil rights issue is not an ephemeral, evanescent domestic issue that can be
> kicked about by hypocritical and reactionary politicians; it is rather an eternal
> moral issue which may well determine the destiny of our nation in the ideological
> struggle with communism.[70]

King tried to reach out to broaden the base of the movement, to bring others,
including whites, into it. He felt that those who would fight to retain racism
were a minority, and he looked to winning the support of the white majority.
He reminded Northern whites that no matter where one lived, "the problem of
injustice is his problem; it is his problem because it is America's problem." In
particular, he looked to the "millions of people of good will [in the white south]
whose voices are yet unheard . . . and whose courageous acts are yet unseen."
To these he held out the prospect of joining with the blacks "who yearn for
brotherhood and respect, who want to join hands with their fellow Southerners
to build a freer, happier land for all."[71] Nonviolent action was central to his
strategy:

> It was in this Gandhian emphasis on love and nonviolence that I discovered the
> method for social reform that I had been seeking for so many months. . . . I
> came to feel that this was the only morally and practically sound method open to
> oppressed people in their struggle for freedom.

Its practicality was based on King's perception that in a violent conflict, blacks
must lose: it would "place them as a minority in a position where they confront
a far larger adversary than it is possible to defeat in this form of combat." This
approach enabled King to make an approach to whites on a new basis. No longer
hat-in-hand, King rejected also what he called "corroding hatred" toward whites.
Nonviolent resistance offered the possibility of reconciliation. "We are out to
defeat injustice and not white persons who may be unjust," was how he put it.
King recognized that whites feared blacks, and he feared that with black shackles
removed, blacks would wish to turn the tables and abuse, oppress, and humiliate
the whites. For that reason, he sought to reassure whites. That would make it
much easier to end the system of oppression. "The job of the Negro," he
exhorted, "is to show them [the whites] that they have nothing to fear. . . ."
When the body that became the Southern Christian Leadership Conference first
met, it adopted as its slogan "Not one hair of one head of one white person
shall be harmed in the campaign for integration."[72]

King was not simply trying to avoid the losing bloodbath that he felt would
inevitably follow from an armed conflict. He was seeking to broaden the ranks
of the movement: "By nonviolent resistance, the Negro can also enlist all men
of good will in his struggle for equality. . . . Nonviolent resistance is not aimed
against oppressors but against oppression. Under its banner consciences, not
racial groups are enlisted."[73]

King stressed that if there was suffering to be done, it would be by the blacks, that they were prepared to take whatever the whites could dish out—they still could not be stopped:

> We will match your capacity to inflict suffering with our capacity to endure suffering. . . . We will soon wear you down by our capacity to suffer.[74]

> Rivers of blood may have to flow before we gain our freedom, but it must be our blood.[75]

These expressions were meant to provide a bridge to reassure whites. But they had a deeper meaning, as well. They were meant to encourage a black population that had been terrorized to feel that white terror could no longer stop and intimidate them. No matter what the whites sought to do to them, blacks would stand up, take it, and not be deterred. That was the central focus of King's approach. What was most important about nonviolent direct action was its impact upon the blacks themselves:

> The nonviolent approach does not immediately change the heart of the oppressor. It first does something to the hearts and souls of these committed to it. It gives them new self-respect; it calls up resources of strength and courage that they did not know they had.

> Nonviolent resistance makes it possible for the Negro to remain in the South and struggle for his rights. The Negro's problem will not be solved by running away.

"To struggle for his rights": that was really the most important part of King's message—to motivate blacks to stand up and fight for their rights.

> First, it must be emphasized that nonviolent resistance is not a method for cowards; it does resist. If one uses this method because he is afraid or merely because he lacks the instruments of violence he is not truly nonviolent. This is why Gandhi often said that if cowardice is the only alternative to violence, it is better to fight.

Not to resist was immoral:

> To accept passively an unjust system is to cooperate with that system; thereby the oppressed became as evil as the oppressor. Noncooperation with evil was so much a moral obligation as is cooperation with good.[76]

> The question is beyond rights. We have a duty to perform.[77]

King was calling on black people to come out into the light of day, to stand up for their rights, to reject the whites' efforts to shame and degrade them by defying whites' oppression. Said Bayard Rustin:

> In the black community going to jail had been a badge of dishonor. Martin made gong to jail like receiving a Ph.D . . . and when Martin would say . . . "As sure as Moses got the children of Israel across the Red Sea, we can stick together and win," he had this ability to communicate victory, and to let everybody know he was prepared to pay for victory.[78]

In the Montgomery experience, King came to understand the power of collective action. It was the solidarity and unity that the black community displayed during the boycott that gave individuals the strength and determination to do things that they had not thought themselves capable of doing. King's program made it easier for blacks to act openly together. It was in this light that he opposed the suggestions of militants such as Robert Williams for armed self-defense: "There is more power in socially organized masses on the march than there is in guns in the hands of a few desperate men." He went on: "Our enemies would prefer to deal with a small armed group rather than with a huge, unarmed but resolute mass of people." If the Negro seeks violence "and organizes it, he cannot win," King warned. But, he emphasized, "the greatest danger is that it will fail to attract Negroes to a real collective struggle, and will confuse the large, uncommitted group, which as yet has not supported either side." Instead, "we must be willing to fill up the jail houses of the south." The best defense against the violence of the whites was not armed counterviolence. It was, rather, "to meet every act of violence toward an individual Negro with the facts that there are thousands of others who will present themselves in his place as potential victims. . . . Once more every Negro must be able to cry out with his fore-fathers: 'Before I'll be a slave, I'll be buried in my grave and go home to my Father and be saved.' " Nonviolence and mass participation in the freedom struggle became a central part of King's contribution to the cause of black freedom. Mass action transformed the character of the struggle itself—making it immeasurably stronger, with a much more rapid pace.[79]

King succeeded in casting the black struggle with an ideology that left little to the other side but tyranny and naked racist aggression. The old justifications of "niggers" and "black apes" wore thin in the face of the human courage and dignity displayed by blacks. King was thus well grounded to appeal for "strong and aggressive leadership from the federal government." And the government had little justification for shrinking from the task except its own powerlessness or the complaint that blacks were asking for too much, too fast.[80]

King did not invent all of these ideas. This discussion has not been an effort to delve into their origins. King emerged from Montgomery with a synthesis of these ideas, a remarkable ability to articulate them to both black and white audiences, and the stature that enabled him to command a hearing based on his baptism and conduct under fire in the city of Montgomery.

Montgomery: The New Negro

Martin Luther King Jr. did not simply appear out of a void; nor did the events in Montgomery just "happen." They were a part of a process in which blacks were changing. Nonetheless, the grip of the old system still held strong, and black consciousness and self-images were still very much shaped by it. King was deeply aware of the demeaning impact of the Southern system of race relations on blacks: "Many Negroes came to the point of losing faith in themselves. They came to feel that perhaps they were less than human. The great tragedy of physical slavery was that it led to mental slavery."[81]

In response to this problem, King railed against black degradation, and he encouraged human dignity. That was so not only because the self-degradation was in itself terrible but because it was necessary to eradicate it if blacks were to fight back. For a people who had had to get off the sidewalk when passing whites, looking these same whites in the eye without flinching required a different self-image.

> Acquiescence—while often the easier way—is not the moral way. It is the way of the coward. The Negro cannot win the respect of his oppressor by acquiescing; he merely increases the oppressor's arrogance and contempt. Acquiescence is interpreted as proof of the Negro's inferiority. The Negro cannot win the respect of the white people of the South or the people of the world if he is willing to sell the future of his children for his personal and immediate comfort and safety.[82]

> Our non-violent protest in Montgomery is important because it is demonstrating to the Negro, North and South, that many of the stereotypes he has held about himself and other Negroes are not valid. Montgomery has broken the spell.[83]

Bayard Rustin assessed King's contribution:

> What King delivered to blacks there, far more important than whether they got to ride on the bus, was the absence of fear, the ability to be men. . . . Dr. King had this tremendous facility for giving people the feeling that they could be bigger and stronger and more courageous and more loving than they thought they could be.[84]

King thus played an important role in motivating blacks and enabling them to find the inner strength to stand up and fight. But King was not alone; the Montgomery boycott changed the character of black efforts for social reform. Previous challenges to segregation, led by the NAACP, had relied upon passive support on the part of most blacks. Lawyers and lobbyists did the work *for* people. But in Montgomery, victory required active participation of the whole black community. That meant that blacks in all walks of life had actively to confront the white supremacists. Mass meetings, the sight of others walking, the formation of car pools all showed a measure of strength, unity, and solidarity that many blacks had felt would not be forthcoming. They had thought "I didn't expect Negroes to stick to it." Mass action made blacks participants in the struggle. They came no longer to sit back and watch others do something for them, but became the authors of their own transformation. There was room for everyone to play his or her part, and doing so deepened commitment, as well as pride and self-respect.[85]

Joseph Lowery, one of the founders of the SCLC, recalled, "What the bus thing did was simply more than withholding patronage from the bus; it was restoring a sense of dignity to the patrons, as best expressed by an oft-quoted black woman in Montgomery who said, 'Since I been walking, my feet are tired, but my soul's rested.' " A group of school children walking home in the rain were invited by a bus driver to board an empty bus to get dry. "Us ain't ridin' no bus today! Us boycotting," they responded. College students who participated in the car pool decided not to return to school but to stay and continue their participation in the struggle. That they felt this decision to be more important than their studies, for which they and their parents had worked and sacrificed so much, indicates how deeply people were being touched. Everyone became swept up by glimpsing what the struggle might mean. Yancey Martin, then a freshman in college, recalled:

> Even the people who were not in attendance at the meetings, who are just sorta like people who don't get involved, decided to abide by the rules. . . . I remember Mrs. A. W. West. Her husband was a dentist, very prominent dentist in town. . . . She was really Mrs. Middle Class Black America in Montgomery . . . and when Mrs. West got involved, even the ladies who were not directly involved and directly participating in meetings were supportive.[86]

On several occasions, blacks acted in ways that surprised their white opponents in Montgomery and, perhaps, even themselves. Frequently, blacks were provoked to greater unity and courage by the whites' efforts to intimidate them. The city sent police to escort the buses and to frighten the black population, but blacks still refused to board the buses. When black taxi drivers were harassed for providing rides at low rates, blacks responded by forming a volunteer car pool. This act, more than any other but the boycott itself, created a unified black population. Middle-class blacks who never rode the bus now had a tangible way of joining the struggle, by offering rides in their cars, and many did so. Similarly, when King was arrested two hours before a mass meeting, so many showed up in response that seven meetings had to be held in place of just one.[87]

This movement was, of necessity, democratic. It did not seek to maintain established hierarchical relations; it sought to overturn them. At its meetings, decisions were made. The leadership had to be scrupulously careful not to exceed the bounds of its new authority, since the success of proposals required mass community involvement, and participation was voluntary. Consequently, the flow of influence between leader and mass was very much a two-way street. This two-way communication was reinforced because the new black leadership had to win its authority against the established leadership. Even King, appointed as leader of the Montgomery Improvement Association, was not always looked to at first as the spokesman for the boycott.

The oft-besieged black population was forced into a solidarity that transcended class and status lines and helped to forge a black consciousness. The black movement of the 1950s was very much a product of the whole black community. It profoundly affected both the organization and the individuals in the black movement. There was a great deal of opportunity, indeed a desperate need, for individuals to be creative, to develop a whole range of skills, to think through and practice strategy, to become orators. All of these are commonly associated with significant social movements, which must and do tap human potential that under "normal" conditions lies unused and therefore unknown. Because of the character of the activities in which they were involved, the black population changed and grew.

When the struggle was already all but over, the Ku Klux Klan organized a motorcade through the black community. King and Rustin planned the response: "Tell everybody to put on their Sunday clothes, stand on their steps, and when the Ku Kluxers come, applaud them." They did so, even though some were frightened, waving at passing cars filled with robed and hooded riders. In a few blocks, the Klan, unable any longer to generate fear, ignominiously turned down a side street and disappeared. Seeing that gave new strength to the population. One night, King reported, "a small boy was seen warming his hands at a burning cross."[88]

At one point in the boycott, a bomb exploded in King's home. A crowd gathered outside, and when one man was told by the police to move, he responded angrily, "You white folks is always pushin' us around. Now you got your .38 and I got mine so let's battle it out." This was no mere back-alley encounter. The man who was challenging the white police, the symbol of oppression to blacks in the South, was giving voice to what many must have felt. That he could utter the words indicated how much many blacks had changed.[89]

The new times had created the New Negro, for as a result of their experiences, they had become new people. Or, rather, they were *becoming* new people, for they had a long journey to travel yet. But they had already changed a great deal; the self-deprecation was being put aside. King quoted a janitor: "We got our head up now, and we won't ever bow down again—no sir—except before God." He noted increased self-respect and respect for others. The old tendency to deprecate other blacks, to feel that they couldn't and wouldn't stand together, was disappearing. In Montgomery the New Negro had taken a big step forward.[90]

These effects of the boycott rippled out far beyond the city of Montgomery. The actions of Montgomery blacks were noted in many cities, and their example inspired others. Direct action to desegregate buses spread to Tallahassee, Birmingham, Mobile, and Atlanta. Blacks in New Orleans decided to boycott the Mardi Gras carnival there to support the efforts in Montgomery and Tallahassee. "It is immoral for Negroes in New Orleans to dance while Negroes in Montgomery walk," they said. In Durham, blacks began an effort to desegregate the schools, and in Greensboro they became more persistent over the same issue. Indicating their desire to avoid such activities in their communities, several cities voluntarily desegregated their bus lines, including Little Rock, Pine Bluff, Fort Smith, and Hot Springs, Arkansas; Charlotte, Greensboro, Durham, and Winston-Salem, North Carolina; Richmond, Norfolk, Portsmouth, Newport News, Petersburgh, Charlottesville, Fredericksburg, Lynchburg, and Roanoke, Virginia; San Antonio, Corpus Christi, and Dallas, Texas; and Knoxville, Tennessee.[91]

In Orangeburg, South Carolina, in a conflict that had begun before the Montgomery bus boycott, whites had retaliated against a black petition for desegregated schools by boycotting and blacklisting the blacks who had signed the petition. The blacks in Orangeburg organized a counterboycott and circulated a list of twenty-three businesses that blacks should avoid; it was effective. The only black college in the state was located in Orangeburg, and the students were an important sector of trade to the local white merchants. When the students joined the boycott, the state legislature passed a law calling for investigation of the college to determine the extent of involvement of the NAACP there. The students and faculty denounced such attempts at intimidation and supported the NAACP. The students went further, demanding that the college administration stop buying from White Citizens' Council businesses. When they were ignored, they burned in effigy the president of the college and the state legislator who had introduced the bill calling for the investigation. The governor responded by threatening to send state police to the campus. The students then went on strike. Within days the governor backed down: police would be available only if they were needed. The outcome was inconclusive, but it was clear that blacks were more determined than ever and had the ability and the will to fight back effectively.[92]

In Tallahassee, black college students played a key role in initiating and organizing a bus boycott. The result of the boycott was a more aroused black community and a more active student body. A study of the impact of the boycott in Tallahassee found that a new leadership had emerged. It refused to approach whites as the old accommodationist leadership had, while the whites refused to negotiate with the new leaders on acceptable terms. Thus, there was really no communication, and confrontation was the only means left open for settling disputes. The authors of the study contended that the change in leadership was permanent, that the old accommodationist leaders would not regain their former eminence. That was so not because of the inherent qualities of the new leaders but "because they adhere vigorously to the *form* of militant leadership which is becoming the trend for Negroes throughout the United States" (emphasis in original). Not content to rest on their laurels, the new leaders "have sought to keep the Negro community of Tallahassee militant and dynamic by continuing weekly meetings of the ICC, the organization formed to promote the bus protest, conducting institutes on nonviolence, taking preliminary steps toward school integration, working to get more Negroes registered and voting. . . ."[93]

In Birmingham, the NAACP was forced by Alabama persecution to close its doors on June 1, 1956. Four days later, the Reverend Fred Shuttlesworth called to order the Alabama Christian Movement for Human Rights, later to become an affiliate of the Southern Christian Leadership Conference.

> The Alabama Christian Movement took up where the N-Double-A-C-P left off. . . . We saw it was going to be a fight to the finish and therefore when we started out, we tried to sit down and talk and to get the whites to voluntarily . . . get these segregation laws off the books. But at that time they refused to talk to us.

They initiated a bus boycott in Birmingham which saw five hundred blacks go to jail, Shuttlesworth's home dynamited, evictions, and firings. They were unable to attain victory then, but their effort helped to prepare them for the struggle yet to come.[94]

Montgomery: A New Leadership

Across the South, a new leadership was emerging based on the new black militancy and on the new impulse toward direct action. Wherever protest took place, there was a substantial change in the leadership. This leadership was not sui generis; it arose out of the one established institution in the black community, the church. The leaders were often black ministers, many of whom were affected by the example of King. Elaine Burgess found a new "radical" leadership emerging in Durham:

> Many are young ministers just out of divinity school—Martin Luther King is their ideal. They want an end to segregation in all areas of life immediately. They are angry young men who prefer boycott and mass demonstration to the slower procedures of arbitration and litigation.[95]

The events that brought these men to prominence were not isolated activities. The Tallahassee bus boycott, begun while Montgomery's was still proceeding, was connected with King, who was becoming a prodigious speaker across the South and the nation. Joseph Lowery, a minister in Mobile, Alabama at the time and already involved in efforts to desegregate the buses there, went to Montgomery in support of the boycott. He soon became part of the network.[96]

King sought not only to win support for the struggle in Montgomery, which he saw as a turning point in the black struggle, but to encourage blacks elsewhere to take similar action. He perceived the importance of leadership and tried continually to create a stratum of leaders who could spur the new movement on. King sought leaders "not in love with money, but in love with justice; leaders not in love with publicity, but in love with humanity; leaders who can subject their particular egos to the greatness of the cause." He demanded of black leaders "a concerted effort . . . to arouse their people from their apathetic indifference. . . ."[97]

This awakening of black militancy was occurring at a time when white racism was becoming increasingly strident. The two were bound together, for every stirring of black hope and impatience brought a new swelling of white racism to defend the imperiled territory of white supremacy. It was where their ground was threatened that the White Citizens' Councils organized. The Montgomery bus boycott had led many whites to join the WCC. And it was during the boycott, in the fall of 1956, that Autherine Lucy had been driven off the University of Alabama campus. The tide of racism was then rising. It was clear that a victory in Montgomery was necessary to permit other such protests to occur. A defeat would have been terribly demoralizing. But a victory in Montgomery was not sufficient; others would be necessary. As Bayard Rustin later wrote:

> In practical terms, this meant that the movement needed a sustaining mechanism that could translate what we had learned during the bus boycott into a broad strategy for protest in the South. At the same time we felt it vital that we maintain the psychological momentum Montgomery had generated.

At a suggestion from the Reverend C. K. Steele, the leader of the Tallahassee boycott, Steele, King, and the Reverend Shuttlesworth (from Birmingham) met. They decided to call for a broader meeting early in 1957. The call was premised on their assessment that "the increasing violence was being carefully planned and organized on the theory that the Negroes would back down when faced with such incidents. Therefore Negroes had no alternative but to extend and intensify this struggle."[98]

This meeting was the first of what became the Southern Christian Leadership Conference. The new organization defined itself around two focal points: non-violent direct action as a means to effect change, and the right to vote. It was organized by a leadership that was different from any the black South had known. King, Steele, Shuttlesworth, and Ralph Abernathy were young men who had attained their stature through open confrontation with the white power structure. They brought together a group of leaders who had been similarly proved, or who intended to proceed by their example. The SCLC thus became the organizational expression of the "New Negro." Its aim was to extend the new militancy and to make room for the new kind of leadership that King and his collaborators represented.

The formation of the SCLC meant that for the first time in American history, Southern blacks were openly organizing to confront the structure of white-ruled society. And for the first time, Southern blacks began openly to provide leadership for blacks in the nation.

The emerging Southern black leadership soon came into conflict not only with the Southern ruling class but with the established black leadership. That was obvious in the struggles in the South between the old accommodationist leadership and the new, more militant leaders. The conflict extended to the older protest leadership, especially the NAACP. This clash was not intentional, and it certainly did not emerge out of personal jealousies. King went out of his way to diffuse it by taking out a personal life membership in the NAACP; the SCLC avoided making itself a membership organization so as not to compete with the NAACP for adherents. The NAACP, for its part, awarded King its Spingarn Freedom Medal, making him the youngest recipient of the prestigious award.[99]

But conflict was unavoidable: it was about policy. The NAACP had carried on the freedom fight for years under the most adverse conditions. It was under the gun in the South at that very time. Its approach had not been to mobilize the black masses, who under earlier conditions could not have been mobilized because of the white terror. The NAACP had been accustomed to lobbying white leaders behind the scenes and to lawsuits that had required the participation of only a few courageous black individuals. Direct action, which include the willingness to break laws, was not in keeping with the NAACP strategy. When bus boycotts were proposed in Miami and St. Petersburg, Florida in the summer of 1956, the NAACP encouraged blacks to obey the law. When King suggested that students "study-in" at white high schools—a tactic that he later successfully adapted in Birmingham—Thurgood Marshall of the NAACP Legal Defense Fund rejected the proposal, stating that it was "neither wise nor heroic to send children to do the work of men."[100]

There was a wide gulf between the two organizations. The SCLC was established out of mass protest, and it envisioned more. It sought to mobilize the black masses, to encourage them to take their destinies in their own hands, to participate in winning their freedom. It sought to inject a note of urgency and impatience into the freedom struggle. "Freedom now!" was the message Martin Luther King, Jr. and the SCLC promulgated.

> We must and we will be free. . . . We do not want freedom fed to us in teaspoons over another 150 years. Under God we were born free. Misguided men robbed of our freedom. We want it back; we would keep it forever. This is not idle chatter, for we know that sacrifice is involved, that brutality will be faced, that savage conduct will need to be endured, that slick trickery will need to be overcome, but we are absolutely prepared for all of this.[101]

> We must speed up the coming of the inevitable.[102]

The new leaders made demands; they did not ask for favors or concessions. And by operating in public, they increased the pressure on themselves to gain a clear and unambiguous victory, unobscured by compromises made behind closed doors. Kenneth Clark noted the problem with the old approach: "Its chief danger is that a primary and understandable concern of civil rights leaders for a posture of respectability might make them more vulnerable to the shrewd psychological exploitation of skillful political leaders."[103] A public, mass movement could not be dealt with in this way. Once matters could no longer be settled quietly and amiably by "influence," the appearance of concessions or agreement with a leader was no longer sufficient, because that agreement would have to be brought back to the "mass." Alfred Sloan, for many years head of General Motors, provided an insight into this process. In 1948 the United Auto Workers and General Motors began closed-door bargaining for the first time. Sloan gave a picture of what the change meant from his point of view:

> In previous years our collective bargaining had come to resemble a public political forum in which the union fed a stream of provocative statements to the press and we felt obliged to answer publicly. The privacy of the negotiations made their tone more realistic from the start.[104]

The Southern white leadership must have longed for the "realism" of the old accommodationist black leaders—but it was disappearing forever.

Toward Black Independence

If these events created a self-confident, though embattled, black population and leadership, their feelings were tempered by disappointment, cynicism, and anger, as the allies to whom blacks had looked demonstrated their unreliability. That was particularly true of the federal government and white liberals.

Blacks had looked to the federal government since the thirties. First the New Deal and later President Truman's concessions had encouraged them. And they had gained much from the federal judiciary. However, the government showed increasing reluctance to act. If the election of 1948 provided the lesson that it was possible for a Democrat to win by courting the black vote and ignoring the white South, it was a lesson that the Democratic candidate, Adlai Stevenson, failed to apply in the 1952 and 1956 elections, as he sought to appease white Southerners. That was why many blacks deserted the party of Roosevelt in 1956 and voted for Eisenhower. Eisenhower, however, did little more.[105]

King and the SCLC were aware of the difficulty of prodding the federal government to act in their favor. King stated at a conference called by the Montgomery Improvement Association two weeks after the boycott victory:

> We must face the appalling fact that we have been betrayed by both the Democratic and Republican parties. The Democrats have betrayed us by capitulating to the whims and caprices of the Southern Dixiecrats. The Republicans have betrayed us by capitulating to the blatant hypocrisy of right-wing reactionary Northerners.[106]

The SCLC sought continually to pressure the federal government to support its struggles. It sent telegrams nine months before Little Rock that urged that President Eisenhower deliver a speech in the South urging Southerners to abide by the Supreme Court decisions as the law of the land, and that Vice-President Nixon tour the South "observing and reporting on the terror to which blacks were subject." The president refused the request; the vice-president ignored it.[107]

When the SCLC leaders met again a month later, they repeated their request to Eisenhower to speak out. "We are confronted with a breakdown of law, order and morality," they warned. "This is a sinister challenge and threat to our government of laws. . . ." They asked the president to call a conference on civil rights and again suggested that Nixon take a "fact-finding trip." When no answer came forth, King approached Roy Wilkins, head of the NAACP, and A. Philip Randolph, leader of the March on Washington movement of the 1940s, to discuss the SCLC's proposal of a pilgrimage to Washington, D.C. On the third anniversary of the *Brown* decision, some 15,000 to 20,000 people, 90 percent black, assembled at the capital "because . . . the Eisenhower Administration was dragging its heels in the matter of voting rights," explained Coretta King. Less than a month later, King and Abernathy met with Vice-President Nixon, but nothing came of that. In his writing and speaking, King continued to stress the necessity of federal government intervention in the increasingly serious struggle in the South.[108]

In June 1958, King, Randolph, Wilkins, and Lester Granger, head of the Urban League, met with the president to discuss what he might do on their behalf. The president responded vaguely and committed himself to nothing. When the group broke up, he said to King, indicating his frame of mind: "Reverend, there are so many problems . . . Lebanon . . . Algeria." So even after the Little Rock confrontation, with the school closing in Little Rock and Virginia yet to come, with the terror operating, with suppression of black voting rights in full swing, there was little the federal government had to offer. King summed up his perceptions of the experience:

> His personal sincerity on the issue was pronounced. . . . However . . . President Eisenhower could not be committed to anything which involved a structural change in the architecture of American society. His conservatism was fixed and rigid, and any evil defacing the nation had to be extracted bit by bit with a tweezer because the surgeon's knife was an instrument too radical to touch his best of all possible societies.[109]

When King complained of "the relatively slow progress being made in ending racial discrimination" and tied that slow progress to "the undue cautiousness of the federal government," he was expressing a growing sentiment. In June 1958, Medgar Evers, leader of the NAACP in Mississippi, wrote the president, requesting that he publicly support compliance with *Brown*. He received a vague reply from the White House staff, which, said Evers's wife, "was no answer at all."[110]

It was not the executive and legislative branches of the government alone that were disappointing in their actions. The judiciary, which had in recent times been the strongest supporter of the black drive for equal rights, now recoiled in response to the aggressive drive of the segregationists. In June 1958, the Supreme Court made a decision that, at the time, was little noticed but came to be very important. The Court upheld Alabama's Pupil Placement Act, which entitled school administrators to place students in schools based on a variety of criteria, including behavior, physical facilities, sociological and psychological factors, and academic background. Race was not formally listed among these, though there was little question that their purpose was to disguise continuing racial discrimination. Complicated and lengthy administrative appeals were required before a plaintiff had the right to seek legal remedies. This law permitted the maintenance of segregation by allowing very minimal token integration. "Tokenism" became the white South's next stand.[111]

Tokenism was an effective stance. By June 1961, Alabama, Georgia, Mississippi, and South Carolina still had no blacks in desegregated schools. Florida, Louisiana, North Carolina, and Virginia had less than .1 percent of their pupils in desegregated schools. Arkansas and Tennessee had less than 1 percent; Texas had 1.2 percent in desegregated schools. After advances in the fall of 1958, progress came virtually to a halt. In Greensboro, North Carolina, where the sit-ins began, token desegregation held the line. A Little Rock school official wrote to an acquaintance in Greensboro: "You North Carolinians have devised one of the cleverest techniques of perpetuating segregation that we have seen." King assessed the disappointing trend the court ruling seemed to portend:

> It raises the prospect of long, slow change without a predictable
> end. . . . This . . . is the danger. Full integration can easily become a distant or
> mythical goal—major integration may be long postponed, and in the quest for
> social calm a compromise firmly implanted in which the real goals are merely
> token integration for a long period to come.[112]

Disappointment was even greater with the white liberals who collapsed before
the onslaught of the Southern establishments. They were silent, or worse. They
ceased urging better conditions for blacks or affirmed their devotion to segregation. They asked blacks to modify their goals, for they were pushing too fast
for the white supremacists, who, said William Faulkner, "will go to any length
and against any odds at this moment to justify and, if necessary defend that
condition [segregation and white supremacy] and its right to it." The truculence
of white supremacy unnerved the moderates and brought them to seek calm the
only way they knew how—by prevailing upon the blacks to return, only temporarily, of course (Faulkner urged the NAACP to "stop now for a moment"),
to the quiet that had prevailed before *Brown* and before Montgomery.[113]

King spoke to this issue and rejected the pleas of white liberals, refusing to
allow them to set the pace of the struggle. He affirmed that blacks would set
their own pace:

> The enlightened white Southerners, who for years have preached gradualism, now
> see that even the slow approach finally has revolutionary implications. This re-
> alization has immobilized the liberals and most of the white church leaders. They
> have no answer for dealing with or absorbing violence. They end in begging for
> retreat, lest things get out of hand and lead to violence.

King alluded to Faulkner's request to "stop now for a moment" and pointed
out in response that "it is hardly a moral act to encourage others patiently to
accept injustice which he himself does not endure." Rather, he asserted: "We
Southern Negroes believe that it is essential to defend the right of equality now.
From this position we will not and cannot retreat."[114]

It was clear that others were feeling the frustration. Louis Lomax expressed
the reaction:

> We . . . had faith in a class of white people . . . who were pillars of the Southern
> community and who appeared to be the power structure of the community. . . . It
> was incredible to a Negro woman who had been a servant in a white home for
> twenty years that her employers would cringe and hide while white trash threw
> bricks at her grandson on his way to school.

Journalist Carl Rowan bitterly characterized the moderate response: " 'When in
doubt do nothing' was rationalizing its way into believing that we would not
face a racial crisis today if only we had thought to do more of nothing sooner."
In Durham, North Carolina, Elaine Burgess caught the trend in one leader's
frustration: "We'll have to keep pushing, pushing, pushing to get what we want."
Daniel Thompson discovered the same sentiments. Speaking of white moderates,
one black leader said: "They have talked a lot but never about the real issue—

segregation. They have agreed with everything the White Citizens' Council advocates except closing schools. I think they are the Negro's worst enemy.'' And another: ''We see them now as they have always been—segregationists, who want us to continue to be satisfied with the crumbs that might fall from their weighty, segregated tables.'' In Memphis blacks were becoming disillusioned with the policy of supporting white liberals, who became increasingly segregationist as the White Citizens' Council pressure was applied.[115]

By the end of the decade, blacks were disabused of their illusions about white liberals and the federal government. These lessons helped to define the course of action blacks would take in the 1960s. More and more, they came to see that they could not rely on anyone to carry their torch for them, and that if others were to act on their behalf, they would have to be pushed into it. In the fall of 1958, Bayard Rustin organized a youth march on Washington for integrated schools, with King's support. Ten thousand attended. Some six months later, another such march brought out twenty-five thousand. In Richmond, Virginia, two thousand participated in a demonstration for integrated schools, the first such in the South.[116]

In Durham, blacks used their voting power in the fall of 1958 to force a proposed industrial education center, which required a bond issue to be passed, to open on a desegregated basis. In 1959 Memphis blacks, constituting 30 percent of the city's registered voters, decided to run their own candidates rather than rely on white liberals. King and Mahalia Jackson were brought in to speak at huge election rallies. Though the blacks lost, they demonstrated real political strength and had begun a move toward political independence.[117]

In Tallahassee, when a black woman student at Florida A & M University was kidnapped and raped by four white youths, students held a mass meeting about this atrocity. National news services were contacted, and the students made the rape an international incident. They forced a trial in which the whites were convicted.[118]

By the end of the decade, blacks, especially students, had begun experimenting with what would become the hallmark of the sixties—direct action. In August 1958, the youth group of the NAACP in Oklahoma City organized a sit-in. This action spread to Enid, Tulsa, and Stillwater, Oklahoma and to Wichita and Kansas City, Kansas. There were sit-ins at Miami department store lunch counters, which included three arrests, and in Nashville just two months before the Greensboro sit-ins, this time without arrests. Neither succeeded. In Louisville the NAACP tried sit-ins in 1959, as did the Charleston, West Virginia and Lexington chapters of CORE, the latter two successfully. And in Atlanta a boycott ended segregated busing in 1959.[119]

By 1960, élan and momentum, which had been broken among the advocates of white supremacy by the defeats in Little Rock and in Virginia, were with the black movement. This momentum was not to leave until the Southern political system was transformed. The stage was now set for the rapid escalation of the pace of struggle that was to begin in Greensboro.

VI

THE SECOND WAVE

Half a decade of black pressure and courage, often exhibited by children who had to face hostile mobs at schoolhouse doors; half a decade of white resistance; and half a decade of federal support for the black struggle all created what amounted to a second wave of the black movement among those who came of age in that period. Teens in the early sixties had a formative experience quite different from that of their predecessors. For these young people, the traditional constraints on blacks had lost their legality and their legitimacy. The emergence of the New Negro provided youth with new role models. They grew up with the sense that they were as good as whites and therefore were entitled to equality. They saw the federal government on their side, and they were not fearful. They refused to abide by the white South's stalling tactics designed to delay implementation of the *Brown* decision into a far distant future.

On February 1, 1960, their action began. Four black college students sat down at the food counter of the local Woolworth's in Greensboro, North Carolina and ordered lunch. When the four were asked to leave, they refused, and though they were denied service, they remained until the store closed. They then returned the next day and for several days thereafter with more participants. Within four days they numbered three hundred, and soon such protests spread across the South. With this "sit-in," they initiated a new phase of the movement, in which younger, even more impatient blacks escalated the struggle. Soon sit-ins, freedom rides, and passive resistance all became well-known characteristics of the movement. The fight for civil rights developed in an intensifying spiral of activity that took in broader and broader layers of people and that challenged more and more of the ideology, customs, and practices of white supremacy.

This second wave of the black movement burst upon the scene with a display of militancy and daring that captured the imagination of many young people. The students soon created their own organization, the Student Nonviolent Coordinating Committee (SNCC), which rapidly displaced the SCLC as the most militant black organization. The militant reputation of SNCC became a point of pride to its members, who continually challenged other black leaders and the nation to come to grips with black oppression in all of its manifestations.

The boldness of these youth proved unsettling to the political world that they entered. Where their allies perceived political considerations, the youth saw injustice and decided it must go, period. They sought consciously to involve the lower-class black population in the black struggle, because they insisted that the liberation of blacks was a task for the broad masses. People, they felt, must have control over their lives and could gain such control only by authoring their own emancipation. The broadened movement and the audacity of the young activists made possible a more effective assault on the bastions of white supremacy. Increasing black anger made it necessary.

The trend put pressure on King, whose leadership came under attack, especially when he suffered defeat in Albany, Georgia. After this defeat, King was forced to demonstrate the ability of nonviolence to bring about change. If he failed, he would lose his base of support and see the black masses abandon nonviolence as the only effective strategy for victory. So confrontation became necessary. It was made more necessary by the lack of will on the part of white allies to insist upon change.

Since the government was a political, not a moral, creature, its support for civil rights was forthcoming only to the extent that moral issues could be made into political imperatives. To attain new legislation, blacks had to win the support of many legislators whose concerns were more particularized than those of the president or the federal judiciary. To overcome the considerable ability of Southern congressmen and senators to block civil rights legislation, the black movement had to make civil rights an issue of national import. It had to enlist the backing of the Northern middle class, thereby expanding the coalition. Blacks did so by exposing Southern brutality to what King called the "light of day," thereby shocking white opinion. Massive confrontations were the means used to create a sense of national crisis.

The site for King's confrontation was the city of Birmingham, Alabama, where he had no choice but to enlist the whole black community. This move began a course of action that King and others had not anticipated. When King appealed to all the members of the black community to participate, they heeded his call, but then they would not be controlled. He had brought into motion the most subdued strata of the population. When they began moving, it was difficult to stop them; they had many of their own scores to settle and would not easily be put aside. One of the ironic results of King's Birmingham campaign was that the great victory for his nonviolent strategy ended in the first of the urban riots: the Birmingham campaign of 1963 began the transition from a movement based in the black middle class, whose goal was civil rights, to one with a much broader base that fought under the slogan of "black power."

As SNCC moved into the heart of the black belt to confront the entrenched source of Southern racism, the young activists faced terrorism on the part of Southern whites and apparent indifference from Washington and the Northern middle class. Within five years, the second wave had transformed both racial politics in America and themselves, as well. As the second half of the sixties began to unfold, blacks were more angry and cynical, proud of themselves for what they had accomplished, and adamant that they would accept no less than their own liberation.

The Second Wave

Political generations can be of short duration; 1960 came only six years after the *Brown* decision, but by that time there was a world of difference in the black population. The "New Negro" had been shaped in the crucible of the fifties. The experiences of this formative period disposed the youths who watched or lived through them to interpret and to respond differently from their predecessors to subsequent events. By 1960, these youths began to emerge as *new* "New Negroes" and began to create a second wave of activism. The protests of the fifties had often been led by young men in their twenties; now it was frequently those in their teens who led the way. They were *able* to do so because they were personally less vulnerable than those older than they: they had no jobs to lose, no homes and families to protect. But the absence of such inhibitions cannot explain why they acted nor why they did so with such alacrity.

What lay behind their action was, in part, the events of the past decade. In school desegregation, young children had borne the brunt of the white mobs. Victories in Montgomery, Little Rock, and elsewhere, as well as the leadership of those who took the risks in the fifties, inspired this new generation. John Lewis recalled the impact that the Montgomery bus boycott had on him:

> Montgomery was only fifty miles away. . . . Seeing Martin Luther King Jr., and the black people of Montgomery organize themselves in such a way that fifty thousand people, for more than a year, walked rather than rode segregated buses had a tremendous impact on me. . . . I think that particular event probably changed the direction of my life more than anything else.[1]

Prior to the sit-ins initiated by four freshmen from Greensboro's Agricultural and Technical School (A & T), the four had rehashed the experiences of Montgomery and Little Rock. These experiences helped to inspire their action: "Before the sit-ins," said one of them, "I felt kinda lousy, like I was really useless. I was ashamed at how those young kids in Little Rock were braving it out. . . ."[2] Like Anne Moody, these youths were hardened by the white attacks they witnessed. They had reflected upon what they had seen, and they were prepared for the harassment they would receive. Joseph Washington of New Orleans, referred to earlier, had been eleven years old when the Little Rock story unfolded. He told psychiatrist Robert Coles he would "never forget if I live to be one hundred. I was walking every inch with those kids." In 1960, when New Orleans began desegregation and experienced serious rioting by whites, Joseph worried about his seven-year-old sister: "I kept on picturing her going through it, and I figured if she did, I'd walk beside her; and just let anyone try anything." When Coles witnessed the treatment endured by Washington, one of the first to desegregate the high school in New Orleans, he frankly wondered, "I don't know how you can take that sort of treatment; I really don't." Coles recorded Washington's response:

> You don't know how I can take it because you haven't ever *had* to take it. You see, when I grew up I had to learn to expect that kind of treatment; and I got it,

so many times I hate to remember and count them. Well, now I'm getting it again, but it's sweet pain this time, because whatever they may say to me or however they try to hurt me, I know that just by sticking it out I'm going to help end the whole system of segregation; and that can make you go through anything. Yes, when they get to swearing and start calling me "nigger" I think of the progress we're making, I'm making, every minute; then I know I can take even worse than we had tonight.[3]

As Washington's comment indicates, many of these youth spent much of their time in the fifties thinking long and hard about the issues that so deeply affected them. By the start of the new decade, they were prepared to act. The actions of this second wave were motivated by anger, pride, and a sense of power, as well as by the frustrating sense that the segregationists, who had been defeated in their efforts at massive resistance, were still successfully holding back integration and any change in black status. The resisters employed tokenism where deseg- regation was legally mandated; they ignored the law where they were left alone to do so; they never voluntarily desegregated anything. This approach meant that by 1960, despite the *Brown* decision and others following it, little progress had been made. Every change required a new lawsuit, or a series of them. It had become apparent to many that past efforts were simply insufficient. Thus, the Greensboro sit-in was not an isolated or surprising move, except to whites: it had been long prepared, and it emerged out of a Southern black youth that was eager to take some dramatic action. Said Cleveland Sellers.

I spent many hours thinking about "the problem." I'd become particularly aware of my environment: the differences between the black and white sides of town, the numerous little indignities that blacks had to endure just to survive from day to day, the awesome poverty suffered by the vast majority of Southern blacks. My thoughts always culminated with the same vow: "I've gotta help do something about this shit!"[4]

After a stint in the Air Force, James Meredith, who was to become the first black to attend the University of Mississippi, returned to his home state in 1960, intending to fight a war against the Southern system. "My objective in this war was total victory: victory over discrimination, oppression, the unequal application of the law, and, most of all, over 'white Supremacy' and all of its manifesta- tions."[5]

The sit-in tactic appeared to solve the problem of how to overcome the frus- trations engendered by the stalling tactics of the segregationists. It was one that students themselves could carry out. Cleveland Sellers told of his reaction:

When reporters asked them [the four who began the first sit-in at Greensboro] "How long have you been planning this?" they replied, "All our lives!" I knew exactly what they meant. . . . My identification with the demonstrating students was immediately personal.[6]

Ebony magazine reporter Ben Bagdikian spoke to many civil rights youth activists in the South in 1962. He noted that while most older black Americans dated the changes in their conditions back to the 1954 *Brown* decision,

> not one Negro student in over a hundred interviewed had any vivid personal recollection of that day. They all regard it as a failure. But almost every student could remember precisely where he was and what time of day it was when he first heard of the event that galvanized them all and launched the new Negro generation into contemporary history: the sit-in at Greensboro.[7]

According to Julian Bond, one of the original members of SNCC:

> Some of these people were active in their high school NAACP, and when they got to college, they were almost in place holding, and they probably didn't know they were waiting, but they were poised and ready to jump in. When the Greensboro sit-ins happened in early 1960, that was it. It wasn't that much of a conscious decision of what to do. Greensboro became the model, almost a blueprint.[8]

The students were galvanized. They felt compelled to follow the "blueprint." John Lewis: "I had the feeling that we was involved in something like a crusade in a sense. *It was a sense of duty, you had an obligation to do it.* . . . ." A student who was expelled from Alabama State University in Montgomery for participating in a sit-in said, "When we discovered that the kids in Greensboro had made a move, *we felt that we were obligated* to show our hand"[9] (emphasis added).

The sense of moral and real victory over the racist restrictions was a lure that could not be ignored. In Greensboro, according to Franklin McCain, one of the original four,

> we actually got to the point where we had people going down in shifts. . . . It got to the point wherein we took all the seats in the restaurant. . . . I think at the height of the sit-in movement in Greensboro, we must have had at least, oh, ten or fifteen thousand people downtown who wanted to sit-in, but obviously there weren't that many chairs in downtown Greensboro for people to sit-in. . . . It spread to places like the shopping centers, the drugstores in the shopping centers, the drive-ins. . . .[10]

It was not long before the Greensboro "blueprint" was applied to other areas. A week after the first sit-in in Greensboro, there were sit-ins in Durham and Winston-Salem, North Carolina. Days later Virginia was hit, then South Carolina. At first the movement apparently spread along A & T's basketball circuit, but it soon flowed beyond those bounds. By the end of February, thirty-two cities in North Carolina, South Carolina, Virginia, Tennessee, Florida, Maryland, Kentucky, and Alabama had experienced sit-ins and other demonstrations protesting racial restrictions. By the end of March another forty-one cities had been subject to these demonstrations, and Georgia, Texas, Louisiana, and Arkansas were added to the list of states struck. In April even Mississippi joined. Students were eagerly drawn in by the drama they saw enacted before them. Support for these activities among black students was nearly universal.[11]

Their effort appears to have been partly sustained by their optimistic assessment of the balance of forces. One activist got on a bus one day and, without having planned it in advance, sat down in front. When he was asked to move, he refused and was arrested. That was the start of his involvement. When it began, he told Robert Coles, he was

> optimistic, that's what I was, plain optimistic. I thought we'd demonstrate and then they'd fold up before us. But it's been tougher than I ever dreamed . . . you know you learn slowly how this country runs and how it's not so easy to get what you want if you're colored. . . . I suppose if I'd known that when I first joined I never would have done it.[12]

This failure to understand the big picture, the structure of power that the civil rights movement was confronting, was widespread among movement participants. In a survey carried out among 827 students in black colleges in Greensboro and Raleigh, North Carolina in May of 1960, the respondents were asked what they thought was the primary reason for white opposition to their goals. Only one-tenth chose the response "They hate Negroes," and only 6.5 percent said "They are protecting economic interests." The students were prone to assume "better" motives among their white opponents. Those most active in the movement were least likely to attribute white opposition to hatred of blacks. Another survey found that student activists tended to be those who underestimated white opposition, while those who did not tended to remain "totally inactive."[13]

In part, their optimism was a product of the still-predominant view that even if Southern whites remained intransigent, their Northern counterparts and the federal government were on the side of blacks and, once made aware of the actual situation, would support them. Julian Bond recalled what he termed the "early naivete of the movement":

> We were operating on the theory that here was a problem, you expose it to the world, the world says "How horrible!" and moves to correct it. . . . We thought there was even a hidden reservoir of support among white Southerners. . . . And we thought that the Kennedy Administration was on our side and that, again, all you had to do was put your case before them and they would straighten out what was wrong.[14]

Perhaps it was because of that naivete that they reacted so strongly once they became disabused of their illusions.

All of their demonstrations took place in cities, especially in larger cities, and tended to steer clear of the black belt, where resistance was strongest. Away from the black belt, threats and intimidation directed to these black demonstrators were commonly ignored. The president of the student body in Columbia, South Carolina, when warned that sit-ins that he and others organized would result in expulsions, responded that "if expulsion is the price of freedom" he was "willing to pay it." A high-school student who had been expelled from school and jailed for six months and then released only on condition that she not return to her home county, all because of her participation in a sit-in, asserted nonetheless that she would continue her protest activities.[15]

Indeed, far from being stopped by the intimidation, the students sometimes appeared to thrive on it. By Saturday of the first week, the Greensboro demonstrators were met by white gang members who sought to stop them. The A & T football team led the march downtown. " 'Who do you think you are?'' demanded the whites. "We the union army,'' responded the football players with an élan that comes through plainly even in print. The demonstration proceeded. In Raleigh, North Carolina the following week, when one student was arrested others replaced him, and when the news spread, a new group arrived, who also demanded to be arrested.[16]

The experiences of these youth in their demonstrations brought about the feelings of self-affirmation that tended to accompany confrontations with white power. Franklin McCain remembered that after sitting at the counter the first day, "We had the confidence of a Mack truck. . . . I probably felt better that day than I've ever felt in my life. I felt as though I had gained my manhood . . . and not only gained it, but developed a lot of respect for it.'' Said another: "I just felt that I had powers within me, a super-human strength that would come forward. I don't know how the crusaders felt, but [I got] a heightened sense of duty . . . once things really started to go.'' And a third:

> I felt entirely different about myself. . . . Before the sit-ins, I felt kinda lousy, like I was really useless. I was ashamed at how those young kids in Little Rock were braving it out . . . at last, we felt we had *done* something, not just talk about things, like in those bull sessions.

John Lewis summed up what many must have felt:

> Being involved tended to free you. You saw segregation, you saw discrimination, and you had to solve the problem, but you saw yourself also as the free man, as the free agent, able to act.[17]

The Student Nonviolent Coordinating Committee

Within weeks of the Greensboro sit-in, black students had burst upon the scene and established a presence within the political landscape. White officials did not know how to respond to them. They tried at first to ignore the students on the theory that they would grow apathetic and give up, but their numbers increased; they tried arresting them, but their numbers still increased. The students slid around the barriers erected to withhold previous challenges to segregation by refusing to accept the old rules of the game, and they acted in blatant disregard of white authority. Perhaps, having learned a lesson from the leaders of massive resistance, they set out deliberately to defy the law. They thus represented a new political trend one more militant, more daring, and more uncompromising than had so far appeared.

By mid-April 1960, students who had been active in the demonstrations called a meeting to form the Student Nonviolent Coordinating Committee. The meeting was organized by the SCLC, and it was addressed by King, who called upon the students to create an organization of volunteers who would be prepared to go to jail and to carry the struggle into all parts of the South. King's call coincided with the developing sentiments of the students involved, who would do much of what he suggested. Yet, the students had already begun to distance themselves from him, and they were openly critical of the NAACP, thereby establishing the precedent for what would become a new and more intense stage of conflict and competition between the civil rights organizations, and between the generations, for leadership of the black movement.[18]

SNCC consolidated and gave organizational form to the new trend of activism and militance represented by the black student activities. Whereas heretofore Martin Luther King and the Southern Christian Leadership Conference had constituted the left pole in the black movement in the South, now King stood in the middle. The creation of SNCC assured the existence of an organizational vehicle to spread and extend the politics of the second wave. With its formation, SNCC completed the organizational cast of characters in the struggle for civil rights in the South.

Idealistic and committed, SNCC would soon be referred to as the "shock troops of the revolution." Its members became the most militant activists of their time. By their refusal to compromise or to be intimidated and by their insistence on tackling even the most entrenched areas of the black belt, they raised the level of intensity of the movement. Charles McDew, who became chairman of the new organization in the fall of 1960, promised that the student movement would continue "until every vestige of racial segregation and discrimination are erased from the face of the earth."[19]

It became a point of pride for many that SNCC was known as the most militant organization. Its leaders and members would, at times, eagerly rush to be arrested. Sometimes they did so in competition with the Northern-based Congress of Racial Equality (CORE), which was also often bold and innovative. They frequently chose to expose themselves to danger that others avoided. Amzie Moore of Cleveland, Mississippi became dissatisfied with the legalistic approach of the NAACP, of which he was a local leader, and he invited SNCC to help with voter registration. Moore said of them:

> SNCC was an organization of strong, intelligent, young people who had no fear of death and certainly did not hesitate to get about the business for which they came here. . . . They met anywhere, at any time. . . . I found that SNCC was for business, live or die, sink or swim, survive or perish. They were moving, and nobody seemed to worry about whether he was gonna live or die.[20]

SNCC did go anywhere; its people took serious risks, accepted beatings and the threat of long-term imprisonment, and continued on their course. They went into the black belt in Mississippi and Alabama, where they had no protection but what they and their supporters could muster. Some were murdered; others were the object of murder attempts.

This experience had an impact on the political views of this growing stratum; it accentuated a tendency that had existed from the first: to view moral courage, rather than political strategy, as the quality most required of leadership. Staughton Lynd and Vincent Harding took note of this tendency in their discussion of the efforts to fill the jails in opposition to segregation in Albany Georgia: "One of the most subtle problems of the whole jail-going movement is the constant temptation to measure a man's courage and worth by the number of times he has gone to jail."[21]

This attitude made many young activists suspicious of the established black leaders, who were frequently too cautious for them, and who tended to avoid situations that would subject them to arrest. In order to gain a hearing with the second-wave youth, one had to be willing to put his or her body "on the line." These activists were not seeking personal glory. Rather, they believed that if people were to be free, they must free themselves, and that therefore they had to be involved in achieving that freedom. Cleveland Sellers explained the SNCC method:

> With SNCC projects . . . emphasis was placed on development of grass roots organizations headed by local people. We called it participatory democracy: local people working to develop the power to control the significant events that affected their lives. Working, eating, sleeping, worshipping and organizing among the people—for years, if necessary—that was the SNCC way.[22]

This approach led them to emphasize a long-term commitment to a project, and to the people with whom they worked. They felt it necessary to win the confidence of these people by becoming part of their community. Lawrence Guyot:

> You learned very quickly that if you got that door slammed in your face, it just takes a day or two of talking to people to find out whose face the door won't be slammed in. . . . There are some towns you go into, and you find a man who has none of the characteristics of leadership as we identify them. He is the leader [of the black community] and has been and is unquestioned, and mess with him wrong—forget it. Don't speed him up too much, dialogue with him, find out what his tempo is, what his objectives are. Then you might alter them a little bit, but don't, don't, don't—don't be careful. We learned over and over again how to find potential leadership, how to groom it, and the most painful lesson for some of us was how to let it go once you've set it into motion. . . . You don't alter the basic format that you walk into. Let's say you're riding past a picnic, and people are cuttin' watermelons. You don't immediately go and say, "Stop the watermelon cuttin', and let's talk about voter registration." You cut some watermelons, or you help somebody else serve 'em.

Amzie Moore testified to the effectiveness of these methods:

> One great thing I think was introduced in the South with reference to SNCC's tactics was the business of organizing leadership. If 'leven people went to jail this evening who the power structure considered leaders, tomorrow morning you had 'leven more out there. And the next morning 'leven more.

And so did Fannie Lou Hamer, a Mississippi sharecropper who became a leader of the movement:

> These kids . . . treated us like we were special and we loved 'em. . . . We didn't
> feel uneasy about our language: might not be right or something. We just felt like
> we could talk to 'em. We trusted 'em. . . .[23]

The SNCC cadre often acted as a leavening agent, coaxing out others and imparting confidence to them, encouraging them to take some risks. The combination of the brave example set by SNCC and the evidence of the gains blacks were winning helped to bring more people into the movement. In one case a young man went to a meeting after the murder of a civil rights worker. He signed up:

> How it got to me . . . was hearing a colored boy my age speaking better than any
> white man I ever heard. I told myself that's no boy, he's a man, and since he's
> about your age, you can be just like him, which after a while I did become.[24]

SNCC Challenges Leaders

The student activists' revolt, by directly challenging segregationist practices and the traditional slow and tedious ways of dealing with them, also challenged the established black leaders. It was not uncommon for these leaders to feel that the brash youth were acting inappropriately. "You young people are trying to go too fast. If you'll just be patient, the courts will decide these matters," NAACP officials told students in Rock Hill, South Carolina. In Greensboro, black professionals, especially ministers and doctors, were slow to support the students. Teachers and college administrators, on public and therefore white-controlled payrolls, were often silent—or, worse, acted to punish their students. There were still occasions when black leaders presented active opposition to the sit-ins. One black newspaper, the *Charlotte Post*, claimed that sit-ins only increased tensions and produced no benefits. In Atlanta, the black leadership—a powerful and well-entrenched group, including Martin Luther King, Sr. ("Daddy" King)—negotiated a settlement after students had initiated sit-ins and a buying boycott. The agreement called for desegregation to begin within ten months and for all movement activities to cease immediately. This deal, made by "leaders" who had no mandate from the troops, was greeted by anger on the part of the students, who booed Daddy King when he presented it. Some referred to it as a "sell-out by the black middle class leadership of Atlanta." Louis Lomax summed up the situation: "I found that established leaders don't have the same fire in their stomachs that the students and the rallying Negro masses have."[25]

The student movement entailed, as Lomax and others pointed out, a challenge to the black leadership, as well as to segregation itself. "If we leave it to the adults, nothing will become of it," was how one eighteen-year-old freshman expressed a widely held sentiment. This challenge was more profound than that of the fifties, because it was far broader and more widespread, and it was deeper, demanding more change. Even with the changes that had already taken place in black leadership, those who spoke for the black masses still tended to enjoy a curiously comfortable status. They negotiated with whites and were in turn anointed as leaders by whites. The students, by bypassing this group and its procedures, threatened to displace it.[26]

Yet, the NAACP and local organizations and leaders supported the students, with money, with legal help, with advice. One of the reasons the students got this support from leaders was the widespread backing often accorded the youth by an enthusiastic black population. In Greensboro, when the sit-ins were not sufficient to compel desegregation, the black community launched an economic boycott against stores that refused to serve blacks. Like the Montgomery bus boycott, this move brought the community together. Soon black businessmen pledged bail money for the demonstrators. Some farmers even offered to put up their land. Ministers helped out—some eagerly, others after being pressured by their congregations. Even more conservative figures, such as Warmouth Gibbs, the president of A & T College, refused to interfere with the students. (Gibbs had been chosen for this position because of his manifest acceptance of white supremacy. He had denied the right to speak on campus in the late fifties to Martin Luther King and to Thurgood Marshall, the general counsel of the NAACP Legal Defense Fund.[27]) John Constable, the director of information of the Southern Regional Council, found substantial community support for the students' efforts in the six North Carolina cities of Charlotte, Raleigh, Durham, Greensboro, High Point, and Winston-Salem and in Rock Hill, South Carolina. "My idea is this," said one woman. "We older people didn't have the guts to do it, but the young people didn't care even if they died." "It's the greatest!" exclaimed another. "I tell you, they have courage I never dreamed of."[28]

Sometimes this support was hard-won. Often the first form it took was a generational conflict. The young would wish to get involved; their parents tried to hold them back out of fear for themselves and for their offspring. The children would insist, and their parents would acquiesce. The adults, once won over, could become militant. In Greensboro, black adults, enraged by the jail conditions to which they saw students subjected, marched several hundred strong through downtown.

The challenge to authority extended beyond the black community. In Atlanta, the SNCC people decided very early to inject themselves into national politics and to challenge King in a friendly but insistent way. In doing so, they had a national impact. The sit-ins, and the heightened sense of urgency that they had created, propelled black concerns into the 1960 presidential campaign. Not since 1948 had an election been so close. This time, because of continued migration to the North, the black vote was of greater significance than ever. Democrat Adlai Stevenson had rejected Truman's strategy and instead wooed the white South. Kennedy, however, had promised to "wipe out discrimination with the stroke of a pen," referring to the power of presidential orders, thereby indicating that he was returning to the lessons of the Truman campaign. And he had "stated categorically" that the civil rights issue was "of overwhelming moral significance to him and if elected President he would use the full prestige and weight of his office to completely eliminate second-class citizenship in America."[29] But he had avoided a direct commitment. SNCC activists sought to use King to force Kennedy to take some overt act.

Their effort began with their plan to sit-in at Rich's department store, the largest and poshest retail business in Atlanta. Their theory was that if Rich's gave in, "all we have to do is just kind of whisper to the others." Julian Bond explained their plan. They

> decided that in order to dramatize this thing, we really ought to get Martin King arrested, if we could. So we called him and asked him would he meet us . . . at Rich's and go to jail with us. . . . We wanted to stage the thing in the middle of October because we wanted to influence . . . the presidential election of 1960. . . . We thought that with Dr. King being involved in it, that would create enough of a national uproar in the black community and we would really see where these guys stand.

Not wishing to cause trouble for Kennedy, King urged that they delay until after the election. When they refused, he turned down the invitation, having scheduled a meeting that day with Kennedy. Bond continued to press him: "Well Martin, you've got to go to jail. You are the spiritual leader of the Movement, and you were born in Atlanta, Georgia, and I think it might add tremendous impetus if you would go." Kennedy canceled the meeting and left King with little choice but to join the sit-in. King was arrested with the others and then sentenced to four months' hard labor on the pretext that he had violated the terms of probation for his conviction on a previous charge of driving without a license. This situation forced Kennedy to commit himself. He phoned Mrs. King to express his concern about her husband and helped to secure King's release.[30]

In response to Kennedy's call and the release of his son, Martin Luther King, Sr. changed his traditional Republican position and strongly endorsed Kennedy. Kennedy supporters got the word of this endorsement out to thousands of black churchgoers in the North just before the election, and it was clear that their turnout carried the election for Kennedy in the key Northern states. This demonstration of black power, together with Kennedy's apparent support for justice for blacks, helped to create new black self-confidence, which in turn hastened the pace of events. It also illustrated the ability of the youth of the second wave to have a significant influence on events.

The Second Wave in Combat: The Growth of Radicalism

The outlook of SNCC and the generation out of which it had been created were deeply affected by these developments: the sit-ins and the role blacks played in the election made a new escalation probable. On February 1, 1961, one year after the first sit-in, James Farmer, the newly appointed national director of CORE, announced plans for a "Freedom Ride." It would be an integrated bus ride that would begin in the North and proceed through the Southern states. It would test a December 1960 Supreme Court ruling that prohibited segregation in bus terminal accommodations—washrooms, cafeterias, waiting rooms—that were used for interstate travel. The travelers would ride together, eat together, and use the white-only restrooms.

This action emerged out of the growing impatience of the black movement. CORE was taking advantage of the new political climate to test the new president's convictions. More, the Freedom Ride represented the sense of the militant wing of the movement that confrontation was necessary to defeat Southern racism. "Our intention," Farmer stated, "was to provoke the Southern authorities into arresting us and thereby prod the Justice Department into enforcing the law of the land." They aimed at filling the jails, "as Gandhi had," said Farmer.[31]

The confrontation was not first and foremost with the federal government but with local authorities, and with mobs. However, movement hostility toward the federal government developed because of its perceived failure to protect the riders adequately. The buses went through Virginia and North Carolina without serious incident. In South Carolina there were beatings and arrests, while in Georgia all was quiet. But in Alabama, one bus was attacked and burned; riders of the other bus were seriously beaten, and the ride was halted. When it looked as though CORE would stop the ride because of these attacks, SNCC resumed the course and refused to give it up. The group was attacked and besieged in Montgomery, where it was forced to spend the night in a church, surrounded by a mob and protected by United States marshals. Now SNCC, SCLC, and CORE formed a joint committee, and the rides continued into Mississippi, where arrests spurred efforts to send in masses in order to "fill the jails." More than 360 were arrested that summer, and the conditions they suffered in the Mississippi jails shocked some. That was SNCC's first encounter with the Deep South. A changed body of activists came out of this episode in the movement. Clayborne Carson wrote in his history of SNCC:

> The rides . . . contributed to the development of a self-consciously radical student movement prepared to direct its militancy toward other concerns. The participants . . . suddenly became aware of their collective ability to provoke a crisis that would attract international publicity and compel federal intervention.[32]

Their experience made them increasingly angry and restive. The government had acted only when faced with terrible violence. How, then, to pressure it; how much could it be trusted? Thus, when the Kennedys pushed for voter registration as an alternative to the confrontationist approach, many militants reacted with suspicion. Although the promise of a voter registration campaign was to alter the balance of power in the South, wasn't it being proposed simply as an effort to avoid the demonstrations that put embarrassing pressure on the government? This attitude hardened over time as the activists observed the Kennedy ad-

ministration vacillate and refuse to commit itself to decisive action. Kennedy
had won a honeymoon with the black population with his verbal support of civil
rights. But he had also raised hopes that ultimately created disappointment and
disillusionment. For a long time after the election, the federal government did
little to encourage civil rights proponents. Kennedy did not carry out his promised
"stroke of a pen." Instead, he attempted on more than one occasion to halt the
freedom rides. When he did act to support civil rights activists, it was in a
situation such as Montgomery in 1961, when the freedom riders and their supporters were literally besieged. King came to feel that Kennedy was lacking the
"moral passion" to do something decisive about civil rights. At one point the
president attempted to persuade King to encourage the freedom riders to accept
bail; King refused and promised instead to keep up the pressure.[33]

The physical attacks upon the nonviolent freedom riders in 1961 shocked
Northern opinion and impelled the Kennedy administration to act to protect them
by mobilizing the National Guard and by pressuring state officials. In one case
the president pressured state troopers to escort a bus through Alabama. This
experience confirmed the civil rights activists in their view that confrontation
and crisis were necessary to compel government action.

When the Kennedys encouraged SNCC to undertake a voter registration campaign, many felt that they had also been offered protection from the violence
such a campaign would be likely to provoke. Robert Moses, who led this campaign, wrote to the Justice Department inquiring about the likely response if the
campaign encountered lawlessness. He was promised that "the government
would vigorously enforce federal statutes forbidding the use of intimidation
threats, and coercion against voter aspirants." Reality, however, was jarring.
Activists frequently called on the Justice Department but received little succor;
they took note of the close relations between the FBI, many of whom were
Southerners, and the local law-enforcement officials. They watched federal marshals calmly take notes as the segregationists openly broke laws and attacked
them.[34]

Such perceptions, at a time when to be in SNCC and in the South meant the
probability of jail and beatings and the possibility of murder, could not help but
take their toll. "Official statements from Washington are usually evasive concerning allegations of police brutality," wrote one white SNCC member.

> A symptom of the attitude of the federal government toward civil rights is Ken-
> nedy's appointment of a judge to the Southwest Georgia district court who had
> consistently rendered unfavorable decisions in cases involving racial issues. His
> views on race relations were well-known before his appointment.[35]

The student activists were becoming aware that their allies were not as deeply
committed to change as they themselves were and that the government was guided
by considerations other than morality or even legality.

The government was not the only target of the students' ire. The freedom
rides had begun what was to be a long and increasingly bitter disillusionment

with King, who had refused to join the rides. The reason, he said, was that he was on probation and another arrest might have landed him a long jail term at a time when his presence was needed to raise money and to give direction to the movement. "I would rather have heard King say, 'I'm scared—that's why I'm not going.' I would have had greater respect for him if he said that," responded one of the riders.[36] Such a remark was symptomatic of the developing tensions.

More fundamental were the political differences that separated King from the second wave. As SNCC and the youth it represented grew increasingly radical and alienated from the older, more conservative black leadership, and from the federal government, King attempted to bridge the gap. He sought united black pressure to lead the civil rights coalition. And he continued his strategic approach to that coalition, insisting that the federal government and the Democratic party were a real and legitimate, and, more important, a necessary, part of the effort to bring about civil rights for blacks in the South. As a result, King increasingly became a centrist, speaking to all parts of the coalition, trying to bridge gulfs that were widening. At one point he recommended a "temporary lull" in the freedom rides, but without effect. When he became an early supporter of the voter registration project, some of those in SNCC who viewed the proposal with suspicion felt that he had been coopted by the Kennedys.[37]

SNCC activists worked with Southern blacks and through this process sought to see the world through their eyes. These youths worked for the enhancement of black self-activity and began to see their goal as developing the power, initiative, and self-confidence of the people with whom they worked. They frequently succeeded in developing local people as leaders of the movement.

SNCC people had little tolerance for King's stance in the face of the enormous task of ending black second-class citizenship and the brutal resistance that activists faced. They were hostile to King's strategy of focusing national attention on a particular city in order to expose a concrete manifestation of the general phenomenon of Southern racism to gain support for federal intervention. They felt that King's efforts were counterproductive, because when the demonstrations were over he would depart, leaving no existing organization or overturning what had previously been built. It was true that King's eye was focused primarily upon the national impact of his efforts; but his successes encouraged and facilitated local black organization and challenges to white authority.

SNCC activists were eager to go into areas of the black belt where no others dared enter. Andrew Young, one of King's collaborators, recalled: "We tried to warn SNCC. We were all Southerners and we knew the depth of depravity of Southern racism. We knew better than to try to take on Mississippi."[38] SNCC preferred to challenge Southern racism at its strongest point, in order to dispose of it entirely, and to make sure that no black brethren would continue to be subjected to it. In adopting this stance, SNCC challenged the black-belt elite on its own turf. Its members and supporters who tried to carry out these policies were subject to brutalization. Their audacity succeeded in making the political transformation more far-reaching than it otherwise would have been. SNCC played an important role in shaping the consciousness and perceptions of the black population, and thus in structuring the reality within which King and other black leaders had to function.

The conflict between SNCC and King's approach was brought out in 1962 in Albany, Georgia. SNCC had begun demonstrations there and had succeeded in creating a broad movement aimed at desegregating all public facilities. But the city refused to make concessions. William Anderson, a black osteopath who was president of the coalition that had been created to lead the effort, invited King to join. Originally, King had intended not to become deeply involved, but he soon took over leadership. Faced with Albany's refusal to grant concessions, King told his listeners not to limit their hopes to the local arena but to take their case before the court of world opinion. He attempted to do just that, with mass marches and defiance of local laws. Again and again, large numbers of people were arrested—several hundred all told. But in the end, more than six months of King's involvement produced no fruit. The police chief, Laurie Pritchet, refused to be provoked. Coretta King wrote of Pritchett:

> He would allow the protesters to demonstrate up to a point. Then he would say, "Now we're going to break this up. If you don't disperse, you'll be arrested." Often they would refuse to disperse, and would drop on their knees and pray. Chief Pritchett would bow his head with them while they prayed. Then of course, he would arrest them and the people would go to jail singing.[39]

No provocation meant little publicity, which produced little concern up North and therefore no outside intervention. The upshot of it all was a humiliating defeat for King, which heightened the tensions between him and the SCLC and SNCC. SNCC workers questioned the utility of nonviolence as a principle rather than a tactic. They were becoming increasingly alienated from King. Their alienation was expressed in the new title they bestowed upon him— "De Lawd."

A militant black youth movement arose as part of the process of building a black movement to confront the Southern power structure. These youth soon developed their own independent stance and began to pressure King and the movement that had given birth to their political selves to escalate tactics. By the end of 1962, this pressure came not only from SNCC but also from the increasingly wide layers of the black population who were being mobilized by all of these confrontations. Albany was one of the first cases in which masses of people became actively involved in protest demonstrations. That happened for a number of reasons. The example of the defiant black students, together with their victories, gave heart to many. Extending the goals of the demonstrations and increasing impatience not only with segregation but also with the demeaning status it represented for blacks provided people with motivation to participate. The dynamic was such that for black leaders to retain their leadership, they would have to devise programs and strategies that would give expression to this increasing militancy.

The Changing Social Base of the Civil Rights Movement

Part of what lay behind the changing political character of the movement was its changing social composition. As it went through its successive phases, it became broader in character, taking in more and more people of an increasingly diverse character. The class and status base of the civil rights movement broadened, and as it broadened both the issues that were raised and the manner in which they were posed changed.

The demands of the civil rights movement have often been called middle-class demands. Equal access to restaurants and theaters, to department stores and hotels, to housing and hospitals could be utilized only by those who had the wherewithal to pay for them, or who expected to have it. In that sense, these demands were middle-class, and most blacks did not fit in that category and therefore could not directly benefit from them. Nonetheless, in the early days of the civil rights movement there was widespread support for these battles, because they were legitimately seen to benefit everyone. The common denominator was human dignity.

The first and most significant of these demands was for desegregated education. That was a very important issue, which encompassed several concerns. Desegregating education generally affirmed black dignity; it also offered opportunities for black advancement. White schools were almost invariably better than those for blacks, and they had a greater orientation to higher education. Given the importance of the schools in preparing students for upper-level occupations, opening the schools to blacks was central to their hopes for social mobility.

There is a widespread consensus that the civil rights movement was based on the black middle class. It is not incidental that its emergence and growth took place during the postwar boom, when opportunities were increasing for blacks and whites. And certainly a more independent black middle class and a more affluent working class affected the ability of the black population to flex its collective muscles. Nonetheless, the matter deserves more careful consideration.

Some observers have noted the conservatism of the more established black middle class and its reluctance to encourage confrontation. I have already mentioned Atlanta, where the established black leadership agreed to halt demonstrations, and where they were severely criticized for doing so. Similarly, in Greensboro the black middle class was slow to support the students. Most of the black press in the South did not support the sit-ins. One survey done in the early sixties was reported by Gary Marx to have shown that "those who have been upper status for a longer period of time are more likely to have developed a vested interest in the system than those who have recently arrived, and the former are therefore less militant." Many established businessmen and professionals had much to lose if whites chose reprisals. They encouraged change, but they did so quietly through the courts. Louis Lomax succinctly noted "a good deal of foot-dragging by moneyed Negroes in high places."[40]

The NAACP was often the organization of this stratum. While it was based in the North, it had a substantial membership in the South. But its modus operandi was hostile to mass action, and especially to breaking the law. That was particularly so among the national staff. That was why on several occasions local NAACP leaders, frustrated by inaction on the part of the national office, called in other groups. Amzie Moore of Cleveland, Mississippi asked for help from SNCC for voter registration; Dr. George Simkins, who headed the Greensboro NAACP, requested help from CORE once the sit-ins began.

The first phase of the civil rights upheaval, examined in the previous chapter, was led by middle-class people. But they were a different stratum from that of the established leaders. They were heavily dominated by preachers but often included doctors and small businessmen. Most were free from direct economic dependence upon whites, and as such they were not easily subject to reprisals. These tended to be the newer arrivals to the middle class. They were usually younger men (and sometimes women) who were less well-established and less tied into the existing structures of power. King, it should be remembered, was asked to assume leadership of the Montgomery bus boycott precisely because he had no such ties. The other ministers who, with King, built the SCLC were similarly placed. They were not reluctant to lead protests and were willing to mobilize broad sectors of the community in order to confront the white centers of power.

Generally, what few studies there are show the black middle class to have been more militant and more likely to participate in politics than lower-class people in those early days before the sit-ins and freedom rides.[41] The movement began under the leadership of a younger, better-educated, more militant, but still middle-class stratum. While this movement involved many more people than the legalistic approach of the NAACP, it did so mainly by asking them to withhold their patronage of businesses. They were not called out to confront white authority. But when there were widespread protests, they inevitably involved, and were based upon, lower-class blacks. In Montgomery, for example, the bus boycott was carried out by lower-class and working-class blacks, including especially the many cooks and domestics. Wealthier blacks, who relied on their automobiles for transportation, became actively involved only when the car pool was organized. Similarly, the boycott in Tuskeegee, Alabama relied upon the farmers to make it work, although it was initiated by the professors who had been slapped in the face by the gerrymander that robbed them of their vote. In fact, any boycott had to depend upon the lower class, because the black middle class was such a small stratum at that time.

The movement of the early sixties passed largely into the hands of the newly mobilized students. Virtually all of these were middle-class. They did not necessarily come from the middle class; few did. But that they or their parents could provide the money necessary to put them through college was an important marker; and once through college, most were bound for a middle-class existence. Yet, they were faced with indignities that were incongruous with the status they expected in life. There was, moreover, a real threat to that status, in that, with the rigid structure of segregation and second-class citizenship, there were not sufficient opportunities to accommodate the expansion of this stratum. Unless these youth broke through the system, many, perhaps most, of them would be forever frustrated.

A number of surveys and other studies were carried out on this body of people in the early sixties.[42] They tend generally to agree on most points: the most active students in the early days tended to be middle-class. The higher the status of the students, the more likely they were to have been active. There were a number of such associations: students in private colleges were more likely to be participants, as were those in higher-quality colleges.[43]

It was these students who imparted the more militant and confrontationist tendency to the movement. They became increasingly concerned about lower-class blacks and sought to mobilize them to change their conditions. That was a significant move. Surveys found that while lower-class students were less likely to get involved at first, when they did so they were likely to be more active than the higher-status students. An implication of this finding was that when lower-class blacks did become involved, they would be even more likely to exhibit militancy and thus would increase the pressure on the black leadership to escalate goals, strategies, and tactics. Generally speaking, lower-class blacks were found to be late joiners of the movement. However, by the mid-sixties, at a time when the movement had broadened in its base, Anthony and Amy Orum reported that there was no longer any class difference in student participation in the movement. And by 1966, Joyce Ladner saw the social base of the activist civil rights movement as including "plantation workers, students, the average lower class Negro, and a small number of ministers, professionals and businessmen."[44]

As a result of the changing social character of the movement, its tenor was changing. As lower-class blacks moved into activity, and as the goals the black movement was seeking began to alter in their class character to accommodate the needs of these newly mobilized strata, the terms of the coalition that had been created to effectuate black gains came into question. As that happened, the coalition itself was shaken. Herein lay the dynamic that led to black power.

Birmingham: The Turn toward Black Power

Criticisms of King attained their greatest strength following the fiasco in Albany. King's leadership and his strategy of nonviolent direct action were portrayed by his opponents as a failure. The growing self-confidence and militancy in the black community would lead it to search for new approaches if nonviolence was discredited. King felt that that would be a serious error; so he was under pressure to produce a dramatic victory using his strategy. He turned to Birmingham, Alabama for an offensive that would dramatically demonstrate the validity of his strategy and gain it new adherents.

Birmingham was to be unlike any civil rights campaign yet. King and his staff carefully pored over the lessons of previous efforts, especially the Albany campaign, as they plotted "Project C" (for Confrontation) in Birmingham. Chief Pritchett's elastic response had made it impossible to create any sense of crisis and disorder. People were quietly arrested, and the movement had slowly weakened. No national indignation had been aroused, and no significant gains had been won. The example of CORE'S freedom rides that provoked the federal government to respond clearly applied to this campaign in Birmingham. Unprovoked attacks upon the protestors who were legitimately and peacefully asking only for their rights as Americans were needed to make civil rights an issue of national concern. Such a spectacle, played out in public and transmitted by the news media to the rest of the nation and to the world, would create indignation and demands to redress blacks' grievances.

King intentionally went after what he knew to be the weak point in the Birmingham power structure: the businessmen. They were the key to victory in the city if they could be made to realize that to refuse to make concessions would be more costly and socially dangerous than to accept them. King's strategy was to bypass the city's elected leaders and to put the pressure on the downtown merchants. He noted:

> You don't win against a political power structure where you don't have the votes. But you can win against an economic power structure when you have the economic power to make the difference between a merchant's profit and loss.[45]

King was aware of the businessmen's vulnerability, and he knew that in Birmingham they had already experienced a black boycott and had perceived what it could do to their sales.

Birmingham was for many reasons an ideal choice for a confrontation. It was the most important industrial city in the South, and it was, in King's words, "a city where brutality directed against Negroes was an unquestioned and unchallenged reality." The movement's chief protagonist in Birmingham was not a Laurie Pritchett but rather "Bull" Connor, whom King described as "a racist who prided himself on knowing how to handle the Negro and keep him in his place." Connor was the man who had arrested Senator Glen Taylor, Henry Wallace's running mate, for holding an unsegregated rally in 1948, and he continued to display "as much contempt for the rights of the Negro as he did defiance for the authority of the federal government." Thus, the confrontation in Birmingham was likely to provoke a response that would compel the federal government to act. Moreover, Birmingham was not just the locus of another demonstration. Rather,

> We believed that while a campaign in Birmingham would surely be the toughest fight of our civil rights careers, it could, if successful, break the back of segregation all over the nation. This city had been the country's chief symbol of racial intolerance. A victory there might well set forces in motion to change the entire course of the drive for freedom and justice.[46]

The way to attain this victory was through massive disruption of commerce. The Albany demonstrations had made apparent the possibility of moving beyond previous efforts that had relied on either a cadre of trained and committed volunteers for active participation, as in the sit-ins and freedom rides, or the less confrontational involvement of the whole black population, as in the Montgomery bus boycott. In Albany a large section of the black population had become involved in the demonstrations through mass marches and arrests. If a similar strategy could be employed in Birmingham, reaching down to involve even deeper layers of the black population, with the aim of disrupting downtown commerce, it could create such chaos that political and economic leaders would be forced to act to accommodate black demands. The disruption would move the businessmen themselves; if it provoked unjustifiable brutality against the demonstrators, it would also bring into motion the other elements of the coalition: Northern middle-class public opinion and the federal government. They, in turn, would add pressure upon the Birmingham power structure and, through civil rights legislation, bring about much broader gains for blacks throughout the South.

In adopting this approach to Birmingham, King was bowing to the growing impatience in the black community. Moreover, he was adopting the approach of the student militants, and even of Malcolm X (who will be discussed in the next chapter)—though they did not perceive it that way—by organizing a massive confrontation on a scale that they had not yet been able to accomplish.

In order to move so substantial a section of the black population, it was necessary to motivate them to take the risks of arrest, physical beating, and economic punishment. King did so by raising what came to be known as the "package deal," calling for the immediate desegregation of all public facilities, stores, theaters, restrooms, anywhere blacks had been humiliated and degraded. He addressed the particular economic concerns of blacks by demanding not only that they be allowed to spend their money freely with whites but that they also be given greater employment opportunities. Jobs in business and industry, and on the public payroll, also became part of the package deal. King was thus responding to the reality that race alone did not make up the totality of black deprivation, that there were classes within the black community, and that the concerns of working- and lower-class blacks demanded attention. The Birmingham campaign thus showed the influence on King of the same social force that affected SNCC and the second wave.

The demonstrations began with the use of trained volunteers. When the protests flagged, in part because Connor acted with a restraint that King had not anticipated, King reached out to the young people. Starting with high-school students, and eventually even using grade-school children, he succeeded in getting masses of people out, over six thousand in all. Adults soon joined them by the thousands. "The protest seemed to become a rallying of the whole Negro community," said the *New York Times*. The participants were no longer only those who had been trained in nonviolence, and—although the SCLC activists tried to prevent it—they took to throwing stones and bricks at the police. Connor responded with force in the form of dogs, firehoses, and clubs, and he did so in front of the newsmen, who promptly transmitted it to the public.[47] King's calculation certainly worked. The spectacle of children being attacked by police dogs, of firehoses being trained on crowds of people who in the eyes of most people were doing nothing wrong, caused a national revulsion.

King was very clear about this strategy. He knew that he was creating a dilemma for the white power structure by forcing it to employ open repression or to accept defeat. Reflecting back a few years later, he said:

> We swept into Southern streets to demand our citizenship and manhood. For the South with its complex system of brutal segregation we were inaugurating a rebellion. Merely to march in public streets was to rock the status quo to its roots. Boycotting buses in Montgomery, demonstrating in Birmingham, the citadel of segregation, and defying guns, dogs, and clubs in Selma, while maintaining disciplined nonviolence, totally confused the rulers of the South. If they let us march, they admitted their lie that the black man was content. If they shot us down, they told the world they were inhuman brutes. They tried to stop us by threats and fear, the tactic that had long worked so effectively. But nonviolence had muzzled their guns and Negro defiance had shaken their confidence. When they finally reached for clubs, dogs and guns, they found the world was watching, and then the power of nonviolent protest became manifest. It dramatized the essential meaning of the conflict and in magnified strokes made clear who was the evildoer and who was the undeserving victim. The nation and the world were sickened and through national legislation wiped out a thousand Southern laws, ripping gaping holes in the edifice of segregation. Those were days of luminous victories. Negroes and whites collaborated for human dignity.[48]

As the demonstrations reached their height, over three thousand blacks were in jail; four thousand more were still demonstrating; blacks were closing Birmingham down. Ed Gardner, a local activist, described what happened:

> They had tried to play as though nothing was happening, but when we marched downtown . . . marched in every department store, every eating joint, and tied up everything, all the traffic, everything was at a standstill. We had 4500 folks in jail, and we had about ten or twenty thousand wanted to get in, and "Bull" Connor had filled up the Bessemer jail, had filled up the Fair Park. He run out of space and when he run out of space he got the firemen and turned the water on, but the more water he would pour, the more they would come.

"This is the first time in the history of our struggle that we have been able literally to fill the jails," said King. "In a real sense this is the fulfillment of a dream. . . ."[49] The businessmen, who were meeting to consider what to do during this massive demonstration, were shocked, and they capitulated. Northern public opinion was terribly inflamed by the sight of brutality employed against children, women, and others who were harming no one. Indeed, the moral issue was so plain that at one point firemen who were ordered to turn the firehoses on the blacks refused to do so. President Kennedy was moved by the spectacle, and by its impact on police opinion, to propose the Civil Rights Bill that was enacted into law after his assassination.

Clearly, King had won a great victory. His calculation of the centrality of Birmingham was proved correct. He had certainly recouped the initiative for his program of nonviolent direct action as the means to win black rights. Yet ironically, the victory in Birmingham prepared the way for the eclipse of that strategy. Birmingham made a qualitative difference in the black movement and gave new strength to elements in the black movement that King bitterly opposed.

Just as black participation was greater than before, so too was the white brutality. It embittered blacks at the very time that they were developing a greater sense of efficacy. White violence did not stop once blacks had won their victory. Bombs were planted at the home of King's brother and at the motel where the movement had been headquartered. The black population of Birmingham responded with the first of the urban riots. They threw stones and bricks and bottles at police and drew their knives in anger; they set fires and looted stores. This response and a general melee that King's lieutenants could neither control nor abate prefigured what was yet to come in the nation's black ghettos. No one was yet aware that black riots would become the most widespread form of political expression. The layers of people that King had tapped in Birmingham—that he had had to tap—went beyond his methods. These people, and those like them, would force a revision of black goals as they began to make their social weight felt.

The impact of Birmingham was very far-reaching. If there were ripples after Montgomery, what followed after Birmingham was a tidal wave. "You got to understand," a Mississippi cotton planter told Theodore White, "that every one of those Negroes on my land has a television set in his shack, and he sits there in the evening and watches." Several hundred boycotts, marches, and sit-ins took place in some two hundred cities and towns in the South in the months following Birmingham. In only one week in June, a Justice Department report listed demonstrations in Gadsden, Alabama; Bradenton, Sarasota, and Tallahassee, Florida; Atlanta and Savannah, Georgia; Cambridge and Ocean City, Maryland; Jackson, Mississippi; Greensboro and Lexington, North Carolina; Beaufort and Charleston, South Carolina; Nashville; Texarkana, Texas; Danville, Virginia; Providence, Rhode Island; Columbus, Ohio; New York City; Rahweh, New Jersey; St. Louis; Los Angeles; and Washington, D.C. According to the Justice Department, that summmer there were 758 demonstrations in the nation and almost 14,000 arrests in the South alone. Barriers to desegregation began tumbling in the face of this onslaught. To provide some indication of the extent of change: before May 27, 1963, in 56 cities, 109 theaters had been desegregated. Four and one-half months later, by November 13, the number had jumped to 253. The count of desegregated restaurants in that same period went from 141 to 270; hotels and motels from 163 to 222; even lunch counters, which had been so widely challenged earlier, went from 204 desegregated to 304 in that short period.[50]

As always, King had stressed in Birmingham the need and ability of blacks to act for themselves. He encouraged and exhorted them to act, and he provided the rationale and the means for them to do so, and they responded. The result was a very powerful demonstration of black will, determination, and power. Blacks confronted white power, and they won. As so often before in such confrontations, black pride and self-confidence were greatly strengthened, and not only in Birmingham. The spectacle had been viewed through television all over the country. The same sights that won white support for legislative action inspired black anger and determination elsewhere. One of the communities in which King followed up his Birmingham victory was St. Augustine, Florida. A series of demonstrations there, including sit-ins, marches, ocean wade-ins, and an economic boycott, all hit hard at businesses in that tourist-based city. The business leaders at first encouraged the Ku Klux Klan, but ultimately, faced with a large drop-off in tourism, they capitulated. King observed the impact of the movement:

> Even if we do not get all we should, movements such as this tend more and more to give a Negro the sense of self-respect that he needs. It tends to generate courage in Negroes outside the movement. It brings intangible results outside the community where it is carried out. There is a hardening of attitudes in situations like this. But other cities see and say "We don't want to be another Albany or Birmingham," and they make changes. Some communities, like this one, had to bear the cross.[51]

Black demands became more far-reaching. The package deal now became the general aim; the sense of black power grew. Said Percy Sutton, lawyer for Malcolm X: "You developed out of Birmingham a number of crazy niggers; you learned that, if you defy the establishment, the establishment responds—it doesn't want to die."[52] That summer, blacks in the North and West began to participate in demonstrations in significant numbers also. While the leadership of the movement was still centered in the South, the urban ghetto blacks began to have a social impact. The issues they raised were not limited, strictly speaking, to civil rights; they were concerned, rather, with economic issues, especially jobs, but also the cost of housing and the trend toward urban renewal; welfare; the quality of schooling; and health care. They mounted militant demonstrations, demanding access to jobs and job training, protesting the slum conditions blacks were forced into, opposing the de facto segregation that existed in Northern schools as a result of segregated housing. And from this movement came the impetus for the Poverty Program, enunciated by President Lyndon Johnson in his State of the Union message in January 1964, after President Kennedy's assassination.

The Birmingham confrontation was a success in King's terms: it defeated the power structure of the city that may have been the most solidly opposed to desegregation of any in the South. It stimulated the passage of civil rights legislation that affected blacks far beyond Birmingham. And it encouraged blacks all over the country more actively to oppose racial discrimination.

At the same time, the effort that was required to accomplish this goal unleashed a dynamic among blacks that began to turn them away from the nonviolent method that had succeeded in Birmingham. It was a matter not merely of anger, but of the need for self-protection, a need that grew in the period following Birmingham, as the civil rights movement entered the black belt.

SNCC Confronts White Power in Mississippi

The swelling of black activity had its greatest impact in the Upper South and in the North and West. There, the black upsurge brought a number of gains as barriers fell. The Deep South, especially those who bitterly resisted desegregation, became more determined in the face of the growing black movement. The White Citizens' Councils attained their greatest strength in Mississippi, where, in the early sixties, the governor appointed their members to high positions, and they advised him on racial matters.[53]

Such polarization brought more bombing and arson. In Mississippi, six churches were burned in June of 1963, and twenty-one more during that summer. Police first used electric cattle prods against civil rights demonstrators that year, as well as guns and clubs, fire hoses, and tear gas. Beatings and legal repression were widespread in Alabama, Georgia, Louisiana, and Mississippi. Car chases on lonely stretches of back-country roads added to the terror that was fostered by murder. Civil rights activity meant the threat of death in Mississippi. While Medgar Evers, a leader of the NAACP in that state, was the most prominent leader murdered that summer, SNCC activists faced the most widespread terror there. Lawrence Guyot, an SNCC organizer, described their circumstances: "The phones were tapped, people knew where we were going, people knew where we bought our gas, where we lived . . . you name it." The counteroffensive succeeded: there were few victories in the Deep South following Birmingham. There, the structure of segregation remained.[54]

The segregationists often broke the law in collaboration with the legal authorities, and the civil rights activists who sought to bring the rule of law to the Southern frontier suffered. Civil rights workers could cite cases of FBI collusion with local police. By the time of the March on Washington at the end of the first long, hot summer of 1963, SNCC chairman John Lewis had been prepared to ask rhetorically, "Which side is the federal government on?" and to note that:

> The party of Kennedy is also the party of [Senator James] Eastland [of Mississippi]. The party of liberal Senator Jacob Javits [of New York], is also the party of Goldwater. Where is our party? . . . We cannot depend on any political party, for the Democrats and Republicans have betrayed the basic principles of the Declaration of Independence.[55]

Despite their feeling of having been left to tough it out alone in the Deep South, the SNCC people refused to abandon their work. In the fall of 1963 an umbrella organization known as the Council of Federated Organizations (COFO), which was dominated by SNCC, carried out a mock election in Mississippi. It was designed to show that people who were disfranchised wished to vote and would do so if given the opportunity. Some 80,000 participated throughout the state. On the basis of these results, the civil rights activists decided to embark upon a massive program to register blacks to vote in the summer of 1964. The Mississippi Summer Project, or, as it came to be known more broadly, Freedom Summer, called upon white college students from the North to descend on Mississippi to aid with this campaign. This tactic reflected the political education that civil rights activists had received in their years of struggle. Dave Dennis of CORE, one of the two organizers of the summer project, explained the reasoning behind it:

> We knew that if we had brought in a thousand blacks, the country would have watched them slaughtered without doing anything about it. Bring a thousand whites and the country is going to react to that in two ways. First of all is to protect. We made sure that we had the children, sons and daughters of some very powerful people in this country over there, including Jerry Brown, who's now governor of California, for instance. . . . The idea was . . . to get the country to . . . respond to what was going on there. They were not gonna respond to a thousand blacks working in that area. They would respond to a thousand young white college students, and white college females who were down there. . . . If there were gonna take some deaths to do it, the death of a white college student would bring on more attention to what was going on than for a black college student getting it.

The cynical attitude about white America illustrated in this comment emerged from the experience of civil rights activists. Several blacks had been murdered in connection with SNCC activity prior to the 1964 summer project. None of these murders had been widely reported, and the government had still refused to protect civil rights workers. According to Dennis, by bringing what were essentially white hostages to Mississippi, they were "speaking the language of this country," meaning, presumably, that the "language of the country" was not morality but power. The whites would add to the power of mainly black activists by forcing the government to provide protection.[56]

As King had chosen Birmingham to win broader gains, SNCC and its collaborators chose Mississippi, because it was the bastion of second-class citizenship for blacks. Just as King had found it necessary to adopt SNCC's confrontationist approach, they were forced to adopt measures for which they had criticized him. Ordinarily, SNCC volunteers stayed with a project for an extended period to demonstrate to the blacks they sought to organize that the outsiders would not disappear when the going got rough. But the college student volunteers were being asked to stay only for the summer. To be sure, while they were there the volunteers lived with the blacks with whom they worked; they shared their food, their living conditions, and their dangers. But when they departed, those they left would still have to face whites who had been enraged by the summer project. SNCC accepted these conditions because it needed the volunteers.

SNCC chose to go to the areas that were most resistant and most violent. They felt that not to do so would be to show fear, and if they showed fear they would be driven out of the state. "To the extent we don't push, they are going to push us," said one activist. The strategy was to force those opposed to black rights to come out into "the light of day" and to expose their violence and repression to the nation. When the state was presented with a massive onslaught of volunteers, the segregationists would be forced to react. Because most of the volunteers were white, the repression they faced would be widely reported. The reports would generate outrage in the North, especially among parents, some of whom were influential. The outrage would force the government to act, as it had been forced to act by Birmingham. Some of the white opposition understood this tactic and tried to counter it. Leaflets appeared in Pascagoula, Mississippi, signed by the KKK, urging people to avoid violence because that was what the demonstrators wished.[57]

The plea, however, went unheeded. The same day it was issued, three men were murdered, one black and two whites. The Schwerner-Chaney-Goodman murder set the scene for a summer of terror. Mississippi prepared for what it called the "invasion" by expanding its police forces and their armaments. The city of Jackson bought a tanklike vehicle that had thick steel walls, bullet-proof windows, shotguns, teargas guns, and a submachine gun. Official repression combined with unofficial terror to produce scars that, said Cleveland Sellers, "are still there, deep inside, where I suspect they will remain for the rest of our lives." Sellers catalogued the list: 1,000 arrests, 35 shooting incidents, 30 homes and other buildings bombed, 35 churches burned, 80 beatings, and at least 6 persons murdered. Dave Dennis recalled that while they were searching for the bodies of Schwerner, Chaney, and Goodman, "it was almost a daily thing. A body was found here. Two bodies were found floating in the river. . . . *They were finding people*, black people, floating in rivers and every place else, and nothing was being done about it"[58] (emphasis in original).

There was the constant danger of harassment, of arrest, or even of death. Robert Coles, who was staff psychiatrist for the summer project, found fear and anxiety to be widespread. Dave Dennis spoke of the "stark terror of day-to-day living . . . wondering whether someone was going to sneak in and dynamite you or firebomb your home." Cleveland Sellers described his reaction after a comrade was killed in an automobile accident, and after Sellers and his coworkers had had to fight with police to get his passenger taken to a hospital:

> We tried to pull ourselves together and "Keep on Keepin' on," but it was impossible. The weeks of tension and strain, coupled with Wayne's brutal death, could not be ignored. Hate and viciousness seemed to be everywhere. We realized that the only thing keeping us from sharing Wayne's fate was dumb luck. Death

could come at any time in any form: a bullet between the shoulder blades, a fire bomb in the night, a pistol whipping, a lynching. I had never experienced such tension and near-paralyzing fear.[59]

The FBI provided little protection. After the Schwerner-Chaney-Goodman killings, FBI director J. Edgar Hoover publicly offered his opinion that there was an overemphasis on civil rights and that the bureau would not offer protection to volunteers. When three men were later arrested by the FBI for threatening two white volunteers, SNCC veteran Stokeley Carmichael remarked angrily that "they let the murderers of Negroes off, but already men have been arrested in Itta Bene just for *threatening* white lives"[60] (emphasis in original).

These experiences brought nonviolence much more seriously into question than ever before. After the Schwerner-Chaney-Goodman murders, leaders stopped telling people not to carry guns to protect themselves. Said one:

This country discouraged nonviolence. There was a real loss of faith in it by Negroes after Medgar and Chaney were murdered. Very few of us accept non-violence as a way of life. It's an unnatural discipline on a natural response. We were willing to accept it as a tactic as long as it was sanity, but it's just not sanity to give your life away. Now it's not a question of violence and nonviolence, but one of survival.

The move to bear arms emerged from below, out of the hands of people SNCC sought to organize. SNCC and CORE activists found that for many of the blacks with whom they worked, being armed was simply a matter of course, that in their view not to arm was plain foolishness. That summer, the Deacons for Self-Defense were organized in Louisiana, and by the end of the summer, many SNCC activists carried guns.[61]

Despite the mayhem, SNCC failed to provoke any confrontation between Mississippi and the federal government, and they were unsuccessful in getting any significant number of blacks registered to vote. So they began instead to register people into a party called the Mississippi Freedom Democratic party. The party would go to the Democratic convention and challenge the regular party's credentials, seeking to fill the seats slated for Mississippi. The MFDP was racially nonexclusive, it was democratically organized, and it declared itself loyal to the party and the party's nominee, which the regular party refused to do.

Many of the participants in the summer project saw this move as the first step in dismantling the power of the Southern bloc and in opening the gates to re-distribute wealth and power within the nation. If successful, they hoped the MFDP venture would spread to other states. This prospect alarmed the white South. President Johnson, who had no intention of alienating the powerful South-ern bloc, reacted by opposing the exclusion of the Mississippi delegation. Instead, the president offered a compromise: the MFDP would get two at-large seats, their occupants to be chosen by the national party rather than the MFDP; the regular Mississippi delegation would get all of its seats; and they were promised that if the same election procedures were used by the regulars in 1968, the MFDP would unseat them.

King, among others, attempted to convince the activists to accept this offer as a genuine step forward, but they rejected his counsel. Fannie Lou Hamer, who had become a leader in the party, warned that "if the Mississippi Freedom Democratic Party is not seated now, I question America." Charles Sherrod, an SNCC leader, explained why they rejected the offer: "We want much more than 'token' positions. We want power for our people." Here was another expression of the political distance that had been traveled by blacks, and particularly by these black activists. Lawrence Guyot and Mike Thilwell of SNCC described the change. The convention experience and the strategy of the summer project, they said, were based on

> confidence in the ultimate morality in national political institutions and practices—
> "They really couldn't know, and once we bring the facts about Mississippi to
> national attention, justice must surely be swift and irrevocable"—which was a
> simplistic faith somewhat akin to that of the Russian peasants under the Czars.
> Caught in the direct kind of oppression and deprivation, the peasants would moan,
> "If the Czar only knew how we suffer. He is good and would give us justice. If
> only he knew." The fact was that he knew only too well.[62]

In response to black rioting in the North, President Johnson urged civil rights leaders to declare a moratorium on demonstrations so as to avoid a backlash. SNCC and CORE refused. At the start of 1965, when the newly elected Congress met, the MFDP sent a delegation to Washington that unsuccessfully challenged the seating of the elected representatives from Mississippi. Mrs. Hamer's words expressed their bitterness at yet another defeat: "Mississippi Negroes are excluded from everything except hanging. Someday we want to be able to teach our children that this really is a democracy."[63]

The anger with which those who had built the MFDP responded to the rebuff handed them by the Democratic party was a product of more than their experience at the convention itself. It emerged from the whole experience of repression and terrorism that they had suffered while they fought for rights that "legally" were already theirs. Freedom Summer, with its increase in terror, had substantially worsened these conditions and had sharpened their sense of isolation from the American mainstream. A sign in the Jackson, Mississippi headquarters cynically marked this feeling:

> There's A Town in Mississippi Called Liberty
> There's A Department in Washington Called Justice.[64]

These experiences provided the background to the hostilities that developed among the blacks toward the whites in SNCC. From the first, the whites who volunteered to participate in Freedom Summer found antagonism directed toward them. Some blacks had originally objected to the project on the ground that most of the volunteers would be white. They charged that whites took over running offices, freedom schools, and campaigns by virtue of their superior education and the sole fact of their being white, and that they thereby prevented blacks from controlling their own movement. White women became sexually involved with black men, which drew anger from all parts. These charges became grounds later for some of the impetus for black power. Behind them lay other, more fundamental concerns. Blacks in SNCC were moving toward greater militancy than whites. Finding little response from white America, their trend toward independent action was sending them toward a break with whites, though that was yet some time off.

The youth of the second wave began to question their goals. Was integration into the existing American society sufficient to deal with the problems black people faced? One participant recalled to historian William Chafe how he and his coworkers felt: "We could go anywhere in Greensboro that we wanted to go, but we were already raising the question, 'what the hell, if people can't afford food on their table at home, it matters not that they can eat at the fancy little restaurants in Greensboro.' "[65]

Even those who knew the facts about black poverty, or who had experienced it themselves, were surprised to learn of its depth and extent. They began to encourage blacks to vote as a means of overcoming the conditions that kept blacks poor, and they began to think in terms of transforming America's economic system, which, they came to feel, kept blacks in subjection. They were now probing the limits of the civil rights coalition. Their experience at the Democratic convention thus ratified a deepening sense of alienation from the government and from the country. "After Atlantic City," affirmed Cleveland Sellers, "our struggle was not for civil rights, but for liberation." Sellers noted the substantial changes that had taken place in the outlook of the second wave. An important part of SNCC questioned the structure of American society: Sellers felt that "our most important conclusion was that it was not possible for poor black people to solve their problems within the structure of the two-party system. We agreed that there was a need for alternative or parallel political structures."[66] The civil rights coalition was being pulled apart as its components pursued their own interests.

King attempted once again to resurrect that coalition and to reassert the validity of his strategy by campaigning for the right to vote in the South, as SNCC had done in Mississippi. He repeated the formula for success in Birmingham by focusing national attention on the issue in a specific campaign in Selma, Alabama. There, Sheriff Jim Clark would serve as another "Bull" Connor and be King's foil for passage of a voting rights act.

Clark performed as expected, and once again television screens were illuminated by the sight of peaceful blacks being mercilessly attacked and beaten by the guardians of Southern law and order. Once again, Northern outrage brought the passage of legislation. The Voting Rights Act was signed into law in August 1965, and it was to have a far-reaching impact on the structure of power in the South. King had successfully reconstructed the civil-rights coalition one more time, and he had established the power of his program for nonviolent direct action and demonstrated its ability to defeat the reactionary forces of racism.

Yet, Selma was the end of the civil rights movement, whose forces soon splintered. SNCC people, who had begun the voter registration campaign in Selma and who had been beaten down by Clark there, were infuriated by King's failure to confront the police. At one point, he turned a march around rather than face a police attack similar to one that had taken place a few days earlier. In response, SNCC removed itself from the demonstrations in response. By refusing to push on with every confrontation, King lost supporters among the militants. In truth, he had already lost them. They were unsatisfied with the results to be gained from the civil rights coalition. They were searching for another route to what Sellers and many others were now calling "liberation." The term itself connoted the struggles against colonialism waged in Africa and Asia—and at that time in Vietnam. Little more than a year after Selma, Stokely Carmichael was elected to lead SNCC. Carmichael's platform involved a commitment to racial separation and militancy that he would call "black power."

VII

GHETTO REVOLTS, BLACK POWER, AND THE LIMITS OF THE CIVIL RIGHTS COALITION

With the passage of the Voting Rights Act in 1965, the civil rights movement finished its program of legal gains. This legislation, and the process by which it was achieved, broke the central thrust of black subjection in the South. By this time the focus of activity was already moving to the North. There, where blacks were legally free and equal, they were consigned to live apart in black "ghettos," many in poverty, almost all substantially worse off than whites, with inferior education and medical care.

These ghettos, where huge numbers gave blacks a sense of strength and power, became the breeding grounds for anger and militance. By 1964 they became the site of a long series of explosive upheavals—the ghetto riots—that eloquently made the case that the black movement had not ended with the civil rights movement, that more was needed to redress black grievances. The riots served notice that racial subjection had ceased to be merely a Southern problem—it was alive and well throughout the nation, even if in a different form.

The actions of the ghetto blacks forced everyone to take notice: the federal government, white liberals, and civil rights leaders all had to respond. The government created a poverty program to ease some of the distress and to get blacks off the streets. When it became clear that this response was inadequate, that some substantive redistribution of wealth and power would be necessary, the former allies of the battle against Southern intransigence—the Northern middle class, the Democratic party, and the federal government—refused to take the path asked of them. More concessions were ruled out.

The youth of the second wave and SNCC were affected by these outbursts. Though they had little connection to them, they understood and sympathized with the frustration and anger that motivated riots. The urban revolt confirmed their own sense of the failures of white society and of the strength of blacks. These youth gave general expression to this sense in their call for black power—a call that echoed through the black ghettos, as the rioters and their defenders adopted it as their own.

King felt the need to respond to the discontent illustrated by the riots and to try to fashion a program consistent with his principles and his strategy that could meet the needs made evident by the rioters. He could not do so with the old civil rights coalition, but his attempt to fashion a new coalition, based on more radical principles, failed.

The civil rights movement had won its victories because blacks had been able to assemble a coalition that altered the balance of power within the nation. That coalition had brought about structural change within the South; but that same coalition put limits on the extent of change it was willing to support. It had cohered around a specific program: abolishing the state-sanctioned forms of discrimination in the South, particularly those having to do with segregation and the right to vote. Completing this program had required an intensive struggle and the defeat of the ruling elite of the region.

All of these developments had added up to the modernization of the South— bringing its politics into alignment with its new economic structure, and with the rest of the country. Support could be won for this program from the federal government, the Northern Democratic party, some businesses, and the middle classes. This support was forthcoming, despite the intensive struggle for power that it entailed, because the social class being displaced from power was anachronistic to modern society, and because second-class citizenship for blacks came to be viewed both as morally unacceptable and as a political liability to the nation. For the Southern middle class and businessmen, the turmoil created when black insistence met white resistance made the status quo a social and economic liability, as well. That was especially so because what blacks were asking for in the civil rights movement was unthreatening to modern capitalism and therefore acceptable even if at times unpalatable. The ghetto revolts, however, raised the specter of class upheaval and seemed to demand the redistribution of wealth and power, and this demand was unacceptable to those who had been the allies of the black movement. Blacks' allies were unwilling to undermine their own power and privileges. Class considerations had shaped the position of blacks originally; a changed class structure had enabled blacks to get the leverage to alter their position. But so long as they operated within that structure, there were limits to what they could achieve. They did not escape its confines.

Race and Class outside the South

The class concerns of disadvantaged blacks were of particular importance outside the South. There, in the ghettos to which Southern blacks had made their way, they encountered circumstances different from those that they had fled. There was still segregation. Many restaurants refused to serve blacks. There were sometimes volatile flareups over the use of parks. If a black person dared to move into a white neighborhood or to use a "white" beach, riots might break out, as they had in the past. But these indignities were not state-sanctioned; they did not have the systematic use of police power behind them; they were not ubiquitous. There was no class whose well-being depended upon the total subordination of blacks, as was the case in the South. In many ways, blacks were free from the overt oppression they had left. They were able to use public facilities, such as restrooms, water fountains, buses, and trains, without discrimination. They could try on clothes, purchase automobiles, go to movies. They could vote and, since the thirties, participate in unions. In that sense, their flight to the North was a success.

But Northern blacks frequently stated that they preferred the South, because there they at least "knew where they stood." This expression meant that while the ideology in the North was one of equality, the reality was quite different. Whites did not openly treat blacks with contempt, as they did in the South: they did not flaunt their hostility. Jobs were not openly denied to blacks because they were black; jobs were simply not offered. Houses and apartments that were available over the telephone had been quickly sold or rented when people with black skin appeared.

Housing was an important component to black suffering in the urban ghettos of the North. Blacks were kept in segregated housing areas by a combination of interests. They were limited to certain areas by "racial steering," in which realtors refused to show blacks housing in areas reserved for whites; by "restrictive covenants" in which contracts were written (and enforced by the courts, until 1948) that forbade the owner to sell to a black person; and by the physical attacks of whites who, when a black family moved into a previously all-white neighborhood, would stop at little to drive them out.

In the fifties, even as court decisions favored blacks in the South, and as the movement there grew, the federal government continued and deepened its involvement in segregated housing. It did so through two programs. The Federal Housing Authority's insured housing loan program refused to underwrite loans to racially mixed areas. In 1959, the United States Commission on Civil Rights estimated that minorities had gotten less than 2 percent of the $120 billion in housing underwritten by the FHA since World War II, and all of that was in segregated housing. The FHA had very early recommended the use of restrictive covenants and continued to underwrite housing that used them for eighteen months after the Supreme Court decision that outlawed them. The massive federally financed highway construction program, carried out in the fifties and sixties, as blacks were arriving in the Northern cities, also reinforced residential segregation. Though it was not established for racial purposes, the program enabled whites to flee these cities and to abandon large parts of them to the blacks.[1]

The result of these policies was the creation of black ghettos—areas of the city where blacks were forced to live and from which most could not escape, even if they had the funds to enable them to buy or rent in more expensive areas of the city or in the suburbs. Renters and landlords were able to obtain substantially higher rents and purchase prices than would be justified by fair market value for apartments and houses when blacks' choices were limited in this way.

For the same dollar, they simply got less than whites, and though they earned less, they had to pay more. In these ghettos, blacks were crammed in. Poorer blacks were forced to double up because of the inadequate space at overly high prices. Huey Newton, founder of the Black Panther party, recalled the house he had lived in as a child in Oakland, California: "The floor was either dirt or cement, I cannot remember exactly; it did not seem to be the kind of floor that 'regular' people had in their homes." In this house,

> I slept in the kitchen. That memory returns often. Whenever I think of people crowded into a small living space, I always see a child sleeping in the kitchen and feeling upset about it; everybody knows that the kitchen is not supposed to be a bedroom. That is all we had, however. I still burn with the sense of unfairness I felt every night as I crawled into the cot near the icebox.[2]

Absentee landlords often compounded these problems by failing to maintain their properties adequately. As a result, slums were created or worsened. Government exacerbated this tendency also, by building public housing in black areas and by providing high-rise housing that packed thousands or even tens of thousands of people into small areas. When "urban renewal" was applied to the impoverished black areas, it forced blacks to move and to crowd into the remaining slums, thereby worsening them, or to expand the boundaries of the ghetto.

The California state legislature tried to come to grips with this issue by passing a law that did away with restrictive covenants and discrimination in housing and rental properties. This law was seen as appropriate to a part of the country that had supported federal action directed toward the South's discriminatory policies. However, in 1964, a referendum was placed on the state ballot to repeal the law, and it passed by a two-to-one vote, thereby administering a stinging rebuff to blacks. Apparently, Northern white support for civil rights was limited to the South. Richard Townsend, a resident of Watts, the black community of Los Angeles, described how the residents of that community reacted to the vote:

> The attitude of the people in Watts was "I didn't really want to move there, but it's just the idea of you didn't want me anyway; it was like a bar you put there, that we didn't want to cross it, but you put it there, so that's pretty mean, it indicates how you feel about me. So, for that reason, I feel a certain way about you."[3]

The extra charges on ghetto residents were not limited to housing. Trapped in the ghetto by poverty and by a lack of good public transportation, they were also forced to pay more than the white middle class for goods and services. They often had inferior merchandise to choose from, and they paid more for it. Because they were short on cash, they frequently bought on credit, for which they were charged exorbitant terms. Thus, they were enveloped in a web of exploitation.[4]

With the neighborhood school system, segregated housing meant segregated schools, and segregated schools generally meant inferior education. In part, that was because white school districts had more money to spend. But it was also a

result of more deliberate policies. Within city districts, less experienced teachers
were assigned to black schools, as was inferior equipment. In Boston in 1963,
CORE reported that 27 percent less was spent per pupil in black than in white
schools, while in Chicago in 1962 it was found that appropriations per pupil
were 21 percent less in all-black schools than in those for whites. According to
Charles Silberman:

> A distinguished Chicago minister who lives in an integrated area was horrified to
> discover that when the Negro registration in his child's school began to climb,
> the school was shifted in mid-year from one District Superintendent to another,
> who had an all-Negro district. After this transfer had been made, the school lost
> its speech therapist, remedial reading teacher and other special services. The fol-
> lowing year, shortages of textbooks began to show up and then the school began
> getting an inordinate number of permanent substitutes.[5]

The problem was not only inferior facilities and staff. It was also the attitude
of the teachers and administrators, mostly white, who denigrated the children.
Anthropologist Gerry Rosenfield told of his experience at a black school in
Harlem: "One teacher's class preceded ours down the stairway at dismissal time
each day. Without fail, every afternoon, she turned to the children, halted them
and shouted: 'Shut those thick lips! Can't you behave like human beings?' "[6]
Dick Gregory recalled his childhood in school bitterly:

> The teacher thought I was stupid. Couldn't speak, couldn't read, couldn't do
> arithmetic. Just stupid. Teachers were never interested in finding out that you
> couldn't concentrate because you were so hungry, because you hadn't had any
> breakfast. All you could think about was noontime, would it ever come? . . . The
> teacher thought I was a troublemaker. All she saw from the front of the room was
> a little black boy who squirmed in this idiots' seat and made noises and poked
> the kids around him. I guess she couldn't see a kid who made noises because he
> wanted someone to know he was there.[7]

Perhaps worst of all, the economic opportunities to which may blacks had
flocked were terribly elusive. They found themselves consigned to the worst
jobs, when they could find work at all. Skilled jobs, white-collar and professional
jobs, were largely closed off to them. Even in manufacturing they were channeled
into the dirtiest, most unsafe, and lowest-paying work. In service industries,
they were kept away from the public. In restaurants, they were dishwashers and
busboys but not waiters or waitresses or managers. In hotels, they were not
allowed to tend bar or serve in the front. Education did not provide an out, as
it did for whites. Studies showed that blacks with a college degree earned no
more than whites who had not gone beyond the eighth grade.[8]

All of these circumstances were worsened by the fact that the postwar boom
came to an end very early for blacks. In 1967, economist Arthur Ross called
1953 "the last year in which Negroes enjoyed relatively good times. . . ." The
recession of the fifties hit blacks hard. During 1954, the black unemployment
rate jumped from 4.1 percent to 8.9 percent, which was double the unemployment

rate of whites, a ratio that has not improved since. And blacks stayed unemployed considerably longer than whites. In 1958 they accounted for 25 percent of the long-term unemployed, and in 1962, 29 percent, even though they were only 11 percent of the labor force. This number was made worse by the fact that a great number of blacks simply dropped out of the labor force, presumably because of discouragement. The number of these would-be workers increased from 270,000 in 1954 to 405,000 in 1964. Those most affected by this trend were the youth. The participation of black teenagers in the labor market fell from 56.1 percent in 1950 to 37.7 percent in 1964, a much more precipitous decline than that among white teenagers.[9]

In their earnings, blacks were losing ground to whites in the fifties and early sixties, and that was true in every region. The losses were not only relative; real wages were falling, as well. Blacks in the city suffered a very high level of poverty: in Los Angeles during the first half of the sixties, the poverty rate among blacks hovered between 30 and 31 percent. That blacks left the South to go to other regions, where they were better paid, kept the overall statistic from appearing worse. Poverty created a great deal of personal strain. Huey Newton recalled of his childhood:

> My father's constant preoccupation with bills was the most profound and persistent memory of my childhood. We were always in debt, always trying to catch up. . . . For me, no words . . . were as profane as "the bills." It killed me a little each time they were mentioned, because I could see the never-ending struggle and agony my father went through trying to cope with them.[10]

As a result of these conditions, a high proportion of blacks were on the welfare rolls. Welfare came with a price: the dignity of those receiving it. Welfare workers were free to inspect the homes of the recipients at any time, and at times they did so at night to see if there was a male breadwinner present. As a result, men were driven from their families to make them eligible for Aid to Families with Dependent Children. Families could be broken up in other ways, as well. Malcolm X and his siblings were taken from their mother and put in foster homes, partly through efforts of the welfare department. A welfare mother described to Robert Coles the demeaning and destructive impact of her lack of power over her life and those of her children. She told him she was

> tired of everything they try to do to help us. They send us those welfare checks, and with them comes that lady who peeks around every corner here, and gives me those long lectures on how I should do everything—like her, of course. Then they take my kids to the Head Start thing, and first thing I hear is the boys' fingernails is dirty, and they don't use the right words, and the words they do use, no one can make them out. They try to take them to those museums and places, and tell them how sorry life is here at home and in the neighborhood, and how they is no good, and something has to be done to make them better—like the rich ones, I guess. But the worst is they just make you feel no good at all. They tell you they want to help you, but if you ask me they want to make you into them, and leave you without a cent of yourself left to hang on to.[11]

Blacks in the cities of the North were everywhere faced with white authority: in the schools, in the welfare department, and especially with the police. Police were mostly white; they sometimes aggressively patrolled high-crime areas, namely, the black ghettos; they stopped people indiscriminately, simply because they were black. In the sixties the police were frequently referred to as an occupying army; they were felt to demean, to harm and attack residents but not to protect them.[12]

The most humiliating conditions in the South did not exist in the North or were relatively easily done away with. A condition of class despair and anger remained, a condition that was substantially worsened by less overt, but still serious, racial discrimination. The anger especially emerged in response to the apparent hypocrisy of a society that proclaimed the equality of all but then denied it to blacks. Jimmie Sherman, who grew up in the Watts area of Los Angeles, recalled:

> As a child I used to dream of being . . . a general, a lawyer, a man who flew those big shiny planes. . . . I even wanted to be President. But sadly enough, dreams withered with time, and age brought me closer to reality—a reality I wanted no part of. I began to notice many things around me—things I did not like, but could do nothing about. I noticed my mother going out to the white folks' houses, scrubbing their floors and serving their food every day. I realized that my father, the man I idolized and imitated, had been cleaning sewers all of his life and getting nowhere. I even heard a white man call him "boy" a couple of times. That really made me mad. It made him mad, too. But what could he do but take it? I noticed the old shacky house we lived in—the cold splintered floors, the torn curtains, the broken chairs we sat in, the pie pans and jelly jars we ate and drank from. I noticed the roaches crawling on the walls, across the floors, and breeding all over the house, and the junk and the trash that piled up and scattered in the yard. And for the first time, *I realized that I was in poverty*. Then I discovered that we weren't the only family in that bag. My friends were in bad shape, too. Their parents were also servants, and they were living on beans and grits and hand me downs, just as we were. And *I discovered that being black had something to do with it*.[13] (emphasis added)

For Sherman, racial subjection meant poverty—without the ideological justification of black inferiority. He was free to dream as a child, but it soon became clear that the dreams of gold were destined to turn into dross—because of his race.

Malcolm X and Northern Lower-Class Blacks

These conditions formed the social base of a new trend toward black militancy that grew up independently of King and the Southern movement. "This sense of despair and futility led us into rebellious attitudes," wrote Huey Newton.[14] Blacks in the North, freed from the heavy hand of Southern police repression, were heartened by the victories won by their brethren and angered by the violence they saw visited upon Southern blacks for no legitimate reason. This anger augmented the hostility they felt toward their own police and other authority figures. They were less accepting than Southern blacks of nonviolence and of exhortations to love their oppressors.

They were thus open to an approach critical of King. One key source of the critique was the Nation of Islam, more popularly known as the Black Muslims, an organization that militantly raised the banner of black nationalism. They, and in particular their spokesman, Malcolm X, rejected the civil rights goal of integration, saw whites simply as an enemy, and pointedly refused to endorse the program of nonviolent resistance. Black solidarity was their program.

Toward the end of the 1950s, the Black Muslims had begun to develop a reputation in the North. In 1957, Minister Malcolm X had led a crowd of some two thousand to a police station in Harlem to demand that a prisoner who had been injured by the police be examined and treated, if necessary. The crowd had its way, whereupon Malcolm sent them home. Word of this incident spread, and with it the reputation of Malcolm and the Muslims. Benjamin Goodman, who became one of Malcolm's followers, described its impact on him:

> Here was a man who could walk boldly into the jaws of the lion, walk proud and tall into the territory of the enemy, the station house of the twenty-eighth precinct, and force the enemy to capitulate. Here was a man who could help restore the heritage, the pride of race and pride of self, that had been carefully stripped from us over the four hundred years of our enslavement here in white America.[15]

Louis Lomax's television documentary "The Hate That Hate Produced" brought a great deal of publicity to the Black Muslim organization when it was broadcast in 1959, and with publicity came rapid growth. Increased numbers meant, in turn, a greater hearing especially for Malcolm X, who abrasively attacked the established civil rights leadership: "We do not want leaders who are handpicked for us by the white men. We don't want any more Uncle Toms. We don't want any more leaders who are puppets or parrots for the white man."[16]

Malcolm, and the Black Muslims generally, called for black separatism. They stressed that blacks should be an independent nation:

> Can you not see that our former "leaders" have been fighting for the wrong thing . . . the wrong kind of freedom? Mr. Muhammed says we must have some land where we can work hard for ourselves, make ourselves equal, and live in dignity. Then and only then we won't have to beg the white man for the crumbs that fall occasionally from his table. No one respects or appreciates a beggar.[17]

Malcolm was criticized for that demand by whites and by more moderate blacks. The idea that the American government could or would yield some of its territory was utopian, they suggested. And it was ridiculous to believe that all or even most blacks would transplant themselves to this new nation. What these critics often missed was that many blacks were stirred not by the demand for land per se but by the connotations expressed by it of militancy and impatience. Many blacks in the 1920s supported Marcus Garvey, who had called upon American blacks to return to Africa, even though they had no thought of really doing so. Malcolm's expression of anger and impatience and the Muslim rejection of integration as a goal had a similar effect:

> When someone sticks a knife into my back nine inches and then pulls it out six inches they haven't done me any favor. They should not have stabbed me in the first place. . . . During slavery they inflicted the most extreme form of brutality against us to break our spirit, to break our will . . . after they did all of this to us for three hundred ten years, then they come up with some so-called Emancipation Proclamation. . . . And today the white man actually runs around here thinking he is doing the black people a favor.[18]

Malcolm rejected nonviolence, and he countered King directly on this issue. It didn't work, he said, because whites were fundamentally immoral:

> Don't change the white man's mind. You can't change his mind, and that whole thing about appealing to the moral conscience of America—America's conscience is bankrupt. She lost all conscience. They don't know what morals are.[19]

To encourage nonviolence on the part of blacks was to mislead disastrously and dangerously. Malcolm X would make this point, using lurid imagery.

> Just as the slavemaster of that day used Tom, the house Negro, to keep the field Negroes in check, the same old slavemaster today has Negroes who are nothing but moderate Uncle Toms, twentieth century Uncle Toms, to keep you and me in check, to keep us under control, keep us passive and peaceful and nonviolent. That's Tom making you nonviolent. It's like when you go to the dentist, and the man's going to take your tooth. You're going to fight him when he starts pulling. So he squirts some stuff in your jaw called novocaine, to make you think they're not doing anything to you. So you sit there and because you've got all of that novocaine in your jaw, you suffer—peacefully. Blood running all down your jaw, and you don't know what's happening. Because someone has taught you to suffer—peacefully.[20]

Instead, he counseled,

> be peaceful, be courteous, obey the law, respect everyone; but if someone puts his hand on you, send him to the cemetery. That's a good religion. In fact, that's that old-time religion. . . . Preserve your life, it's the best thing you've got. And if you've got to give it up, let it be even-steven.[21]

Malcolm insisted that the civil rights movement's white allies—those to whom King looked for support in the struggle against the segregationists: the federal government, the Northern Democratic party, and the white middle class—could not be trusted:

> Roosevelt promised, Truman promised, Eisenhower promised. Negroes are still knocking on the door begging for civil rights. Do you mean to tell me that in a powerful country like this, a so-called Christian country, that a handful of men from the South can prevent the North, the West, the Central States and the East from giving Negroes the rights the Constitution says they already have? No! I don't believe that and neither do you. *No white man really wants the black man*

to have his rights, or he'd have them! The United States does everything else it
wants to do.[22] (emphasis in original)

The Black Muslims were rooted in and speaking directly to Northern, urban,
lower-class blacks. Malcolm himself was one of many who were recruited out
of the prisons, and others came from the streets. The bulk were laborers or
unemployed. They were less directly concerned with the issue of segregation
that confronted blacks in the South except and so far as they identified with their
kinsmen. But the treatment blacks received in the South, and their own concerns,
angered these ghetto blacks. It was their anger that Malcolm X both articulated
and encouraged.

Malcolm was well aware of who his constituency was, and he was pleased
about it and comfortable with it. Alex Haley, with whom Malcolm worked closely
in producing his autobiography, recalled:

> Where I witnessed the Malcolm X who was happiest and most at ease among
> members of our own race was when sometimes I chanced to accompany him on
> what he liked to call "my little daily rounds" around the streets of Harlem, among
> the Negroes that he said the "so-called black leaders" spoke of "as black masses
> statistics." On these tours, Malcolm X generally avoided the arterial 125th Street
> in Harlem; he plied the side streets, especially in those areas which were thickest
> with what he described as "the black man down in the gutter where I came from,"
> the poverty-ridden with a high incidence of dope addicts and winos. Malcolm X
> here indeed was a hero. Striding along the sidewalks, he bathed all whom he met
> in the boyish grin, and his conversation with any who came up was quiet and
> pleasant. . . .[23]

Malcolm encouraged his followers to think of themselves as different from what
he viewed as King's middle- and upper-class supporters, and he pointedly charged
that King's approach was not relevant to his people:

> When you have two different people, one sitting on a hot stove, one sitting on
> the warm stove, the one sitting on the warm stove thinks progress is being made.
> He's more patient. But the one who is sitting on the hot stove, you can't let him
> up fast enough. You have the so-called Negro in this country, the upper-class
> Negro or the so-called high-class Negro or, as Franklin Frazier calls them, the
> "black bourgeoisie." They aren't suffering the extreme pain that the masses of
> the black people are. And it is the masses of the black people today, I think you'll
> find, who are the most impatient, the most angry, because they're the ones who
> are suffering the most.[24]

These lower-class blacks did indeed suffer from different problems and saw
solutions different from those favored by the constituency mobilized by King.

Malcolm X and the Black Movement outside the South

Despite this trend, the civil rights movement outside the South began with
middle-class demands. There was, for example, some substantial emphasis on
desegregating housing. As with the right to use public accommodations in the

South, that was largely for the benefit of those who could afford to move to more expensive areas but were prohibited from doing so by racial discrimination. Over time, increasing concern was given to issues of greater importance to lower-class blacks. CORE and other organizations held demonstrations around the needs of those displaced by urban renewal; they raised demands for black jobs—on retail establishments, on banks and other businesses, on the construction trades. Civil rights activists made an issue of school segregation in the North.

Increasingly, the issue of police brutality was brought into relief by the highly publicized attacks on blacks in the South. Outside the South, police mistreatment of blacks was an issue of common concern. A study of blacks in Los Angeles, after the outbreak of racial unrest in the Watts area, showed that large percentages of blacks had seen or had themselves been subject to police mistreatment. (Almost one-quarter asked said that they had personally been treated with lack of respect by the police, and almost 40 percent had seen it happen to others. One-fifth had been unnecessarily rousted and frisked, and two-fifths had seen it happen; almost the same numbers applied to people who were stopped while driving and whose cars were searched; 5.1 percent had had their homes searched, and 15.2 percent had seen it; 7.8 percent had experienced unnecessary force in being arrested, and 36.9 percent had seen it; 3.9 percent had been beaten while in police custody, and over 20 percent had witnessed such conduct.[25]) The Black Muslims, led by Malcolm X, hammered at this issue and set themselves apart from the civil rights movement by their ridicule of nonviolence as a response to such mistreatment.[26]

Organizations such as CORE became concerned over their class composition, and as they did so, they also began to question the utility of an interracial movement. They demanded black leadership on principle, but in actuality the proposal reflected the perception that the needs, concerns, and and interests of whites diverged from those of blacks, especially when the blacks represented were of a different class from the middle- and upper-class whites who supported or were active in the movement.[27]

The demonstrations in Birmingham had an electrifying effect upon blacks in the North, just as they did in the South. Demonstrations proliferated as the movement mushroomed. Ministers, unions, student organizations, and others provided financial and political backing for the black movement. One hundred thousand marched in San Francisco, and King joined with Walter Reuther in the summer of 1963, after Birmingham, to lead a march of 125,000 on a Freedom Walk in Detroit. Data from a national *Newsweek* poll taken in that summer showed widespread backing for and involvement in the black movement: 80 percent thought that demonstrations worked; 46 percent felt a personal obligation to get involved; 48 percent were prepared to demonstrate even if it meant going to jail.[28]

As the tempo of black struggle grew in 1963, Malcolm increasingly spoke to concerns. King's confrontation in Birmingham helped to provide Malcolm with an audience that was far more receptive to his ideas. But the Birmingham movement and its aftermath slowed recruitment into the Black Muslims, to whom many had previously turned because of their militancy. The Muslims spoke in militant terms, but they remained inactive. Those blacks who wished to participate in the struggle for black equality, and who previously might have been attracted to the Muslims, began to look elsewhere. The civil rights movement now provided a place for them to put their energy. Malcolm himself wanted to play a role in the racial conflicts of the sixties, and ultimately that goal lay behind his rupture with Muhammed. Malcolm explained the impact this tendency was having:

> Privately, I was convinced that our nation of Islam could be an even greater force in the American black man's overall struggle—if we engaged in more *action*. It could be heard increasingly in the Negro communities: "Those Muslims *talk* tough, but they never *do* anything, unless somebody bothers Muslims." I moved around among outsiders more than most other Muslim officials. I felt the very real potentiality that, considering the mercurial moods of the black masses, this labeling of Muslims as "talk only" could see us, powerful as we were, one day suddenly separated from the Negro's front-line struggle. (emphasis in original)

Malcolm did not wish to be separated from that struggle. So, while the Black Muslims continued to refrain from black activity, Malcolm's pronouncements became increasingly harsh and political. His departure from the organization was only months away.[29]

As this conflict developed, Malcolm was able to stay at the center of black and white consciousness by articulating the growing black mood of anger. He persistently hammered away at the viciousness of the whites and at the apparent limitations put on the actions of blacks by their leaders.

> You don't have to criticize Reverend Martin Luther King, Jr. His actions criticize him. Any Negro who teaches other Negroes to turn the other cheek is disarming the Negro. . . . And men like King—their job is to go among Negroes and teach Negroes "Don't fight back." He doesn't tell them "don't fight each other." "Don't fight the white man" is what he's saying in essence, because the followers of Martin Luther King, Jr. will cut each other from head to foot, but they will not do anything to defend themselves against the attacks of the white man. . . . *White* people follow King. *White* people pay King. *White* people subsidize King. *White* people support King. But the masses of black people don't support Martin Luther King, Jr.[30] (emphasis in original)

"They controlled you," he said of the civil rights leaders, "but they have never incited you or excited you. . . . They contained you."[31]

The anger articulated by Malcolm X reflected the wounds that had been rubbed raw in the Northern black population. They had seen the brutality of Southern police and of those who flagrantly and successfully violated the law. They themselves had gained little from the civil rights movement, and their material concerns had not been addressed at all. The angry mood deepened in both the South and the North when a bomb exploded in a church in Birmingham about a month after the March on Washington, in the fall of 1963. Four young black girls were killed, and Malcolm's angry words rang out:

As long as the white man sent you to Korea, you bled. He sent you to Germany, you bled. He sent you to the South Pacific to fight the Japanese, you bled. You bleed for people, but when it comes to seeing your own churches being bombed and little black girls murdered, you haven't got any blood. You bleed when the white man says bleed, you bite when the white man says bite; and you bark when the white man says bark. I hate to say this about us, but it's true. How are you going to be nonviolent in Mississippi, as violent as you were in Korea?[32]

Malcolm counseled militancy as necessary for blacks to achieve their goals:

When I was in Africa, I noticed some of the Africans got their freedom faster than others. . . . I noticed that in the areas where independence had been gotten, someone got angry. And in areas where independence had not been achieved yet, no one was angry.[33]

He stressed to his followers the culpability of Northern whites in black oppression, and he contended that it was not only Southern blacks who suffered:

What has Mississippi got to do with Harlem? It isn't actually Mississippi; it's America. America is Mississippi. . . . There's no such thing as the South—it's America. If one room in your house is dirty, you've got a dirty house. . . . Don't say that that room is dirty but the rest of my house is clean. You're over the whole house. . . . And the mistake that you and I make is letting these Northern crackers shift the weight to the Southern crackers. . . . This country is a country whose governmental system is run by committees. . . . Out of 46 committees that govern the foreign and domestic direction of this country, 23 are in the hands of Southern racists . . . because in the areas from which they come, the black man is deprived of his right to vote. . . . So, what happens in Mississippi and the South has a direct bearing on what happens to you and me here in Harlem.[34]

Malcolm felt that blacks had to have control over their lives:

We're against a segregated school system. . . . But this does not mean that a school is segregated because it's all black. A segregated school means a school that is controlled by people who have no real interest in it whatsoever. . . . They never refer to the white section as a segregated community. It's the all-Negro section that's a segregated community. Why? The white man controls his own school, his own bank, his own economy, his own politics, his own everything, his own community—but he also controls yours. When you're under someone else's control you're segregated.[35]

Control was necessary in order to enable blacks to attain the benefits to which they were entitled:

Just because you're in this country doesn't make you an American. No you've got to go farther than that before you can become an American. You've got to enjoy the fruits of Americanism.[36]

Ghetto Rebellions

Malcolm's biting words expressed and focused a mood of anger that festered while the organized civil rights movement grew. The extent of his influence cannot be measured; that it was substantial cannot be doubted. As the movement in the North grew, it produced a variety of manifestations: school boycotts protesting not only segregation but also the unequal allocation of resources; demonstrations at construction sites, as blacks demanded a share of the well-paying jobs in the industry; ''shop-ins,'' where demonstrators filled grocery carts with goods and then walked off and left them in order to pressure the stores to hire blacks; sit-ins in hotels for the same purpose; and a threat to block the entrances to the New York World's Fair during the summer of 1964. Over and over, the charge of police brutality reverberated as the demonstrators encountered the police. This experience provided a common point of reference to the travails of the civil rights workers in the South.

It was the charge of police brutality after a white police lieutenant shot a fifteen-year-old boy that precipitated the Harlem riot in the summer of 1964. This upheaval was the first of the ghetto rebellions in the Northern cities. It may have been coincidence that this riot, and almost all of those that followed that year, took place within weeks of the Democratic convention, either before, during, or after. But it was the summer of the Schwerner-Charey-Goodman murders, and information about the terrible harassment to which civil rights workers were subject had been well aired in the North. Fannie Lou Hamer testified on television to the Democratic Credentials Committee concerning the brutal beatings she suffered that summer for her activity; it was after her testimony that Malcolm reminded blacks of the similarity between Mississippi and the rest of the nation.

Shooting incidents such as the one in Harlem were not uncommon, but the response was. Before the Harlem riot was over, riots had spread to Brooklyn and Bedford-Stuyvesant. And immediately thereafter, new riots broke out in Rochester, New York; then Jersey City, New Jersey. During the Democratic convention, there was more rioting in Patterson and Elizabeth, New Jersey, and somewhat later in Philadelphia.

These riots were not minor disturbances. In Rochester, for example, 4 people died, hundreds were injured, and 976 were arrested. Property damage was estimated at near three million dollars, and the Governor of New York mobilized 1,500 National Guardsmen. Thus was inaugurated a new period in the black movement. Malcolm X warned after the summer bout of 1964 that ''more and worse riots will erupt. The black man has seen the white man's underbelly of guilty fear.'' He was right about there being more to come. The riots took place for the most part outside the South, in the new urban ghettos. They illustrated a depth of alienation and disaffection from the American mainstream previously unimagined by white society.[37]

The summer of 1964 was only the first wave in what was to become a sea of riotous upheaval. The next summer saw an uprising in Watts, the black ghetto of Los Angeles, that dwarfed those of the previous year. The riot proceeded for six days. When it was over, 35 people had been killed, 28 of them black; 900 were injured, and over 3,500 had been arrested. The police had been unable to cope with the dimensions of the uprising, and over 12,000 National Guardsmen were called in; entire city blocks were burned to the ground; buses and ambulances were stoned; snipers fired at police and fireman, and even at airplanes. David Sears and John McConahay noted that the number of law enforcement agents employed was "equal to the 17,000 troops necessary to conquer Cuba in the Spanish-American War."[38]

Watts was the largest, but by no means the only, such riot that year. There were others in Chicago and San Diego. In 1966, over two dozen cities were struck by riots. The summer of 1967 saw many more such upheavals, including one in Detroit that substantially exceeded the scale even of the Watts rebellion: 43 dead, over 1,000 injured, 7,000 arrested, and fifty million dollars of property destruction. More followed through the rest of the sixties, with a big wave in 1968, after the murder of Martin Luther King.

The riots had an immense political impact: they shifted both the geographical and the political focus of the black movement. They went beyond the matter of civil rights to raise a wide variety of political, economic, and social issues. They forced the government to respond with new programs, the civil rights leaders to reshape their strategies and even their goals; they intensified the political struggles within the black movement, and they confronted white society with the dilemma of how to respond. Finally, their impact on blacks themselves was profound.

Riots or Revolt?

These riots proceeded for several years, during which there was heated debate over who had participated in them, what they were about, and why they occurred. Because they were first and primarily a Northern urban phenomenon, they were a shock to Northern liberals, who had supported and been moved by the black struggle in the South, and who felt that conditions in the North were superior. They upset the big-city political machines and bosses, who had provided an important share of the support for the civil rights movement in the South, and the riots forced these officials to reconsider their relations with the black community resident in their localities.

Politicians often tried to deflect the political impact of the upheavals by terming them mere riots rather than expressions of protest. They contended that the riots were irrational, senseless acts and that the rioters were either an urban underclass—the dregs of society—or newly arrived from the South, and hence really protesting, irrationally, Southern conditions when they were safely in the North. In any case, they charged that the rioters represented a tiny part of the black population and were in no sense representative. They thus implied that the riots did not represent a general feeling of black discontent with conditions in the Northern cities.

There were several critiques of this view, but it was most sharply attacked by Sears and McConahay, T. M. Tomlinson, and Nathan Caplan. These scholars held that the riots were the work of what Sears, McConahay, and Tomlinson called "the new urban black" and what Caplan called the "new ghetto man." The rioters, they held, were socialized in the North and were responding specifically to Northern grievances, using Northern-engendered responses. Moreover, they argued that these "new urban blacks" were relatively well educated and of a higher class status than blacks in general. Tomlinson referred to the rioters as the "cream of Negro youth in particular and urban Negro citizens in general." The political implication of this contention ran directly counter to the politicians' characterization of the riots and rioters. The riots were seen as a response to real grievances and thus as a legitimate form of political expression.[39] (This thesis was, in its turn, attacked by Abraham Miller, Louis H. Bolce, and Mark R. Halligan. They charged that Sears and McConahay had seriously miscalculated their data by confusing dependent and independent variables. They argued that Caplan, who summarized a whole series of studies, erred by collapsing categories, and that he thereby confused civil rights protestors with rioters, a distinction that Miller et al. felt had to be retained. They contended that the rioters were part of the unstable underclass and not necessarily raised in the North.[40])

The evidence indicates something different from these analyses. The rioters included a large part of the eligible population in the areas of the city in which rioting took place—generally from 10 to 20 percent. They were representative of the broader populace, a large percentage of which was quite sympathetic to the rioters and their actions. There was participation of the underclass in these outbursts, but in general the participants lived in the riot areas and were not the hard-core unemployed. Their income was basically the same as the nonrioters', and their employment status does not appear to have diverged sharply from the nonrioters', although the lower-status occupations were overrepresented.[41]

A survey in Newark found the very poor to be less supportive of violence than those who were better off, and the study in Watts found that the most active churchgoers were most likely to have been participants, indicating the stable character of the rioters (although the next most likely were those who went to church least). Rioters tended to believe in the work ethic about the same as nonrioters; and they had a crime rate prior to the riots similar to that of nonrioters, but they tended to have committed *fewer* serious crimes prior to the riot.[42]

Robert B. Hill and Robert M. Fogelson, who looked at those actually arrested in the riots, concluded that "the occupational distributions of the arrestees and the residents are quite similar" and that "if age is . . . held constant, the rioters were about as likely to be unskilled and unemployed as the potential rioters." It appears, then, reasonable to conclude that the rioters were fairly representative of the black, urban population. While that means they were not necessarily an underclass, they were without question an overwhelmingly lower-class population.[43]

The participants in these upheavals did not lash out blindly. They were selective: public facilities, such as libraries, went untouched; so did black-owned stores and those that were felt to treat ghetto residents fairly. In one study of the residents of one of the areas of conflagration in Detroit, most thought that the riot was not a product of impulsive behavior. Fifty-seven percent thought that "most of the people who started the trouble in Detroit had been thinking about it for a long time."[44]

These lower-class black riots were the product of the first generation of blacks raised in the North. Robert Fogelson, using a sample of those arrested, demonstrated that in a large number of riots in different cities over several years, on the first day of rioting young men raised in the urban ghettos outside the South constituted the largest share of the arrestees. Moreover, he noted that in later years, blacks socialized in the North came increasingly to be represented among those arrested. He concluded:

> Apparently the upcoming generation of urban blacks, the young and single blacks born in the Northern ghettos, joined in the riots first; and it was particularly active in the rioting and burning. The current generation of urban blacks, the mature and married blacks born in the rural South, joined in thereafter; and it was particularly active in the rioting and looting. What is more, the upcoming (and presumably more militant) generation has increased its participation over time much more rapidly than the older generation. Hence the fairly typical young adults born and raised in the Northern ghettos who reached maturity in the 1950's and 1960's were not just the main source of rioters. They were also the rioters who joined in at the beginning, who engaged in the most serious forms of violence and who in all likelihood, will predominate in future riots.

The riots were carried out to a significant extent by people who were raised in the conditions of the Northern urban ghettos and who had their own distinctive response to those conditions. Even the Southern blacks who participated in the riots evidently were not simply expressing resentment over Southern conditions and circumstances; they were also responding to distinctly Northern conditions. They were aware of, concerned about, and affected by the Southern drama, and the successes of the civil rights movement had provided them with a sense of power. But they had their own problems, and it was to these they were responding.[45]

Angus Campbell and Howard Schuman, in a study of blacks in fifteen cities that experienced riots in 1968, found significant grievances directed toward any number of features of ghetto life. When people were asked a series of questions concerning their experiences with the police, over 50 percent stated that the police did not come quickly enough when called; almost 40 percent felt they were disrespectful and insulting; 36 percent felt they searched people in their neighborhood without good reason; 35 percent felt they roughed people up unnecessarily. These findings were corroborated in the Los Angeles study of blacks after the Watts upheaval. Said one man:

> If they stop a white man, they don' bother him, but a Negro they hope to find dope or pills [or] stolen merchandise. They hope to "get lucky" on a Negro and get him to do or say the wrong thing, or call in on you. On a Sunday afternoon, you can't even go out for a decent ride. . . . The police is always hiding out

trying to sneak up on people. You are tense and nervous looking for them at all times. Even the children are afraid. They start running when they see the police because they have heard how the policemen beat their fathers and brothers. They have seen how they stop them for nothing.[46]

Findings were similar with respect to feelings about merchants. People felt that the merchants overcharged them, served them inferior merchandise, and treated them with a lack of respect. In the Los Angeles study, people felt aggrieved about their treatment by public agencies, public officials, the white-dominated media, and their own representatives. Racial discrimination was felt to be still pervasive:

I've run into more prejudice here than I did in the South. The kids in the South can go to school anywhere now, but here we are zoned so that we are still segregated *de facto*. When a white kid gets out of school, he can qualify for a job in aircraft with his high school training, but not our kids. Here at Centinela High they give them woodburning and mess like that and they get bad grades because they aren't interested. They don't fail them anymore, they just pass them along and when they get sixteen, they kick them out.[47]

Thus, real grievances existed, based on distinctly Northern conditions. But grievances alone were not sufficient to bring about upheaval. The young men and women who grew up in the urban ghettos of the North and West were much freer than those who had come before them of the debilitating effects of racial self-hatred. They had been socialized to believe they were equal to whites. They were much less inclined to self-derogation than their Southern counterparts or those older than they in the cities. They exhibited racial pride. This new generation of urban blacks was politically sophisticated and well informed. It felt capable of affecting policy.[48]

These blacks were, at the same time, quite militant; they had grown up learning not, as had many Southern blacks, to contain their anger but rather to express it effectively. Huey Newton recalled:

In our working and lower class community we valued the person who successfully bucked authority. Group prestige and acceptance were won through defiance and physical strength. . . . Fighting has always been a big part of my life, as it is in the lives of most poor people. . . . We were really trying to affirm our masculinity and dignity, and using force in reaction to the social pressures exerted against us. For a proud and dignified people fighting was one way to resist dehumanization.[49]

Joe R. Feagin and Harlan Hahn argued that prior to and during the course of the riots, there was growing support among blacks for the use of violence. Many others were prepared to justify the use of violence, even if they themselves would not use it. Increasingly, support grew for use of these means, so that James Geschwender contended that the distinction between protest and riots was disappearing.[50]

The riots took place in a climate of increasing protest. Northern blacks had been watching the civil rights movement and the treatment blacks received in the South. They were infuriated by it. Cries of "Selma!" were heard in the Watts riot, which took place only months after the demonstrations in Alabama, indicating how extensive was the impact of the events there. Douglas Glasgow, who studied a group of the black underclass who had participated in the riot, reported that the group had watched the civil rights struggles on television. They had observed the white violence and blacks' accepting it by turning the other cheek. "The men resolved that they would never passively accept this treatment from the 'man.' Whereas earlier they had turned much of the anger in on themselves . . . their rage and resentment now arose to a new high and was externalized."[51]

Many Northern blacks were disillusioned with the federal government, and a large number of those who rioted had also participated in civil rights demonstrations. They and others had little faith in the procedures that existed for handling grievances. In Watts, 40 percent were found to have lost faith in conventional approaches. Again and again, researchers found that blacks viewed the riots as an expression of protest and as a way of forcing changes. James Geschwender noted that, as a result of these riots, negotiations proceeded in several cases between the authorities and black leaders, sometimes including black youth. The riots emerged as a form of protest, a way to win black gains, under conditions where most participants felt that there was no other way to win them. Said one:

> It was an attempted emergence from passivity. Too long now we Negroes have had things done *to* and *for* us, but seldom *by* us. This was our initial try. . . . I feel that it was something that the white folks had been inviting. They set the stage and wrote most of the script leading to this drama. (emphasis in original)

That was why many called the riots revolts, or even insurrections, indicating that they had a political character and were not merely outbursts of looters and hoodlums.[52]

Ghetto Revolts and the Break with White America

The protest character of these ghetto revolts was further illustrated by the way in which the black community viewed them. King toured the riot area in Watts during the last day of the riot. There a young man proudly told him: "We won!" Looking at the mayhem and destruction, King asked how he could say that. "Because we made them pay attention to us," was the response. His was not an isolated sentiment. In a survey of Watts, 58 percent of the area residents and 57 percent of the arrestees thought that the effect of the riot would be favorable, while only 18 percent and 27 percent respectively anticipated unfavorable results. Thirty-eight percent of the residents and 54 percent of the arrestees thought that the Watts riot "helped the Negro's cause"; 84 percent and 80 percent respectively thought that it made whites "more aware of Negro problems"; 51 percent and 49 percent thought that it made "whites more sympathetic to Negro problems."

One respondent commented: "Things will be better. We will have new buildings and the whites now realize that the Negro isn't going to be pushed around like before."[53]

Real gains were won as a result of the riots. The funds generally allocated to the poverty program were increased during the riot period and those cities that experienced riots got the largest share of antipoverty money. One study showed that the amount of antipoverty money allocated to Los Angeles dramatically increased after the Watts uprising. James Button argued that his statistical analysis of the allocation of these funds demonstrated that "the black riots had a greater direct positive impact than any other independent variable upon total Office of Economic Opportunity expenditure increases in the latter 1960's." Jobs were also provided for the unemployed.[54]

King contended that the gains produced by the riots were small and that those who argued they were significant

> always end up with stumbling words when asked what concrete gains have been won as a result. At best, the riots have produced a little anti-poverty money allotted by frightened government officials, and a few water-sprinklers to cool the children of the ghettos. It is something like improving the food in the prison while the people remain securely incarcerated behind bars.[55]

A great deal had to do with perception. An important part of the riots was their impact on black self-esteem, which was similar to that of the civil rights demonstrations: black pride grew. This effect was evidenced in many ways. Sears and McConahay found that black pride increased over time in Watts, as people had the opportunity to discuss and assimilate the impact of the upheaval. Campbell and Schuman found that racial pride was widespread in the cities they surveyed.[56]

During the riot period, this changing attitude had its reflection in a number of developments. The term *Negro* fell into disrepute; those wanting to emphasize racial pride called themselves "blacks," the linguistic counterpart to "whites." The use of hair straighteners was greatly diminished, and the process of males' "conking" their hair—soaking it in lye to take out the curl—came virtually to an end. Young blacks wore "naturals"—they let their hair grow out in a way that no white hair could. "Black is beautiful" became a widespread slogan that emphasized the new attitude. In the colleges and universities, black students fought for and frequently won the establishment of black studies programs.

Nationalism grew, particularly among the young. Campbell and Schuman reported that from about 10 to 20 percent of those aged sixteen to nineteen agreed with a variety of statements that could be described as nationalist, or as separatist, and among these Malcolm X was particularly well regarded. Nationalist and separatist organizations grew and proliferated in the latter years of the sixties and the early years of the seventies. Cooperative political relations between blacks and whites on college campuses diminished during the late sixties, and even social relations became severely curtailed.[57]

This growing nationalist sentiment was only partially a product of a sense of black strength. In part also, it emerged from a growing sense, mirrored in the young black activists in the South, that whites would not support them in their efforts to restructure American society so as to improve substantially their life chances. The rebuff administered by Californians in 1964 to middle-class blacks who wanted to expand their housing selection was one such indication. There were many others.

Campbell and Schuman found that whites and blacks had very different assessments about the riots. Close to 50 percent of whites felt that riots were wholly or partially for the purpose of looting; over 60 percent attributed the causes of the riots to radicals, looters, and Communists; almost 85 percent thought they had been planned in advance; nearly 50 percent felt that the best way to prevent future riots was to increase police control. Perhaps most dramatic, given the black perception that the ghetto rebellions would improve their circumstances and the way whites viewed them, was that about 65 percent of the whites felt that the riots hurt the black cause, most because they felt that those upheavals increased antiblack sentiments. Sixty-eight percent of whites interviewed in Los Angeles after Watts felt that blacks were pushing too fast, and 56 percent thought blacks were "asking for special treatment from whites to which they were not entitled." William Brink and Louis Harris, in a poll done for *Newsweek* magazine in 1966, found that the whites' assessment of racial matters was entirely different from the blacks': 85 percent felt that demonstrations hurt the black cause, and certainly that riots did so. Seventy percent thought blacks were moving too fast. As in California, most whites (58 percent) did not want blacks moving into their neighborhood, "and this figure rises to 76 per cent among whites living in the areas where Negroes would like to move." For this reason a national open-housing bill was defeated in the election year of 1966.[58]

These sentiments were reflected in government action. While at first monies were poured into rioting ghettos, by the summer of 1967 the then-secretary of the Department of Housing and Urban Development stated: "We were very careful *not* to allow a riot city to receive a lot of new money, as we didn't want to appear to respond to violence" (emphasis in original). Instead, both federal and local governments began emphasizing repression. President Johnson mobilized the army in 1967, not to protect integration, as President Eisenhower had done in Little Rock a decade earlier, but to suppress the Detroit uprising; and the National Guard was mobilized for the same purpose twenty-nine times that summer. City after city stockpiled armaments; new legislation was passed to prevent riots and to suppress crime.[59]

There was thus ample reason for blacks to feel that their needs were not being met, and perhaps would not be met. Though they gained antipoverty money and jobs, these did not begin to deal with the problems they faced. The very fact of the rioting itself, in which invariably more blacks were hurt than whites, and in which black neighborhoods were seriously damaged, often losing most or all of their stores, indicated a sense of despair and alienation. That was particularly so among lower-class blacks. The Brink and Harris survey found that while Southern blacks, especially those of the middle class, had made some substantial progress, "the Negroes who have shared the least in the rewards of progress are those living in the big-city slums and ghettos, mainly in the North." While 70 percent of the black population said that they had seen progress, only 29 percent of lower-class blacks did. "In the case of jobs, only 24 percent of them feel they are better off now, compared with 54 percent of Negroes overall." Economist Vivian Henderson corroborated this sense when he testified before the National Advisory Commission on Civil Disorders:

> No one can deny that all Negroes have benefited from civil rights laws and desegregation in public life in one way or another. The fact is, however, that the masses of Negroes have not experienced tangible benefits in any significant way. This is so in education and housing. It is critically so in the area of jobs and economic security. Expectations of Negro masses for equal job opportunity programs have fallen short of fulfillment. Negroes have made gains. . . . But . . . the masses of Negroes have been virtually untouched by these gains.

The commission itself summed up in its conclusion what many blacks felt: "Our nation is moving toward two societies, one black and one white—separate and unequal."[60]

It was not, however, merely a matter of color. Blacks outside the South met a rebuff because whites, who were willing to support changes in the South to accommodate blacks there, were unwilling to do so when demands for change were brought in their own backyards. That was one important element of the situation. But the needs of blacks in the North and the demands raised by them for jobs, housing, health, welfare—for a slice of the American pie—went far beyond what blacks in the South had demanded. Blacks in the North and West were seeking a restructuring not just of the South but of American society generally, and as such they ran up against the interests that had supported the civil rights movement. They began to lose those allies, and it was largely out of this process of isolation that the demand for black power emerged and became the dominant tendency among these new urban blacks.

Ghetto Revolts and Black Power

The anger that emanated from the black ghettos of the North was particularly important because the social weight of these black concentrations was so great. By the mid-sixties, one-half of the black population lived in the North, almost all crowded into the big cities. The disturbances blacks created in those metropolises were magnified because the extensive destruction and the widespread challenge to authority took place in the nation's cultural, financial, manufacturing, and political centers. Turmoil in Little Rock or Montgomery was significant; in Chicago or New York or Los Angeles it was far more so. And the riots had a national impact, as they began to eclipse the civil rights struggle and to exert a great pull on the civil rights activists themselves. Cleveland Sellers recalled:

> We were all very conscious of the fact that the axis of the struggle appeared to be shifting away from the rural South to the cities in the North. The totally unexpected rebellions in Harlem, Watts, Chicago and Philadelphia made a big impact on our thinking.[61]

SNCC and CORE had already begun to turn away from both the goals and the strategy of the civil rights movement. After the MFDP experience, many SNCC activists began to look more carefully at Malcolm X, and they began to explore ties with him. They drew the conclusion that the effort to attain civil rights was insufficient. One SNCC activist wrote that she understood this point only after winning the Voting Rights Act:

> We found that it was a shallow victory. After the earlier sit-ins, the civil rights movement had had to stop and ask: "What have we gained by winning the right to a cup of coffee downtown?" In the same way, we who had worked for voting rights now had to ask ourselves what we had gained. In both cases the answer was the same: Negroes were in fact not basically better off with this new right than they had been before; they were still poor and without the power to direct their own lives.[62]

In part because of their own experiences, in part because the ghetto revolts demanded a new black agenda, SNCC and CORE activists began to propose major structural changes in America. In the manifesto *Black Power*, SNCC leader Stokeley Carmichael and Charles V. Hamilton explained black power. Elsewhere, Hamilton argued that the ghetto riots were

> acts which deny the very legitimacy of the system itself. The entire value structure which supports property rights over human rights, which *sanctions* the intolerable conditions in which the black people have been *forced* to live is questioned.

This statement, and many others like it, indicated clearly that the effort to resolve issues of *racial* concern had led many black activists to challenge the *class* structure. Now they were going beyond the anachronistic form of class domination that had characterized the South to attack the structure of modern American capitalism.[63]

In the spring of 1966, after the Selma campaign and the Watts riots, a bitter faction fight in SNCC resulted in the election of radical Stokeley Carmichael as chairman of the organization. As a result, those who were leaning toward nationalism took over the leadership of the most militant civil rights organization. That summer, during a civil rights march in Mississippi that was jointly sponsored by SNCC, CORE, and the SCLC, Carmichael seized the opportunity to make known and to popularize his position. There, in front of the media, he raised the cry of "black power" as the new slogan for the black movement. The cry grew out of the experiences and disillusionment of the civil rights workers in the South, but it was fueled by the ghetto uprisings. Had it expressed only the sentiments of frustrated civil rights activists in the South, its impact would have been minimal. But it clearly tapped into the developing consciousness of masses of urban ghetto blacks. With the help of the media, the cry spread across the country, and Carmichael became a major national black spokesman.

Black riots had helped to give rise to the slogan; they also helped to provide it with meaning. While talking with King, Carmichael endowed the slogan with a relatively innocuous meaning: "Martin, you know as well as I do that practically every other ethnic group in America has done just this. The Jews, the Irish and the Italians did it, why can't we?" But circumstances gave the slogan a much angrier tone. The expression "black power" was articulated in the midst of the fourth long, hot summer of angry black activity. The summer of 1966, and those that followed with their massive explosions of human anger in the black ghettos, endowed the phrase "black power" with the connotations of militance and nationalism, of black anger and hostility to whites. Above all, it seemed to signify the willingness of blacks to seek their course alone, unencumbered by whites, who did not share the same oppressive conditions to which blacks were subject and who, many blacks felt, did not and could not share the deep sense of urgency to transform their lives and their conditions.[64]

In adopting the slogan "black power," Carmichael and others were consciously rejecting the limits set by the civil rights coalition. It was a mistake, said Carmichael and Hamilton, to assume that "a politically and economically secure group can collaborate with a politically and economically insecure group." Such alliances were held to be unviable because the coalition partners had widely differing goals. While blacks needed fundamental social transformation, the others didn't: "At bottom, those groups accept the American system and want only—if at all—to make peripheral, marginal reforms in it. Such reforms are inadequate to rid the society of racism." Thus, given the "power-oriented nature of American politics," the partners in the civil rights coalition "are unpredictable allies when a conflict of interest arises."[65]

King responded to the ideological offensive represented by black power by arguing that the slogan was self-defeating because it did not provide a strategy capable of success. "No one has ever heard the Jews publicly chant a slogan of Jewish power, but they have power. Through group identity, determination and creative endeavor, they have gained it. The same thing is true of the Irish and Italians." He objected to the slogan of "black power" because, he maintained, it isolated blacks.[66]

"Black power" did isolate the black movement, and whites certainly did turn away from it in the later sixties and early seventies. But in truth it should be plain that black power was also a *response* to the isolation of the black movement that was already taking place. As blacks perceived the need to go beyond the simple struggle for civil rights and to extend their demands to dig deeper into the foundation of American society, they saw themselves increasingly isolated as whites deserted them.

Black power, and indeed the riots themselves, were as much an expression as a cause of the disintegration of the civil rights coalition, and of the isolation of blacks that was attendant upon it. That alliance had made the movement victorious in its effort to end legal segregation and discrimination against blacks in the South. It was possible because the dominant section of the nation had an interest in ending segregation, owing to the political and economic difficulties it caused. But neither the federal government nor any of the other allies of blacks had any interest in carrying out the far-reaching social and economic changes that would be necessary to deal with the full range of black needs. There was no pressure from the middle classes to do so. On the contrary, many actually opposed black demands when they were directed at social issues that went beyond simple racial discrimination. Even in this realm, they often did not view issues such as housing and school desegregation with sympathy. Whereas in the South turmoil created by blacks again and again had brought the business and middle classes to seek to conciliate the demand for change, the disorder of the ghetto riots had no such effect; if anything, attitudes hardened in response to these outbursts. The result was for many blacks to turn inward, but the turn inward was a response to the turn away from the black movement by whites.

Ghetto Revolts and Martin Luther King: Search for a New Coalition

King and his supporters could not escape the turmoil outside the South that had such a great impact on the black movement and on civil rights activists, organizations, and leaders. They too were moved by it and felt compelled to respond to it by altering their agenda. If King and his strategy of nonviolent direct action were to retain their leadership, he had now to turn to the ghettos, where, Bayard Rustin stated, "Roy [Wilkins, then head of the NAACP], Martin and I haven't done a thing about it. We've done plenty to get votes in the South and seats in lunch rooms, but we've had no progress for these youngsters." So, King proposed a project in Chicago, to begin in 1966.[67]

In making this move, King was, in one sense, gambling. The problems he was facing—poverty and slumlords; black exclusion from jobs; housing that was segregated because whites refused to sell or rent to, or live near, blacks—were very different from and much more difficult to resolve than the legal discrimination he had fought with such success in the South. Moreover, as Northern blacks and those in SNCC had already found, King's allies in the Southern campaigns—the Northern Democratic party and liberal white opinion—now turned out to be his adversaries. In Chicago, King was not dealing with an outlawed section of the country that had kept blacks in their place and prevented modernization. Mayor Daley's political machine was the bedrock of the national Democratic party. But that party saw little that needed change in Chicago or elsewhere outside of the South. When King entered this territory, he did so without the backing of the potent civil rights coalition. In this circumstance, he was risking failure. But in another sense it was no gamble at all: if he didn't undertake this campaign, he would be abandoning the field.

King was able to develop impressive support. He got some from the AFL-CIO unions; the United Auto Workers sent in organizers to set up a rent strike. He had a meeting with the powerful leaders of the black gangs in Chicago and persuaded them to give nonviolence a try. He was able to hold some large demonstrations. However, he succeeded in winning little.

In the midst of this campaign, from the rural backlands of Mississippi, intruded the drama that recast the movement. When James Meredith had enrolled at the University of Mississippi in 1962, he had precipitated a white riot, which forced President Kennedy to federalize the Mississippi National Guard. Now, in the summer of 1966, Meredith had begun a "March against Fear" in that state to prove that blacks could go anywhere they wished. He had not gone far when he was shot and seriously wounded. King and other civil rights leaders immediately flew down to Mississippi to visit Meredith and to continue his march.

There were deep differences between the groups represented, ranging from the newly installed heads of SNCC and CORE, Stokeley Carmichael and Floyd McKissick, to the far more conservative Roy Wilkins of the NAACP and Whitney Young of the Urban League. Wilkins and Young balked over demands for a march manifesto that charged the federal government with failure to carry out a real civil rights program. King accepted the manifesto but had to battle over two other issues: whether whites should be allowed on the march and whether it would be nonviolent. King prevailed on the first issue, and ostensibly on the second, as well. But a group from Louisiana, the Deacons for Self-Defense, escorted the march, and they were quietly armed. It was on this march that Carmichael had raised the cry of black power.

All of that made the Chicago campaign more crucial for King. If he could succeed there, his nonviolent approach would be proved against the advocates of black power. But he did not succeed in Chicago: in the summer of 1966 a riot broke out in that city, followed shortly by another riot in Cleveland. King, without the support of the civil rights coalition, was able to secure little in the way of real concessions from the Daley machine, and eventually he packed up and returned to Atlanta. By the time the summer was over, the black movement had a new face: it was more radical, more militant, more nationalist.

King thus faced a new situation. He perceived that the civil rights coalition had run its course, and in his last book, *Where Do We Go from Here: Chaos or Community?* he wrote that:

> It evokes happy memories, to recall that our victories in the past decade were won with a broad coalition of organizations representing a wide variety of interests. But we deceive ourselves if we envision the same combination backing structural changes in the society. It did not come together for such a program and will not reassemble for it.

This perception did not lead King to abandon the pursuit of coalition politics. Rather, he attempted to counter the isolating trend of black power. "In a multiracial society," he affirmed, "no group can make it alone." So, he sought to create a new coalition. Who would the new allies be? He was groping toward a solution that put more emphasis on class politics. "There are, in fact, more poor white Americans than there are Negro," he pointed out. And these whites were indeed, in his view, potential allies:

> Racism is a tenacious evil, but it is not immutable. Millions of underprivileged whites are in the process of considering the contradiction between segregation and economic progress. White supremacy can feed their egos but not their stomachs. They will not go hungry or forego the affluent society to remain racially ascendant.[68]

It was to these people, as well as to the well-intentioned middle-class whites, that King hoped to turn in what had to be a much more radical confrontation with American society than he had heretofore attempted. One example of his thinking is found in his address before the tenth-anniversary convention of the SCLC in 1967:

> We must honestly face the fact that the Movement must address itself to the question of restructuring the whole of American society. There are 40 million poor people here. And one day we must ask the question, "Why are there 40 million poor people in America?" And when you begin to ask that question, you are raising questions about the economic system, about a broader distribution of wealth. When you ask that question, you begin to question the capitalistic economy. And to ask questions about the whole society. We are called upon to help the discouraged beggars in life's market place. But one day we must come to see that an edifice which produces beggars needs restructuring. It means that questions must be raised. You see, my friends, when you deal with this, you begin to ask the question, "Who owns the oil?" You begin to ask the question, "Who owns the iron ore?" You begin to ask the question, "Why is it that people have to pay water bills in a world that is two-thirds water?" These are questions that must be asked.

King denied the inevitable charge that he was a Marxist. Nonetheless, he went on to contend that:

> When I say question the whole society, it means ultimately coming to see that the problem of racism, the problem of economic exploitation, and the problem of war are all tied together. . . . A nation that will keep people in slavery for 244 years will "thingify" them, make them things. Therefore they will exploit them, and poor people generally economically. And a nation that will exploit economically will have to have foreign investments . . . and will have to use its military might to protect them. All of these problems are tied together. What I am saying today is that we must go from this convention and say, "America, you must be born again!"[69]

It was in this spirit, and in hope of creating a new coalition that could successfully tackle the economic issues that had been raised by the black movement, that King began preparation for the Poor People's March on Washington, which he envisioned as a confrontation. He also turned to union organizing. That was the new strategy he had to offer. If successful, he felt that it would restore nonviolent direct action as the centerpiece of social change and enable blacks to break out of the isolation that was being imposed upon them as they refused to cease their struggles. A class program that posed issues in terms of economic equality might, he hoped, create a new spirit of unity. King and the SCLC embarked upon a serious campaign that involved them in strikes and union organizing in Atlanta; Memphis; Detroit; Birmingham; St. Petersburg, Florida; and Charleston, Georgetown, and Florence, South Carolina. His murder in Memphis took place when he was involved in such activity. That was part of his alternative to what he considered the blind alley of black power.

The new alliance, however, never emerged. King's death cut short his efforts to create it, so we can never know what might have happened. But there is no indication that in those prosperous times any substantial section of whites would have heeded his call. If black power was a blind alley, King does not appear to have had an approach that at that time was more likely to be successful. The Black Panther party attempted to create such a coalition, within the framework of black power, in 1968 and 1969. While it was able to gain some white support from the anti-Vietnam War movement, it was not sufficiently powerful to have any major impact on the structure of American society. The black movement appeared to have gone about as far as it was capable of going at that time, given the political alignments.

VIII

CLASS AND RACE:
A RETROSPECTIVE
AND PROSPECTIVE

This study of the growth and development of the civil rights movement has had a dual focus: first, the impact of class politics upon the system of racial domination and of racial politics upon the class structure; second, the transformation of the black self, both individual and collective. At this point it is appropriate to ask, What is gained from such an approach? What insights does it yield?

Class and Race

First, the examination of class and race highlights what the black movement was about, what it was facing as it sought civil rights. It was not merely prejudice, hatred, or entrenched customs that stood in the way of blacks' being treated as humans, but also the vested interest of the agrarian elite. This class had mobilized for massive resistance to segregation to defend its own power and position in the name of the whole white population of the South. Black victory meant the defeat of this class. That is why the term *Second Reconstruction* applied to the civil rights movement is apt: the first Reconstruction attempted but failed to do away with the power of the Southern landed elite. The Second Reconstruction succeeded where the first failed; it accomplished this change by carrying out what was, in effect, a social revolution.

What had to be changed were not merely laws and customs. The vested interests maintaining those laws and customs had to be confronted. That was the aspect of the civil rights movement that made it seem like a revolutionary movement: the regime of the black-belt, upper class had to be removed forcibly from power. In carrying out this task, blacks fulfilled may of the broken promises from the original Reconstruction era—a period that, in its own way, was tinged with revolution. Because the federal government acted on the side of blacks, the transition of the mid-twentieth century was a mere upheaval rather than an actual overthrow of the government. But this difference should not obscure the social meaning of the outcome: a historic regime was ushered out against its will.

The impact of the 1962 Supreme Court ruling in *Baker* v. *Carr* was to reinforce the loss of power of the agrarian elite. Known as the one-man, one-vote decision, *Baker* v. *Carr* ruled illegal all districting that gave disproportionate power to the voters of any one district. The agrarian elite had retained its dominance partly by its disproportionate representation in the legislature and the United States Congress. Georgia even maintained an electoral college type of arrangement for electing the governor, which greatly augmented the electoral strength of the black-belt whites. *Baker* v. *Carr* hastened the transfer of power to the cities.

Second, the focus on class and race illuminated the social and historical changes necessary for a black victory in the mid-twentieth century. New economic circumstances diminished the significance of the agrarian elite in the Southern economy; new classes—the business and middle classes—emerged, with different needs and interests. Although these classes had no intention of challenging the power of the old ruling class, they acted when their interests were threatened. In case after case, business and middle classes intervened to counter the resistance to civil rights demands and to accommodate blacks. These steps were often taken grudgingly—businessmen were often no less hostile toward blacks than anyone else—but they were taken. The businessmen acted in this way because they were economically and socially vulnerable to black pressures in ways that the agrarian elite had never been and could never be. A glance at some cases other than those already discussed illustrates how decisive this trend was:

*In New Orleans there was resistance to desegregation. Fears of school closing brought business leaders to support publicly a moderate for the school board, "for the future of our children and for the continued growth of New Orleans as a major industrial center in the South." When mobs and violence persisted, hotels, restaurants, and department stores suffered steep declines in sales. Victor Schiro, appointed as mayor by the city council in the midst of the turmoil, told the public that he was "putting all on notice that law and order will be maintained at any cost." Schiro was supported by business leaders, and these joint efforts brought an end to the crisis. Desegregation was implemented.[1]

*In Atlanta, which was the financial center of the Southeast, businessmen did not wait for disorder; they moved to forestall it. The Chamber of Commerce and other influential business leaders put their full weight behind open schools, because "disruption of our public school system would have a calamitous effect on the economic climate outside of Georgia."[2]

*In Columbia, South Carolina, the experience of other cities convinced the business leaders, who sought *Look* magazine's All-American City Award all through the fifties and sixties (they won it twice), that they had to desegregate peacefully.[3]

*Newspaper accounts of events in Little Rock warned business executives in Dallas of the cost of failure to desegregate peacefully. Fifteen industries were lost in the Arkansas capital, they were told. The Dallas business community supported compliance to desegregation.[4]

*In Augusta, Georgia, threats to disrupt the Masters Golf Tournament and the experience in New Orleans brought some concessions. But it is interesting to note that in Augusta, when blacks pressed for their demands in the courts rather than the streets, steps toward integration proceeded much more slowly, indicating once again that social disruption was necessary to produce results.[5]

*Even in Jackson, Mississippi, said one observer: "Mississippi business opinion generally came to believe that the state's economic development would be hurt by racial disorder. When they reached this conclusion, the weight of their influence moved toward easing the conflict through compliance with the federal law."[6]

Third, a class and race analysis explained the form that the civil rights movement took. The process of social change is uneven. New economic and social conditions were not accompanied by a different way of treating blacks, or by an altered distribution of political power in the region. The "fit" between these spheres was no longer tight. Numan Bartley first characterized the South as a classic example of what William Ogburn termed "cultural lag." The differing situation of the new urban classes meant that they could be split from the black-belt upper class. That split did not take place of itself. The unevenness of social change helped to set the stage for a social movement to establish a new stable equilibrium; but to attain it required social upheaval.

The Southern upper class had two distinct social and economic bases, each with a different relationship to the segregation system and to blacks themselves. While for the small-town agrarian group the maintenance of the old color line was of vital importance, it simply was not for the urban business interests. This difference provided space for the black movement to develop, space that was greatly augmented by the shift of the federal government in favor of civil rights. Indeed, the division within the Southern elite invited a black movement, for while the new business class could be induced through pressure to throw its weight on the side of the blacks, it would not do so of itself. The black-belt elite did everything in its power to block change, and the federal government moved ponderously. Therefore, blacks had to act. At the same time, the divisions made it easier for blacks to act and more difficult for the segregationists to repress them.

Normally, a monolithic elite is much more difficult to confront than one that is divided. A unified elite is able to mobilize the population in its support, to point to all the prestigious and powerful centers of the society in support of its position and to contend that its point of view represents a consensus. A monolithic elite is thereby able to isolate those who seek to challenge its power. When there is an open split, an elite cannot so readily isolate its opposition, and so that opposition gains access to a broader hearing in the society. Moreover, because the elite is split, the opposition can, as blacks did, render the split wider, increasing its social power.

The civil rights movement created a new racial etiquette and recast political alignments. It helped to close the fissures that had opened between the agrarian and urban centers of power within the Southern states, and between these states and the federal government, but on a new basis. The system became stable once again.

Finally, the focus on class and race explained the shift of the movement to the North, and with that move the decline of civil rights as a unifying slogan and the emergence of black power. The swelling of black activity in the North, and its relative decline in the South, indicated that the civil rights movement had accomplished its goals. The move to the North also heralded a new set of goals defined by problems unique to the black urban experience and especially felt in the North. These problems arose from the position of most blacks on the bottom of the class structure of modern America—their class position was exacerbated by their racial status. Black efforts to alter this position demanded changes in the class system; these were structural changes that the civil rights coalition would not and could not carry out. So, as the focus of the movement changed, blacks were left alone in their efforts, an isolation that ultimately led to the move toward black power.

The civil rights coalition, which had been vital to the success of the movement, was an unstable phenomenon. As a coalition, it was never negotiated, nor did it have any explicitly agreed-upon program. The blacks' allies often had to be dragged into support. As the movement proceeded into the sixties, and the tasks the blacks set for themselves were more far-reaching, the demands that they made on their coalition "partners" were more significant, as well. Much more was asked of businessmen in Birmingham than in Montgomery or Little Rock, and of the federal government, as well. At the same time, the struggle moved from the Upper South to the Deep South, where the agrarian elite was stronger and the racial patterns more entrenched. As a result, resistance to desegregation and to black political rights was greater. The stronger position of the agrarian elite in the Deep South meant a more aggressive struggle for civil rights—massive confrontations ensued. Such confrontations served two tactical functions: to demonstrate the strength of the movement to those in power and to elicit support from allies. The tactics were successful: concessions were made on the local level, and the federal government was prodded to intervene much more deeply in Southern social and political life.

The success of confrontation, however, contributed to the disintegration of the civil rights coalition. In one sense that should have been expected, because the coalition succeeded in attaining its goals. In another sense it was not expected; there was no clearly defined statement of goals that the coalition as such was seeking. The federal government did attempt to accommodate itself to the newly expressed aims of the black movement for equality with its multifaceted Poverty Program, begun in 1964. This program also raised expectations, especially with the Community Action Programs, through which it mandated "maximum feasible participation" by the poor. But these were expectations that could not be fulfilled without altering the structure, not of an outmoded social system such as had been dominant in the South but of modern America. It was these raised expec-

tations that called into relief the limits of the civil rights coalition and foretold
its disintegration.

The rallying cries of the movement may have signaled its fragile character.
Coalitions are created with slogans and concepts that are of sufficient generality
to appeal to broad sectors of the society. The broad slogan of white supremacy,
for example, became the banner under which the Southern agrarian elite was
able to grasp and consolidate its power. The goals of the civil rights movement
were similarly framed in the simple and appealing calls for "freedom" and
"equality." The development of the doctrine of nonviolence and the search for
"brotherhood" were also part of the ideological appeal of the black movement—
waged under virtually the same slogans as the French Revolution: liberty,
equality, and brotherhood.

These slogans made it possible to draw in a broad spectrum of groups to
support the civil rights movement. The usual fate of coalitions that include such
a broad spectrum is to fall apart once the broad aim that brought them together
has been achieved. Because they involve disparate forces with differing needs,
they group themselves under a single banner, using the most general of terms.
But the various parties give such terms very different meanings. *Freedom* for
the middle class may mean the removal of governmental control, and particularly
the provision of free access to the market place, while for the working class it
may mean access to jobs and social services, the absence of hunger and poverty.
The two classes may unite against the power of the old regime, but when a new
regime is brought into being, they then have to come to terms concerning its
content. It is not surprising, therefore, that stresses emerged in the civil rights
coalition, as a result of the differing concerns of its component parts. The "freedom" from segregation and overt racial discrimination was acceptable to the
coalition; the "freedom" from economic misery was not. So, as the goal
changed, the binding force of the coalition dissolved.

Race and Class

There were other ways in which the politics of class and race influenced one
another. It was not merely that the class structure shaped the possibilities for
racial action. There were classes within the black community, and these classes
also affected black action. Consider:

1.–The dynamics of the old system had divided blacks along class lines. The
divisions in the old system had a weak objective basis. Those considered of
higher social rank often had a tenuous hold on their status. That was all the more
reason for their subjective insistence upon an exaggerated social distance separating them from poorer and (in their view) less cultured blacks.

2.–The social distance separating blacks from each other was a significant
obstacle to be overcome if blacks were successfully to confront white power.
Overcoming it often came about when higher-status blacks realized that they

were still only "niggers" to whites and that they needed to stand with lower-class blacks to be successful in advancing their own ends.

3.–While the demands of the civil rights movement were of benefit to all in the sense that they were a step toward the recognition of blacks as worthy of human dignity, it was primarily middle-class blacks, who were financially independent of whites, who led the assault and who were able to make use of its victories.

4.–As the movement proceeded, it drew in broader layers of people, who began to influence its goals and methods, as well as the general thinking process that permeated the period. The fact that the black population was overwhelmingly lower- and working-class in the 1960s meant that the black movement would inevitably have to champion their cause and to raise issues that would trouble middle-class white America. Ultimately, it became these issues that divided blacks from their white allies.

These points demonstrate that the class structure of the black community, which was itself shaped by the class system of American society, played an important role in the development of black consciousness and in the course of action chosen.

At the same time, the interpenetration of race and class was such that race was very important in shaping the class structure. I have argued that race was the lynchpin of the class settlement that emerged out of the post-Civil War period: the positioning of blacks at the bottom of the class structure, circumscribed by law and by terror, was necessary for the political power and for the economic well-being of the agrarian elite. Moreover, in carrying through the reforms of the civil rights movement, blacks caused a reshuffling of the distribution of class political power. This change had economic as well as political consequences. As representatives of the business and middle classes came to power, they made decisions that were of benefit to business and to the urban economy in general. All of that is to indicate that the interrelationship between class and race, race and class is most complex and not subject to any simple formula.

The New Negro

While the impact of class on racial politics was profound, it was not determinant. The interaction of races, of classes, and of individuals provided the framework through which changes emerged. In the old system, accommodation became the dominant path for black advancement. The prolonged period of white supremacy took its toll on blacks, who developed a sense of inferiority, the custom of acceding to white power, and a leadership that made its way by winning favors from whites.

Challenging the entrenched system necessitated a self-transformation that involved a difficult struggle both within and between individuals. People had to confront themselves and to steel themselves to make it possible to confront white power. It is not surprising that youth played such an important role in this process. They did so not only because they were relatively free of the encumbrances of life—of homes, jobs, families—but also because they were still in the process of defining themselves as individuals and had sufficient personal flexibility to attempt the difficult process of refashioning themselves. Standing up to white power necessitated restructuring the black community: new leaders were required, as well as a new style of leadership.

Southern blacks entered the decade of the fifties with the naive expectation that segregation and white supremacy would be ended voluntarily by the white leadership once it became clear that these policies were illegal and unfair. This expectation was based upon the concessions that had been made to blacks in the postwar period prior to the *Brown* ruling and upon the lingering attachment to the system of white paternalism. But the concessions were made primarily to maintain the system of white supremacy, and when it became clear, with the *Brown* decision, that white supremacy was in jeopardy, the response of the Southern elite changed. Irrespective of the law, they meant to have their own way, and they began to fight for it.

The actions of the agrarian elite forced the blacks, in their turn, to organize in response, and several confrontations ensued. The result was a new sense of self-worth and power; by the end of the decade, blacks had changed a great deal. They were angry, disillusioned with the federal government and with white liberals, and they recognized that their opponents, the advocates of white supremacy, were perfectly prepared to break the law. It became increasingly clear that it would take direct action on the part of blacks to defeat segregation. It was also evident that direct action might well entail breaking the local laws, which were structured to defeat the purpose of the federal law to which the blacks adhered. It was plainly a matter of whose laws would prevail. In this case, given the actions of leaders of the Southern resistance, one or the other—state or federal law—was bound to be broken. Thus, the lawbreaking that became almost a hallmark of the black movement in the sixties, and that spread by example to the student and antiwar movements of that time, was inspired and effectively taught by the Southern conservatives who chose to defy the Supreme Court.

It is possible that, had the Southern black population encountered in the fifties the viciousness and brutality that it met in the sixties, it would have been turned back. But in the fifties blacks won a series of victories, some larger, some smaller—with the high points in Montgomery and Little Rock—and thus they entered the sixties with a sense of growing self-confidence and militancy and with an organization that embodied these sentiments: the Southern Christian Leadership Conference. And when they faced the implacable resistance in the Deep South, they could not be turned back by it—they meant to have their victory. It was this sentiment, when carried into the later sixties, and when faced with the bitter resistance of the Deep South and the relative (to blacks) indifference of the white North, that brought about the alienation that was manifested in black riots and in the ideology of black power.

The New Negro, though made possible by changes in the class structure, was a product of black effort: blacks were creating themselves anew in may respects. Knowing that right and even the law were on their side was one thing, and seeing themselves act cohesively, courageously, and effectively was another. As blacks tried themselves and discovered their abilities under what were often adverse conditions, they grew and developed. Their perceptions and their consciousness changed through their efforts. Thus, the process of refashioning the world had as its byproduct a rather substantial reconstruction of black character. That is not a novel occurrence or finding; it frequently happens in a social movement, though each time in a unique way. It is no less significant a development for that, and to the participants it was certainly both very new and very important.

The Impact of the Civil Rights Movement

I began this study with a perception of the significance of the civil rights movement. It had deeply affected American society. The student movement of the sixties, the anti-Vietnam War movement, the movements for women's rights and gay rights emerged largely as a product of the civil rights movement. The struggles of American Indians, Hispanics, and Asians were profoundly influenced by this movement. The civil rights movement shattered the extraordinary social quiet that had settled upon the nation in the 1950's. It put an end to the view that a consensus prevailed in American society, that ideological conflict was over, and that most of the fundamental problems associated with inequality had ceased to be in the United States. As my research proceeded, I came to realize that the legacy of this social movement was far greater even than these important developments.

The civil rights movement ended an era in American history and began a new one. It was a vital part of the modernization of the South. That was evident in the political realm, where blacks not only won the right to vote but, in doing so, brought a new class to political leadership within the region. Blacks played an important role in the industrial development of the South, as well. As the South developed its industry, failure to confront the racial patterns would have been likely to fetter industrial production; as industry expanded, business leaders would be saddled with segregation, limiting their use of labor. So the civil rights movement, which was made possible by industrial expansion in the South, in its turn cleared the way for further industrial expansion.

As a result of these changes, the particular structures, customs, economy, and political culture that had kept the South apart all deteriorated as the agrarian elite ceased to be the dominant class of the region. The South had become one with the nation. The election of Jimmy Carter of Georgia as president was indicative of this new situation. Carter was the first Southerner to attain that office by election since before the Civil War; until the civil rights movement it was unthinkable that anyone from the South could be the nation's leader.

There has been much discussion and speculation about the end of the civil rights movement, and with it of the Second Reconstruction. Will blacks be returned to their position of second-class citizenship, as they were following the original Reconstruction period? If the analysis presented here is correct, there will be no turning back. The Second Reconstruction was more thoroughgoing than the first. It was premised on the structural changes that had already begun reshaping both the economy and the demographic make-up of the South, as well as the distribution within the nation. After the Civil War and Reconstruction, the South had continued to develop along lines radically different from those of the rest of the country. Its culture and politics reflected this different development. Later, as the South came to resemble the rest of the country economically and sociologically, the basis for its distinctive political structure and racial practices disappeared. The Second Reconstruction succeeded in removing from political power the representatives of a class that could no longer reassert its former control. The particular form that Southern racism had taken was the legacy of a system that was in the process of disappearing and that could not be restored. So, while racism is not ended in this country, its peculiar Southern form is, and so are some of its features that had become instituted nationally. That is not to say that blacks do not or will not suffer from what President Nixon called "benign neglect," or that there has not been an effort to roll back some of the gains of the sixties and seventies. It is to say, however, that, short of some major catastrophe, state-sanctioned segregation and second-class citizenship for blacks are gone for good.

As a result, blacks have more opportunities for access to the benefits as well as the problems of the American class system. In that sense, the shift of the locus of black struggle from the South to the North had an important symbolic significance. Blacks in the North were not protesting primarily the segregated racial system of Southern oppression; they were protesting the American class system as it particularly affected blacks. As the South changed, it became more like the North. And the problems of blacks in the South became basically the same as those confronted by blacks in the North. Thus, the protests of Northern blacks were concerned with issues that did or would soon affect blacks everywhere.

The black civil rights victories, by opening some of the barriers of caste, left greater room for class differentiation within the black population. Many blacks have risen; the black middle class has substantially expanded. While E. Franklin Frazier could write critically in 1957 about a black bourgeoisie that was more pretense than substance,[7] today the black community has a real stratification pyramid.* Affirmative action programs, instituted as a result of the civil rights movement, are one reason for the expansion of the black middle class.

A result of class differentiation within the black community has been the emergence of class conflict among blacks. This trend was evident in Atlanta in the 1970s. Garbage workers there, who were overwhelmingly black, went out

---

*In truth, it is only a partial pyramid. There is no black stratum comparable in power and wealth to the upper stratum of whites.

on strike in 1970 against the white mayor. They were supported by the Southern Christian Leadership Conference, which joined their picket lines and turned the strike into something of a moral crusade, and by Maynard Jackson, the black vice-mayor of the city, who called the wages of the strikers "a disgrace before God." As a result, the union backed Jackson in the next election, and he won, becoming the first black mayor of the city in 1973. Early in 1977 the workers again went out on strike. But by then Jackson had switched sides: as mayor, he fired one thousand strikers and effectively broke the union. In all probability no white mayor could have done that: in 1977 few members of the city's black civil rights leadership spoke out in favor of the union. The SCLC was silent, while Martin Luther King, Sr., the Urban League, and other important black organizations sided with Jackson. The mayor had been bitterly opposed in his first election bid by the white business community in Atlanta, and bitter relations had persisted throughout his first term. But when he announced his candidacy for a second term shortly after the strike, he was embraced by these same business figures. One can expect other such occurrences, though perhaps not so dramatic as that in Atlanta.

That is not to say that blacks who move up into the middle class will or do find themselves in conflict with their poorer brethren. Black unity still has vitality, because race and racism persist as powerful forces in American society. An example is provided by the racially divided city of Chicago. There, Harold Washington was elected as the first black mayor of the city in 1983, on a reform platform. The city council retained a white, machine-dominated majority. When Washington nominated Dorothy Tillman, a longtime civil rights activist and foe of the machine, who represented poor blacks, to replace a black alderman who had been convicted of corruption, the city council sat on the nomination, refusing to confirm it. While her nomination was held in limbo, Ed Gardner, owner of Sof-Sheen, a prominent black hair products company, and John Johnson of Johnson Publications, which produces *Jet* and *Ebony* magazines, paid her aldermanic salary and picked up her office expenses. Here, class differences were minimized in the face of a racial conflict.

In recent times, the black movement has shown signs of advancing. The black power trend, as it was manifested in the late sixties, was something of a blind alley, and the riots soon ended. The protest organizations were either crushed (as was the Black Panther party by police attacks) or coopted, or they withered away. But many of the gains remained, and blacks progressed in some areas while losing out in others. The continued consolidation of the black presence within the cities and the flight of whites to the suburbs have extended the black political base. Political control, in its turn, provides an increasingly deep layer of people with leadership ability and experience and a base for extending black political influence. More black people are registering to vote, and more are voting. These voters are people who have been profoundly changed by the impact of the civil rights movement, and the American political system will have to come to terms with this developing black political savvy and strength.

Moreover, blacks have increasingly become a central part of the labor force, and often the most union-conscious sector. That has been happening at a time when labor is under assault from business, from the shocks provided by international competition, and more recently from a conservative administration. What will be the outcome? Will there be a new labor upheaval? Will a coalition like the one Martin Luther King, Jr. envisioned of black and white poor, or of black and white labor, come into existence? Perhaps. If such a movement does cohere, there is no reason to assume that black members of the middle class will oppose it or be indifferent to it. Many will undoubtedly support it, and some will be among its leaders. Such a movement would not be able to forsake issues of racial discrimination and equality or allow them to be subsumed under the notion of class unity. More likely, such a movement would have forthrightly to come to terms with racial issues, because the social power of blacks simply cannot be ignored.

BIBLIOGRAPHY

Adams, Sherman. *First-Hand Report*. New York: Harper and Brothers, 1961.

Ahmann, Mathew H., ed. *The New Negro*. Notre Dame, Ind.: Fides Publishers, 1961.

Anderson, Eric. *Race and Politics in North Carolina, 1872–1901*. Baton Rouge: Louisiana State University Press, 1981.

Anderson, Jervis. *A. Philip Randolph*. New York: Harcourt, Brace, Jovanovich, 1973.

Ashmore, Harry S. *The Other Side of Jordan*. New York: W. W. Norton and Co., 1960.

Bagdikian, Ben H. "Negro Youth's New March on Dixie." *Saturday Evening Post*, September 8, 1962.

Baker, Ray Stannard. *Following the Color Line*. New York: Harper and Row, 1964.

Barnard, William. *Dixiecrats and Democrats*. Alabama: University of Alabama Press, 1974.

Baron, Harold. "The Demand for Black Labor: Historical Notes on the Political Economy of Racism." *Radical America* 5 (March-April 1971).

Barr, Alwyn. *Reconstruction to Reform: Texas Politics, 1876–1904*. Austin: University of Texas Press, 1971.

Bartley, Numan V. *The Rise of Massive Resistance*. Baton Rouge: Louisiana State University Press, 1969.

Bass, Jack, and Walter DeVries. *The Transformation of Southern Politics*. New York: Basic Books, 1976.

Bates, Daisy. *The Long Shadow of Little Rock*. New York: David McKay Co., 1970.

Beardslee, William R. *The Way Out Must Lead In*. Atlanta: Center for Research in Social Change, Emory University, 1977.

Bennett, Lerone Jr. *Confrontation: Black and White*. Baltimore: Penguin Books, 1965.

———. *The Negro Mood*. New York: Ballantine Books, 1964.

———. *What Manner of Man?* Chicago: Johnson Publishing Co., 1964.

Berger, Peter L., and Thomas Luckmann. *The Social Construction of Reality*. New York: Anchor Books, 1967.

Berman, William. *The Politics of Civil Rights in the Truman Administration*. Columbus: Ohio State University Press, 1970.

Bernstein, Barton. "The Ambiguous Legacy: The Truman Administration and Civil Rights." In Barton Bernstein, ed., *Politics and Policies of the Truman Administration*. Chicago: Quadrangle Books, 1970.

Berry, Mary Francis. *Black Resistance, White Law*. New York: Appleton-Century-Crofts, 1971.

Billings, Dwight. *Planters and the Making of a "New South"*. Chapel Hill: University of North Carolina Press, 1979.

Billington, Monroe Lee. *The Political South in the Twentieth Century*. New York: Charles Scribner's Sons, 1975.

Bleiweiss, Robert M., ed. *Marching to Freedom*. New York: New American Library, 1969.

Blumer, Herbert. *Symbolic Interactionism*. Englewood Cliffs, N.J.: Prentice-Hall, 1969.

Bonacich, Edna. "Abolition, the Extension of Slavery, and the Position of Free Blacks: A Study of Split Labor Markets in the United States, 1830–1863." *American Journal of Sociology* 81, no. 3 (November 1975): 601–628.

———. "Advanced Capitalism and Black/White Race Relations in the United States: A

Split Labor Market Interpretation." *American Sociological Review* 41 (February 1976): 34–51.

———. "A Theory of Ethnic Antagonism: The Split Labor Market." *American Sociological Review* 37 (October 1972): 547–59.

Bond, Julian. "The Movement Then and Now." *Southern Exposure*, 1976.

Bracey, John Jr.; August Meier; and Elliott Rudwick, eds. *Black Nationalism in America*. Indianapolis: Bobbs-Merrill Co., 1970.

Brandon, Robert H. *Cotton Kingdom of the New South*. Cambridge: Harvard University Press, 1967.

Brink, William, and Louis Harris. *Black and White*. New York: Simon and Schuster, 1967.

———. *The Negro Revolution in America*. New York: Simon and Schuster, 1964.

Brisbane, Robert H. *Black Activism*. Valley Forge: Judson Press, 1974.

———. *The Black Vanguard*. Valley Forge: Judson Press, 1970.

Brock, Clifton. *Americans for Democratic Action*. Washington, D. C.: Public Affairs Press, 1962.

Brooks, Thomas R. *Walls Come Tumbling Down*. Englewood Cliffs, N.J.: Prentice-Hall, 1974.

Brophy, William. "Active Acceptance—Active Containment, the Dallas Story." In Elizabeth Jacoway and David R. Colburn, eds., *Southern Businessmen and Desegregation*. Baton Rouge: Louisiana State University Press, 1982.

Bullock, Paul, ed. *Watts: The Aftermath*. New York: Grove Press, 1969.

Burgess, Elaine. *Negro Leadership in a Southern Town*. New Haven: College and University Press, 1976.

Burns, W. Haywood. *The Voices of Negro Protest in America*. New York: Oxford University Press, 1963.

Button, James. *Black Violence*. Princeton: Princeton University Press, 1978.

Campbell, Angus, and Howard Schuman. " Racial Attitudes in Fifteen American Cities." In *Supplemental Studies for the National Advisory Commission on Civil Disorders*. Washington, D.C.: Government Printing Office, 1968.

Caplan, Nathan. "The New Ghetto Man: A Review of Recent Empirical Studies." In David Boesel and Peter H. Rossi, eds., *Cities under Siege: An Anatomy of the Ghetto Riots, 1964–1968*. New York: Basic Books, 1971.

Carmichael, Stokeley, and Charles V. Hamilton. *Black Power*. New York: Vintage Books, 1966.

Carson, Claybonne. *In Struggle*. Cambridge: Harvard University Press, 1981.

Carter, Hodding III. *The South Strikes Back*. Garden City, N.Y.: Doubleday and Co., 1959.

Carter, Wilmoth H. *The Negro of the South*. New York: Exposition Press, 1967.

———. *The Urban Negro in the South*. New York: Vantage Press, 1961.

Cash, W. J. *The Mind of the South*. New York: Vintage Books, 1969.

Caute, David. *The Great Fear*. New York: Simon and Schuster, 1979.

Cell, John W. *The Highest Stage of White Supremacy: The Origin of Segregation in South Africa and the American South*. New York: Cambridge University Press, 1982.

Chafe, William. *Civilities and Civil Rights*. New York: Oxford University Press, 1980.

Chalmers, David M. *Hooded Americanism*. Garden City, N.Y.: Doubleday and Co., 1965.

Civil Rights Congress. *We Charge Genocide*. New York, 1951.

Clark, John Henrik, ed. *Malcolm X: The Man and His Times*. Toronto: Collier Books, 1969.

Clark Kenneth. *Dark Ghetto*. New York: Harper and Row, 1965.

————. "Observations on Little Rock." *New South*, June 1958, pp. 3–8.

————. "The Civil Rights Movement: Momentum and Organization." In James Geschwender, *The Black Revolt*. Englewood Cliffs, N.J.: Prentice-Hall, 1971.

Clark, Thomas. *The Emerging South*. New York: Oxford University Press, 1968.

Clark, Thomas, and Albert Kirwan. *The South since Appomattox*. New York: Oxford University Press, 1967.

Cobb, James C. "Yesterday's Liberalism, Business Boosters and Civil Rights in Augusta, Georgia." In Elizabeth Jacoway and David R. Colburn, eds., *Southern Businessmen and Desegregation*. Baton Rouge: Louisiana State University Press, 1982.

Cohen, Robert Carl. *Black Crusader*. Secaucus, N.J.: Lyle Stuart, 1972.

Colburn, David R. "The Saint Augustine Business Community." In Elizabeth Jacoway and David R. Colburn, eds., *Southern Businessmen and Desegregation*. Baton Rouge: Louisiana State University Press, 1982.

Coleman, James S. "Race Relations and Social Change." In Irwin Katz and Patricia Gunn, eds., *Race and the Social Sciences*. New York: Basic Books, 1969.

Coles, Robert. *Children of Crisis, Volume I*. Boston: Little, Brown and Co., 1967.

————. "Children of the American Ghetto." *Harper's*, September 1967.

————. "Social Struggle and Weariness." *Psychiatry* 27 (1964).

Coles, Robert, and Joseph Brenner. "American Youth in a Social Struggle: The Mississippi Summer Project." *American Journal of Orthopsychiatry*, October 1965.

Constable, John. "Negro Student Protestors Challenge North Carolina Leaders." *New South* 15 (1960).

Cook, James Graham. *The Segregationists*. New York: Appleton-Century-Crofts, 1962.

Cothran, Tilman C., and William Phillips, Jr. "Negro Leadership in a Crisis Situation." *Phylon* 22, no. 2 (1961): 107–118.

Coulter, E. Merton. *The South during Reconstruction*. Baton Rouge: Louisiana State University Press, 1947.

Cox, Oliver C. "Leadership among Negroes in the United States." In Alvin Gouldner, ed., *Studies in Leadership*. New York: Russell and Russell, 1965.

Crain, Robert L. et al. *The Politics of School Desegregation*. Chicago: Aldine Publishing Co., 1968.

Cushman, Robert. "Our Civil Rights Become a World Issue." *New York Times Magazine*, January 11, 1948, pp. 12, 22, 24.

Davis, Allison, and John Dollard. *Children of Bondage*. New York: Harper and Row, 1940.

Davis, Allison; Burleigh B. Gardner; and Mary R. Gardner. *Deep South*. Chicago: University of Chicago Press, 1965.

Degler, Carl N. *The Other South*. New York: Harper and Row, 1974.

Dittmer, John. *Black Georgia in the Progressive Era, 1900–1920*. Urbana: University of Illinois Press, 1977.

Divine, Robert. "The Cold War and the Election of 1948." *Journal of American History* 59 (June 1942): 90–110.

Dollard, John. *Caste and Class in a Southern Town*. Garden City, N.Y.: Doubleday and Co., 1957.

DuBois, W. E. B. *Black Reconstruction*. New York: Russell and Russell, 1963.

Dykeman, Wilma, and James Stokely. *Neither Black nor White*. New York: Rinehart and Co., 1957.

Editors of *Freedomways. Paul Robeson: The Great Forerunner*. New York: Dodd, Mead and Co., 1978.

Edmonds, Helen. *The Negro and Fusion Politics in North Carolina*. Chapel Hill: University of North Carolina Press, 1951.

Ehle, John. *The Free Men*. New York: Harper and Row, 1965.

Ellsworth, Ralph E., and Sarah Harris. *The American Right Wing*. Washington, D.C.: Public Affairs Press, 1962.

Encylopedia Britannica. vol. 17, New York, 1903.

Evers, Mrs. Medgar, with William Peters. *For Us the Living*. Garden City, N.Y.: Doubleday and Co., 1967.

Feagin, Joe A. "Social Sources of Support for Violence and Nonviolence in a Negro Ghetto." *Social Problems* 15, no. 4 (Spring 1968): 432–41.

Feagin, Joe, and Harlan Hahn. *Ghetto Revolts*. New York: Macmillan Co., 1973.

Ferman, Louis A.; Joyce L. Kornbluh; and J. A. Miller. *Negroes and Jobs*. Ann Arbor: University of Michigan Press, 1968.

Fischer, Roger A. *The Segregation Struggle in Louisiana, 1862–1877*. Urbana: University of Illinois Press, 1974.

Flaming, Karl H. *Who "Riots" and Why? Black and White Perspectives in Milwaukee*. Milwaukee Urban League, 1968.

Fogelson, Robert M. *Violence as Protest: A Study of Riots and Ghettos*. Garden City, N.Y.: Doubleday and Co., 1971.

Fogelson, Robert M., and Robert B. Hill. "Who Riots? A Study of Participation in the 1967 Riots." In *Supplemental Studies for the National Advisory Commission on Civil Disorders*. Washington, D.C.: Government Printing Office, 1968.

Franklin, John Hope. *From Slavery to Freedom*. New York: Alfred A. Knopf, 1964.

―――. *Reconstruction*. Chicago: University of Chicago Press, 1961.

Frazier, E. Franklin. *Black Bourgeoisie*. New York: Collier Books, 1962.

Freidel, Frank. *F.D.R. and the South*. Baton Rouge: Louisiana State University Press, 1965.

French, Edgar N. "Beginnings of a New Age." In Glenford E. Mitchell and William H. Peace III, *The Angry Black South*. New York: Corinth Books, 1962.

Fuller, Helen. "Southern Students Take Over." *New Republic*, May 2, 1960, pp. 14–16.

―――. "We Are All So Very Happy." *New Republic*, April 25, 1960, pp. 13–16.

Garfinkel, Herbert. *When Negroes March*. Glencoe, Ill.: Free Press, 1959.

Garrow, David. *Protest at Selma*. New Haven: Yale University Press, 1979.

Gates, Robbins L. *The Making of Massive Resistance*. Chapel Hill: University of North Carolina, 1964.

Geschwender, James. "Civil Rights Protests and Riots: A Disappearing Distinction." *Social Science Quarterly* 49, no. 3 (December 1968). Reprinted in Norval D. Glenn and Charles M. Bonjean, *Blacks in the United States*. San Francisco: Chandler Publishing Co., 1969.

Gillette, Paul J., and Eugene Tillinger. *Inside the Ku Klux Klan*. New York: Pyramid Books, 1965.

Glasgow, Douglas G. *The Black Underclass*. New York: Vintage Books, 1981.

Going, Allen Johnston. *Bourbon Democracy in Alabama, 1874–1890*. Montgomery: University of Alabama Press, 1951.

Goldman, Peter. *The Death and Life of Malcolm X*. Urbana: University of Illinois Press, 1979.

Goodman, Benjamin, ed. *Malcolm X: The End of White World Supremacy*. New York: Merlin House, 1971.

Gossett, Thomas F. *Race: The History of an Idea in America*. New York: Schocken Books, 1968.

Grant, Joanne. *Black Protest*. Greenwich, Conn.: Fawcett Publications, 1968.

Grantham, Dewey. *The Democratic South*. Athens: University of Georgia Press, 1963.

Graves, John Temple. *The Fighting South*. New York: G. P. Putnam's Sons, 1943.

Greenberg, Stanley. *Race and State in Capitalist Development*. New Haven: Yale University Press, 1980.

Greenstone, J. David, and Paul E. Peterson. "Reformers, Machines, and the War on Poverty." In James Q. Wilson, ed., *City Politics and Public Policy*. New York: Wiley, 1968.

Gregory, Dick. *Nigger*. New York: Pocket Books, 1965.

Griffith, Winthrop. *Humphrey*. New York: William Morrow and Co., 1965.

Grimshaw, Allen D., ed. *Racial Violence in the United States*. Chicago: Aldine Publishing Co., 1969.

Hackney, Sheldon. *Populism to Progressivism in Alabama*. Princeton: Princeton University Press, 1969.

Haley, Alex, ed. *The Autobiography of Malcolm X*. New York: Grove Press, 1965.

Hamilton, Charles. *The Black Experience in American Politics*. New York: G. P. Putnam's Sons, 1973.

Handlin, Oscar. *Fire-Bell in the Night*. Boston: Little, Brown and Co., 1964.

Harding, Vincent, and Staughton Lynd. "Albany, Georgia." *Crisis*, February 1963.

Hare, William Ivy. *Bourbonism and Agrarian Protest*. Baton Rouge: Louisiana State University Press, 1967.

Harris, Marvin. *Cultural Materialism*. New York: Vintage Books, 1980.

Heard, Alexander. *A Two-Party South?* Chapel Hill: University of North Carolina Press, 1952.

Henderson, Vivian W. "Regions, Race, and Jobs." In Arthur Ross and Herbert Hill, ed., *Employment, Race, and Poverty*. New York: Harcourt, Brace and World, 1967.

Higham, John, *Strangers in the Land*. New York: Atheneum, 1973.

Hill, Robert B., and Robert M. Fogelson. "A Study of Arrest Patterns in the 1960's Riots." Unpublished manuscript, 1969.

Hine, Darlene Clark. *Black Victory: The Rise and Fall of the White Primary in Texas*. Millwood, N.Y.: KTO Press.

Hirshon, Stanley P. *Farewell to the Bloody Shirt*. Chicago: Quadrangle Paperbacks, 1968.

Holley, William C.; Ellen Winston; and T. J. Woofter, Jr. *The Plantation South, 1934–1937*. New York: DaCapo Press, 1971.

Holloway, Harry. *The Politics of the Southern Negro*. New York: Random House, 1969.

Holt, Len. *The Summer That Didn't End*. New York: William Morrow and Co., 1965.

Hoover, Calvin B., and B. U. Ratchford. *Economic Resources and Politics of the South*. New York: Macmillan Co., 1951.

Hornsby, Alton, Jr. "A City That Was Too Busy to Hate: Atlanta Businessmen and Desegregation." In Elizabeth Jacoway and David R. Colburn, eds., *Southern Businessmen and Desegregation*. Baton Rouge: Louisiana State University Press, 1982.

Howe, Irving, and Lewis Coser. *The American Communist Party*. New York: Frederick A. Praeger, 1962.

Huggins, Nathan. *Harlem Renaissance*. New York: Oxford University Press, 1973.

Hughes, Langston. *Fight for Freedom*. New York: W. W. Norton and Co., 1962.

Hunter, Floyd. *Community Power Structure*. Garden City, N.Y.: Anchor Books, 1963.

Inger, Morton. "The New Orleans School Crisis of 1960." In Elizabeth Jacoway and David R. Colburn, eds., *Southern Businessmen and Desegregation*. Baton Rouge: Louisiana State University Press, 1982.

Johnson, Charles. *Background to Patterns of Negro Segregation*. New York: Thomas Y. Crowell Co., 1970.

Johnson, Charles; Edwin R. Embree; and W. W. Alexander. *The Collapse of Cotton Tenancy*. Chapel Hill: University of North Carolina Press, 1935.

Jones, Jesse. *Fifty Billion Dollars: My Thirteen Years with the RFC*. New York: Macmillan Co., 1951.

Joubert, William H. *Southern Freight Rates in Transition*. Gainesville: University of Florida Press, 1949.

Kahn, Tom. *The Economics of Equality*. New York: League for Industrial Democracy, 1964. Reprinted in Louis A. Ferman, Joyce L. Kornbluh, and J. A. Miller, *Negroes and Jobs*. Ann Arbor: University of Michigan Press, 1968.

Kardiner, Abram, and Lionel Ovesey. *The Mark of Oppression*. Cleveland: Meridian Books, 1964.

Key, V. 0. *Southern Politics*. New York: Alfred A. Knopf, 1949.

Killian, Lewis. "Leadership in the Desegregation Crisis: An Institutional Analysis." In Muzafer Sherif, *Intergroup Relations and Leadership*. New York: John Wiley and Sons, 1962.

———. *The Impossible Revolution?* New York: Random House, 1968.

Killian, Lewis, and Charles Grigg. *Racial Crisis in America*. Englewood Cliffs, N.J.: Prentice-Hall, 1964.

Killian, Lewis, and Charles Smith. "Negro Protest Leaders in a Southern Community." In John Bracey, August Meier, and Elliott Rudwick, *Conflict and Competition: Studies in the Recent Black Protest Movement*. Belmont, Calif.: Wadsworth Publishing Co., 1970.

Killingsworth, Charles C. "Negroes in a Changing Labor Market." In Arthur Ross and Herbert Hill, eds., *Employment, Race, and Poverty*. New York: Harcourt, Brace and World, 1967.

King, Coretta Scott. *My Life with Martin Luther King, Jr.* New York: Holt, Rinehart and Winston, 1969.

King, Martin Luther, Jr. "A View of the Dawn." *Interracial Review*, May 1957, pp. 81–85.

———. "Facing the Challenge of a New Age." *Phylon* 18 (Spring 1957): 25ff.

———. "Our Struggle." *Liberation*, April 1956, pp. 3–6.

———. *Strength to Love*. New York: Harper and Row, 1963.

———. *Stride toward Freedom*. New York: Harper and Row, 1964.

———. "The President's Address to the Tenth Anniversary Convention of the Southern Christian Leadership Conference, Atlanta, Georgia, August 16, 1967." In Robert L. Scott and Wayne Brockside, eds., *The Rhetoric of Black Power*. New York: Harper and Row, 1969.

———. "The Social Organization of Nonviolence." *Liberation*, October 1959, pp. 5–7.

———. *The Trumpet of Conscience*. New York: Harper and Row, 1968.

———. "Who Speaks for the South?" *Liberation*, March 1958, pp. 13ff.

———. *Where Do We Go from Here: Chaos or Community?* New York: Harper and Row, 1967.

Kirby, Jack Temple. *Darkness at the Dawning: Race and Reform in the Progressive South*. Philadelphia: J. B. Lippincott, 1972.

Kirwan, Albert. *Revolt of the Rednecks*. New York: Harper and Row, 1965.

Kluger, Richard. *Simple Justice*. New York: Vintage Books, 1977.

Knowles, Louis L., and Kenneth Prewitt, eds. *Institutional Racism in America*. Englewood Cliffs, N.J.: Prentice-Hall, 1969.

Kolko, Joyce, and Gabriel Kolko. *The Limits of Power*. New York: Harper and Row, 1972.

Kousser, J. Morgan. "Progressivism—For Middle Class Whites Only: North Carolina Education, 1880–1910." *Journal of Southern History* 46, no. 2 (May 1980): 169–94.

————. *The Shaping of Southern Politics: Suffrage Restriction and the Establishment of the One-Party South, 1880–1910.* New Haven: Yale University Press, 1974.

Krueger, Thomas A. *And Promises to Keep.* Nashville: Vanderbilt University Press, 1967.

Ladd, Everett Carl Jr. *Negro Political Leadership in the South.* Ithaca, N.Y.: Cornell University Press, 1966.

Ladner, Joyce. "What 'Black Power' Means to Negroes in Mississippi." *Transaction* 5 (November 1967): 7–15.

Larkins, J. R. *Patterns of Leadership among Negroes in North Carolina.* Raleigh, N.C.: Irving-Swain Press, 1959.

Lawson, Steven F. *Black Ballots: Voting Rights in the South.* New York: Columbia University Press, 1976.

Lester, Julius. *Look Out, Whitey! Black Power's Gon' Get Your Mama.* New York: Dial Press, 1968.

Leuchtenberg, William E., *Franklin D. Roosevelt and the New Deal.* New York: Harper Torchbooks, 1963.

Lewis, Anthony. *Portrait of a Decade.* New York: Random House, 1964.

Lewis, David L. *King: A Critical Biography.* New York: Praeger Publishers, 1970.

Lewis, Hylan. *Blackways of Kent.* Chapel Hill: University of North Carolina Press, 1955.

Lewison, Paul. *Race, Class, and Party.* New York: Grossett and Dunlap, 1965.

Lincoln, C. Eric. *Sounds of the Struggle.* New York: William Morrow and Co., 1967.

Litwack, Leon F. *Been in the Storm So Long.* New York: Vintage Books, 1980.

Lively, Robert. "The South and Freight Rates: Political Settlement of an Economic Argument." *Journal of Social History* 14, no. 3 (August 1948): 357–84.

Lofton, Paul S. Jr. "Calm and Exemplary: Desegregation in Columbia, South Carolina." In Elizabeth Jacoway and David R. Colburn, eds., *Southern Businessmen and Desegregation.* Baton Rouge: Louisiana State University Press, 1982.

Logan, Frenise. *The Negro in North Carolina, 1876–1894.* Chapel Hill: University of North Carolina Press, 1964.

Lokos, Lionel. *House Divided.* New Rochelle, N.Y.: Arlington House, 1968.

Lomax, Louis. "The Negro Revolt Against the 'Negro Leaders,' " *Harper's,* June, 1960.

————. *The Negro Revolt.* New York: New American Library, 1963.

————. *To Kill a Black Man.* Los Angeles: Holloway House Publishing Co., 1968.

Louis, Debbie. *And We Are Not Saved.* Garden City, N.Y.: Doubleday and Co., 1970.

Lubbell, Samuel. *The Future of American Politics.* Garden City, N.Y.: Doubleday and Co., 1956.

————. *White and Black.* New York: Harper and Row, 1964.

Lynd, Staughton H. *Nonviolence in America.* Indianapolis: Bobbs-Merrill, 1966.

McAdam, Doug. *Political Process and the Development of Black Insurgency, 1930–1970.* Chicago: University of Chicago Press, 1982.

McCoy, Ronald, and Richard Ruetten. "The Civil Rights Movement: 1949–1954." In *Midwest Quarterly* 11 (October 1969): 11–34.

MacDougall, Curtis. *Gideon's Army,* vol. 1. New York: Marzani and Munsell, 1965.

McGill, Ralph. *The South and the Southerner.* Boston: Little, Brown and Co., 1964.

McLaughlin, Glenn E., and Robock Stefan. *Why Industry Moves South.* Kingsport, Tenn.: Kingsport Press, 1949.

McLaurin, Melton. *Paternalism and Protest.* Westport, Conn.: Greenwood Publishing, 1971.

McMillen, Neil R. "Black Enfranchisement in Mississippi: Federal Enforcement and Black Protest in the 1960's." *Journal of Southern History* 43 (August 1977): 351–72.

————. *The Citizen's Council.* Urbana: University of Illinois Press, 1971.

Malcolm X. *Autobiography.* New York: Grove Press, 1965.

————. *By Any Means Necessary*. Edited by George Breitman. New York: Pathfinder Press, 1970.

————. *Malcolm X Speaks*. Edited by George Breitman. New York: Grove Press, 1965.

————. *The End of White World Supremacy*. Edited by Benjamin Goodman. New York: Merlin, 1971.

————. *The Speeches of Malcolm X at Harvard*. Edited by Archie Epps. New York: William Morrow and Co., 1968.

Mannheim, Karl. "Conservative Thought." In *Essays on Sociology and Social Psychology*. New York: Oxford University Press, 1953.

————. *Ideology and Utopia*. New York: Harcourt Brace and World, 1936.

Martin, John Bartlow. *The Deep South Says 'Never'*. New York: Ballantine Books, 1957.

Marx, Gary. *Protest and Prejudice*. New York: Harper and Row, 1967.

Marx, Karl. *The Eighteenth Brumaire of Louis Bonaparte*. New York: International Publishers, 1963.

————. *The German Ideology*. New York: International Publishers, 1960. Matthews, Donald R., and James W. Prothro. *Negroes and the New Southern Politics*. New York: Harcourt, Brace and World, 1966.

Mayfield, Julien. "Challenge to Negro Leadership." *Commentary* 31 (April 1961): 297–305.

Meier, August, ed. *Black Protest in the Sixties*. Chicago: Quadrangle Books, 1970.

Meier, August, and Elliott Rudwick. *CORE*. New York: Oxford University Press, 1973.

————. *From Plantation to Ghetto*. New York: Hill and Wang, 1966.

Meredith, James. *Three Years in Mississippi*. Bloomington: Indiana University Press, 1966.

Miller, Abraham H., Louis H. Bolce, and Mark R. Halligan. "The New Urban Blacks." *Ethnicity* 3 (1976).

Moody, Anne. *Coming of Age in Mississippi*. New York: Dell, 1968.

Moon, Henry. *Balance of Power: The Negro Vote*. New York. Doubleday and Co., 1948.

Moore, Barrington Jr. *Social Origins of Dictatorship and Democracy*. Boston: Beacon Press, 1966.

Moore, F. Henderson. "School Desegregation." In Glenford E. Mitchell and William H. Peace III, *The Angry Black South*. New York: Corinth Books, 1962.

Moore, John Robert. "The New Deal in Louisiana." In John Braeman, Robert H. Bremner, and David Brody, *The New Deal*, vol. 2. Columbus: Ohio State University Press, 1975.

Morris, Aldon D. *The Origins of the Civil Rights Movement*. New York: Free Press, 1984.

Morris, Richard T., and Vincent Jeffries. "The White Reaction Study." In Nathan Cohen, ed., *The Los Angeles Riots*. New York: Praeger, 1970.

Murphy, Raymond J., and James W. Watson. "The Structure of Discontent: Relationship between Social Structure, Grievance, and Riot Support." In Nathan Cohen, ed., *The Los Angeles Riots*. New York: Praeger, 1970.

Murray, Pauli. *States' Laws on Race and Color*, Women's Division for Christian Science, 1950.

Muse, Benjamin. *Ten Years of Prelude*. New York: Viking Press, 1964.

————. *Virginia's Massive Resistance*. Bloomington: Indiana University Press, 1961.

Myrdal, Gunnar. *An American Dilemma*. New York: Harper and Row, 1962.

National Committee against Discrimination. *How the Federal Government Builds Ghettos*. New York, 1967. Reprinted in Helen Ginsburg, ed., *Poverty, Economics, and Society*. Boston: Little, Brown and Co., 1972.

Nelson, Harold. "The Defenders: A Case Study of an Informal Police Organization."

In James Geschwender, ed., *The Black Revolt*. Englewood Cliffs, N.J.: Prentice-Hall, 1971.

Newman, Dorothy K.; Nancy J. Amidei; Barbara L. Carter; Dawn Day; William J. Kruvant; and Jack S. Russell. *Protest, Politics, and Prosperity: Black Americans and White Institutions, 1940–75*. New York: Pantheon, 1978.

Newton, Huey. *Revolutionary Suicide*. New York: Ballantine, 1973.

Nicholls, William. *Southern Tradition and Regional Progress*. Chapel Hill: University of North Carolina Press, 1960.

Norris, Hoke, ed. *We Dissent*. New York: St. Martin's Press, 1962.

Northrup, Herbert R. "Industry's Racial Employment Policies." In Arthur Ross and Herbert Hill, *Employment, Race, and Poverty*. New York: Harcourt, Brace and World, 1967.

Novak, Daniel A. *The Wheel of Servitude*. Lexington: University Press of Kentucky, 1978.

Oates, Stephen. *Let the Trumpet Sound*. New York: Harper and Row, 1982.

Oberschall, Anthony. *Social Conflict and Social Movements*. Englewood Cliffs, N.J.: Prentice-Hall, 1973.

Oppenheimer, Martin. "The Genesis of the Southern Negro Student Movement (Sit-in)." Ph.D. dissertation, University of Pennsylvania, 1963.

Orbell, John M. "Protest Participation among Southern Negro College Students." In James Geschwender, *The Black Revolt*. Englewood Cliffs, N.J.: Prentice-Hall, 1971.

Orum, Anthony. *Black Students in Protest*. Washington, D.C.: American Sociological Association, n.d.

Orum, Anthony, and Amy W. Orum. "The Class and Status Bases of Negro Student Protest." *Social Science Quarterly* 49 (December 1968).

Oshinsky, David. *Senator Joseph McCarthy and the American Labor Movement*. Columbia: University of Missouri Press, 1976.

Osofsky, Gilbert, ed. *The Burden of Race*. New York: Harper and Row, 1967.

Parsons, Talcott, and Kenneth Clark, eds. *The Negro American*. Boston: Houghton Mifflin Co., 1966.

Peeks, Edward. *The Long Struggle for Black Power*. New York: Charles Scribner's Sons, 1971.

Perdew, John. "Difficult to Organize Poorest and Wealthiest among Negroes." *I.F. Stone's Weekly*, December 9, 1963.

Peters, William. *The Southern Temper*. Garden City, N.Y.: Doubleday and Co., 1959.

Pierce, Truman M. et al. *White and Negro Schools in the South*. Englewood Cliffs, N.J.: Prentice-Hall, 1955.

Pinard, Maurice; Jerome Kird; and Donald Von Eschen. "Processes of Recruitment in the Sit-in Movement." *Public Opinion Quarterly* 33 (Fall 1969).

Piven, Frances Fox, and Richard Cloward. *Poor People's Movements*. New York: Pantheon, 1977.

Powdermaker, Hortense. *After Freedom*. New York: Russell and Russell, 1968.

President's Committee on Civil Rights. *To Secure These Rights*. Washington, D.C.: Government Printing Office, 1947.

Pulley, Raymond H. *Old Virginia Restored*. Charlottesville: University Press of Virginia, 1968.

Quint, Howard. *Profile in Black and White*. Washington, D.C.: Public Affairs Press, 1958.

Rabinowitz, Howard N. "From Exclusion to Segregation: Southern Race Relations, 1865–1890." *Journal of American History* 63 (June 1976): 325–50.

Raine, Walter J. "The Perception of Police Brutality in South Central Los Angeles." In Nathan Cohen, ed., *The Los Angeles Riots.* New York: Praeger, 1970.

Raines, Howell. *My Soul Is Rested.* New York: Bantam Books, 1978.

Ransom, Roger, and Richard Sutch. *One Kind of Freedom.* New York: Cambridge University Press, 1977.

Reddick L. D. *Crusader without Violence.* New York: Harper and Brothers, 1959.

Redding, Jack. *Inside the Democratic Party.* New York: Bobbs-Merrill Co., 1958.

Redding, J. Saunders. *No Day of Triumph.* New York: Harper and Brothers, 1942.

Roark, James L. *Masters without Slaves.* New York: W. W. Norton and Co., 1977.

Robinson, Armsted L. "Beyond the Realm of Social Consensus: New Meanings of Reconstruction for American History." *Journal of American History* 68, no. 2 (September 1981): pp. 276–97.

Rogers, William Warren. *The One-Gallused Rebellion.* Baton Rouge: Louisiana State University Press, 1970.

Rohrer John H., and Munro Edmunson. *The Eighth Generation Grows Up.* New York: Harper Torchbooks, 1964.

Rosenfield, Gerry. *Shut Those Thick Lips: A Study of Slum School Failures.* New York: Holt, Rinehart and Winston, 1971.

Ross, Arthur M. "The Negro in the American Economy." In Arthur Ross and Herbert Hill, eds., *Employment, Race, and Poverty.* New York: Harcourt, Brace and World, 1967.

Rowan, Carl. *Go South to Sorrow.* New York: Random House, 1957.

———. *South of Freedom.* New York: Alfred A. Knopf, 1952.

Rubin, Morton. *Plantation County.* Chapel Hill: University of North Carolina Press, 1951.

Salisbury, Harrison. *Without Fear or Favor.* New York: New York Times Books, 1980.

Sallis, Charles, and John Quincy Adams. "Desegregation in Jackson, Mississippi." In Elizabeth Jacoway and David R. Colburn, eds., *Southern Businessmen and Desegregation.* Baton Rouge: Louisiana State University Press, 1982.

Saloutos, Theodore. *Farmer Movements in the South, 1865–1933.* Lincoln: University of Nebraska Press, 1960.

Schapsmeier, Edward L., and Frederick H. Schapsmeier. *Henry A. Wallace of Iowa: the American Years, 1910–1940.* Ames: Iowa State University Press, 1968.

Schlesinger Arthur M. Jr. *The Coming of the New Deal.* Boston: Houghton Mifflin Co., 1959.

———. *The Crisis of the Old Order.* Boston: Houghton Mifflin Co., 1957.

Schmidt, Karl. *Henry A. Wallace.* Syracuse: Syracuse University Press, 1960.

Schwartz, Michael. *Radical Protest and Social Structure.* New York: Academic Press, 1976.

Searles, Ruth, and J. Allen Williams, Jr. "Negro College Students' Participation in Sit-ins." *Social Forces* 40 (March 1962).

Sears, David O., and John B. McConahay. *The Politics of Violence: The New Urban Blacks and the Watts Riot.* Boston: Houghton Mifflin Co., 1973.

Sellers, Cleveland. *River of No Return.* New York: William Morrow and Co., 1973.

Shannon, Jasper Berry. *Toward a New Politics in the South.* Knoxville: University of Tennessee Press, 1949.

Sherman, Jimmie. "From the Ashes." *Antioch Review* 27, no. 3 (1967): 285–93.

Sherrill, Robert. *Gothic Politics in the Deep South.* New York: Grossman Publishers, 1968.

Sherrill, Robert, and Harry Ernst. *The Drugstore Liberal.* New York: Grossman Publishers, 1968.

Shugg, Roger. *Origins of Class Struggle in Louisiana.* Baton Rouge: Louisiana State University Press, 1966.

Sickle, John Van. *Planning for the South*. Nashville: Vanderbilt University Press, 1943.

Silberman, Charles. *Crisis in Black and White*. New York: Random House, 1964.

Sindler, Allan P., ed. *Change in the Contemporary South*. Durham, N.C.: Duke University Press, 1963.

Sitkoff, Harvard. "Harry Truman and the Election of 1948: The Coming of Age of Civil Rights in American Politics." *Journal of Southern History* 37 (November 1971): 597–616.

——. *The Struggle for Black Equality*. New York: Hill and Wang, 1981.

Sloan, Alfred. *My Years with General Motors*. New York: MacFadden Books, 1963.

Smith, Bob. *They Closed Their Schools*. Chapel Hill: University of North Carolina Press, 1965.

Smith, Charles. "The Sit-ins and the New Negro Students." In Earl Raab, *American Race Relations Today*. Garden City, N.Y.: Anchor Books, 1962.

Smith, Jean. "I Learned to Feel Black." In Floyd Barbour, ed. *The Black Power Revolt*. Boston: Extending Horizons Books, 1968.

Smith, Kenneth, and Ira Zapp, Jr. *Search for the Beloved Community*. Valley Forge: Judson Press, 1974.

Solomon, Fredric, and Jacob R. Fishman. "Youth and Social Action: II. Action Identity Formation in the First Student Sit-in Demonstration." *Journal of Social Issues* 20 (April 1964).

Somers, Dale A. "Black and White in New Orleans: A Study in Urban Race Relations, 1865–1900." *Journal of Southern History* 60 (February 1974): 30–36.

Sosna, Morton. *In Search of the Silent South*. New York: Columbia University Press, 1977.

Southeastern Regional Planning Commission to the National Resources Planning Board. *Southeastern Regional Development Plan for 1942*. Atlanta.

Stamp, Kenneth. *The Era of Reconstruction*. New York: Alfred A. Knopf, 1965.

Sternberg, Fritz. *Capitalism and Socialism on Trial*. New York: John Day Co., 1950.

Stocking, George. *Basing Point Pricing and Regional Development*. Chapel Hill: University of North Carolina Press, 1954.

Stone, I. F. *In a Time of Torment*. New York: Random House, 1964.

Sullivan, Neil V. *Bound for Freedom*. Boston: Little, Brown and Co., 1965.

Taylor, Arnold H. *Travail and Triumph*. Westport, Conn.: Greenwood Press, 1976.

Theoharis, Athan. "The Rhetoric of Politics: Foreign Policy, Internal Security, and Domestic Politics in the Truman Era, 1945–1950." In Barton Bernstein, ed., *Politics and Policies of the Truman Administration*. Chicago: Quadrangle Books, 1970.

Thompson, Daniel. *The Negro Leadership Class*. Englewood Cliffs, N.J.: Prentice-Hall, 1963.

Tindall, George Brown. *South Carolina Negroes, 1877–1900*. Baton Rouge: Louisiana State University Press, 1966.

——. *The Emergence of the New South, 1913–1945*. Baton Rouge: Louisiana State University Press, 1967.

Tomlinson, T. M. "The Development of a Riot Ideology among Urban Negroes." *American Behavioral Scientist* 11 (March-April 1968).

Trelease, Allen. *White Terror*. New York: Harper and Row, 1971.

Trotsky, Leon. *The Russian Revolution*. Ann Arbor: University of Michigan Press, 1960.

Tussman, Joseph. *The Supreme Court on Racial Discrimination*. New York: Oxford University Press, 1963.

United States Commission on Civil Rights. *Freedom for the Free*. Washington, D.C.: Government Printing Office, 1963.

United States Department of Commerce. *Bicentennial Statistics*. Washington, D.C.: Government Printing Office, 1976.

United States National Emergency Council. *Report on Economic Conditions of the South.* Washington, D.C.: Government Printing Office, 1938.

Vander Zanden, James W. *Race Relations in Transition.* New York: Random House, 1965.

Von Hoffman, Nicholas. *Mississippi Notebook.* New York: David White Co., 1964.

Walton, Hanes Jr. *The Political Philosophy of Martin Luther King, Jr.* Westport, Conn.: Greenwood Publishing, 1971.

Walzer, Michael. "A Cup of Coffee and a Seat." *Dissent* 7 (Spring, 1960): 111–120.

———. "The Politics of the New Negro." *Dissent* 7 (Summer, 1960): 235–243.

Warren, Earl. "The Memoirs of Earl Warren." In Peter Woll, *American Government.* Boston: Little, Brown and Co., 1978.

Washington, Booker T. "Cast Down Your Buckets." In Thomas Clark, *The South since Reconstruction.* New York: Bobbs-Merrill Co., 1973.

Watters, Pat. *The South and the Nation.* New York: Vintage Books, 1956.

Watts, Marzette. "Sit-ins and Pickets." *New University Thought*, 1960.

Weldon, James. "The South's Own Civil War." In Don Shoemaker, ed., *With All Deliberate Speed.* New York: Harper and Brothers, 1957.

Westin, Alan F. *Freedom Now!* New York: Basic Books, 1964.

Wharton, Vernon. *The Negro in Mississippi, 1865–1900.* New York: Harper and Row, 1965.

White, Theodore. *The Making of the President 1960.* New York: New American Library, 1961.

———. *The Making of the President, 1964.* New York: Atheneum, 1965.

White, Walter. *How Far the Promised Land?* New York: Viking Press, 1955.

Wiener, Jonathan M. "Planters, Merchants, and Political Power in Reconstruction Alabama." In Maurice Zeitlin, *Classes, Class Conflict, and the State.* Cambridge: Winthrop Publishers, 1980.

———. *Social Origins of the New South: Alabama, 1860–1865.* Baton Rouge: Louisiana State University Press, 1978.

Wilhelm, Sidney. *Black in a White World.* Cambridge: Schenkman, 1983.

Wilhoit, Francis M. *The Politics of Massive Resistance.* New York: George Braziller, 1973.

Wilkins, Roy. "At the Beginning of a New Era." In August Meier, Elliott Rudwick, and Francis L. Broderick, *Black Protest Thought in the Twentieth Century.* Indianapolis: Bobbs-Merrill Co., 1965.

Williams, Robert. *Negroes with Guns.* New York: Marzani and Munsell, 1962.

Williamson, Joel. *After Slavery.* New York: W. W. Norton and Co., 1975.

Wilson, William Julius. *The Declining Significance of Race.* Chicago: University of Chicago Press, 1980.

Wofford, Harris. *Of Kennedys and Kings.* New York: Farrar, Straus, Girous, 1980.

Wolff, Eric. *How It All Began.* New York: Stein and Day, 1971.

Wolters, Raymond. *Negroes and the Great Depression.* Westport, Conn.: Greenwood Publishing, 1970.

Woodman, Harold. "Sequel to Slavery: The New History Views the Postbellum South." *Journal of Southern History* 43, no. 4 (November 1977): 523–54.

Woodward, C. Vann. *American Counterpoint.* Boston: Little, Brown and Co., 1971.

———. *Origins of the New South, 1871–1913.* Baton Rouge: Louisiana State University Press, 1951.

———. *Reunion and Reaction.* Garden City, N.Y.: Doubleday and Co., 1956.

———. "The Edifice of Domination." *New Republic*, December 1982, pp. 33–35.

———. "The New Reconstruction in the South." *Commentary*, June 1956.

———. *The Strange Career of Jim Crow.* New York: Oxford University Press, 1966.

————. *Tom Watson, Agrarian Rebel.* New York: Oxford University Press, 1963.

Woofter, T. J. Jr. *Landlord and Tenant on the Cotton Plantation.* Washington, D.C.: Government Printing Office, 1936.

Wynes, Charles. *Race Relations in Virginia, 1870–1902.* Charlottesville: University of Virginia Press, 1961.

Yarnell, Allen. *Democrats and Progressives.* Los Angeles: University of California Press, 1974.

Young, Richard P., ed. *Roots of Rebellion.* New York: Harper and Row, 1970.

Zinn, Howard. *New Deal Thought.* Indianapolis: Bobbs-Merrill, 1966.

————. *SNCC: The New Abolitionists.* Boston: Beacon Press, 1964.

NOTES

Introduction

1. Barrington Moore, Jr., *Social Origins of Dictatorship and Democracy* (Boston: Beacon Press, 1966); see also Eric R. Wolf, *Peasant Wars of the Twentieth Century* (New York: Harper and Row, 1969).

2. John W. Cell, *The Highest Stage of White Supremacy: The Origin of Segregation in South Africa and the American South* (New York: Cambridge University Press, 1982), p. 104.

3. Edna Bonacich, "Abolition, the Extension of Slavery, and the Position of Free Blacks: A Study of Split Labor Markets in the United States, 1830–1863," *American Journal of Sociology* 81, no. 3 (November 1975): 601–628; idem, "A Theory of Ethnic Antagonism: The Split Labor Market," *American Sociological Review* 37 (October 1972): 547–59; idem, "Advanced Capitalism and Black/White Race Relations in the United States: A Split Labor Market Interpretation," *American Sociological Review* 41 (February 1976): 34–51.

4. Bonacich, "Abolition," p. 602.

5. William Julius Wilson, *The Declining Significance of Race* (Chicago: University of Chicago Press, 1980), pp. 57–59. C. Vann Woodward, *American Counterpoint*, (Boston: Little, Brown and Co., 1971), p. 259, 254–55.

6. Ibid., p. 258.

7. C. Vann Woodward, *Origins of the New South, 1877–1913* (Baton Rouge: Louisiana State University Press, 1951), p. 179.

8. C. Vann Woodward, *The Strange Career of Jim Crow*, (New York: Oxford University Press, 1966), pp. 78–79.

9. James S. Coleman, "Race Relations and Social Change," in Irwin Katz and Patricia Gunn, eds., *Race and the Social Sciences* (New York: Basic Books, 1969), p. 294.

10. Karl Marx, *The German Ideology* (New York: International Publishers, 1960), p. 69.

11. Peter Berger and Thomas Luckmann, *The Social Construction of Reality* (New York: Anchor, 1969).

12. Anthony Oberschall, *Social Conflict and Social Movements* (Englewood Cliffs, N.J.: Prentice-Hall, 1973), p. 211.

13. Frances Fox Piven and Richard A. Cloward, *Poor People's Movements* (New York: Vintage Books, 1979), p. 182.

14. Ibid., pp. 183, 252.

15. Doug McAdam, *Political Process and the Development of Black Insurgency, 1930–1970* (Chicago: University of Chicago Press, 1982).

16. Ibid., pp. 34, 48, 108, 109–110.

17. Alden Morris, *The Origins of the Civil Rights Movement* (New York: Free Press, 1984).

I. The Political Economy of Southern Racism

1. Armsted L. Robinson, "Beyond the Realm of Social Consensus: New Meanings of Reconstruction for American History," *Journal of American History* 68, no. 2 (September 1981): 285.

2. Martin Luther King, Jr., *Where Do We Go from Here: Chaos or Community?* (New York: Harper and Row, 1967), pp. 13–14.

3. James L. Roark, *Masters without Slaves* (New York: W. W. Norton and Co., 1977), p. 108.

4. E. Merton Coulter, *The South during Reconstruction* (Baton Rouge: Louisiana State University Press, 1947), pp. 5, 2; John Van Sickle, *Planning for the South* (Nashville: Vanderbilt University Press, 1943), p. 170; Thomas Clark and Albert Kirwan, *The South since Appomattox* (New York: Oxford University Press, 1967), pp. 20–21, 60; W. E. B. DuBois, *Black Reconstruction* (New York: Russell and Russell, 1963), p. 210.

5. Clark and Kirwan, *The South*, pp. 88–89; William Ivy Hare, *Bourbonism and Agrarian Protest* (Baton Rouge: Louisiana State University Press, 1967), p. 54; U.S. National Emergency Council, *Report on Economic Conditions of the South*, Prepared for the President (Washington, D.C.: Government Printing Office, 1938), pp. 49, 51.

6. Kenneth Stampp, *The Era of Construction* (New York: Alfred A. Knopf, 1965), pp. 174–76; Vernon Wharton, *The Negro in Mississippi, 1865–1900*, (New York: Harper and Row, 1965), p. 178; Joel Williamson, *After Slavery* (New York: W. W. Norton and Co., 1975), pp. 151, 148; Roger Shugg, *Origins of Class Struggle in Louisiana* (Baton Rouge: Louisiana State University Press, 1966), p. 229.

7. Coulter, *South during Reconstruction*, p. 92; Leon F. Litwack, *Been in the Storm So Long* (New York: Vintage Books, 1980), p. 337; DuBois, *Black Reconstruction*, p. 138.

8. Jay R. Mandle, *The Roots of Black Poverty* (Durham, N.C.: Duke University Press, 1978), pp. 17–18; Jonathan M. Wiener, *Social Origins of the New South, Alabama, 1860–1865* (Baton Rouge: Louisiana State University Press, 1978), pp. 37–47; Litwack, *Been in the Storm*, pp. 326, 392.

9. Wharton, *Negro in Mississippi*, pp. 82–83, 81–82; Williamson, *After Slavery*, p. 108; Litwack, *Been in the Storm*, p. 252; Harold Woodman, "Sequel to Slavery: The New History Views the Postbellum South," *Journal of Southern History* 43, no. 4 (November 1977): 537; Roger Ransom and Richard Sutch, *One Kind of Freedom* (New York: Cambridge University Press, 1977), pp. 3–5.

10. Ray Stannard Baker, *Following the Color Line* (New York: Harper and Row, 1964), p. 78.

11. Shugg, *Origins*, p. 254; Litwack, *Been in the Storm*, pp. 351–52; Coulter, *South during Reconstruction*, p. 105.

12. W. J. Cash, *The Mind of the South* (New York: Vintage Books, 1969), pp. 110, 154–56, 157; Williamson, *After Slavery*, p. 153; Shugg, *Origins*, p. 244.

13. Theodore Saloutos, *Farmer Movements in the South, 1865–1933*, (Lincoln: University of Nebraska Press, 1960), p. 1; Rasom and Sutch, *One Kind*, pp. 78–79; Shugg, *Origins*, pp. 24, 272; Dwight B. Billings, Jr., *Planters and the Making of a "New South"* (Chapel Hill: University of North Carolina Press, 1979), p. 73; Michael Schwartz, *Radical Protest and Social Structure* (New York: Academic Press, 1976), pp. 80–88; Woodward, *Origins*, pp. 179, 407.

14. Woodward, *Origins*, pp. 179–80; Shugg, *Origins*, pp. 248–49; Wiener, *Social Origins*, pp. 5–16.

15. Williamson, *After Slavery*, p. 173; Shugg, *Origins*, p. 250.

16. Wharton, *Negro in Mississippi*, p. 72; George Brown Tindall, *South Carolina Negroes, 1877–1900*, (Baton Rouge: Louisiana State University Press, 1966), pp. 108–109; Woodward, *Origins*, p. 184; Schwartz, *Radical Protest*, p. 59.

17. Schwartz, *Radical Protest*, p. 58; Wiener, *Social Origins*, pp. 112–14.

18. Billings, *Planters*, pp. 36–37, 50, 77–92, 100–101.

19. William Nicholls, *Southern Tradition and Regional Progress*, (Chapel Hill: University of North Carolina Press, 1960), p. 51; Jonathan M. Wiener, "Planters, Merchants,

and Political Power in Reconstruction Alabama,'' in Maurice Zeitlin, *Classes, Class Conflict, and the State* (Cambridge: Winthrop Publishers, 1980).

20. Clark and Kirwan, *The South*, pp. 90–91; Cash, *The Mind*, p. 152; Ransom and Sutch, *One Kind*, p. 130; John Dollard, *Caste and Class in a Southern Town* (Garden City, N.Y.: Anchor Books, 1954), p. 140; Woodward, *Origins*, p. 180.

21. Cash, *The Mind*, p. 167.

22. Williamson, *After Slavery*, pp. 174–75.

23. Schwartz, *Radical Protest*, pp. 43–45.

24. Woodward, *Origins*, pp. 4–14, 116–20.

25. Ibid., p. 181; Clark and Kirwan, *The South*, p. 89.

26. DuBois cited in Clark and Kirwan, *The South*, p. 61; Schwartz, *Radical Protest*, pp. 75–79; Wiener, *Social Origins*, p. 81.

27. Wharton, *Negro in Mississippi*, p. 95; Baker, *Color Line*, p. 80.

28. Litwack, *Been in the Storm*, p. 365; Dollard, *Caste and Class*, p. 117.

29. Cited in Woodman, ''Sequel to Slavery,'' pp. 541–42.

30. Clark and Kirwan, *The South*, p. 99; Woodward, *Origins*, p. 182; Cash, *The Mind*, pp. 150, 152; Tindall, *South Carolina Negroes*, p. 112.

31. Cash, *The Mind*, pp. 150–52, 159–61.

32. Clark and Kirwan, *The South*, p. 92; Cash, *The Mind*, p. 287.

33. Williamson, *After Slavery*, p. 72; Wharton, *Negro in Mississippi*, pp. 85, 87; Paul Lewinson, *Race, Class, and Party* (New York: Grossett and Dunlap, 1965), p. 33; Daniel A. Novak, *The Wheel of Servitude* (Lexington: University Press of Kentucky, 1978), pp. 2–3.

34. Barrington Moore, Jr., *Social Origins of Dictatorship and Democracy* (Boston: Beacon Press, 1966), pp. 144–46; Lewinson, *Race, Class, and Party*, pp. 41, 44–45.

35. Litwack, *Been in the Storm*, pp. 177–78.

36. Carl N. Degler, *The Other South* (New York: Harper and Row, 1974), pp. 209–212, 217–18.

37. Robinson, ''Beyond the Realm,'' pp. 283, 285–86, 287; Wharton, *Negro in Mississippi*, p. 175.

38. Stampp, *Construction*, pp. 134–35; Howard Quint, *Profile in Black and White* (Washington, D.C.: Public Affairs Press, 1958), p. 1; Williamson, *After Slavery*, pp. 112–13; Tindall, *South Carolina Negroes*, p. 108; Wiener, *Social Origins*, p. 67; Truman M. Pierce et al., *White and Negro Schools in the South* (Englewood Cliffs, N.J.: Prentice-Hall, 1955), p. 47.

39. Allen Trelease, *White Terror* (New York: Harper and Row, 1971), p. xxv.

40. Degler, *The Other South*, pp. 222–23, 225; Robinson, ''Beyond the Realm,'' p. 288.

41. Robinson, ''Beyond the Realm,'' pp. 285–89.

42. Charles Wynes, *Race Relations in Virginia, 1870–1902* (Charlottesville: University of Virginia Press, 1961), p. 11.

43. Cash, *The Mind*, pp. 131–32; Frenise A. Logan, *The Negro In North Carolina, 1876–1894* (Chapel Hill: University of North Carolina Press, 1964), p. 19.

44. Wharton, *Negro in Mississippi*, p. 157; Trelease, *White Terror*, p. 196; Lewinson, *Race, Class, and Party*, pp. 52–53; Williamson, *After Slavery*, p. 375, fn.; C. Vann Woodward, *Reunion and Reaction* (Garden City, N.Y.: Doubleday and Co., 1956), p. 45; Degler, *The Other South*, p. 254.

45. Trelease, *White Terror*, pp. 178–79, 123, 289; Lewinson, *Race, Class, and Party*, p. 51; Wiener, *Social Origins*, pp. 61–66.

46. Trelease, *White Terror*, p. xivii; see also pp. 96, 122, 128, 135–36, 175, 190–91; John Hope Franklin, *Reconstruction* (Chicago: University of Chicago Press, 1961), pp. 157–58.

47. Trelease, *White Terror*, pp. 214–15, 139, 140, 52, 82–83, 96, 62–63; Williamson, *After Slavery*, p. 264.
48. Trelease, *White Terror*, p. 28.
49. Degler, *The Other South*, p. 266; Sarah Wollfolk Wiggins, "Democratic Bulldozing and Republican Folly," in Otto H. Olson, ed., *Reconstruction and Redemption in the South* (Baton Rouge: Louisiana State University Press, 1980), pp. 60–66.
50. Stanley Hirshon, *Farewell to the Bloody Shirt* (Chicago: Quadrangle Paperbacks, 1968), pp. 21–62.
51. Alwyn Barr, *Reconstruction to Reform: Texas Politics, 1876–1904* (Austin: University of Texas Press, 1971), p. 9; Degler, *The Other South*, p. 271; Woodward, *Origins*, pp. 59, 57–58; Tindall, *South Carolina Negroes*, p. 113.
52. Woodward, *Origins*, p. 55.
53. Albert Kirwan, *Revolt of the Rednecks* (New York: Harper and Row, 1965), pp. 35–36; Logan, *Negro in North Carolina*, pp. 49–50; Allen Johnston Going, *Bourbon Democracy in Alabama, 1874–1890* (Montgomery: University of Alabama Press, 1951), pp. 33, 30; Woodward, *Origins* p. 51.
54. Kirwan, *Rednecks*, pp. 35–36, 27–28; Woodward, *Origins*, p. 79; Clark and Kirwan, *The South*, pp. 62–63; Going, *Bourbon Democracy*, p. 29.
55. Woodward, *Origins*, pp. 55–58; Wynes, *Race Relations*, pp. 12–22; Going, *Bourbon Democracy*, pp. 33–34, 37–38.
56. Wiener, *Social Origins*, pp. 90–118.
57. Woodward, *Origins*, p. 79; Degler, *The Other South*, pp. 239–41.
58. Wharton, *Negro in Mississippi*, pp. 200, 202–203; Woodward, *Origins*, p. 217; Kirwan, *Rednecks*, pp. 10–17; Wynes, *Race Relations*, p. 8; Tindall, *South Carolina Negroes*, p. 32; Woodward, *Origins*, p. 209; J. Morgan Kousser, *The Shaping of Southern Politics: Suffrage Restriction and the Establishment of the One-Party South: 1880–1910* (New Haven: Yale University Press, 1974), p. 28.
59. Going, *Bourbon Democracy*, p. 42; Cash, *The Mind*, p. 132; Logan, *Negro in North Carolina*, pp. 50–55.
60. Billings, *Planters*, p. 213; Kousser, *Shaping*, p. 27; Barr, *Reconstruction to Reform*, p. 63; Logan, *Negro in North Carolina*, pp. 19–20; Degler, *The Other South*, p. 265.
61. Kirwan, *Rednecks*, pp. 22, 46; Woodward, *Origins*, pp. 80–81; Wynes, *Race Relations*, pp. 16–38.
62. Degler, *The Other South*, pp. 277–78.
63. Wynes, *Race Relations*, pp. 21, 22–25; Degler, *The Other South*, pp. 280–85; Raymond H. Pulley, *Old Virginia Restored* (Charlottesville: University Press of Virginia, 1968), pp. 41–45.
64. Pulley, *Old Virginia*, pp. 36, 44; Degler, *The Other South*, p. 293.
65. Degler, *The Other South*, pp. 293–300; Pulley, *Old Virginia*, pp. 41–45; Wynes, *Race Relations*, pp. 22–25.
66. C. Vann Woodward, *Tom Watson, Agrarian Rebel* (New York: Oxford University Press, 1963), p. 132; Saloutos, *Farmer Movements*, p. 139; Lewinson, *Race, Class, and Party*, p. 69; Woodward, *Origins*, pp. 185, 270.
67. Coulter, *South during Reconstruction*, p. 245; Clark and Kirwan, *The South*, p. 61; Woodward, *Origins*, p. 193.
68. Sheldon Hackney, *Populism to Progressivism in Alabama* (Princeton: Princeton University Press, 1969), pp. 58–60.
69. Kirwan, *Rednecks*, p. 70; Clark and Kirwan, *The South*, p. 70; Hackney, *Populism to Progressivism*, p. 58; Degler, *The Other South*, p. 344; Kousser, *Shaping*, pp. 186–87; Helen Edmonds, *The Negro and Fusion Politics in North Carolina* (Chapel Hill:

University of North Carolina Press, 1961), pp. 41, 153; Woodward, *Origins*, p. 193; Clark and Kirwan, *The South*, p. 71.

70. C. Vann Woodward, *The Strange Career of Jim Crow* (New York: Oxford University Press, 1966), p. 61; Lewinson, *Race, Class, and Party*, pp. 72–73; Kirwan, *Rednecks*, p. 73.

71. Woodward, *Strange Career*, pp. 62, 63; August Meier and Elliot Rudwick, *From Plantation to Ghetto* (New York: Hill and Wang, 1966), pp. 159–60; Degler, *The Other South*, pp. 340–47; Barr, *Reconstruction to Reform*, p. 151; Roscoe C. Martin, *The People's Party in Texas* (Austin: University of Texas Press, 1970), p. 54; Woodward, *Tom Watson*, p. 239; Hackney, *Populism to Progressivism*, p. 40; Eric Anderson, *Race and Politics in North Carolina, 1872–1901* (Baton Rouge: Louisiana State University Press, 1891), p. 228.

72. Woodward, *Origins*, pp. 192, 274, 261, 277–78; Martin, *People's Party*, p. 143; Lewinson, *Race, Class, and Party*, p. 76; Hackney, *Populism to Progressivism*, p. 3; Woodward, *Tom Watson*, p. 269; Kirwan, *Rednecks*, p. 99; Edmonds, *Negro and Fusion Politics*, pp. 37–38; Degler, *The Other South*, pp. 333–34.

73. Woodward, *Strange Career*, pp. 78–79; Pulley, *Old Virginia*, pp. 66–67; Hackney, *Populism to Progressivism*, pp. 42–43.

74. Woodward, *Origins*, p. 277; Woodward, *Strange Career*, pp. 79, 86; Edmonds, *Negro and Fusion Politics*, p. 141; Anderson, *Race and Politics*, pp. 264, 269; Woodward, *Tom Watson*, p. 223; Kirwan, *Rednecks*, p. 95; Kousser, *Shaping*, pp. 37–38.

75. Cash, *The Mind*, p. 173; cited in Edmonds, *Negro and Fusion Politics*, p. 149; Kousser, *Shaping*, p. 193; Woodward, *Origins*, p. 259; Degler, *The Other South*, pp. 316–17; Barr, *Reconstruction to Reform*, pp. 197–200; Martin, *People's Party*, p. 238.

76. Hackney, *Populism to Progressivism*, pp. 34–40; Logan, *Negro in North Carolina*, pp. 20–22; Tindall, *South Carolina Negroes*, pp. 62–64, 66–67.

77. Kirwan, *Rednecks*, p. 101; Hackney, *Populism to Progressivism*, pp. 22, 62; William Warren Rogers, *The One-Gallused Rebellion* (Baton Rouge: Lousiana State University Press 1970), p. 222.

78. Barr, *Reconstruction to Reform*, pp. 196, 207; Rogers, *One-Gallused Rebellion*, pp. 222–24; Going, *Bourbon Democracy*, p. 39; Edmonds, *Negro and Fusion Politics*, pp. 151, 158–74; Degler, *The Other South*, pp. 359–66; Kousser, *Shaping*, pp. 47, 172; Martin, *People's Party*, pp. 236–37.

79. Edmonds, *Negro and Fusion Politics*, pp. 158–72; Woodward, *Strange Career*, pp. 80, 83–85; Woodward, *Tom Watson*, p. 371; Steven F. Lawson, *Black Ballots: Voting Rights in the South* (New York: Columbia University Press, 1976), p. 89.

80. Those who have challenged Woodward include Williamson, Roger A. Fischer *(The Segregation Struggle in Louisiana, 1862–1877)*, and Howard N. Rabinowitz ("From Exclusion to Segregation: Southern Race Relations, 1865–1980," *Journal of American History* 63 [June, 1976]). The quote comes from the Rabinowitz article, p. 349. On racial relations in the South in the 1870s and 1880s, see Dale A. Somers, "Black and White in New Orleans: A Study in Urban Race Relations, 1865–1900," *Journal of Southern History* 60 (February 1974): 30–36; John Dittmer, *Black Georgia in the Progressive Era, 1900–1920* (Urbana: University of Illinois Press, 1977), pp. 87, 16; Jack Temple Kirby, *Darkness at the Dawning: Race and Reform in the Progressive South* (Philadelphia: J.B. Lippincott Co., 1972), pp. 22–23.

81. Woodward, *Strange Career*, pp. 97–102.

82. Hirshon, *Farewell*, pp. 216–22, 252.

83. Thomas F. Gossett, *Race: The History of an Idea in America* (New York: Schocken, 1965), pp. 271–72, 287–88, 329, 332; John Higham, *Strangers in the Land* (New York: Atheneum, 1973), pp. 35–87.

84. Joseph Tussman, ed., *The Supreme Court on Racial Discrimination* (New York: Oxford University Press, 1963), pp. 66, 68, 73, 74.

85. *Encyclopedia Britannica* (New York, 1903), vol. 17, pp. 317–18.

86. W. E. B. DuBois, *Black Reconstruction in America, 1860–1880* (New York: Atheneum, 1970), chap. 17.

87. Booker T. Washington, "Cast Down Your Buckets," in Thomas Clark, ed., *The South since Reconstruction* (New York: Bobbs-Merrill Co., 1973), pp. 521–24.

88. Wiener, "Planters, Merchants," pp. 42–43.

89. Woodward, *Origins*, p. 211; Clark and Kirwan, *The South*, p. 111.

90. Degler, *The Other South*, pp. 347–48.

91. Woodward, *Origins*, p. 328; Woodward, *Strange Career*, p. 85.

92. Kousser, *Shaping*, pp. 238–40.

93. Ibid., pp. 139–81.

94. Hackney, *Populism to Progressivism*, p. 229; Kousser, *Shaping*, p. 180; Darlene Clark Hine, *Black Victory: the Rise and Fall of the White Primary in Texas* (Millwood, N.Y.: KTO Press, 1979), p. 235; Barr, *Reconstruction to Reform*, p. 205.

95. Kousser, *Shaping*, p. 247;

96. Ibid., pp. 144, 169, 191.

97. Ibid., pp. 48, 130, 181, 208, 195; Barr, *Reconstruction to Reform*, p. 208; Woodward, *Origins*, pp. 336–67.

98. Cash, *The Mind*, pp. 254–55; Clark and Kirwan, *The South*, p. 111.

99. Hackney, *Populism to Progressivism*, pp. 232–34, 278–83; T. Harry Williams, *Huey Long* (New York: Batan Books, 1970), p. 433. See also George Brown Tindall, *The Emergence of the New South, 1913–1945* (Baton Rouge: Louisiana State University Press, 1967), pp. 20–21; Woodward, *Origins*, pp. 393–94; Cash, *The Mind*, pp. 254–59; Kirby, *Darkness*, pp. 27–31 for other references.

100. Williams, *Huey Long*, p. 434, Billings, *Planters*, pp. 211–12; Kousser, *Shaping*, p. 238; Cash, *The Mind*, p. 258.

101. Woodward in the *New Republic*, December 27, 1982, p. 33.

102. Somers, "Black and White," p. 23; Logan, *Negro in North Carolina*, p. 161; Kirby, *Darkness*, p. 25; Dittmer, *Black Georgia*, p. 21; table compiled from Pauli Murray, *States' Laws on Race and Color* (Women's Division for Christian Service, 1950).

103. Murray, *States' Laws*.

104. Woodward, *Strange Career*, p. 98.

105. Murray, *States' Laws*, pp. 17–18; cited in Clark and Kirwan, *The South*, p. 152.

106. Billings, *Planters*, p. 102; Melton McLaurin, *Paternalism and Protest* (Westport, Conn.: Greenwood Publishing, 1971), pp. 60, 64; Stanley Greenberg, *Race and State in Capitalist Development* (New Haven: Yale University Press, 1980), p. 215.

107. Robert Margo, "Race Differences in Public School Expenditures," *Social Science History* 6, no. 1 (Winter 1982):12.

108. J. Morgan Kousser, "Progressivism—For Middle Class Whites Only: North Carolina Education, 1880–1910," *Journal of Southern History* 46, no. 2 (May 1980):174.

109. Margo, "Race Differences," p. 11.

110. Kousser, "Progressivism," p. 174.

111. Ibid., p. 181.

112. Woodward, *Tom Watson*, p. 404; T. J. Woofter, Jr., *Landlord and Tenant on the Cotton Plantation*, Research Monograph 5 (Washington, D. C.: Works Progress Administration, 1936), p. xxi; Tindall, *Emergence*, p. 409; Woodward, *Origins*, p. 319; Thomas Clark, *The Emerging South* (New York: Oxford University Press, 1968), p. 15; Van Sickle, *Planning*, p. 61.

113. Nicholls, *Southern Tradition*, p. 28; Clark, *Emerging South*, p. 15.

114. Clark and Kirwan, *The South*, p. 297.

115. Woodward, *Origins*, p. 2.
116. Ibid, p. 22; Cash, *The Mind*, p. 205.
117. Clark, *Emerging South*, p. 18; Nicholls, *Southern Tradition*, p. 125.

II. The Old Order Changes

1. Ralph McGill, *The South and the Southerner* (Boston: Little, Brown and Co., 1964), p. 15.
2. T. J. Woofter, Jr., *Landlord and Tenant on the Cotton Plantation*, Research Monograph 5 (Washington, D. C.: Works Progress Administration, 1936), pp. xxxii-xxxiii; W. J. Cash, *The Mind of the South* (New York: Vintage Books, 1969), pp. 281–82.
3. George Stocking, *Basing Point Pricing and Regional Development* (Chapel Hill: University of North Carolina Press, 1954), p. 104.
4. Pat Watters, *The South and the Nation* (New York: Vintage Books, 1969). pp. 79–80.
5. Vivian W. Henderson, "Regions, Race, and Jobs," in Arthur Ross and Herbert Hill, *Employment, Race, and Poverty* (New York: Harcourt, Brace and World, 1967), p. 81.
6. Arthur M. Ross, "The Negro in the American Economy," in Ross and Hill, *Employment, Race, and Poverty*, pp. 17–18; Charles C. Killingsworth, "Negroes in a Changing Labor Market," in ibid., p. 52; Henderson, "Regions, Race, and Jobs," p. 86; Herbert R. Northrup, "Industry's Racial Employment Policies," in Ross and Hill, *Employment, Race, and Poverty*, pp. 293, 295–96.
7. Thomas Clark and Albert Kirwan, *The South since Appomattox* (New York: Oxford University Press, 1967), p. 239.
8. Fritz Sternberg, *Capitalism and Socialism on Trial* (New York: John Day Co., 1950), pp. 277, 289–90; Arthur M. Schlesinger, Jr., *The Crisis of the Old Order* (Boston: Houghton Mifflin Co., 1957), p. 248; William E. Leuchtenburg, *Franklin D. Roosevelt and the New Deal* (New York: Harper Torchbooks, 1963), p. 1; Arthur M. Schlesinger, Jr., *The Coming of the New Deal* (Boston: Houghton Mifflin Co., 1959), p. 297.
9. Calvin B. Hoover and B. U. Ratchford, *Economic Resources and Policies of the South* (New York: Macmillan Co., 1951), p. 52; Cash, *The Mind*, p. 369; George Brown Tindall, *The Emergence of the New South, 1913–1945* (Baton Rouge: Louisiana State University Press, 1967), p. 254; Frank Freidel, *F.D.R. and the South* (Baton Rouge: Louisiana State University Press, 1965), pp. 37–38.
10. Hoover and Ratchford, *Resources*, pp. 170–71; Monroe Lee Billington, *The Political South in the Twentieth Century* (New York: Charles Scribner's Sons, 1975), p. 59.
11. Charles S. Johnson, Edwin R. Embree, and W. W. Alexander, *The Collapse of Cotton Tenancy* (Chapel Hill: University of North Carolina Press, 1935), p. 47; John Robert Moore, "The New Deal In Louisiana," in John Braeman, Robert H. Bremner, and David Brody, eds., *The New Deal*, vol. 2 (Columbus: Ohio State University Press, 1975), p. 137; Freidel, *F.D.R.*, p. 38; Woofter, *Landlord and Tenant*, p. 146.
12. Leuchtenberg, *Roosevelt*, pp. 41–62; Howard Zinn, ed., *New Deal Thought* (Indianapolis: Bobbs-Merrill Co., 1966), pp. xxix-xliii.
13. U. S. National Emergency Council, *Report on Economic Conditions of the South* (Washington, D.C.: Government Printing Office, 1938), pp. 1–2.
14. Ross in Ross and Hill, *Employment, Race, and Poverty*, p. 14; Cash, *The Mind*, p. 410; Tindall, *Emergence*, p. 429.
15. Cash, *The Mind*, p. 375; Hoover and Ratchford, *Resources*, p. 55.
16. Clark and Kirwan, *The South*, p. 239; Johnson et al., *Collapse*, pp. 52–54; Gunnar Myrdal, *An American Dilemma* (New York: Harper and Row, 1962), p. 257; John Dollard,

Caste and Class in a Southern Town (Garden City, N.Y.: Doubleday and Co., 1957), p. 125; Edward L. and Frederick H. Schapsmeier, *Henry A. Wallace of Iowa: The Agrarian Years, 1910–1940* (Ames: Iowa State University Press, 1968), p. 197; Myrdal, *Dilemma*, p. 248.

17. Tindall, *Emergence*, p. 478; Clark and Kirwan, *The South*, p. 240; Cash, *The Mind*, p. 406.

18. Jesse Jones, *Fifty Billion Dollars: My Thirteen Years with the RFC* (New York: Macmillan Co., 1951), pp. 94–95; William C. Holey, Ellen Winston, and T. J. Woofter, Jr., *The Plantation South, 1934–1937*, Research Monograph 22, WPA (New York: DaCapo Press, 1971), p. 25.

19. Glenn E. McLaughlin and Stefan Robock, *Why Industry Moves South* (Kingsport, Tenn.: Kingsport Press, 1949), p. 53; Tindall, *Emergence*, pp. 455–57; Clark and Kirwan, *The South*, p. 264.

20. Tindall, *Emergence*, p. 470.

21. Robert Lively, "The South and Freight Rates: Political Settlement of an Economic Argument," *Journal of Southern History* 14, no. 3 (August 1948): cited pp. 360–62, 363; William H. Joubert, *Southern Freight Rates in Transition* (Gainesville: University of Florida Press, 1949), p. 342.

22. Allison Davis, Burleigh Gardner, and Mary Gardner, *Deep South* (Chicago: University of Chicago Press, 1965), p. 260.

23. U.S. Department of Commerce, *Bicentennial Statistics*, Bureau of the Census (Washington, D.C.: U.S. Government Printing Office, 1976), p. 394.

24. William H. Nicholls, *Southern Tradition and Regional Progress* (Chapel Hill: University of North Carolina Press, 1960), p. 12 fn.; Hoover and Ratchford, *Resources*, p. 90; Tindall, *Emergence*, pp. 703, 432.

25. Hoover and Ratchford, *Resources*, p. 59; Tindall, *Emergence*, p. 699; Hoover and Ratchford, *Resources*, p. 120; Report of the Southeastern Regional Planning Commission to the National Resources Planning Board, *Southeastern Regional Development Plan for 1942*, Region Three, Atlanta.

26. Tindall, *Emergence*, pp. 694, 701–703; Hoover and Ratchford, *Resources*, p. 60; *Southeastern Regional Development Plan for 1942*, p. 8.

27. *Southeastern Regional Development Plan for 1942*, p. 4; Hoover and Ratchford, *Resources*, pp. 96, 101.

28. McLaughlin and Robock, *Why Industry*, pp. 32–33, 73; McGill, *South and Southerner*, p. 209.

29. McLaughlin and Robock, *Why Industry*, p. 70.

30. Hoover and Ratchford, *Resources*, p. 413.

31. McGill, *South and Southerner*, p. 209; *Bicentennial Statistics*, p. 403; James W. Vander Zanden, *Race Relations in Transition* (New York: Random House, 1965), p. 12.

32. Cash, *The Mind*, pp. 419–20; Tindall, *Emergence*, pp. 479–80.

33. Tindall, *Emergence*, p. 710; McGill, *South and Southerner*, p. 170.

34. McGill, *South and Southerner*, pp. 161–63; Jasper Berry Shannon, *Toward a New Politics in the South* (Knoxville: University of Tennessee Press, 1949), p. 44.

35. Billington, *Political South*, p. 78.

36. Tindall, *Emergence*, p. 443.

37. Leuchtenberg, *Roosevelt*, pp. 266, 267–69; Steven F. Lawson, *Black Ballots: Voting Rights in the South* (New York: Columbia University Press, 1967), p. 57.

38. Samuel Lubbell, *The Future of American Politics* (Garden City, N.Y.: Doubleday and Co., 1956), pp. 120–21; Numan V. Bartley, *The Rise of Massive Resistance* (Baton Rouge: Louisiana State University Press, 1969), p. 18.

39. Tindall, *Emergence*, pp. 611, 613;

40. Irving Howe and Lewis Coser, *The American Communist Party* (New York: Frederick A. Praeger, 1962), p. 331.

41. Tindall, *Emergence*, pp. 623–24.

42. Freidel, *F.D.R.*, p. 93.

43. Leuchtenberg, *Roosevelt*, pp. 252, 254, 269.

44. Tindall, *Emergence*, pp. 491, 707.

45. Ibid., pp. 710, 724; John Temple Graves, *The Fighting South* (New York: G. P. Putnam's Sons, 1943), p. 245.

46. Bartley, *Massive Resistance*, p. 29.

47. Ibid., pp. 341, 35.

III. Nineteen Forty-Eight: The Opening of the Breach

1. Irwin Ross, *The Loneliest Campaign*. (New York: New American Library, 1968), p. 122; *New York Times*, July 14, 1948.

2. Barton Bernstein, "The Ambiguous Legacy: The Truman Administration and Civil Rights," in Barton Bernstein, ed., *Politics and Policies of the Truman Administration* (Chicago: Quadrangle Books, 1970), p. 289; Jack Redding, *Inside the Democratic Party* (New York: Bobbs-Merrill Co., 1958), p. 192.

3. V. O. Key, *Southern Politics* (New York: Vintage Books, 1949), pp. 318–19; William Barnard, *Dixiecrats and Democrats* (Alabama: University of Alabama Press, 1974), p. 3; Henry Moon, *Balance of Power: The Negro Vote* (New York: Doubleday and Co., 1948), pp. 20–21, 33; William Berman, *The Politics of Civil Rights in the Truman Administration* (Columbus: Ohio State University Press, 1970), p. 86.

4. Joyce Kolko and Gabriel Kolko, *The Limits of Power* (New York: Harper and Row, 1972), pp. 11–29, 69–73.

5. Frances Piven and Richard Cloward, *Poor People's Movements* (New York: Pantheon, 1977), pp. 191–192; Thomas Brooks, *Walls Come Tumbling Down* (Englewood Cliffs, N.J.: Prentice-Hall, 1974), p. 17; Gunnar Myrdal, *An American Dilemma* (New York: Harper and Row, 1962), p. 183; Moon, *Balance*, p. 198.

6. Moon, *Balance*, pp. 240–44; Berman, *Civil Rights*, p. 7; Pat Waters and Reese Cleghorn, *Climbing Jacob's Ladder* (New York: Harcourt, Brace and World, 1967), p. 12.

7. Brooks, *Walls*, p. 54; Moon, *Balance*, pp. 198, 199; John Hope Franklin, *From Slavery to Freedom* (New York: Alfred Knopf, 1964), p. 518.

8. Robert Cushman, "Our Civil Rights Become a World Issue," *New York Times Magazine*, January 11, 1948, pp. 12, 22, 24; Richard Dalfiume, *Desegregation of the U.S. Armed Forces* (Columbia: University of Missouri Press, 1969), p. 139; Richard Kluger, *Simple Justice* (New York: Vintage Books, 1977), p. 335.

9. Lee Nichols, *Breakthrough on the Color Front* (New York: Random House, 1954), pp. 83–84; Dalfiume, *Desegregation*, p. 139.

10. Donald McCoy and Richard Ruetten, "The Civil Rights Movement: 1949–1954," in *Midwest Quarterly* 11 (October 1969): 16.

11. Myrdal, *Dilemma*, p. 409; Herbert Garfinkel, *When Negroes March* (Glencoe, Ill.: Free Press, 1959), pp. 31, 38, 57, 92–96.

12. *Hearings on Senate Bill S. 380*, Subcommittee of the Committee on Banking and Currency, 1945; Daisy Bates, *The Long Shadow of Little Rock* (New York: David McKay Co., 1962), p. 44; Berman, *Civil Rights*, pp. 50–51; President's Committee on Civil Rights, *To Secure These Rights* (Washington, D.C.: U.S. Government Printing Office, 1947), p. vii.

13. Berman, *Civil Rights*, pp. 65–66; Moon, *Balance*, p. 203.

14. Berman, *Civil Rights*, p. 97; Jervis Anderson, *A. Philip Randolph* (New York: Harcourt, Brace, Jovanovich, 1973), pp. 276–80.

15. Moon, *Balance*, p. 9.

16. Karl M. Schmidt, *Henry A. Wallace* (Syracuse: Syracuse University Press, 1960), pp. 5–6, 22; Curtis MacDougall, *Gideon's Army*, vol. 1 (New York: Marzani and Munsell, 1965), pp. 7–11, 13–14, 22–54; Allen Yarnell, *Democrats and Progressives* (Berkeley and Los Angeles: University of California Press, 1974), p. 23; Clifton Brock, *Americans for Democratic Action* (Washington, D.C.: Public Affairs Press, 1962), pp. 88–92; Dalfiume, *Desegregation*, p. 144.

17. Schmidt, *Wallace*, pp. 102–103, 146–49.

18. Robert Divine, "The Cold War and the Election of 1948," *Journal of American History* 59 (June 1952): 93.

19. Athan Theoharis "The Rhetoric of Politics: Foreign Policy, Internal Security and Domestic Politics in the Truman Era 1945–1950," in Bernstein, *Truman Administration*, pp. 219, 229, 221.

20. Ibid.; Redding, *Democratic Party*, p. 143; Divine, "Cold War," p. 93; Schmidt, *Wallace*, p. 143.

21. Brock, *Americans*, p. 75; Berman, *Civil Rights*, p. 91; Redding, *Democratic Party*, p. 145.

22. Editors of *Freedomways*, *Paul Robeson: The Great Forerunner* (New York: Dodd, Mead and Co., 1978), p. 118; Harvard Sitkoff, "Harry Truman and the Elections of 1948: The Coming of Age of Civil Rights in American Politics," *Journal of Southern History* 37 (November 1971): 597–616; Berman, p. 115.

23. Berman, *Civil Rights*, p. 76; MacDougall, *Gideon's Army*, p. 220; Schmidt, *Wallace*, pp. 75–80, 204–209.

24. Bernstein, "Ambiguous Legacy," p. 288; Berman, *Civil Rights*, p. 124; ibid., p. 128.

25. Brock, *Americans*, p. 51.

26. Ibid., pp. 81, 88, 92–94.

27. Bernstein, "Ambiguous Legacy," p. 284; Berman, *Civil Rights*, pp. 86–87, 92, 95.

28. Berman, *Civil Rights*, p. 85.

29. Ibid., pp. 102–103.

30. Ibid., pp. 110, 108.

31. Brock, *Americans*, p. 96; Berman, *Civil Rights*, pp. 111, 107; Ross, *Campaign*, p. 123; Robert Sherrill and Harry Ernst, *The Drugstore Liberal* (New York: Grossman Publishers, 1968), p. 124; Winthrop Griffith, *Humphrey* (New York: William Morrow and Co., 1965), p. 155; Bernstein, "Ambiguous Legacy," pp. 288–89.

32. Sherrill and Ernst, *Drugstore Liberal*, p. 124; Griffith, *Humphrey*, pp. 157–58.

33. Griffith, *Humphrey*, p. 159; Brock, *Americans*, p. 99.

34. Berman, *Civil Rights*, pp. 116–20; Bernstein, "Ambiguous Legacy," pp. 290–91.

35. Bernstein, "Ambiguous Legacy," pp. 290–91; Berman, *Civil Rights*, pp. 116–20.

36. Ross, *Campaign*, pp. 246–47; Berman, *Civil Rights*, pp. 129–30.

37. Berman, *Civil Rights*, p. 129; Myrdal, *Dilemma*, p. 496.

38. U.S. Commission on Civil Rights, *Freedom for the Free* (Washington, D.C., 1963), pp. 109–111; Numan Bartley, *The Rise of Massive Resistance* (Baton Rouge: Louisiana State University Press, 1969), pp. 4–6; McCoy and Ruetten, "Civil Rights Movement," pp. 30–32.

39. Bartley, *Massive Resistance*, p. 32.

IV. The Splitting of the Solid South

1. Steven F. Lawson, *Black Ballots: Voting Rights in the South* (New York: Columbia University Press, 1976), pp. 175–76.

2. C. Vann Woodward, "The 'New Reconstruction' in the South," *Commentary*, June 1956, p. 501; Neil R. McMillen, *The Citizens' Council* (Urbana: University of Illinois Press, 1971), p. 358.

3. Gunnar Myrdal, *An American Dilemma* (New York: Harper and Row, 1962), pp. xlvii-xlxiii; V. O. Key, *Southern Politics* (New York: Random House, 1949).

4. Richard Kluger, *Simple Justice* (New York: Random House, 1977), pp. 282–83, 238; Hodding Carter III, *The South Strikes Back* (Garden City, N.Y.: Doubleday and Co., 1959), p. 13.

5. Kluger, *Justice*, p. 236; Numan Bartley, *The Rise of Massive Resistance* (Baton Rouge: Louisiana State University Press, 1969), pp. 8, 9.

6. Bartley, *Resistance*, p. 37; Lawson, *Ballots*, p. 134.

7. Joseph Tussman, ed., *The Supreme Court on Racial Discrimination* (New York: Oxford University Press, 1963), p. 42; Earl Warren, "The Memoirs of Earl Warren," in Petter Woll, *American Government* (Boston: Little, Brown and Co., 1978), p. 552; Carter, *South Strikes*, pp. 16–17.

8. Bob Smith, *They Closed Their Schools* (Chapel Hill: University of North Carolina Press, 1965), pp. 87–88; Howard Quint, *Profile in Black and White* (Washington, D.C.: Public Affairs Press, 1958), p. 8; M. Elaine Burgess, *Negro Deadership in a Southern Town* (New Haven: College and University Press, 1965), p. 169.

9. Benjamin Muse, *Virginia's Massive Resistance* (Bloomington: Indiana University Press, 1961); p. 5; Woodward, "New Reconstruction," p. 503.

10. James Weldon, "The South's Own Civil War," in Don Shoemaker, ed., *With All Deliberate Speed* (New York: Harper and Brothers, 1957), p. 24; Robbin L. Gates, *The Making of Massive Resistance* (Chapel Hill: University of North Carolina, 1964), p. 51; Muse, *Virginia's Resistance*, pp. 4–5; William Chafe, *Civilities and Civil Rights* (New York: Oxford University Press, 1980), pp. 59, 65; William Peters, *The Southern Temper* (Garden City, N.Y.: Doubleday and Co., 1959), p. 59.

11. Francis M. Wilhoit, *The Politics of Massive Resistance* (New York: George Braziller, 1973), p. 28; McMillen, *Council*, p. 17; John Bartlow Martin, The *Deep South Says "Never"* (New York: Ballantine Books, 1957), p. 27.

12. Muse, *Virginia's Resistance*, p. 17; Carter, *South Strikes*, p. 46; McMillen, *Council*, pp. 7–8.

13. Samuel Lubbell, *White and Black* (New York: Harper and Row, 1964), p. 89; Gates, *The Making*, pp. 57–58; Martin Luther King, Jr., *Stride toward Freedom* (New York: Harper and Row, 1964), p. 102; Carter, *South Strikes*, p. 159.

14. Wilma Dykeman and James Stokely, *Neither Black nor White* (New York: Rinehart and Co., 1957), p. 109; Martin, *"Never"*, p. 6; Warren, "Memoirs," p. 556.

15. Carl Rowan, *Go South to Sorrow* (New York: Random House, 1957), pp. 200, 210.

16. Carter, *South Strikes*, p. 12; Bartley, *Resistance*, p. 343; see also Burgess, *Leadership*, p. 96.

17. David Oshinsky, *Senator Joseph McCarthy and the American Labor Movement* (Columbia: University of Missouri Press, 1976), pp. 161–69; Fred J. Cook, *The Nightmare Decade* (New York: Random House, 1971), p. 63.

18. Cook, *Nightmare Decade*, pp. 13, 20, 462.

19. David Caute, *The Great Fear* (New York: Simon and Schuster, 1979), pp. 102–103, 360–62.

20. Cook, *Nightmare Decade*, pp. 291–97; Alexander Heard, *A Two-Party South?*

(Chapel Hill: University of North Carolina Press, 1952), pp. 258–59; Carter, *South Strikes*, p. 73; Bartley, *Resistance*, p. 133; Ralph E. Ellsworth and Sarah M. Harris, "The American Right Wing," A Report to the Fund for the Republic (Washington, D.C.: Public Affairs Press, 1962), pp. 5–6.

21. Quint, *Profile*, p. 8; McMillen, *Council*, pp. 17, 197; Rowan, *Go South*, pp. 93–94; Carter, *South Strikes*, p. 35.

22. Bartley, *Resistance*, pp. 119–20; Rowan, *Go South*, pp. 84–85, 91; Lawson, *Ballots*, pp. 153–54.

23. Carter, *South Strikes*, p. 18; Daniel Thompson, *The Negro Leadership Class* (Englewood Cliffs, N.J.: Prentice-Hall, 1963), pp. 74, 136; McMillen, *Council*, p. 198; David L. Lewis, *King: A Critical Biography* (New York: Praeger Publishers, 1970), p. 131.

24. Oshinsky, *McCarthy and Labor*, pp. 166–69.

25. Karl Marx, *The Eighteenth Brumaire of Louis Bonaparte* (New York: International Publishers, 1963), p. 15.

26. Muse, *Virginia's Resistance*, p. 22.

27. Quint, *Profile*, p. 25.

28. Carter, *South Strikes*, p. 28.

29. Bartley, *Resistance*, p. 121; McMillen, *Council*, p. 18; Carter, *South Strikes*, pp. 31–32, 139.

30. Bartley, *Resistance*, pp. 76–77.

31. Martin, "Never," pp. 17, 20–21.

32. Rowan, *Go South*, pp. 38–39; Benjamin Muse, *Ten Years of Prelude* (New York: Viking Press, 1964), pp. 51, 29; Mrs. Medgar Evers with William Peters, *For Us, the Living* (Garden City, N.Y.: Doubleday and Co., 1967), p. 162; Muse, *Virginia's Resistance*, p. 53.

33. McMillen, *Council*, p. 18; Bartley, *Resistance*, p. 121.

34. Carter, *South Strikes*, pp. 31–32; Martin, "Never," p. 21.

35. Carter, *South Strikes*, pp. 28–29.

36. Martin, *"Never"*, p. 25; Carter, *South Strikes*, pp. 141–45, 147, 154–55; Bartley, *Resistance*, p. 192.

37. James Graham Cook, *The Segregationists* (New York: Appleton-Century-Crofts, 1962). pp. 34–43.

38. Carter, *South Strikes*, pp. 159–60, 119; Rowan, *Go South*, pp. 191–97; McMillen, *Council*, pp. 209, 217; Smith, *They Closed*, p. 135.

39. Carter, *South Strikes*, pp. 122–23; McMillen, *Council*, pp. 210–11; Bartley, *Resistance*, p. 193.

40. McMillen, *Council*, pp. 220–26; Cook, *Segregationists*, p. 60.

41. King, *Stride*, p. 151.

42. Carter, *South Strikes*, pp. 14–15, 21; McMillen, *Council*, pp. 216–17; Rowan, *Go South*, pp. 60–75.

43. McMillen, *Council*, p. 217; Carter, *South Strikes*, p. 119.

44. Evers and Peters, *For Us*, pp. 169–70.

45. Ibid., pp. 170–71; Rowan, *Go South*, p. 41.

46. Anne Moody, *Coming of Age in Mississippi* (New York: Dell Publishing Co., 1968).

47. Pat Watters and Reese Cleghorn, *Climbing Jacob's Ladder* (New York: Harcourt, Brace and World, 1967), pp. 27, 28; McMillen, *Council* p. 219; Carter, *South Strikes*, pp. 124–25.

48. Martin, *"Never"*, p. 6; Bartley, *Resistance*, pp. 96, 85, 87, 91, 93, 114; McMillen, *Council*, pp. 19, 24, 43, 101; Carter, *South Strikes*, p. 210; Muse, *Virginia's Resistance*, pp. 8–9.

49. Martin, *"Never"*, p. 105; Carter, *South Strikes*, pp. 196–97, 19–20.

50. McMillen, *Council*, pp. 17, 11, 75, 82, 84, 101, 106; Muse, *Virginia's Resistance*, p. 2; Lewis, *King*, pp. 59–60.

51. Bartley, *Resistance*, pp. 111–12; Lubbell, *White and Black*, p. 89; Chafe, *Civilities*, pp. 27, 28.

52. Martin, *"Never"*, p. 15; McMillen, *Council*, pp. 20–21, 50–56.

53. Muse, *Ten Years*, pp. 82–84; Carter, *South Strikes*, p. 111.

54. King, *Stride*, p. 164.

55. Muse, *Virginia's Resistance*, p. 22.

56. Bartley, *Resistance*, pp. 150–69.

57. Martin, *"Never"*, pp. 49–54; Wilhoit, *Politics*, pp. 43–44.

58. Martin, *"Never"*, pp. 28–30.

59. Warren, "Memoirs," pp. 556–57.

60. Anthony Lewis, *Portrait of a Decade* (New York: Random House, 1964), pp. 105–107.

61. Muse, *Ten Years*, pp. 73–74; Wilhoit, *Politics*, p. 44.

62. Warren, "Memoirs," p. 557.

63. Gates, *The Making*, pp. 66–69, 75–79.

64. Ibid., p. 123; Muse, *Virginia's Resistance*, pp. 24, 19.

65. Muse, *Ten Years*, p. 29.

66. Muse, *Virginia's Resistance*, p. 21; Gates, *The Making*, pp. 104–108.

67. Martin, *"Never"*, pp. 38–41; Bartley, *Resistance*, p. 146; Sherman Adams, *First-Hand Report* (New York: Harper and Brothers, 1961), p. 338.

68. Martin, *"Never"*, p. 37; Lubbell, *White and Black*, p. 93; Bartley, *Resistance*, pp. 260, 144.

69. Bartley, *Resistance*, pp. 116–17; Wilhoit, *Politics*, pp. 52–53.

70. Bartley, *Resistance*, pp. 116–17; Lewis, *Portrait*, p. 45.

71. Bartley, *Resistance*, pp. 171, 180–81, 178–79.

72. Ibid., pp. 212–24; Quint, *Profile*, pp. 85–87.

73. Gates, *The Making*, pp. 126–27, 130, 133; Bartley, *Resistance*, pp. 135, 143.

74. Muse, *Ten Years*, p. 88.

75. Ibid., pp. 88–92.

76. Martin, *"Never"*, p. 180.

77. Adams, *Report*, p. 340.

78. Muse, *Ten Years*, pp. 140–41.

79. Ibid., pp. 112–21.

80. McMillen, *Council*, p. 285.

81. Ibid., p. 251.

82. Muse, *Ten Years*, p. 128; Bartley, *Resistance*, p. 261.

83. McMillen, *Council*, pp. 271–72; Bartley, *Resistance*, p. 257.

84. Bartley, *Resistance*, p. 259; Daisy Bates, *The Long Shadow of Little Rock* (New York: David McKay Co., 1970), pp. 3–4.

85. Bates, *Long Shadow*, pp. 1–5, 57–58; Bartley, *Resistance*, p. 258.

86. Bartley, *Resistance*, pp. 276–77.

87. Lewis, *Portrait*, pp. 47–48; Muse, *Ten Years*, pp. 123–24; Bartley, *Resistance*, pp. 266, 267.

88. Bates, *Long Shadow*, pp. 88–97; Lewis, *Portrait*, p. 50.

89. Lewis, *Portrait*, p. 61.

90. McMillen, *Council*, pp. 276–77; Bates, *Long Shadow*, pp. 107–109; Bartley, *Resistance*, p. 269.

91. Muse, *Ten Years*, pp. 168, 287–89; idem, *Virginia's Resistance*, p. 63.

92. Muse, *Ten Years*, pp. 151–56.

93. Lubbell, *White and Black*, pp. 96–102; Muse, *Virginia's Resistance*, p. 86.

94. Muse, *Virginia's Resistance*, pp. 87–94; Bartley, *Resistance*, pp. 327–28; Muse, *Ten Years*, p. 192.

95. Muse, *Ten Years*, p. 192.

96. Muse, *Virginia's Resistance*, pp. 93–94; James, "South's Own," pp. 30–31.

97. Muse, *Virignia's Resistance*, pp. 93–94.

98. Ibid., pp. 93–94; Bartley, *Resistance*, p. 322.

99. Muse, *Virginia's Resistance*, pp. 120–25, 129, 132–35.

100. Bartley, *Resistance*, pp. 328, 330–31; Muse, *Ten Years*, p. 192.

101. Bartley, *Resistance*, pp. 326, 332.

102. Myrdal, *Dilemma*, p. 65; Key, *Politics*, pp. 19–20, 184.

103. Bartley, *Resistance*, p. 333; Lubbell, *White and Black*, p. 102; Thompson, *Leadership Class*, p. 65.˚

V. The Defeat of White Power and the Emergence of the "New Negro" in the South

1. Nathan I. Huggins, *Harlem Renaissance* (New York: Oxford University Press, 1973), pp. 52–60.

2. John Dollard, *Caste and Class in a Southern Town* (Garden City, N.Y.: Doubleday and Co., 1957), p. 359.

3. Gunnar Myrdal, *An American Dilemma* (New York: Harper and Row, 1962), p. 530, chaps. 24–27, pp. 523–72; Dollard, *Caste and Class*, p. 260; Hortense Powdermaker, *After Freedom* (New York: Russell and Russell, 1968), p. 33.

4. Charles S. Johnson, *Background to Patterns of Negro Segregation* (New York: Thomas Y. Crowell Co., 1970), p. 248.

5. Ibid., p. 249; interview in Howell Raines, *My Soul Is Rested* (New York: Bantam Books, 1981), p. 101.

6. Johnson, *Background*, p. 251.

7. Ibid., p. 264.

8. Hylan Lewis, *Blackways of Kent* (Chapel Hill: University of North Carolina Press, 1955), p. 173.

9. Lewis, *Blackways*, pp. 54, 296; Powdermaker, *After Freedom*, pp. 29, 50–51, 44; Raines, *My Soul*, p. 70; Johnson, *Background*, p. 269.

10. Dollard, *Caste and Class*, pp. 259, 257.

11. Dollard, *Caste and Class*, pp. 259–60, 309; Lewis, *Blackways*, p. 112; interview in Robert Coles, *Children of Crisis*, vol. 1 (Boston: Atlantic Monthly Press, 1967), p. 66.

12. Dollard, *Caste and Class*, pp. 262–63; Johnson, *Background*, p. 246; William H. Chafe, *Civilities and Civil Rights* (New York: Oxford University Press, 1980), p. 29.

13. Davis, Gardner, and Gardner, *Deep South*, p. 235.

14. Morton Rubin, *Plantation County* (Chapel Hill: University of North Carolina Press, 1951), pp. 90–93; Myrdal, *Dilemma*, pp. 786–87, 391–92; Johnson, *Background*, pp. 268–69, 273; Allison Davis, Burleigh B. Gardner, and Mary R. Gardner, *Deep South* (Chicago: University of Chicago Press, 1965), pp. 232–40, Lewis, *Blackways*, p. 197.

15. Allison Davis and John Dollard, *Children of Bondage* (New York: Harper Torchbooks, 1940), p. 124; Davis, Gardner, and Gardner, *Deep South*, pp. 232–40.

16. Lewis, *Blackways*, p. 168; Davis, Gardner, and Gardner, *Deep South*, p. 237; Mrs. Medgar Evers with William Peters, *For Us, the Living* (Garden City, N.Y.: Doubleday and Co., 1967), p. 147.

17. John H. Rohrer and Munro S. Edmonson, *The Eighth Generation Grows Up* (New York: Harper Torchbooks, 1964), p. 53; E. Franklin Frazier, *Black Bourgeoisie*

(New York: Collier Books, 1962), p. 158, Davis, Gardner, and Gardner, *Deep South*, pp. 200, 202–203; Davis and Dollard, *Children*, pp. 44, 87.

18. Martin Luther King, Jr., *Stride toward Freedom* (New York: Harper and Row, 1964), p. 22.

19. Lewis, *Blackways*, pp. 56–61; Dollard, *Caste and Class*, pp. 67–71; Davis, Gardner, and Gardner, *Deep South*, pp. 204–206; Frazier, *Black Bourgeoisie*, pp. 112–26; Powdermaker, *After Freedom*, pp. 175–92; Abram Kardiner and Lionel Ovesey, *The Mark of Opression* (Cleveland: Meridian Books, 1964); King, *Stride*, p. 22.

20. Dollard, *Caste and Class*, pp. 267–86.

21. Myrdal, *Dilemma*, pp. 727, 770; see also Frazier, *Black Bourgeoisie*, p. 158; Everett Carl Ladd, Jr., *Negro Political Leadership in the South* (Ithaca, N.Y.: Cornell University Press, 1966), pp. 42–44.

22. Ladd, *Negro Leadership*, p. 160; Oliver C. Cox, "Leadership among Negroes in the United States," in Alvin Gouldner, *Studies in Leadership* (New York: Russell and Russell, 1965), pp. 245–46; Evers and Peters, *For Us*, p. 148.

23. See Rubin, *Plantation County*, pp. 64–66, for an illuminating example; Myrdal, *Dilemma*, p. 773; Ladd, *Negro Leadership*, p. 171; Chafe, *Civilities*, pp. 54–55.

24. Elaine Burgess, *Negro Leadership in a Southern Town* (New Haven: College and University Press, 1976), p. 49.

25. Bayard Rustin, *Strategies for Freedom* (New York: Columbia University Press, 1976), P. 26; Chafe, *Civilities*, p. 28.

26. Myrdal, *Dilemma*, pp. 770–71.

27. Coles, *Children*, p. 67.

28. Rubin, *Plantation County*, p. 97.

29. Carl T. Rowan, *South of Freedom* (New York: Alfred A. Knopf, 1952), pp. 28–49.

30. Bob Smith, *They Closed Their Schools* (Chapel Hill: University of North Carolina Press, 1964), pp. 169–73.

31. Lerone Bennett, Jr., *Confrontation: Black and White* (Baltimore: Penguin Books, 1965), pp. 169–73, John M. Orbell, "Protest Participation among Southern Negro College Students," in James A. Geschwender, *The Black Revolt* (Englewood Cliffs, N.J.: Prentice-Hall, 1971), pp. 159–65; Ladd, *Negro Leadership*, pp. 177–178, 223–26; William Peters, *The Southern Temper* (Garden City, N.Y.: Doubleday and Co., 1959), p. 182.

32. Floyd Hunter, *Community Power Structure* (Garden City, N.Y.: Anchor Books, 1963), pp. 138–39, Chafe, *Civilities*, pp. 38–39, 32–37; Harry Holloway, *The Politics of the Southern Negro* (New York: Random House, 1969), pp. 240–42; Lewis, *Blackways*, pp. 298–99, 186, 257; Chafe, *Civilities*, pp. 32–37; Daniel Thompson, *The Negro Leadership Class* (Englewood Cliffs, N.J.: Prentice-Hall, 1963), p. 86; Burgess, *Negro Leadership*, pp. 20–21; Robert H. Brisbane, *Black Activism* (Valley Forge: Judson Press, 1974), p. 23; Burgess, *Negro Leadership*, p. 21; Evers and Peters, *For Us*, pp. 98–99, 151–53; Smith, *They Closed*, p. 21.

33. Edgar N. French, "Beginnings of a New Age," in Glenford E. Mitchell and William H. Peace III, *The Angry Black South* (New York: Corinth Books, 1962), p. 32; Thompson, *Leadership Class*, pp. 167–68; Walter White, *How Far the Promised Land?* (New York: The Viking Press, 1955), p. 47.

34. Smith, *They Closed*, pp. 39, 55, 59.

35. Ibid., pp. 20, 59.

36. Lewis, *Blackways*, p. 41; Bennett, *Confrontation*, p. 170; Howard H. Quint, *Profile in Black and White* (Washington, D.C.: Public Affairs Press, 1958), p. 22.

37. Louis E. Lomax, *The Negro Revolt* (New York: New American Library, 1963), p. 84; Bennett, *Confrontation*, p. 189; Benjamin Muse, *Ten Years of Prelude* (New York: Viking Press, 1964), p. 19; Raines, *My Soul*, p. 70; King, *Stride*, p. 168.

38. Evers and Peters, *For Us*, p. 145; Roy Wilkins, "At the Beginning of a New Era," reprinted in August Meier, Elliott Rudwick and Francis L. Broderick, *Black Protest Thought in the Twentieth Century* (Indianapolis: Bobbs-Merrill Co., 1965), pp. 282–83.

39. Chafe, *Civilities*, pp. 61, 83–84; Lewis M. Killian, "Leadership in the Desegregation Crisis: An Institutional Analysis," in Muzafer Sherif, ed., *Intergroup Relations and Leadership* (New York: John Wiley and Sons, 1962), p. 154; Quint, *Profile*, pp. 80–81; Thompson, *Leadership Class*, p. 97; Thomas R. Brooks, *Walls Come Tumbling Down* (Englewood Cliffs, N.J.: Prentice-Hall, 1974), pp. 104–105.

40. Evers and Peters, *For Us*, pp. 112–14, Chafe, *Civilities*, p. 62; Neil R. McMillen, *The Citizens' Council* (Urbana: University of Illinois Press, 1971), pp. 207–208; Quint, *Profile*, pp. 77–79.

41. Robert H. Brisbane, *The Black Vanguard* (Valley Forge: Judson Press, 1970), p. 247.

42. Lomax, *Revolt*, p. 85.

43. Muse, *Ten Years*, pp. 38–39, Quint, *Profile*, p. 52.

44. Rowan, *South of Freedom*, p. 200; Muse, *Ten Years*, p. 39.

45. Burgess, *Negro Leadership*, pp. 125, 165–66; Lewis Killian and Charles Grigg, *Racial Crisis in America* (Englewood Cliffs, N.J.: Prentice-Hall, 1964), p. 29; Ladd, *Negro Leadership*, pp. 127, 119–21.

46. Brooks, *Walls*, p. 129; Evers and Peters, *For Us*, p. 141.

47. Interview in Raines, *My Soul*, pp. 142–43.

48. Evers and Peters, *For Us*, pp. 143, 160; Peters, *Southern Temper*, pp. 261–65.

49. Anne Moody, *Coming of Age in Mississippi* (New York: Dell, 1968), pp. 127–28.

50. Ibid., p. 129.

51. Ibid., pp. 130–37, 138.

52. Killian in Sherif, *Intergroup Relations*, p. 153; Peters, *Southern Temper*, pp. 182, 189; Evers and Peters, *For Us*, p. 149; King, *Stride*, pp. 103–106, 133–37; Burgess, *Negro Leadership*, pp. 118–21.

r 53. Evers and Peters, *For Us*, p. 151; Muse, *Ten Years*, p. 203; Quint, *Profile*, p. 74; F. Henderson Moore, "School Desegregation," in Mitchell and Peace, *Angry Black South*, pp. 60-62.

54. Brooks, *Walls*, p. 126; Chafe, *Civilities*, p. 86; French, "Beginnings," pp. 40–41.

55. Thompson, *Leadership Class*, p. 6; King, *Stride*, p. 68.

56. Burgess, *Negro Leadership*, p. 23; Holloway, *Southern Negro*, pp. 96–99, 117 fn.

57. Muse, *Ten Years*, p. 203; Thompson, *Leadership Class*, p. 79; Burgess, *Negro Leadership*, p. 136; Tilman C. Cothran and William Phillips, Jr., "Negro Leadership in a Crisis Situation," *Phylon* 22, no. 2 (1961): 112.

58. McMillen, *Citizens' Council*, pp. 28–31.

59. Wilkins, "At the Beginning," p. 283; Brisbane, *Black Activism*, p. 33.

60. Brooks, *Walls*, p. 96; David L. Lewis, *King: A Critical Biography* (New York: Praeger Publishers, 1970), p. 49; King, *Stride*, pp. 15–16.

61. Robert M. Bleiweiss, ed., *Marching to Freedom* (New York: New American Library, 1969), p. 63; King, *Stride*, pp. 127–28; ibid., p. 26.

62. Interview in Raines, *My Soul*, pp. 33–34, 35; Lewis, *King*, p. 60; interview in Joanne Grant, ed., *Black Protest*, (Greenwich, Conn.: Fawcett Publications, 1968), pp. 277–79.

63. Interview with Rosa Parks from Highlander Center Archives.

64. Brisbane, *Black Activism*, p. 38.

65. Lerone Bennett, Jr., *What Manner of Man?* (Chicago: Johnson Publishing Co., 1964) pp. 79–80.

66. King, *Stride*, p. 7; Brisbane, *Black Activism*, p. 425; Coretta Scott King, *My Life with Martin Luther King, Jr.* (New York: Holt, Rinehart and Winston, 1969), pp. 163–64.

67. L. D. Reddick, *Crusader without Violence* (New York: Harper and Row, 1959), p. 133; King, *Stride*, pp. 35–36, 67; Lewis, *King*, p. 72.

68. King, *Stride*, pp. 39–40, 111; Raines, *My Soul*, p. 38.

69. King, *Stride*, pp. 90, 94; Edward Peeks, *The Long Struggle for Black Power* (New York: Charles Scribner's Sons, 1971), pp. 302–303; Brooks, *Walls*, pp. 1, 117; French, "Beginnings," p. 44; Raines, *My Soul*, p. 146.

70. Martin Luther King, Jr., "A View of the Dawn," *Interracial Review*, May 1957, pp. 82–85; King, *Stride*, pp. 173, 32.

71. King, *Stride*, pp. 191, 176, 178.

72. Ibid., pp. 79, 196, 84, 192; Martin Luther King, "The Social Organization of Nonviolence," *Liberation*, October 1959, pp. 5–7; Bayard Rustin, "Even in the Face of Death," *Liberation*, February 1957, p. 12.

73. King, *Stride*, p. 191.

74. Lewis, *King*, p. 194.

75. King, *Stride*, p. 85.

76. Ibid., pp. 196, 190, 83, 188.

77. Martin Luther King, Jr., "Who Speaks for the South?" *Liberation*, March 1958, p. 15.

78. Interview in Raines, *My Soul*, p. 50.

79. King, "Social Organization," p. 6; Martin Luther King, Jr., "Facing the Challenge of a New Age," *Phylon* 18 (Spring 1957): 25–34, pp. 33–34.

80. King, *Stride*, p. 174.

81. King, "Facing the Challenge," pp. 26–27.

82. King, *Stride*, p. 189.

83. Martin Luther King, Jr., "Our Struggle," *Liberation*, April 1956, p. 4.

84. Interview in Raines, *My Soul*, p. 49.

85. King, "Our Struggle," p. 4.

86. Interviews in Raines, *My Soul*, pp. 54, 67, French, "Beginnings," p. 46.

87. King, "Our Struggle," p. 5.

88. Interview in Raines, *My Soul*, p. 49; King, *Stride*, pp. 142, 152.

89. Lewis, *King*, p. 70.

90. King, *Stride*, p. 164.

91. C. S. King, *My Life*, pp. 150–51; Thompson, *Leadership Class*, p. 104; Burgess, *Negro Leadership*, p. 125; Chafe, *Civilities*, pp. 84–86; Robert F. Williams, *Negroes with Guns* (New York: Marzani and Munsell, 1962), p. 53.

92. Quint, *Profile*, pp. 50–54; Moore "Desegregation," pp. 56–58.

93. Rowan, *South of Freedom*, p. 146; Charles U. Smith, "The Sit–ins and the New Negro Students," in Earl Raab, *American Race Relations Today* (Garden City, N.Y.: Anchor Books, 1962), pp. 71–72; Killian and Grigg, *Racial Crisis*, p. 87; Lewis M. Killian and Charles U. Smith, "Negro Protest Leaders in a Southern Community," reprinted in John Bracey, August Meier, and Elliott Rudwick, *Conflict and Competition: Studies in the Recent Black Protest Movement* (Belmont, Calif.: Wadsworth Publishing Co., 1970), p. 40.

94. Raines, *My Soul*, pp. 150–51.

95. Ladd, *Negro Leadership*, p. 134; Burgess, *Negro Leadership*, p. 185.

96. Brooks, *Walls*, pp. 126, 140; Raines, *My Soul*, p. 62.

97. King, "Facing the Challenge," p. 33; King, *Stride*, p. 199.

98. Rustin, *Strategies*, p. 38; Lewis, *King*, p. 88; Rustin, "Face of Death," p. 12.

99. Lewis, *King*, p. 93; Brooks, *Walls*, p. 138.

100. Brooks, *Walls*, p. 127.

101. King, "Who Speaks?" p. 15.

102. King, "Facing the Challenge," p. 31.

103. Kenneth Clark, "The Civil Rights Movement: Momentum and Organization," in Geschwender, *Black Revolt*, p. 53.

104. Alfred P. Sloan, Jr., *My Years with General Motors* (New York: MacFadden Books, 1963), p. 398.

105. Steven F. Lawson, *Black Ballots: Voting Rights in the South* (New York: Columbia University Press, 1976), pp. 161–63.

106. King, "Facing the Challenge," p. 32.

107. Reddick, *Crusader*, pp. 184–85.

108. Ibid., pp. 184–97; C. S. King, *My Life*, pp. 159–60; Lewis, *King*, pp. 88–95; Bennett, *What Manner?*, p. 91.

109. Reddick, *Crusader*, pp. 216–25; C. S. King, *My Life*, p. 162.

110. Martin Luther King, Jr., *Strength to Love* (New York: Harper and Row, 1963), p. 104; Evers and Peters, *For Us*, p. 162.

111. Numan V. Bartley, *The Rise of Massive Resistance* (Baton Rouge: Louisiana State University Press, 1969), pp. 78–79, 249, 292.

112. Lomax, *Negro Revolt*, p. 268; King, "Social Organization," p. 5; Chafe, *Civilities*, p. 97.

113. Lerone Bennett, *The Negro Mood* (New York: Ballantine Books, 1964), pp. 58–63.

114. King, "Our Struggle," p. 6.

115. Lomax, *Negro Revolt*, pp. 85, 88; Carl Rowan, *Go South to Sorrow* (New York: Random House, 1957), p. 198; Burgess, *Negro Leadership*, p. 173; Thompson, *Leadership Class*, pp. 158–59; Holloway, *Southern Negro*, p. 282.

116. Brooks, *Walls*, pp. 144–45; Debbie Louis, *And We Are Not Saved* (Garden City, N.Y.: Doubleday and Co., 1970), p. 93.

117. Burgess, *Negro Leadership*, pp. 110–18; Holloway, *Southern Negro*, pp. 282–86.

118. Raab, *Race Relations*, pp. 72–73.

119. Louis, *And We*, p. 93; August Meier and Elliott Rudwick, *CORE* (New York: Oxford University Press, 1973), p. 91; Raines, *My Soul*, p. 98; Brooks, *Walls*, p. 144.

VI. The Second Wave

1. William R. Beardslee, *The Way Out Must Lead In* (Atlanta: Center for Research in Social Change, Emory University, 1977), p. 4.

2. Fredric Soloman and Jacob R. Fishman, "Youth and Social Action: II. Action Identity Formation in the First Student Sit-in Demonstration," *Journal of Social Issues* 20 (April 1964): 41.

3. Robert Coles, *Children of Crisis, Volume I* (Boston: Little, Brown and Co., 1967), pp. 107–117.

4. Cleveland Sellers, *The River of No Return* (New York: William Morrow and Co., 1973), pp. 16–17.

5. James Meredith, *Three Years in Mississippi* (Bloomington: Indiana University Press, 1966), pp. 20–21.

6. Sellers, *River*, p. 18.

7. Ben H. Bagdikian, "Negro Youth's New March on Dixie," *Saturday Evening Post*, September 8, 1962, p. 16.

8. Julian Bond, "The Movement Then and Now," *Southern Exposure*, 1976, p. 7.

9. Howell Raines, *My Soul Is Rested* (New York: Bantam, 1978), p. 101; Marzette Watts, "Sit–Ins and Pickets," *New University Thought*, 1960, p. 16.

10. Raines, *My Soul*, p. 81.

11. Martin Oppenheimer, "The Genesis of the Southern Negro Student Movement (Sit–in)" (Ph.D. dissertation, University of Pennsylvania, 1963), pp. 63–64.

12. Robert Coles, "Social Struggle and Weariness," *Psychiatry* 27 (1964): 313.

13. Ruth Searles and J. Allen Williams, Jr., "Negro College Students' Participation in Sit–ins," *Social Forces* 40 (March 1962): 218, 219; Donald R. Matthews and James W. Prothro, *Negroes and the New Southern Politics* (New York: Harcourt, Brace and World, 1966), pp. 413, 422.

14. Bond, "The Movement," p. 10.

15. Oppenheimer, *The Genesis*, pp. 136–45; Michael Walzer, "A Cup of Coffee and a Seat," *Dissent* 7 (Spring, 1960): 114; Helen Fuller, "We Are All So Very Happy," *New Republic*, April 25, 1960, p. 14; Bagdikian, "March on Dixie," p. 17.

16. William H. Chafe, *Civilities and Civil Rights* (New York: Oxford University Press, 1980), p. 119; Walzer, "Cup of Coffee," p. 117.

17. Chafe, *Civilities*, p. 116; Solomon and Fishman, "Youth and Social Action: II," p. 41; Beardslee, *The Way Out*, p. 8.

18. Oppenheimer, *The Genesis*, pp. 91–95; Clayborne Carson, *In Struggle* (Cambridge: Harvard University Press, 1981), pp. 19–30; Sellers, *River*, pp. 33–45; Helen Fuller, "Southern Students Take Over," *New Republic*, May 2, 1960, p. 16.

19. Sellers, *River*, p. 44.

20. Interview in Raines, *My Soul*, p. 225.

21. Vincent Harding and Staughton Lynd, "Albany, Georgia," *Crisis*, February 1963, p. 73.

22. Sellers, *River*, p. 117.

23. Interviews in Raines, *My Soul*, pp. 260, 261, 255, 251.

24. Coles, *Children of Crisis*, p. 209.

25. Sellers, *River*, p. 26; Miles Wolff, *How It All Began* (New York: Stein and Day, 1971), p. 163; Louis Lomax, "The Negro Revolt against the 'Negro Leaders,' " *Harper's*, June 1960, pp. 42, 48; Oppenheimer, *The Genesis*, pp. 208–210; interview with Julian Bond in Raines, *My Soul*, pp. 94–97.

26. Michael Walzer, "The Politics of the New Negro," *Dissent* 7 (1960): 257–58; Mathews and Prothro, *Negroes*, p. 412.

27. Wolff, *How It All Began*, pp. 163–66.

28. See Chafe, *Civilities*, pp. 130–36; John Constable, "Negro Student Protestors Challenge North Carolina Leaders," *New South* 15 (1960); Mathews and Prothro, *Negroes*, p. 438.

29. Harris Wofford, *Of Kennedys and Kings* (New York: Farrar, Straus, Giroux, 1980), pp. 47–48.

30. Interview in Raines, *My Soul*, pp. 89, 87–94; Wofford, *Of Kennedys*, p. 12.

31. Harvard Sitkoff, *The Struggle for Black Equality* (New York: Hill and Wang, 1981), p. 98; interview in Raines, *My Soul*, p. 115.

32. Carson, *In Struggle*, p. 37.

33. Wofford, *Of Kennedys*, pp. 129, 155.

34. Neil McMillen, "Black Enfranchisement in Mississippi: Federal Enforcement and Black Protest in the 1960's," *Journal of Southern History* 43 (August 1977): 360.

35. John Perdew, "Difficult to Organize Poorest and Wealthiest among Negroes," *I.F. Stone's Weekly*, December 9, 1963, p. 3.

36. Stephen Oates, *Let the Trumpet Sound* (New York: Harper and Row, 1982), p. 117.

37. Harry S. Ashmore, *Hearts and Minds* (New York: McGraw Hill, 1982), p. 335.

38. Ibid., p. 336.

39. Coretta Scott King, *My Life with Martin Luther King, Jr.* (New York: Holt, Rinehart and Winston, 1969), p. 204.

40. Walzer, "New Negro," p. 240; Gary Marx, *Protest and Prejudice* (New York: Harper and Row, 1967), pp. 56–57; Lomax, "Negro Revolt," p. 48;

41. Marx, *Protest and Prejudice*, pp. 56–57; 61–62; Mathews and Prothro, *Negroes*, p. 87.

42. John M. Orbell, "Protest Participation among Southern Negro College Students," *American Political Science Review* 61 (June 1967): 446–56; Anthony M. Orum and Amy W. Orum, "The Class and Status Bases of Negro Student Protest," *Social Science Quarterly* 49 (December 1968): 521–33; Anthony M. Orum, *Black Students in Protest* (Washington, D.C.: American Sociological Association, n.d.).

43. Orbell, "Protest Participation," pp. 448–50; Orum and Orum, "Class and Status Bases," pp. 526–27; Searles and Williams, "Negro Students' Participation," p. 218; Mathews and Prothro, *Negroes*, pp. 418–19, 426.

44. Orum and Orum, "Class and Status Bases," p. 532–33; Maurice Pinard, Jerome Kirk, and Donald Von Eschen, "Processes of Recruitment in the Sit–in Movement," *Public Opinion Quarterly* 33 (Fall 1969): 218–20; Anthony Orum, "A Reappraisal of the Social and Political Participation of Negroes," *American Journal of Sociology* 72 (July 1966): 32–46, p. 30; Joyce Ladner, "What 'Black Power' Means to Negroes in Mississippi," *Transaction* 5 (November 1967): 8.

45. Oates, *Trumpet*, p. 211.

46. Martin Luther King, Jr., *Why We Can't Wait* (New York: New American Library, 1964), pp. 49, 54.

47. Reprinted in August Meier, ed., *Black Protest in the Sixties* (Chicago: Quadrangle Books, 1970), p. 67; Ashmore, *Hearts and Minds*, pp. 352–55.

48. Martin Luther King, Jr., *The Trumpet of Conscience* (New York: Harper and Row, 1968).

49. Interview in Raines, *My Soul*, p. 156; Oates, *Trumpet*, p. 237.

50. Theodore White, *The Making of the President, 1964* (New York: Antheneum, 1965), p. 170; Thomas Brooks, *Walls Come Tumbling Down* (Englewood Cliffs, N.J.: Prentice-Hall, 1974), pp. 210–11.

51. David R. Colburn, "The Saint Augustine Business Community," in Elizabeth Jacoway and David R. Colburn, eds., *Southern Businessmen and Desegregation* (Baton Rouge: Louisiana State University Press, 1982), pp. 223–24.

52. Peter Goldman, *The Death and Life of Malcolm X* (Chicago: University of Illinois Press, 1979), p. 102.

53. Charles Sallis and John Quincy Adams, "Desegregation in Jackson, Mississippi," in Jacoway and Colburn, *Southern Businessmen*, p. 237.

54. Ashmore, *Hearts and Minds*, p. 375; Debbie Louis, *And We Are Not Saved* (New York: Doubleday and Co., 1970), pp. 134–37; interview in Raines, *My Soul*, p. 315; August Meier and Elliott Rudwick, *CORE* (New York: Oxford University Press, 1973), p. 223.

55. Allen Matusow, "From Civil Rights to Black Power: The Case of SNCC, 1960–1966," in John Bracey, August Meier, and Elliott Rudwick, eds., *Conflict and Competition: Studies in the Recent Black Protest Movement* (Belmont, Calif.: Wadsworth Publishing Co., 1971), p. 139.

56. Interview in Raines, *My Soul*, p. 301; see also Julius Lester, *Look Out, Whitey! Black Power's Gon' Get Your Mama* (New York: Dial Press, 1968), pp. 20–22; Len

Holt, *The Summer That Didn't End* (New York: Wiliam Morrow and Co., 1965), p. 47; Carson, *In Struggle*, p. 98.

57. Nicholas Von Hoffman, *Mississippi Notebook* (New York: David White Co., 1964), p. 33.

58. Sellers, *River*, p. 89; interview in Raines, *My Soul*, p. 306.

59. Robert Coles and Joseph Brenner, "American Youth in a Social Struggle: The Mississippi Summer Project," *American Journal of Orthopsychiatry*, October 1965, p. 923; interview in Raines, *My Soul*, p. 283; Sellers, *River*, p. 106.

60. Carson, *In Struggle*, p. 121.

61. Meier and Rudwick, *CORE*, p. 298; Von Hoffman, *Mississippi Notebook*, p. 96; Sellers, *River*, pp. 68–69, 91; Raines, *My Soul*, p. 293.

62. Carson, *In Struggle*, pp. 125, 127; Lawrence Guyot and Mike Thilwell, "The Politics of Necessity and Survival in Mississippi," *Freedomways*, Spring 1966, pp. 131–32, cited in Carson, *In Struggle*, p. 128.

63. I. F. Stone, *In a Time of Torment* (New York: Random House, 1968), p. 54.

64. Von Hoffman, *Mississippi Notebook*, p. 28.

65. Chafe, *Civilities*, p. 213; Julius Lester, *Look Out, Whitey!*

66. Sellers, *River*, pp. 96–97, 115.

VII. Ghetto Revolts, Black Power, and the Limits of the Civil Rights Coalition

1. Dorothy K. Newman, Nancy J. Amidei, Barbara L. Carter, Dawn Day, William J. Kruvant, and Jack S. Russell, *Protest, Politics, and Prosperity: Black Americans and White Institutions, 1940–75* (New York: Pantheon, 1978), pp. 162–64; National Committee against Discrimination, *How the Federal Government Builds Ghettos* (New York, 1967; reprinted in Helen Ginsburg, *Poverty, Economics, and Society* [Boston: Little, Brown and Co., 1972], pp. 249–52).

2. Huey Newton, *Revolutionary Suicide* (New York: Ballantine, 1973), pp. 14–15.

3. Paul Bullock, ed., *Watts: The Aftermath* (New York: Grove Press, 1969), p. 27.

4. Newman et al., *Protest, Politics, and Prosperity*, pp. 146–48; Louis L. Knowles and Kenneth Prewitt, eds., *Institutional Racism in America* (Englewood Cliffs, N.J.: Prentice–Hall, 1969), pp. 25–26; Paul Jacobs.

5. Sidney M. Wilhelm, *Black in a White America* (Cambridge: Schenkman, 1983), p. 523; Charles E. Silberman, *Crisis in Black and White* (New York: Random House, 1964), pp. 262–63.

6. Gerry Rosenfield, *Shut Those Thick Lips: A Study of Slum School Failure* (New York: Holt, Rinehart and Winston, 1971), p. 43.

7. Dick Gregory, *Nigger* (New York: Pocket Books, 1965), p. 30.

8. Louis A. Ferman, Joyce L. Kornbluh, and J. A. Miller, "Introduction," in Louis A. Ferman, Joyce L. Kornbluh, and J. A. Miller, eds., *Negroes and Jobs* (Ann Arbor: University of Michigan Press, 1968), p. 13; Tom Kahn, *The Economics of Equality* (New York: League for Industrial Democracy, 1964, reprinted in Ferman, Kornbluh, and Miller, *Negroes and Jobs*, p. 23; Newman et al., *Protest, Politics, and Prosperity*, p. 34; Harold Baron, "The Demand for Black Labor: Historical Notes on the Political Economy of Racism," *Radical America* 5 (March–April 1971): 26; Kenneth B. Clark, *Dark Ghetto* (New York: Harper and Row, 1965), p. 35.

9. Arthur M. Ross, "The Negro in the American Economy," in Arthur M. Ross and Herbert Hill, *Employment, Race, and Poverty* (New York: Harcourt, Brace and World, 1967), pp. 29, 30, 21, 22; cited in Kahn, *Economics*, p. 20.

10. Charles C. Killingsworth, "Negroes in a Changing Labor Market," in Ross and

Hill, *Employment, Race, and Poverty* p. 52; Silberman, *Crisis*, pp. 41–42; Knowles and Prewitt, *Racism*, p. 19; Newton, *Suicide*, pp. 41–42.

11. Robert Coles, "Children of the American Ghetto," *Harper's Magazine*, September 1967, pp. 21–22.

12. Joe R. Feagin and Harlan Hahn, *Ghetto Revolts* (New York: Macmillan Co., 1973), p. 152.

13. Jimmie Sherman, "From the Ashes," *Antioch Review* 27, no. 3 (1967): 286–87.

14. Newton, *Suicide*, p. 19.

15. Benjamin Goodman, ed., *Malcolm X: The End of White World Supremacy* (New York: Merlin House, 1971), p. 4.

16. Reprinted in John Bracey, Jr., August Meier, and Elliott Rudwick, eds., *Black Nationalism in America* (Indianapolis: Bobbs–Merrill Co., 1970), p. 416.

17. Ibid., p. 420.

18. Goodman, *Malcolm X*, pp. 102–103.

19. George Breitman, ed., *Malcolm X Speaks* (New York: Grove Press, 1965), p. 40.

20. Ibid., p. 12.

21. Ibid., pp. 12–13.

22. C. Eric Lincoln, *Sounds of the Struggle* (New York: William Morrow and Co., 1967), pp. 36–37.

23. Alex Haley, ed., *The Autobiography of Malcolm X* (New York: Grove Press, 1965), pp. 405–406.

24. John Henrik Clarke, ed., *Malcolm X: The Man and His Times* (Toronto: Collier Books, 1979), pp. 155–56.

25. Raine, "Police Brutality," p. 386.

26. Walter J. Raine, "The Perception of Police Brutality in South Central Los Angeles," in Nathan Cohen, *The Los Angeles Riots: A Socio–psychological Study* (New York: Praeger, 1970), p. 386.

27. August Meier and Elliott Rudwick, *CORE: A Study in the Civil Rights Movement, 1942–1968* (New York: Oxford University Press, 1973), pp. 287–88, 292–93.

28. William Brink and Louis Harris, *The Negro Revolution in America* (New York: Simon and Schuster, 1964), pp. 66–67, 204.

29. Haley, *Malcolm X*, pp. 293–94.

30. Clarke, *Malcolm X*, p. 176.

31. Peter Goldman, *The Death and Life of Malcolm X* (Urbana: University of Illinois Press, 1979), p. 74.

32. Breitman, *Malcolm X Speaks*, p. 7.

33. Ibid., p. 107.

34. Ibid., pp. 108–109.

35. Ibid., p. 42.

36. Ibid., p. 172.

37. James Button, *Black Violence* (Princeton: Princeton University Press, 1978), p. 27; citation in Lewis M. Killian, *The Impossible Revolution* (Washington, D.C.: University Press of America, 1975), p. 86.

38. David O. Sears and John B. McConahay, *The Politics of Violence: The New Urban Blacks and the Watts Riot* (Boston: Houghton Mifflin Co., 1973), p. 13.

39. Sears and McConahay, *Politics of Violence*, pp. 29, 33, 22; T. M. Tomlinson, "The Development of a Riot Ideology among Urban Negroes," *American Behavioral Scientist* 11 (March–April 1968): 28; Nathan Caplan, "The New Ghetto Man: A Review of Recent Empirical Studies," in David Boesel and Peter H. Rossi, eds., *Cities under Siege: An Anatomy of the Ghetto Riots, 1964–1968* (New York: Basic Books, 1971).

40. Abraham H. Miller, Louis H. Bolce, and Mark R. Halligan, "The New Urban Blacks," *Ethnicity* 3 (1976).

41. Robert M. Fogelson, *Violence as Protest: A Study of Riots and Ghettos* (Garden City, N.Y.: Doubleday and Co., 1971), p. 30–41; Robert M. Fogelson and Robert B. Hill, "Who Riots? A Study of Participation in the 1967 Riots," in *Supplemental Studies for the National Advisory Commission on Civil Disorders* (Washington, D.C.: GPO, 1968), pp. 241–43; 235–36; Angus Campbell and Howard Schuman, "Racial Attitudes in Fifteen American Cities," in ibid., pp. 51–52, 55; Sears and McConahay, *Politics of Violence*, p. 14; Robert B. Hill and Robert M. Fogelson, "A Study of Arrest Patterns in the 1960's Riots" (unpublished manuscript, 1969), pp. 21–22; Karl H. Flaming, *Who "Riots" and Why? Black and White Perspectives in Milwaukee* (Milwaukee Urban League, 1968), p. vii; Caplan, "New Ghetto Man," p. 42.

42. Sears and McConahay, *Politics of Violence*, p. 21; Caplan, "New Ghetto Man," p. 349–50.

43. Hill and Fogelson, "Arrest Patterns," p. 19.

44. Joe R. Feagin and Harlan Hahn, *Ghetto Revolts: The Politics of Violence in American Cities* (New York: Macmillan Co., 1973), pp. 274–75.

45. Miller, Bolce, and Halligan, "New Urban Blacks," p. 351; Fogelson, *Violence as Protest*, pp. 46–47; Flaming, *Who "Riots"*, p. vii; Caplan, "New Ghetto Man," p. 350; Fogelson and Hill, "Who Riots?", p. 235; J. R. Feagin, "Social Sources of Support for Violence and Nonviolence in a Negro Ghetto," *Social Problems* 15, no. 4 (Spring 1968): p. 437; Raymond J. Murphy and James W. Watson, "The Structure of Discontent: Relationship between Social Structure, Grievance, and Riot Support," in Cohen, *Los Angeles Riots*, pp. 145–47.

46. Campbell and Schuman, "Racial Attitudes," pp. 42–44; Murphy and Watson, "Structure of Discontent," p. 166.

47. Sears and McConahay, *Politics of Violence*, pp. 56–63; Murphy and Watson, "Structure of Discontent," pp. 157–60, 162.

48. Sears and McConahay, *Politics of Violence*, pp. 44, 45, 77; Caplan, "New Ghetto Man," pp. 351, 353–54; Campbell and Schuman, "Racial Attitudes," pp. 15–20; Miller, Bolce, and Halligan, "New Urban Blacks," pp. 362–64.

49. Newton, *Suicide*, pp. 21, 23–24.

50. Feagin and Hahn, *Ghetto Revolts*, pp. 132–34. James Geschwender, "Civil Rights Protests and Riots: A Disappearing Distinction," *Social Science Quarterly* 49, no. 3 (December 1968), reprinted in Norval D. Glen and Charles M. Bonjean, *Blacks in the United States* (San Francisco: Chandler Publishing Co., 1969), pp. 403–404.

51. Douglas Glasgow, *The Black Underclass* (New York: Vintage Books, 1981), pp. 106, 117–19.

52. Feagin and Hahn, *Ghetto Revolts*, pp. 132, 271–72; Sears and McConahay, *Politics of Violence*, pp. 99–101, 63, 105; Campbell and Schuman, "Racial Attitudes," pp. 47–48; James A. Geschwender, "Civil Rights Protests," pp. 403–404.

53. Martin Luther King, Jr., *Where Do We Go from Here: Chaos or Community?* (New York: Harper and Row, 1967), p. 112; Sears and McConahay, *Politics of Violence*, pp. 161–62; Murphy and Watson, "Structure of Discontent," p. 180.

54. J. David Greenstone and Paul E. Peterson, "Reformers, Machines, and the War on Poverty," in James Q. Wilson, ed., *City Politics and Public Policy* (New York: Wiley, 1968), pp. 287–88; Button, *Black Violence*, pp. 34–40, 62–86.

55. Martin Luther King, Jr., "The President's Address to the Tenth Anniversary Convention of the Southern Christian Leadership Conference, Atlanta, Georgia, August 16, 1967," in Robert L. Scott and Wayne Brockside, eds., *The Rhetoric of Black Power* (New York: Harper and Row, 1969).

56. Sears and McConahay, *Politics of Violence*, pp. 188–89; Campbell and Schuman, "Racial Attitudes," p. 20.

57. Campbell and Schuman, "Racial Attitudes," p. 19.

58. Ibid., pp. 47–49; Richard T. Morris and Vincent Jeffries, "The White Reaction Study," in Cohen, *Black Crusader*, pp. 511–12; William Brink and Louis Harris, *Black and White* (New York: Simon and Schuster, 1967), pp. 121, 220, 131.

59. Button, *Black Violence*, pp. 68, 129, 126–27.

60. Brink and Harris, *Black and White*, p. 28; *Report of the National Advisory Commission on Civil Disorders* (New York: Bantam Books, 1968), p. 1.

61. Cleveland Sellers, *River of No Return* (New York: William Morrow and Co., 1973), p. 147.

62. Jean Smith, "I Learned to Feel Black," reprinted in Floyd B. Barbour, ed., *The Black Power Revolt* (Boston: Extending Horizons Books, 1968), pp. 210–11.

63. Stokeley Carmichael and Charles V. Hamilton, *Black Power* (New York: Vintage Books, 1967); Charles V. Hamilton, "Riots, Revolts, and Relevant Response," in Barbour, *Black Power Revolt*, p. 174.

64. King, *Where Do We Go*, p. 30.

65. Carmichael and Hamilton, *Black Power*, pp. 66, 61, 47, 76.

66. King, *Where Do We Go*, pp. 30–31.

67. David Lewis, *King: A Critical Biography* (New York: Praeger Publishers, 1970), p. 306.

68. King, *Where Do We Go*, pp. 50, 51, 152.

69. King, "President's Address," pp. 161–63.

VIII. Class and Race: A Retrospective and Prospective

1. Morton Inger, "The New Orleans School Crisis of 1960," in Elizabeth Jacoway and David R. Colburn, eds., *Southern Businessmen and Desegregation* (Baton Rouge: Louisiana State University Press, 1982).

2. Alton Hornsby, Jr., "A City That Was Too Busy to Hate, Atlanta Businessmen and Desegregation," in ibid., p. 132.

3. Paul S. Lofton, Jr., "Calm and Exemplary, Desegregation in Columbia, South Carolina," in ibid.

4. William Brophy, "Active Acceptance—Active Containment, The Dallas Story," in ibid.

5. James C. Cobb, "Yesterday's Liberalism, Business Boosters and Civil Rights in Augusta, Georgia," in ibid.

6. Charles Sallis and John Quincy Adams, "Desegregation in Jackson, Mississippi," in ibid., p. 247.

7. E. Franklin Frazier, *Black Bourgeoisie* (New York: Collier Books, 1962).

INDEX

Abernathy, Ralph, 149, 151

AFL–CIO, 211

Alabama Christian Movement for Human Rights, 147

American Association of University Women, 115

Americans for Democratic Action: and civil rights, 82–83

Anderson, William, 170

Bagdikian, Ben, 158

Baker, Ray Stannard, 22

Bartley, Numan, 93, 116, 216; on the massive resistance movement, 86

Bates, Daisy, 112, 113

Berger, Peter, and Thomas Luckman: *The Social Construction of Reality*, 9

Billings, Dwight, Jr., 25, 37

Birmingham: civil rights campaign, 156, 173–78, 179

Black Codes, 28, 29, 30, 34

Black movement, 196, 211; and class relations, 187, 214–17; and class structure in America, 208; development and decline of, 12–14, 15; leadership of, 121, 126–28, 130, 133, 145, 147–51, 163–65; militancy of, 155–56; and Student Nonviolent Coordinating Committee, 162. *See also* Civil rights movement

Black Muslims, 197; and nonviolence, 196; their program, 193–95

Black power, 7, 14, 208–209, 211, 217, 220, 223

Blacks: black consciousness, 6, 7, 15, 76, 85, 121–22, 126, 130, 131–32, 135, 136–37, 138, 144, 145, 146, 157–58, 159, 178, 192–93, 203, 205–206, 209, 219–20; and civil rights movement, 78, 87; class distinctions among, 10, 125–26, 218–19, 222–23; and class system in America, 222; and Democratic Party, 2, 5, 36, 42, 69, 186; and desegregation, 104, 129, 158–59, 160–61, 177–78; disfranchisement of, 34–36, 43, 47–48, 100; economic boycotting of, 99–100; and education, 53–56, 190; employment of, 60, 190–91, 223–24; and federal government, 121, 151–52, 156, 160, 175, 180, 186, 204, 206, 214; generational conflict, 164, 165, 169–70; and Kennedy administration, 166–68; nationalist sentiments of, 193, 205–206; New Negro concept, 7, 14, 120–21, 128, 138, 155, 157, 221; and Northern public opinion, 176–77; migration of, 68,
76, 207; paternalism towards, 19, 20, 36, 57, 58, 124–25, 133; political power of, 75–76, 85, 154; school integration, 106–107; school segregation, 114–15, 123–24, 152, 171; violence against, 100–101, 122, 133–35, 177, 179, 181, 196; voter registration, 90, 101, 180, 223; welfare, 191; and whites, 4, 6, 151, 153–54, 160, 175, 176, 186. *See also* South

Blumer, Herbert, 9

Bolce, Louis H., 201

Bonacich, Edna, 47, 53; labor market theory of racism, 3–4

Bond, Julian, 159, 166; on civil rights movement, 160

Brady, Thomas, 101, 102, 104; his Black Monday speech, 94, 96; and Southern resistance to desegregation, 97, 98, 99

Brink, William, 206, 207

Bryan, William Jennings, 71

Burgess, Elaine, 153; on black movement leadership, 148; on Southern whites and desegregation, 91

Button, James, 205

Campbell, Angus: on black nationalism, 205; on ghetto life, 202; on ghetto riots, 206

Caplan, Nathan, 200, 201

Carmichael, Stokeley, 182, 185; and black power, 14, 211; "Black Power" manifesto, 208; and civil rights coalition, 209

Carter, Hodding III: on desegregation in the South, 90, 93; on White Citizens' Councils, 102

Carter, Jimmy, 221

Cash, W. J., 42; on Southern economy, 23, 25; on Southern politics, 37

Chafe, William, 184; on white supremacy, 127

Civil Rights Bill, 177

Civil rights movement, 1; and Americans for Democratic Action, 82–83; Birmingham campaign, 156, 173–78, 179; and blacks, 78, 87; class politics of, 218; demise of, 208, 209, 217; development of, 5, 7–8; and federal government, 156, 180; impact of, 221–24; and national politics, 221; and Northern public opinion, 184; Selma campaign, 184–85; social composition of, 170–73; and Southern business, 178, 215–16; and Student Nonviolent Coordinating Committee, 169–70. *See also* Black movement

Civil War, 2, 6; and class system, 19

Jack M. Bloom has taught at Wayne State University and the University of Detroit and spent some years as a movement activist. He is currently Assistant Professor of Sociology at Indiana University Northwest.